# The Poetics of Childhood

# CHILDREN'S LITERATURE AND CULTURE
Jack Zipes, *Series Editor*

# THE POETICS OF CHILDHOOD

BY RONI NATOV

ROUTLEDGE
NEW YORK AND LONDON

Published in 2003 by
Routledge
29 West 35th Street
New York, NY 10001
www.routledge-ny.com

Published in Great Britain by
Routledge
11 New Fetter Lane
London EC4P 4EE
www.routledge.co.uk

*Routledge is an imprint of the Taylor & Francis Group.*
Printed in the United States of America on acid-free paper.

Library of Congress Cataloging-in-Publication Data

Natov, Roni.
    The poetics of childhood/by Roni Natov.
        p.   cm.—(Children's literature and culture; 24)
    Includes bibliographical references and index.
    ISBN 0-8153-3882-1 (acid-free paper)
    1. English literature—History and criticism.   2. Children in literature.   3. Children's literature, English—History and criticism.   I. Title.   II. Children's literature and culture (Routledge (Firm)); 24.
    PR151.C57 N37 2002
    820.9′352054—dc21

                                                                            2002069800

# Contents

For my son, Jonathan,
who, in so many ways,
gave me back my childhood

# Series Editor's Foreword

Dedicated to furthering original research in children's literature and culture, the Children's Literature and Culture series includes monographs on individual authors and illustrators, historical examinations of different periods, literary analyses of genres, and comparative studies on literature and the mass media. The series is international in scope and is intended to encourage innovative research in children's literature with a focus on interdisciplinary methodology.

Children's literature and culture are understood in the broadest sense of the term children to encompass the period of childhood up through adolescence. Owing to the fact that the notion of childhood has changed so much since the origination of children's literature, this Routledge series is particularly concerned with transformations in children's culture and how they have affected the representation and socialization of children. While the emphasis of the series is on children's literature, all types of studies that deal with children's radio, film, television, and art are included in an endeavor to grasp the aesthetics and values of children's culture. Not only have there been momentous changes in children's culture in the last fifty years but also there have been radical shifts in the scholarship that deals with these changes. In this regard, the goal of the Children's Literature and Culture series is to enhance research in this field and, at the same time, point to new directions that bring together the best scholarly work throughout the world.

Jack Zipes

# Acknowledgments

No one creates in a vacuum. All my work, my deepest thoughts and feelings, have been informed by conversations with my friends, colleagues, and with the students I've been blessed to teach at Brooklyn College, and the faculty and doctoral students I've worked with at the Union Institute and University in Cincinnati. I want to acknowledge them all. I want to thank my friends, Nancy Abrams, Judy Meiselman, Amy Lubelski, and Jane and Vicki Sufian for their love and support. I want to thank Ellen Tremper and Wendy Fairey for their interest and enthusiasm. I want to thank Steve London for his love and patience and for his thoughtful reading of my work; often it is hardest for those we live with to bear our shifts in mood during such intense times. I want to thank my son, Jonathan, with whom I share so much, and whose very presence makes me smile. I want to thank Laura Atkins for generously offering excellent suggestions about contemporary children's books. And I want to thank Geri DeLuca, my work partner and dear friend, for her kind, thoughtful, and tireless attention to my work. I have been blessed in her empathic intellectual companionship for the thirty years we have worked together.

I want to thank Jack Zipes for his guidance; Lois Kuznets for her encouragement and belief in my work; Emily Vail at Routledge for the care she took with my book. I want to thank Larry Hobson for the reproduction of all the art for this book. I am most grateful to the Research Foundation of the City University of New York for the generous PSC-CUNY Grant I received to do this work.

*The Poetics of Childhood* contains a generous sampling, of various proportions, of articles I published previously. I am grateful to those who kindly granted me permission to reprint parts or all of my original publications. Part of Chapter 8 originally appeared as "Harry Potter and the Extraordinariness of the Ordinary," *The Lion and the Unicorn*, 25,2, Johns Hopkins University Press (April 2001): 310–37. Part of Chapter 2 originally appeared as "Dickens's David and Carroll's Alice: The Liminality of Victorian Childhood," written with Wendy Fairey, in *The*

*Australasian Victorian Studies Journal* 5 (1999): 143–55. Part of Chapter 3 originally appeared as "Mothers and Daughters: Jamaica Kincaid's Pre-Oedipal Narrative, in *Children's Literature* 18, eds. Francelia Butler, Margaret Higgonet, and Barbara Rosen, by the Children's Literature Foundation, Yale University Press © 1990: 1–16. Parts of Chapter 4 and parts of Chapter 6 originally appeared as "Internal and External Journeys: The Child Hero in *The Zabajaba Jungle* and *Linnea in Monet's Garden*," *Children's Literature in Education*, 20,2 (June 1989): 91–107, with kind permission from Kluwer Academic Publishers.

# Introduction

Within us, still within us, always within us, childhood is a state of mind.

—GASTON BACHELARD[1]

**1.**

Among the sunny memories of my childhood, I remember some dark moments of what I would now call dislocation, a separation from the harmony I felt with the world, a harmony I came to think of as belonging, as "being normal." They didn't necessarily emerge from fighting with my family or with other children. Rather, these moments hinted at something wrong with the way I was, or almost worse, the way my family was. They involved pockets of shame, which I experienced physically in the pit of my stomach. But they were not pervasive, and I remember recovering easily from them, and feeling, when they passed, almost wholly restored to the world that once again opened to me. I don't remember a lot of anxiety around these moments, although when I look back at notes my mother saved in which I begged her and my father to "forgive me," including boxes for them to check yes or no, I have to admit I must have been distressed. I must have distrusted that I would be welcomed back into their good graces.

However, my real fall from grace came violently and suddenly at the age of thirteen with the appearance of my first real boyfriend. I was from then on a stranger to my family. My sexuality, of which I myself was fairly innocent, was the prime mover that plummeted me into darkness. This rupture from my family was also (and in childhood how could it not be) a rupture within myself. I became suspicious of my desires and pleasures, and I acted in ways to ensure that I was deserving of the abuse I suffered. As Alice Miller so clearly articulated in *The*

*1*

*Drama of the Gifted Child*[2] and in *Pictures of a Childhood*,[3] it was less threatening to believe I was the culprit than to see my parents as seriously flawed and
inept. I had depended so entirely on their vision for so long; I had been so in love
with them and they with me. I would spend much of my adulthood repairing this
sense of myself as tainted.

However discrete each stage of childhood appears, however abrupt or gradual this fall from innocence, I believe the resulting breach occurs as states of feeling layered into the consciousness, so that recovering these memories of felt
experience, restoring them to their original vibrancy, whether positive or negative,
is the imaginative work of a lifetime. Obviously, these memories can never be
recalled wholly without all kinds of projections and distortions. Even if that were
possible, how would we recognize their pure and imaginatively unaltered state?
They are, then, often retrieved, layer by layer, as shards pieced together
metaphorically in bits of dreams, waking and sleeping, from various layers of
consciousness, subconsciousness, and unconsciousness. This is the playing field,
the arena of the poetics of childhood, which has long intrigued writers, particularly since the Romantics recognized the value of childhood in "the search for the
lost realm of the adult's past."[4]

No childhood is without pain; no parent without injury that in turn causes
injury; no community completely nurturing and inclusive, so that there are always
childhood wounds; the more serious, the more potential for damage to memory.
Our sense of the past and of a coherent self is often represented in our postmod-
ern world by a shifting consciousness, by multiplicity and fragmentation. It is apt
and not uncommon to characterize adulthood as severed, to one degree or another,
from childhood memory, and therefore, from the imagination—from a natural
sense of wonder and originality of thought. Behind the fractured adult a child
hides, estranged from his or her own history, deprived of the psychological and
cultural richness of memory that is, as the British educator Peter Abbs claimed,
our "biological inheritance, part of what it means to be human."[5]

## 2.

How close can we, as adults, get to the inner life, where the profusion of our
memories lies? And how much of that richness are we able to express? The dominant images embedded and stored in the imagination are so personal and idiosyncratic—based, as they are, on the unique experiences of each of us and on the
singular way in which we each view those experiences—that they seem untranslatable. Yet, when expressed artistically through the eye and in the voice of childhood memory, they can resonate deeply for others. This is the poetics of
childhood. It involves the images that cluster around childhood, the voices and
tones, the smells and textures that make up the larger landscape that recalls to us
our earliest states of mind. "In the child's reverie," Bachelard wrote, "the image

takes over everything else. . . . The reverie toward childhood returns us to the beauty of the first images" (Bachelard, 43). In a process of "gathering the poetry" of childhood, "it is necessary to give memories their atmosphere of images" (Bachelard, 44). They seem to need to surface and to be expressed, so that as adults we retain a fluidity of thought and feeling, spontaneity and wholeness, a sense of personal authenticity.

This book explores the literature of childhood through a variety of texts, both those conceived and written for children and those that engage an exclusively adult readership. Its focus is those works that provide a shared area where adult and child come together. Perhaps this is the space where all great children's books are located. This study rests on the assumption that the connection between childhood and adulthood is essential to the potential coherence of consciousness. The majority of works considered here belong as much to adults as to children, as the world of childhood belongs to adults in memory as well as to children temporally. The literature of childhood moves between innocence and experience, between initiation and reflection. And, in establishing such a poetics, the child at the center, presently and retrospectively, is, as Carolyn Steedman says, "the story waiting to be told" (Steedman, 11). Childhood narratives bring us to an exquisitely liminal place in adulthood, one that generates—in its attempt to mediate levels of perspective and experience—a rich variety of expression of psychological and aesthetic possibility.

The literature of childhood is inclusive in two ways. It embraces whatever children read and is read to them—the stories they select and those selected for them. And it engages childhood as remembered and imagined by adults. So we are always to some degree or other talking about the imagined child and "the place of childhood in the imaginative life of adults" (Steedman, 4). It explores the various ways in which the child is used as a metaphor for adult states of mind. In her brilliant study of Goethe's *Wilhelm Meister's Apprenticeship*,[6] Steedman points out how Goethe uses the child figure, Mignon, the acrobat, to expose the ways in which adults relate to children (Steedman, ix). Mary Shelley's *Frankenstein*[7] suggests another perspective, the child as monster, as potential threat to adult autonomy and, essentially, to early-nineteenth-century European culture. The child—dependent, powerless, and submissive—evokes an ambiguity of feeling reflected in the literature of childhood. Previous to Rousseau, children were seen as potentially sinister, their sinful nature contained and socialized. But long after their innocence was recognized, they continued to be viewed as threatening in their sensuousness, envied for the youth that our culture distorts and fetishizes. Such adult hostility, however, does not preclude the protective impulses also embedded in stories of adult-child relations. Perhaps, as James Kincaid claimed in his study of childhood and eros:

The child carries for us things we somehow cannot carry for ourselves, sometimes anxieties we want to be divorced from and sometimes pleasures so great we would not, without the child, know how to contain them. People, we know, sometimes beat children because the child can be filled up with whatever must be beaten. It's the same with love.[8]

## 3.

During the eighteenth century, the Romantic child, envisioned by Rousseau, Blake, and Wordsworth as an embodiment of natural goodness, became central in the ways childhood was imagined. And this Romantic conception of childhood drew attention to the corrupting social order it opposed. Blake's construction of childhood innocence was intricately connected with its complementary state of wisdom in adulthood. Wordsworth also believed that in adulthood one could reclaim this instinctual and spiritual knowledge, and that in it one could find the seeds of imaginative life. However, adults' suspicion of children, of their own childhood impulses and of the body, continued to be expressed imaginatively as the other side of Blake's and Wordsworth's spiritual child.

From the eighteenth century on, the concept of the self and identity became more internal. Interest in recognizing that self along with the belief that "each individual self has a history" gave rise to the construction of childhood as "the lost child within all of us" (Steedman, 4). The child became "representative of a lost realm, lost in the individual past, and in the past of the culture," the reclaiming of which suggests a larger historical retrieval as well, so that the idea of childhood and the modern idea of history emerged together. Steedman claims that:

> In establishing psychoanalysis as a body of theory . . . Sigmund Freud worked with the imaginative legacy of cell theory . . . with notions of littleness, of entities composed of smaller parts, and with the idea of the smallest possible entity as the birthplace, or progenitor, of memory and consciousness of time. (Steedman, 77)

She goes on to argue that the cell provided an analogy for "an individual's childhood history laid down inside its body, a place . . . that was indeed very small, but that carried with it the utter enormity of a *history*" (Steedman, 92). From the Romantics through the twentieth century, then, the child became associated with the deepest parts of the self and of one's personal history, and the unconscious became seen as a "meta-theory of childhood" (Steedman, 95). As the child was linked closely with the past, and retrieving the past with the potential of the creative realm, the study of childhood also served to illuminate the nature of adult fear and desire in imaginative literature written by adults about childhood.

This book, in its focus on the imagination of childhood, on how its formation and development is portrayed, raises several questions: How has the freshness through which a child sees the world been approximated? How has the literature of childhood conveyed the ways in which the child's experience is retained and renewed in adulthood? What language expresses and contains this sense of deep and intimate experience? Dickens wrote about the child Nell in *The Old Curiosity Shop*, "As it was she seemed to exist in a kind of allegory."[9] The complexity of the child's reality—layered, at once allegorical and realistic—reflects the child's ability to pass in and out of the imaginative and "realistic" realms, to live often fully and without much discomfort in both, in a kind of spontaneity, so that the literature of childhood often contains narrative, dramatic, and poetic, as well as visual modes. Often it seems "cross-genred," and driven by clusters of images and metaphors that draw us closer to our own early experience. Like much experimental literature, the literature of childhood requires a simultaneity of expression that disrupts chronology and topography.

Consider the ways Lewis Carroll's *Alice*[10] stories use poems, songs, fantastic images, and figures that shape-shift while retaining a realism and directness of expression (most notably Alice herself). While the characters are dreamlike, they suggest the daily world with its obsessions with food, manners, rules, and routines. Carroll records the literalness of the child's imagination visually in the Mouse's tale, by shaping the text into a tail—a precursor of the concrete poetry of contemporary writers, in which the shapes of the words suggest the poem's images. Juliet Dusinberre, in *Alice to the Lighthouse*: *Children's Books and Radical Experiments in Art*, points out the influence of the spirit of "words as play" and "[t]he absence of a . . . linear direction in narrative . . . pioneered in children's books in the latter half of the nineteenth century," on the work of Virginia Woolf and her contemporaries.[11] "By the time of Carroll's death in 1898," she writes, "*Alice* had supplanted *The Pilgrim's Progress* in the popular imagination" (Dusinberre, 1). She asserts, "Radical experiments in the arts in the early modern period began in the books which Lewis Carroll and his successors wrote for children" (Dusinberre, 5). Gertrude Stein, in her experimental story of childhood, *The World Is Round*,[12] engages a narrative as accumulative tale in ring form—at once a story, poem, and nonsense work that, of course, speaks sense, but by indirection. It embodies the aesthetic principles of the modernist hybrid form in an extended children's nursery rhyme and picture book. Stein attempted to make language "innocent" again with the word play that returns us to the child's delight in the sounds and shape of words. The literature of childhood, like children themselves, seems to tolerate, in fact, to inspire and cultivate paradoxical worlds and an exploration of our early ways of ordering the world, notably through language.

Through exploring this literature and the states of mind inherited from childhood, we might identify the images through which we saw the world; we might approximate the lenses through which we view the world even now. This most difficult and continuous task is often dismissed and unexamined in adulthood, even by those who are sophisticated and who regard the world with a developed sense of consciousness. The poetics of childhood draws attention to the ways in which we might see the flux of our imaginations more clearly. We might be able to distinguish between projection of the values and attitudes we associate with images from our early experiences and an illumination of the object or moment itself, as it stands more revealed.

The poetics of childhood addresses the persistent longing for childhood in adulthood and those states of mind we connect with childhood: openness and a sense of mystery and awe, as they are imaginatively expressed in the language and literature of childhood. Through language, the adult can recapture in part what can never fully be reclaimed, what has been twice removed, leaving two empty chambers: in one, the negative space of the first great loss, the body of the mother; in the other—what comes with the growing consciousness and socialization of the child—the loss of the immediacy of a primal response to the natural world. With the awareness of time that embodies and represents consciousness, we lose that early intuitive and instinctive encounter of the body of the world and of the body in the world. Following in the footsteps of D. W. Winnicott, Christopher Bollas notes, "Language succeeds the mother as a transformational object informed by one's personal aesthetic."[13] Language—images, both metaphoric and metonymic, rhythms and forms of meter—affords us what Winnicott called "a holding environment." Situated "in the potential space between inner and outer reality" (Bollas, xvii), language patterned into literature provides a way that we, as adults, can recreate or approximate childhood states. Our need for creativity— whether it be expressed in an active, conscious exploration, or held in stasis, in a fumbling chaos of the unconscious—involves the search for an objective correlative for those states of mind associated with the landscape of childhood. In harmony with the work of Wordsworth and the Romantics, we look for the sublime, sought so instinctually in the mother, in nature, and in the language of memory— idiosyncratically recalled, reconfigured, and transformed by the imagination. This process is not linear. It involves layers of consciousness, of images embedded in that longing, preserved in childhood memory. As Bachelard noted, "Not only our memories, but the things we have forgotten are 'housed.' They bear within themselves a kind of aesthetics of hidden things."[14] And for the urban child, for those of us whose primal landscapes did not include "natural settings," our early imaginative landscapes (natural to us) are infused with city streets, lots, parks, playgrounds, as well as the adored objects of childhood memorabilia. Children's early stories, those first voices heard through tones of pleasure, terror, despair, the sights and sounds of the neighborhood—all inhabit the landscape of childhood, what Bachelard calls "the oneiric house of memory" or the realm of dreams and imagination.

Northrop Frye, in writing about Blake's treatment of the child-archetype, made a strong claim for the urgency of "the child in us who cries for the moon [and who] will never stop crying until the moon is his plaything, until we are delivered from the tyranny of time, space, and death, from the remoteness of a gigantic nature and from our own weakness and selfishness."[15] Perhaps this is an expression of the largest sense of the poetics of childhood, the imaginative construct with which Frye connects the dreamer and the child: "the dreamer whose space is inside his mind . . . [is like] the child who is not yet fully conscious of the iron chain of memory that binds his ego to time and space, [and therefore] still ha[s] some capacity for living in the present" (Frye, 513). So it is the "dreamer" in us that embodies desire, the part Blake identified in his drawing of a small person climbing a huge ladder that reaches the moon, under which he wrote, "I want, I want." It is the capacity for immediacy and revelation of hidden memory that this book attempts to explore, the desire for reaching beyond the grasp that it hopes to illuminate and even retrieve from its origins in childhood.

## 4.

By the late eighteenth century, childhood was established as a distinct and separate state of being.[16] As the Romantics linked childhood and the imagination, the child became established not only as "father of the man" but also as internalized keeper of memory and, therefore, potential healer of the adult who does not remember. However, to be lost in childhood moments also signifies frozenness, so that as adults we need to seek a balance. Language—the reading and writing of it in particular—offers a container for the "wise passivity" of adult remembering, through which the breach with nature and with our nature can be repaired. Whether childhood is regarded as "the shape of a life as a result of happenings" or "the shape already latent," the child has come to be used, in modern study of the self, as identity "constituted in memory" and "expressed in self-narration . . . " (Steedman, 11). Not only the retrieval of childhood memory but its expression brings us close to achieving a harmony between what Wordsworth saw as the "two consciousnesses." The childhood self, as reconstructed by images, pieces of narrative, and pockets of poetic moments, can be reclaimed in adult memory by the functional self of adult consciousness. And imaginative expression of such realms has the power to bring fragments of the self into alignment, to heal the fractures of socialization between mind and body, between the spiritual and the temporal, between the analytical and the meditative. The poetics of childhood represents both to the reader and the writer, the creator and the witness to the creation, the potential of even our darkest moments of dislocation to metamorphose into a rejuvenating and creative energy, what Denise Levertov called "a white source of light." And the child, as guide to this body of literature, remains a source of hope and suggests that, no matter how devastating the world, healing can come through the use of childhood to create a poetics, an imagined but tangible state, inspired and illuminated by the child, to return to.

# 1

# Constructions of Innocence

## I. WILLIAM BLAKE

**1.**

Without Contraries is no progression.

—WILLIAM BLAKE, *THE MARRIAGE OF HEAVEN AND HELL*

Peter Ackroyd, Blake's recent biographer, began his work by declaring, "In the visionary imagination of William Blake there is no birth and no death, no beginning and no end, only the perpetual pilgrimage within time towards eternity."[1] Blake portrayed Innocence as a layered and fluctuating state. Between 1793 and 1818, various editions of *Songs of Innocence* were published, in which "no two copies ever contain[ed] the poems in the same order" (Ackroyd 118). Blake's decision to move certain poems from *Innocence* to *Experience* reflected his sense that the two "contrary states of the human soul" were fluid. He saw Innocence as a singularly fragile state that can only be approximated in its articulation—and then only in art, where it could be captured metaphorically in moments, almost like a still life. For, as Ackroyd said, "there is no birth and no death" for Blake but, rather, always the movement "towards eternity," Blake's higher innocence, the origins of which can be glimpsed in visions rather than fully realized in the world. Nonetheless, through description of the shapes it takes in the real world, most directly seen in the figure of the child, we can approach its meaning for Blake in his best-known work, *Songs of Innocence and of Experience.*

Harold Pagliaro claims that, "Understood from the child's point of view, and not from Blake's . . . or our own, Innocence is a condition of unself-conscious identification with the world."[2] And when the child runs up against experience that defies Innocence, such as the restraints and various institutions that sever us from our natural selves, the instinct is toward denying anything that threatens it. What makes Blake's Innocence "poignant," says Jean Hagstrum, is "its capacity for being blighted by society. There passes now and then over it the shadow of Experience, a cloud that suggests the coming dark but that does not destroy the day."[3]

Certainly, *Songs of Innocence* celebrates the state of Innocence. Some of the simpler lyrics seem without shadows. "Laughing Song" resonates with the spontaneity of laughter: "the green woods laugh with the voice of joy/ . . . the air does laugh/ . . . And the green hill laughs with the noise of it./ . . . [T]he meadows laugh . . . the grasshopper laughs," and the children who all laugh are "merry and join with me," says the speaker, in one incantation of harmony. "Infant Joy" also celebrates the singular state of peace and happiness associated with innocence—before the infant is cast out of such harmony and propelled into the patriarchal world of language and law. Here the infant speaker says, " 'I have no name/ I am but two days old.—/ . . . I happy am/Joy is my name." All other lyrics of *Innocence* involve tears—of loss, of fear, of separation—or suggest their imminence.

The central devastating impulse of innocence is to create myths, rationalizations, and projections, as the innocent child cannot conceive of or tolerate the cruelty of its world. If we extend what modern psychoanalysts such as Winnicott and Alice Miller describe as the "false self," created as an accommodation to parental needs, to society's demands that further necessitate denial, we might be close to the sense of Blake's dramatic lyrics. In a much-quoted lyric of *Innocence*, the child speaker of "The Little Black Boy" has incorporated the lessons of his mother that depict God as benign protector who purposely created "black bodies and this sun-burnt face" so "[t]hat we may learn to bear the beams of love." There he declares, of the little white boy, "I'll stand and stroke his silver hair,/ And be like him and he will then love me." In "The Chimney Sweeper," the child-speaker is sold, as poor children were at four through seven years of age, "while yet my tongue/ Could scarcely cry weep weep weep weep." He relates the story of little Tom Dacre, a fellow sweeper, whose vision of an Angel opening the coffins of "thousands of sweepers" and setting them free, which leads him to conclude, "So if all do their duty, they need not fear harm."

There seem to be two types of innocents in Blake's *Songs*: those who feel "unself-consciously united with the world," like the speaker of "Infant Joy," and those who "unself-consciously prolong" that state (Pagliaro, 11), like the speakers of "The Little Black Boy" and "The Chimney Sweeper." And their caretakers similarly consist of two types: those adults who sympathize with the children and those entrenched in restraining structures of the world that Blake despised. But even the guardians of innocence can't protect the children from entry into the invariably unjust world. And children sense this, hence their tears. This painful truth is revealed in the "magic" or otherworldliness that necessarily accompanies such protection. As Thomas R. Frosch notes, children are saved only through the intervention of an angel, a glowworm, God, or the vision of an afterlife.[4] A child can't help but notice, whether that observation is tolerated in consciousness or driven into the unconscious, how lost and vulnerable he or she is likely to be at any given moment. Just as any childhood dream of separation suggests the inevitable severing of child from parent, similarly the figure of the magic helper implies the ways in which we are helplessly torn from each other, and this is intuited by the child speakers even in the poems of *Innocence*. Frosch notes how each of the lyrics "focuses on a crisis of Innocence, its moment of transition into something else" (Frosch, 75). Innocence is an unstable state, difficult to locate or sustain. The central concern of the *Songs of Innocence and of Experience* seems to be not so much Innocence or Experience, "but the borderline between them" (Frosch, 75).

Blake lived in the liminal spaces between "contrary states" of mind. His reality required negotiating the demands of daily life and the visions that grew in intensity throughout his life. Even as a child, he saw visions that Ackroyd claims were eidetic, images "seen as real sensory perceptions" (Ackroyd, 24). His first vision of "a tree filled with angels," appeared when he was eight or ten years old and he believed all people would see such visions, that they are therefore universal, were it not for worldliness " 'which blinds the spiritual eye' " (Ackroyd, 24). Ackroyd offers, "Perhaps there is a sense in which, with all his contrariness and extreme sensitivity, he remained a child. . . . [H]is visions became a way both of lending himself a coherent identity and of confirming a special fate; they afforded him authenticity and prophetic status in a world that ignored him" (Ackroyd, 25). However we interpret his visionary sensibility, it is clear that for Blake Innocence was palpable in these visions and that they were representations of the unity of past and future, and of the connection between all things— the worldly glimpsed in visions of the heavenly, the heavenly reflected in the world; that "heaven longs to see itself in material form, while the world aspires to be reunited with its spiritual essence" (Ackroyd, 48). As he says in "The Divine Image" of *Innocence*,

Mercy has a human heart
Pity, a human face:
And Love, the human form divine
...
Where Mercy, Love and Pity dwell
There God is dwelling too.

And in "A Divine Image" of *Experience*, "Cruelty has a Human Heart/ And Jealousy a Human Face/ Terror the Human Form divine" as well. Those who repress or deny what they see in the world remain frozen or regress into Ignorance, the potential stasis of Experience. However, Blake suggests a dialectic as the driving force toward the wisdom he sought in a state of higher Innocence.

For Blake, Experience was the fallen world. Critics have had some success in pinning down this realm, the essence of which, according to Frye, "appears to be discreteness or opacity . . . a self-enclosed entity unlike all others" (Frye, 516). Hagstrom saw Blake's Experience as "blighted Innocence . . . a purgatory" on the way to heaven. "Experience is related to Innocence as a fossil is to a living creature. . . . [It] is not primarily a state of nature. It is psychological, political, social—a condition of man and his institutions. . . . Experience is the work of church, state, and man in society" (Hagstrum, 530), which locates Blake as politically radical and as a dissenter.

The child became for Blake the creature furthest and freest from the fallen world, and childhood the state most distant from its corrupting influence. But, within the child, who resides in this fallen world, Innocence battles with Experience toward some vision of release from its shackles. Thus, "The Chimney Sweeper" of *Experience* is conscious of having retained a sense of self, as he describes himself, "A little black thing among the snow:/ Crying weep, weep in notes of woe!" He learns to feign a public image of "happiness" before the authority figures of his life—his " 'father & mother . . . [who] are both gone up to the church to pray./ . . . to praise God & his Priest & King/ Who make up a heaven of our misery.' " However, he privately asserts,

"They clothed me in the clothes of death,
And taught me to sing the notes of woe.
And because I am happy, & dance & sing,
They think they have done me no injury."

Although this image of the chimney sweeper's state is bleak, there is no self-blame, as he is able to locate the source of his pain and the truth of its origins. Aware of the oppressive forces that imprison him, he is free to express a sense of self, that separates him from the darkness, albeit in the imagination—which is where Blake saw the harmony of Innocence and Experience resolve in higher Innocence. For him, Innocence and Wisdom were natural partners, while Ignorance resided with Experience and with those who, in their denial of the worldliness of the world, ultimately denied the spiritual as well. As David Wagenknecht notes, "Blake's secular and religious concerns are one: to demonstrate that the ordinary world of extensive, fallen vision includes the imaginative wherewithal for that world's intensive visionary transformation."[5] Blake worked throughout his life to find forms that could contain such expression.

Within the past ten years, the unity of word and image in Blake's work has been widely discussed.[6] Blake as painter, engraver, and poet created a harmony between his gifts, demonstrated in the illuminated manuscripts of *Songs of Inno-cence and of Experience*. Just as he sought a reconciliation of all contraries—the generic ones, such as male and female, youth and age, and such modes as expansive and contracted, opaque and translucent, attractive and repulsive (Ackroyd, 144)—he worked to create an art that would join image and word. *Songs of Inno-cence and Experience* were printed, poems of Experience on the back plates of the poems of Innocence, so that they "could be held as one object in the hand" (Ackroyd, 143). He etched into the copper plates the words of the poems, backward, so that they would appear as images right side up. Words, thus, were imaged as sketches, each poem an illumination.[7] Only in the poetic imagination and in the work of art it issued could such harmony be secured.

The pairings of the poems by their titles, Innocence with Experience, directed by the subtitle, "Shewing the Two Contrary States of the Human Soul," compel us to read them as opposites. But I find myself struck by the permeable boundaries and the interpenetration of the two states. Certainly we find shadows of Experience in the poems of *Innocence*, as mentioned earlier, and glimmers of Innocence in the voices and images of the poems of *Experience*. Read separately, which also is valid, and considering the shifting of order noted above, one might focus on each poem's resolution, the point at which each poem comes to rest. But, when read in pairs or even within a particular image, they suggest not synthesis or reconciliation but a tension sustained by the shifting voices and echoes, and the images that capture a turning point in process, a corner not yet turned.

The "Introduction" to *Innocence*, for example, is a complex lyric, which introduces the various states that will recur throughout the poems. The child "on a cloud," heavenly in its innocence, directs the more experienced piper—initially revealing the complexity of the child's innocence, while the speaker/poet seems to have moved through Experience into a state of higher Innocence. The child begins with laughter, a spontaneous expression of Innocence, but then weeps at the piper's song of "merry chear." I assume that he is intuiting some loss, some sadness from a knowledge earlier and perhaps deeper than words, since the piping is wordless, sound without signifier, its meaning suggestive and primal. "Sing thy songs of happy chear," the child demands, and weeps "with joy to hear" the movement from pure music into song. The conjoining of joy and sadness, expressive of emotional freedom, also transcends the boundaries of the either/or thinking Blake's dialectic worked against—which is always at the core of complexity. The song unifies sound and word which can attain a permanence in writing, as the child instructs the piper "to sit thee down and write/ In a book that all may read." The movement here is from the one child/listener to the many, so that "Every child may joy to hear."

Art provides for the many a source of inspiration and healing, as the single child vanishes and the piper goes on to narrate his creative process. There also is the suggestion of the loss of the childlike and spontaneous as the child disappears and words emerge. The ambiguous image at the end of the poem, when he says, "And I made a rural pen,/ And I stain'd the water clear," always brings tears to my eyes. Whether it is the resonance of the primal biblical cadences or the haunting image they portray, I feel a sense of awe as I pause at those lines: at how he stained the water clear, at how he also cleared it with his song. Some suggest that Blake is simply inverting the word order, that with his pen the piper is staining the clear water; however, the tension between opposites contained in the one image captures most closely the dynamic of these poems. The water has been sullied, but impurity produces an awareness, the expression of which illuminates experience, as poems, in their concise and suggestive language, often do. The poem does seem, however, to resolve in its assertion of the universality and primariness of art.

The one child united with "Every child" marks a connection with the "Introduction" to *Songs of Experience*, where the Bard, a more evolved version of the piper,

> Present, Past, & Future sees,
> Whose ears have heard
> The Holy Word,
> That walk'd among the ancient trees.

The Bard has transcended Experience, and as visionary poet, keeper and teller of the story of humanity, like the piper and the divine child-director of *Innocence*, he implores "the lapsed Soul . . . [to] fallen fallen light renew!" Earth is in a fallen state and its answer to the Bard does not inspire hope—

> Earth rais'd up her head,
> From the darkness dread and drear.
> Her light fled:
> Stony dread!
> And her locks cover'd with grey despair.

But the Bard evokes an ambiguous image of timelessness in the time-bound world when it implores Earth not to turn away: "The starry floor,/ The watry shore/ Is giv'n thee till the break of day." Similar to the lessons of "The Pretty Rose Tree" and "Ah! Sun-Flower," it warns against turning away from beauty, love, and desire or from the richness of this Earth. Against "the pale Virgin shrouded in snow," Blake places "the Lilly white, [who] in Love delight[s],/ Nor a thorn nor a threat stain her beauty bright." The sorrow and joy of "Introduction" to *Innocence* and the beauty of the expansive sweep from "the starry floor" to "the watry shore," along with the "slumberous mass" of *Experience*, express a full range of human emotion—large and ever-renewing as the dawn that "rises" continually from the darkness. There is a harmony in the voices of the child, the piper, and the Bard, who "Present, Past, & Future sees," a design for the protection, expression, and renewal of Innocence that draws on Experience for its transformation into the *Songs*.

## 2. Children Lost and Found

The pleas of "The Little Boy Lost" of *Innocence* express the single primal fear of children—that of being lost and abandoned, and cut off from their very source of safety in the world. " 'Father, father, where are you going/ O do not walk so fast,' " the little boy implores. He grows more desperate, " 'Speak father, speak to your little boy/ Or else I shall be lost.' " Even in the resolution of the poem that follows, "The Little Boy Found," where he is led by God, who "Appeard like his father in white," and restored him to his "weeping" mother, he never hears a response from his father. In these poems of *Innocence*, spiritual guides may take the place of the parent-deserter, or another parent may still embrace the child. However, often the child is left with an unhealed wound, a silence, a void from the original guardian that can't be easily filled. This is what happens in *Innocence*. In *Experience*, the sense of being lost expands from its most primal expression to a more subtle state of fragility. Here it is a little girl who is lost. Interestingly, "The Little Girl Lost" and the companion piece, "The Little Girl Found," originally placed in *Innocence*, were later moved by Blake into *Experience*, where they appeared as expressions of a young girl's vulnerability. Here the suggestion is sexual. Her primal self and instinctive nature are asserted as the beasts tenderly, "Loos'd her slender dress,/ And naked they convey'd/ To caves the sleeping maid." At the center of the poem, two verses appear curiously and tenuously poised. They read,

> "Lost in desart wild
> Is your little child.
> How can Lyca sleep,
> If her mother weep?
> If her heart does ake,
> Then let Lyca wake:
> If my mother sleep,
> Lyca shall not weep."

The child's consciousness of the mother's grief is at stake here—not just her safety. Or, rather, her safety is dependent on her mother's emotional state. The child, here, in Experience, can freely enjoy her sexuality only if her mother is not upset by the "loss" of her child. The "desart wild" can not be transformed into "a garden mild" if Lyca is not allowed to rest after wandering off to "Hearing wild birds' song." She urges, " 'Frowning frowning night' " to " 'Let the moon arise/ While I close my eyes.' "

We leave Lyca in the cave sleeping until the resolution of her tale in "The Little Girl Found," which follows "The Little Girl Lost" in both printed versions. In "The Little Girl Found," her parents search for her over valleys and through deserts, dreaming of her "Famish'd, weeping, weak/ With hollow piteous shriek." They come upon a lion who leads them to her, urging, " 'Weep not for the maid;/ In my palace deep,/ Lyca lies asleep.' " As they follow their vision, they see "their sleeping child,/ Among tygers wild." This poem rests on a vision of unity and peace: parents no longer "fear the wolvish howl,/ Nor the lions' growl," for they have seen their child safely sleeping among the beasts, which, in turn, liberates them to recognize and accept their affinity with the beasts and be restored to their own primal nature. For Blake, acceptance of desire is essential to the state of higher Innocence.

In fact, freedom to love is natural to the human spirit. In "A Little Boy Lost," it is self-love for which the child is "strip'd," "bound," and "burn'd . . . in a holy place,/ Where many had been burn'd before" for innocently expressing his feelings. Blake prepares us for the horror of his criminalization and torture in the first verse, which reads, surely and directly:

"Nought loves another as itself
Nor venerates another so.
Nor is it possible to Thought
A greater than itself to know."

After this simple and honest affirmation, the little boy openly acknowledges:

"And Father, how can I love you,
Or any of my brothers more?
I love you like the little bird
That picks up crumbs around the door."

At once, he is seized by the Priest, while "all admired the Priestly care," his cries and those of his parents submerged, as Blake cries out against such sacrifice of nature to the tyranny of authority: "Are such things done on Albions shore?"

In its closest pairing, "A Little Girl Lost," Blake begins with an epigraph:

Children of the future Age,
Reading this indignant page:
Know that in a former time,
Love! Sweet Love! Was thought a crime.

In this homily, in reverse of those children's verses popular in his time, Blake creates Ona, the primal child suggestive of her name, who loses her fear: "the holy

holy light,/Had just removed the curtains of the night" and "To the holy light,/ [Ona] [n]aked in the sunny beams delight[s]" in the "kisses sweet" of her lover. The playfulness of the "youthful pair" is described as "Fill'd with softest care." But when she goes home "To her father white," "his loving look,/ Like the holy book,/ All her tender limbs with terror shook." He demands,

"Ona! pale and weak!
To thy father speak:
O the trembling fear!
O the dismal care!
That shakes the blossoms of my hoary hair."

This lyric does not suggest the brutality and child-sacrifice of "A Little Boy Lost." But we are left here to imagine Ona's fate, her natural joy in sexuality, the freedom of her spirit will be crushed and blighted. The "blossoms" of her father's "hoary hair" seem paradoxical, deathlike, pitted against the "the holy light" and "the garden bright" of her innocence. Many such images combine to create allegories of repression and cruelty.

It is interesting to note the movement from the definite to the indefinite article in the otherwise identical poems of the title, from "The Little Boy Lost" to "A Little Boy Lost." The cruelty becomes overt—unrelenting and unredeemable. Similarly, while "The Little Girl Lost" ends with the child's freedom and safety, and "The Little Girl Found" in the parents' acceptance, in "A Little Girl Lost," her pleasure is met with fear and trembling. In the poems of the definite articles, there seems to be a belief in the individual care of the child who is seen as distinct, "the" little boy or "the" little girl, as opposed to "a" child—who can be any child, unprotected by the particular love of a specific parent or set of parents. What makes us feel loved and therefore safe at such a tender age and at the times in our lives when we are most vulnerable, when our sense of self is completely constructed and determined by those who raise us and care for us? Blake suggests that it comes to us in an offering of ourselves as special, as belonging to someone to whom we are visible, distinct. The indefinite article renders the child just that—indefinite, undefined, fragile, and disconnected in the harsh and unviable world of Experience.

**3.**

"To see a World in a Grain of Sand"

—WILLIAM BLAKE, *AUGURIES OF INNOCENCE*

How do we touch the infinite, find "Eternity in an hour," transcend the self, and retrieve the sense of harmony that children assume in their earliest state? Blake never lost his sense of the unity of all things vividly imagined in his many recurring eidetic visions. He was haunted by images of his brother Robert, who died at nineteen and appeared to him continuously throughout his life as his idealized self. Arrested in youth, Robert became for Blake an icon of Innocence, a source of inspiration and creativity.[8] For Blake, the gift of the child was to evoke such innovation and connection.

In the only paintings that appear without words, the frontispieces for both *Innocence* and *Experience*, a child emerges as a source of divine inspiration. The piper of the "Introduction" to the *Songs of Innocence* is looking up at a child who flies above him, illuminated in a kind of celestial light, while below at the piper's feet sheep, also illuminated, although not as brightly, graze, heads down to the green earth. The glow of the painting connects child and sheep in pastoral innocence, a vision that guides the piper. The frontispiece to *Experience* depicts a man walking with an angel/child who sits on his head, their hands joined, as they both look directly out at us. Under them, the same sheep graze, positioned as in *Innocence*. The sun lights the sky in tones similar to but brighter than the golden sheep—another vision of pastoral. But here, the gaze of both the angel—itself a figure of innocence past and reborn—and the man suggest the consciousness born of Experience, but connected to Innocence—the higher Innocence Blake saw as the ultimate spiritual connection of all things.

The unity we knew—although we were unconscious of it as children—may be found again in connection, each with the other, often in compassion for the suffering and injustice Blake saw around him. In "On Another's Sorrow" from *Innocence*, Blake offers to the child empathy and solace for all wounds in his song of compassion:

> Can I see anothers woe,
> And not be in sorrow too.
> …
> Can a father see his child,
> Weep, nor be with sorrow fill'd.
> …
> Can a mother sit and hear.
> An infant groan an infant fear—
> No no never can it be,
> Never never can it be.

The movement is from those close to the infant to He who looks over us all—from the most frail of humans watched over by less frail humans, who are finally all watched over by Christ, who, in His infinite compassion, "becomes an infant small/ . . . a man of woe/ He doth feel the sorrow too." And in his sorrow for us,

Figure 1. *Songs of Innocence* by William Blake: Innocence, Frontispiece (plate 1), 1789. By permission of Yale Center for British Art, Paul Mellon Collection.

O! he gives to us his joy.
That our grief he may destroy;
Till our grief is fled & gone
He doth sit by us and moan.

—an expression of the utmost emotional connection, the absolute caretaker.

In this sense, Blake's vision is ultimately "holistic." He saw the many in the one, which represented the potential for higher Innocence in every element and every living thing. Northrop Frye so eloquently articulated the heart of Blake's philosophical and spiritual stance:

The real form of human society is the body of one man; the flock of sheep is the
body of one lamb; the garden is the body of one tree, so-called tree of life. The city
is the body of one building or temple, a house of many mansions, and the building
itself is the body of one stone, a glowing and fiery precious stone, the unfallen stone
of alchemy which assimilates everything else to itself, Blake's grain of sand which
contains the world. (Frye, 517)

Everywhere are "Auguries of Innocence." Whether it is "A dog starved at his
Master's Gate/ [that] Predicts the ruin of the State/ [or] A Horse misusd upon
the Road/ [that] Calls to Heaven for Human blood," Blake sees in microcosm
the grand cosmos reflected—no creature too insignificant to wreak tremors in
the earth in its abuse and suffering. Even the perpetrators are connected in
mercy to their victims, as "The Lamb misusd breeds Public strife/ And yet
forgives the Butcher's Knife." Even "The Catterpiller on the Leaf/ Repeats to
thee thy Mother's grief." Everything miniscule marks something more exalted, every thing a sign of every other, all intricately linked. The one stands in
for the many and Blake says, "It is right it should be so:/ Man was made
for Joy & Woe." These seemingly paradoxical emotional states are resolved,
in that

> Joy & Woe are woven fine,
> A Clothing for the Soul divine;
> Under every grief & pine
> Runs a joy with silken twine.

In the largest picture, Blake's spirituality allows that:

> Every Night & every Morn
> Some to Misery are Born.
> Every Morn & every Night
> Some are Born to sweet delight.
> Some are Born to sweet delight,
> Some are Born to Endless Night.

This is only catastrophic if we see ourselves as separate units, of which "sweet
delight" and "Endless Night" are discrete rather than only parts of a whole. Frye
says, "In a completely human society man would not lose his individuality, but he
would lose his separate and isolated ego" (516). This happens, according to
Blake, "When we see not Thro the Eye." He sees, in "Auguries of Innocence,"
signs of all the rightness of the world, a pattern of justice, a balance of light and
dark in the whole universe—seen and transformed by the imagination of the poet.
He concludes:

God Appears & God is Light
To those poor Souls who dwell in Night,
But does a Human Form Display
To those who Dwell in Realms of day.

In the literature of childhood, Blake provides a connection between our earliest states of infancy and our growing awareness, the movement from Innocence through Experience, to a higher Innocence retained and contained in the imagination. The child is the guide to the natural world; she keeps us honest—if we stay close by. If we don't—if, in our painful engagement with the world, we turn away from her, we deny ourselves access to that richest and for Blake truest source of feeling, reborn again in the figure of Christ, the Son, who "became a child." And this vision of the child imaginatively cast leads us to resist and survive what Blake saw in the religious and social institutions of his day as the force of the punitive and unforgiving Father.

## II. WILLIAM WORDSWORTH

Wordsworth discovered childhood as the great source of inspiration, the primal force which drives all creativity. He was interested in the consciousness of childhood because he connected it deeply with the consciousness of the poet. He understood how the world becomes suffused with our earliest images, how we drink in with the mother's milk—symbolically, maybe even literally—our earliest impressions, and see the world ever after through those primal lenses. The source of our creativity becomes more remote as we grow away from childhood and from our self in nature; yet, we continue to depend on these early "spots" of memory for our poetic images and for our truest moments of feeling. And if we lose touch with our childhood memories, we inevitably have lost touch with our original feelings, from which all our feeling-infused thinking derives.

### 1. The Natural Child

"Mighty Prophet! Seer blest!"
"Thou Eye among the blind!"

Many of Wordsworth's early poems (published in 1798) contain children, usually in dialogue with an adult. Often it is a parent who does not understand the child, who has lost touch with his own childhood. The child becomes the teacher; the adult learns to listen to the child-speaker and to the outside world, rather than to his own inner preoccupations or conventional responses, in order to eventually retrieve significant lessons originally embedded in childhood.

In these poems, Wordsworth's child is both spiritual and real. He comes to us "trailing clouds of glory" from heaven, which "is our home." And, Wordsworth believed, it is to this home that we are always returning. As "Mighty Prophet" and as "Seer blest," the child is Christ, who warns us: Except ye be converted, and become as children, ye shall not enter the kingdom of heaven. The child prophesies the ways in which the adult's life will be played out—by generating those strengths and frailties that are dictated by the quality of a particular child in her particular childhood. The child is the "Eye among the blind," the one who sees what slips from our adult vision. In poems such as "We are Seven" and "Anecdote for Fathers," she teaches us to forget the self.

There is evidence that Wordsworth was moved by real children, particularly by his love for those close to him. The boy who inspired "Anecdote for Fathers" is identified as "a son of my friend, Basil Montagu, who had been two or three years under our care."[9] He also was impressed by those child acquaintances who attracted his attention, such as the muse of "We are Seven," whom he referred to as, "the heroine I met within the area of Goodrich Castle . . . in the year 1793" (*Selected Poems*, 505). Essentially, however, his interest in childhood had less to do with children *per se* than with the adult's need of the child, with what adults learn from children and what they need from childhood.

In "We are Seven" and "Anecdote for Fathers," we hear the child-voice and see moments of child-movement from opposite perspectives. In "Anecdote" the adult is so separate from the child, so far away in his self-absorption, that he doesn't notice the child's experience. And in "We are Seven," although he is similarly preoccupied, he is not separate enough, so that he assumes the child's vision to be identical to and in harmony with his own.

These early poems are exemplars, subtly and delicately conceived. In some, the adult speaker understands and is able to articulate the moral; in others, the adult reader, as opposed to the speaker, gleans the message, which, although unstated, is powerfully urged. In "We are Seven," the "simple child," who "feels its life in every limb," is a child of nature, an embodiment of connection. Although Wordsworth himself said that in this poem he was writing about "the perplexity and obscurity in childhood that attend our notion of death, or rather our utter inability to admit that notion" (*Selected Poems* 448), the little girl he presents understands intuitively that life and death are on a continuum. This sense of unity exists in her imagination, unquestioned and instinctual, so that although two of her siblings "in the church-yard lie," she insists that they be counted as part of her family. She says, " 'These graves are green, they may be seen/ . . . Twelve steps or more from my mother's door" (ll. 37–9). Far from denying their death, she clearly sets them in chronological order—first Jane died, then John; she notes the time of year, the way in which each was affected by illness. It is the meaning of it that she asserts, her sense that these two are away, like her two siblings who are "gone to sea," only closer in proximity—"in the church-yard. I/ Dwell near them with my mother," she informs the adult narrator, who is struck at first by her "rustic, woodland air" and "[h]er beauty [which] made me glad." However many times he insists that there cannot be seven children if two are dead, this child asserts " 'Nay, we are seven!' " Although the narrator sees her as willful, it is his own lack of imagination, his inability to comprehend her sense of death as continuous with life, that results in his protests: " 'But they are dead; those two are dead!/ Their spirits are in heaven!' "

Wordsworth seems to share the child's vision. When he speaks of children as "trailing clouds of glory . . . [coming] [f]rom God, who is our home," he concludes that "Heaven lies about us in our infancy!" (*Ode* ll. 64–6). Although the conflict in "We are Seven" has been said to be between reason and the imagination,[10] it seems to me to be about different ways of reasoning. The child reasons correctly that they are still a family of seven, although two are buried in the churchyard and two are at sea; but the adult's reasoning here excludes hers, and Wordsworth leaves the adult reader with what the adult speaker couldn't understand or tolerate—the power and veracity of the child's imagination.

"Anecdote for Fathers" illuminates a similar tension between the vision of the adult and that of the child. This most poignant narrative poem begins with an epigraph in Latin that questions the effects of adult demands on children. It first bore the subtitle that translated as, "Shewing How the Art of Lying May Be Taught." Later it was replaced with another Latin epigraph that gives voice to a stronger child or suggests a strong identification with the child. Translated, it reads, "Restrain that force of yours, for I shall tell lies if you drive me to it" (*Selected Poems*, 506). Either way, the conclusion of the adult narrator here acknowledges the wisdom he gleans from the child, when he finally hears the child's subtle story.

This is the story of a conversation between a father and his young son, as they walk together. The poem begins with the adult carried into reverie after being touched initially by the beauty of the child, as with "We are Seven." He says,

> I have a boy of five years old;
> His face is fair and fresh to see;
> His limbs are cast in beauty's mould,
> And dearly he loves me. (ll. 1–4)

He goes on to speak of a particular day, "when I could bear/ Some fond regrets to entertain;/ With so much happiness to spare,/ I could not feel a pain" (ll. 14–17). He leaves the boy behind as his thoughts "on former pleasures ran" to Kilve, last year's seaside vacation place, while he walks through the pastoral setting of Liswyn farm—the birds warbling, the lambs bounding.

> The green earth echoed to the feet
> Of lambs that bounded through the glade,
> From shade to sunshine, and as fleet
> From sunshine back to shade. (ll. 18–21)

Nature is harmonious in its fluctuations, inclusive of both light and shadow. But the man creates a disjuncture, with the dichotomous thinking of the adult world (mind/body, youth/age, seaside/farmland, better/worse). He suddenly asks the child, " 'Now tell me, had you rather be/ . . . [o]n Kilve's smooth shore, by the green sea,/ Or here at Liswyn farm?' " When the child answers, spontaneously, "at Kilve," the adult is disturbed and insists on the reason—which the five year old cannot provide. "And three times to the child" he demands the answer, insisting that "here are woods, hills smooth and warm," while the child "hung down his head . . . blushed with shame," and finally answers arbitrarily, utterly relieved to have come up with anything at all. We don't know and can't know what he really means, partially because he is only five and can't articulate his "reasons," but, most important, because he has had to contrive a reason. Finally, the adult seems to understand something significant, as he says:

"O dearest, dearest boy! My heart
For better lore would seldom yearn,
Could I but teach the hundredth part
Of what from thee I learn." (ll. 57–60)

What the adult learns is never spelled out, but Wordsworth implies that it has to do with lying. Even more so, it has to do with shame, that killer of spontaneity and truth; how we teach children to feel ashamed of their responses, and to substitute their tastes for ours—in other words, to "reason."

A poem from that same period, "The Idiot Boy," combines two of Wordsworth's chief concerns—children and idiots, linked through their marginal status in this society, and therefore through their distance from the worldliness of the world. "The Idiot Boy" is about the child who will not grow into reason, who for the most part resists socialization, and therefore comes to represent a kind of purity of response. He is a being naturally close to the spiritual realm.

Wordsworth was attacked for writing a poem about such a subject as idiots (*Selected Poems*, 508) and wrote in a letter, defending himself,

But where are we to find the best measure of this [what is a fit subject for poetry]? I answer, [from with]in; by stripping our own hearts naked, and by looking out of ourselves to[wards those] who lead the simplest lives, and those most according to nature.

In the *Preface to the Lyrical Ballads* (1800), Wordsworth claimed to be "tracing . . . the primary laws of our nature: chiefly, as far as regards the manner in which we associate ideas in a state of excitement." He chose "[h]umble and rustic life . . . because, in that condition, the essential passions of the heart find a better and speak a plainer and more emphatic language; because in that condition of life our elementary feelings co-exist in a state of greater simplicity, and, consequently, may be more accurately contemplated" (*Selected Poems*, 447). The simplest of children, the idiot boy-hero, Johnny, has not been inducted into the language of the world. He is, for Wordsworth, immersed in nature and resides eternally in spontaneity, particularly as there is no possibility for reflection. He is closest to the owl who shouts, "Halloo!" and the owlets who "hoot" and "curr,/ and Johnny's lips they burr, burr, burr," in harmony with nature's creatures. Wordsworth declares, "His lips with joy they burr," he "makes the noise he loves."

Some critics find Wordsworth sentimental here in his focus on the love of Betty Foy, Johnny's mother, for her child.[11] However, I believe that rather than maternal love, the poem centers on the child's unconscious rescue of the adult. In the story, Betty Foy sends Johnny, her most beloved "idiot boy," out into the night to fetch the doctor because her neighbor, Susan Gale, is ill and in extreme pain. Johnny's epithet, "Him whom she loves," defines him and determines his joy—which defines him as well. In joy, he "forgot his holly whip,/ and all his skill in horsemanship" and, thus, wanders off, oblivious to his mission. But this spirited child of nature is clearly Wordsworth's mute spokesperson. And as we leave the horse and rider in the moonlight, we pick up Betty's story. As she sits by Susan's side, her murmurs of reassurance that Johnny will be back with the doctor are contrapuntal to Susan's moans. But as time passes, Susan urges Betty to leave her bedside to find Johnny, and it is Susan's concern with Johnny that propels her out of her bed and ultimately heals her.

Each of the characters represents a position with regard to childhood. Johnny is the spirit of the eternal child; Susan Gale is the sick adult, bereft of any energy, isolated and severed from nature and her own vitality; and Betty Foy is the mother, who, in love with her perpetually childlike child, retains her childhood. She appears at times foolish and inept, and much like Johnny she forgets the task before her as she searches for her child. But in her search, she listens so hard, and we with her, that "The grass you almost hear it growing." Surely this is the glimmer of a divine state. She worries that Johnny, like the divinely attuned numbskull-hero of fairy tales, will have stopped along the way to try "To lay his hands upon a star,/ And in his pocket bring it home," as he does not differentiate between self and nature, or between the natural boundaries of near and far. When she finds him, "Johnny burrs, and laughs aloud./ . . . She kisses o'er and o'er again/ Him whom she loves, her Idiot Boy;/ . . . She pats the Pony, where or when/ She knows not," and even the Pony is sentient, part of the unity of all feeling nature. Then Susan joins them, for as "her mind [had grown] worse and worse [with worry over the child],/ [h]er body—it grew better." The four travel home, reunited and in harmony with the song of the owls.

As the poem ends, Betty implores her son to tell her, " 'Where all this long night you have been,/ What you have heard, what you have seen.' " He replies,

" 'The cocks did crow to-whoo, to-whoo,/ And the sun did shine so cold!' "
Johnny remains in the sensuous realm of infancy, free from "reason" and reflection, not located temporally or spatially, but rather in the mythic time of childhood.

## 2. The "Immortality" *Ode* and the Longing for Childhood

In the "Immortality" *Ode*, the "Intimations of Immortality" are sources of spirituality that resonate from "recollections" of childhood. The *Ode* is a tribute to the
child as "Prophet" and "Seer," and, as elusive as that may be, it holds the key to
the poet's consciousness. Throughout his life as a poet, Wordsworth was in a constant state of inquiry into the nature of consciousness and into this relationship of
child to adult. From "We are Seven," "Anecdote for Fathers," and "The Idiot Boy"
(1798) through *The Prelude* (1799, 1804–1805, and so until Wordsworth's death
in 1850), the relationship is explored as a dynamic one. It is dialectical and shifting, reflexive when internalized, but always, in ever-transforming and extending
ways, the child remains "father of the man." According to Winnicott, who felt an
affinity between Wordsworth's poems and his own psychoanalytic work,
Wordsworth's "idea of eternity comes from the memory traces in each one of us of
our infancy before time started."[12] Psychoanalysts and critics have seen
Wordsworth's "Immortality" *Ode* as representing a great shift in consciousness
that led to the development of psychoanalysis. According to John Turner, the
underlying tenets of the *Ode* suggest that the quality of an adult's life depends on
the quality of his or her childhood and that we can understand the present only in
relation to the past (Turner, 163). Through reading the *Ode*, he claims, "we are
made aware of a disjunction . . . that the child may see and not know it sees; that
the adult may know what he [or she] has seen but may no longer see it" (Turner,
168), and other such paradoxes that Wordsworth foreshadows in his epigraph "the
Child is Father of the Man." Turner notes that Wordsworth located self-
understanding in "the capacity to relive the past as it survives in the present,"
which is dependent on "keep[ing] alive the child in the adult, together with their
very different experiences of time" (Turner, 168). More than the integration of the
self, more than the memory that binds past, present, and future together, "the cop-
resence of the child's vision still active within the adult" (Turner, 169) is the
essence of the poetic imagination. Self-knowledge and wisdom are intimately
connected with the imagination of childhood and with the power of the poet to
move beyond repetition toward originality and creativity.

The *Ode* begins with the commonplace, with "meadow, grove, and stream"
but "[a]ppareled in celestial light,/ The glory and the freshness of a dream." It
traces the harmonious and radiant settings of our childhood. Wordsworth notices
the reciprocal "call" of the natural world and its creatures, which the heavens
echo. He is immersed in "[t]he fulness of . . . bliss," which, while he "feel[s] it
all," and "with joy" hears it all, a "Tree" and the "single Field which I have looked

upon,/ . . . speak of something that is gone"—and he asks, "Where is it now, the glory and the dream?"

It took Wordsworth two years to brave an answer (*Selected Poems*, 536). After asking that question in Section IV, Wordsworth stopped working on the *Ode*. In 1804, two years later, he began again tracing what we lose as we grow out of childhood and how we become unnatural and constrained. He writes of youth hovering in the "shades of the prison house," then becoming a "little Actor . . . [a]s if his whole vocation/ Were endless imitation" (ll. 106–7). He bemoans the loss of the original self, that "Eye among the blind,/ That . . . read'st the eternal deep,/ Haunted for ever by the eternal mind," the "Mighty Prophet" and "Seer blest!/ On whom those truths do rest,/ Which we are toiling all our lives to find." Wordsworth laments but also affirms the struggle of the adult to recover the early instinctual knowledge, the inarticulate but deep feeling of childhood. He expresses regret that we live out our lives with "custom l[ying] upon [us] with a weight,/ Heavy as frost, and deep almost as life!" (ll. 127–8). This depth is sepulchral, rather than liberating. It is not grounded in the depth of feeling he comes to in the last three stanzas of the *Ode*.

The resting place for Wordsworth, for the adult, is the compassion and insight born of such struggle. As in Blake, with the loss of innocence and entry into and through experience, a brighter light emerges from the shadows, an illumination of a higher innocence. Wordsworth reminds us that there is joy "that in our embers . . . doth live,/ That nature yet remembers/ What was so fugitive!" (ll. 129–32). Through memory and thought, through consciousness, "those shadowy recollections" can still be "the fountain light of all our day,/ . . . a master light of all our seeing; . . ." "Our Souls [do] have sight of that immortal sea," which is childhood. We can still "see the Children sport upon the shore,/ and hear the might waters rolling evermore" (ll. 167–8). He affirms,

> Though nothing can bring back the hour
> Of splendour in the grass, of glory in the flower;
> We will grieve not, rather find
> Strength in what remains behind;
> In the primal sympathy . . .
> In the soothing thoughts that spring
> Out of human suffering. (ll. 177–84)

The *Ode* is circular in structure, connecting the natural world with both the child and adult selves. At the end, he returns to the pastoral setting, to the birds and the young lambs. The last stanza restores us to the first, in which the "meadow, grove and stream," "appareled in celestial light," are transformed through memory, where we find "the faith that looks through death" and "the philosophic mind." The early landscape evolves into Meadows and Groves, capitalized, mythicized, and apostrophized. The mountains of the first stanza become Hills, smaller but archetypal; the Fountains, contained and crafted, but eternal, as opposed to the more natural and unencumbered streams. Wordsworth seems resolved. The "glory and the dream" can be retrieved through the sympathetic imagination, that which was imbibed with the infant's love for its mother, that which infused all the world with its original "celestial light." Wordsworth gives "Thanks to the human heart by which we live/ . . . [through which] the meanest flower that blows can give/ Thoughts that do often lie too deep for tears" (ll. 200–3). We still respond to the simplest beauty but, rather than with the unadulterated pleasure of childhood, with a depth of feeling that engages sadness as well as joy, and reflection that integrates thought with feeling.

### 3. *The Prelude* and the Search for Consciousness

> Our simple childhood, sits upon a throne
> That hath more power than all the elements. (V, ll. 508–9)

*The Prelude* was Wordsworth's lifetime work through which he traced, as underscored in the subtitle, "the growth of a poet's mind." Sometimes in tranquillity, sometimes in turmoil, but always with profound commitment, he pursued the double consciousness of the child in the adult. His interest was in the development of the sympathetic imagination—how it comes to be the great source of integration. The imagination, so natural to childhood, reconciles opposing forces—those in the natural world and in human nature. There both child and adult vision can reside, without eternal conflict, although perhaps only in moments.

In *The Prelude*, Wordsworth seeks to establish a paradigm for such a dual vision in several ways: he looks at the doubleness of time, of structure, and of character that such a large and grand work implies—and he meant it to be epic in proportion, although he died before completing it. As an epic, *The Prelude* focuses on a hero who represents a community, in the broadest sense here, the community of humankind. His quest is for the hope and creative power of renewal found in the imagination. Wordsworth understood that in most, "the first Poetic spirit of our human life" would be "abated or suppressed." But he believed that in some of us, the poetic spirit would resist "every change of growth and of decay" and would remain "[p]re-eminent till death." He believed this was possible for all those who worked to live in the two realms of childhood and adulthood, of daily temporal life and of the eternal life of the imagination. The poet/hero's quest, then, takes him back to the origins of his consciousness, so that one movement of the poem is downward into the unconscious, where he finds childhood memories stored as "spots of time." Steven

Marcus describes these spots of time as "certain special moments from our usually early pasts that have the power of resisting the normal workings of erosion . . . that ordinary memory regularly performs in us . . . whether they be traumatically frightening, or ecstatic and transcendent. . . . [They] recur to us unbidden and with all the freshness and impressiveness of their original occurrence."[13] Wordsworth's task is to make manifest these experiences whose impressions remained imprinted on our consciousness almost the way they were experienced, not in their entirety but with an authenticity of feeling. They are clusters of images distilled from the original sensations, so that they may be recalled as Proust's *petite madeleine* recalls the elaborate memory that forms the basis of *Remembrance of Things Past*.[14] With original sensations intact, the imagination is propelled into a series of free associations that form the very structure of *The Prelude*. Like Blake, Wordsworth seemed to have lived in close contact with his early childhood memories. He "recalled having to clutch at external objects—walls and trees—to assure himself that they were materially real and not part of the internal representations of his own mind" (Marcus, 16).

As well as moving down into the depths of consciousness, Wordsworth's double vision propels us forward. As a quest story, *The Prelude* proceeds from event to event, through time and space, toward its resolution. Its narrative line, however, is interrupted by pockets of deep reflection. The structure, then, is both linear and circular, suggesting that the discrete moments and movements are unified by a kind of reflective memory. In *Villette*, Charlotte Brönte's novel about the life of the mind, the incidents of one's life, each seeming "independent of its successor," are first perceived as "a handful of loose beads; but threaded through." Lucy Snowe, Brönte's character in search of consciousness, asks, "Where lay the link of junction, where the little clasp . . . ? I saw or felt union, but could not yet find the spot, or detect the means of connection."[15] In *The Prelude* Wordsworth provides the connection and the means to its discovery.

*The Prelude* begins with the "gentle breeze . . . [that] [d]oth seem half-conscious of the joy it brings/ From the green fields, and from yon azure sky" (I, ll. 1–4). It becomes the "correspondent breeze" that marks the connection between the inner self and the outer world of Nature. Wordsworth has just come from "the vast city" and the breeze corresponds to his longing for "the sweet breath of heaven," to reconnect with nature. He comes in search of "[a] perfect stillness," which he finds in the "sunshine on the grass,/ And in the sheltered and the sheltering grove" (I, ll. 68–9). However, he is tossed in and out of "[t]he many feelings that oppressed [his] heart" (I, 1. 124). His "days are pas[sed]/ In contradiction; with no skill to part/ Vague longing . . . / From paramount impulse" (I, ll. 238–40). What helps balance him is his use of an internal voice to echo what his consciousness articulates. He says,

My own voice cheered me, and, far more, the mind's
Internal echo of the imperfect sound;
To both I listened, drawing from them both
A cheerful confidence in things to come. (I, ll. 55–8)

His own double voices can be brought into harmony in a moment of respite. This alignment of conscious and unconscious offers a sense of wholeness, instrumental in allowing the poet to stand before a gaping hole, to look down into a dark chaos out of which he creates. He needs to become receptive to and negotiate with his thoughts and memories. He needs to listen with the "third ear," so that his mind, split into conscious and unconscious, reflects both voices.

The two voices here are also turned outward as Wordsworth speaks to his friend, soulmate, and fellow poet, Coleridge, although he is never named. Several times throughout the poem, at particularly difficult moments, he invokes him, "O Friend!" to serve as witness to his experience and by doing so, to affirm and encourage. At one such point, right before he plunges into a most primal moment of himself as an infant "babe,/ Nursed in his mother's arms," he apostrophizes,

". . . Thou, my friend! art one
More deeply read in thy own thoughts . . .
To thee, unblinded by these formal arts,
The unity of all hath been revealed. . . ." (II, ll. 210–20)

And in Book V, subtitled "Books," right before he describes his most penetrating and apocalyptic dream, he recalls how his "studious friend" had "oftentimes given way [t]o kindred hauntings" (V, ll. 55–6).

His fluctuation in moods, another doubleness, reflects his early childhood, here suggested as a paradigm of how we develop morally and spiritually. He says, "Fair seed-time had my soul, and I grew up/ Fostered alike by beauty and by fear" (I, ll. 301–2), and reflects,

Dust as we are, the immortal spirit grows
Like harmony in music; there is a dark
Inscrutable workmanship that reconciles
Discordant elements, makes them cling together
In one society. How strange that all
The terrors, pains, and early miseries,
Regrets, vexations, lassitudes interfused
Within my mind, should e'er have borne a part,
And that a needful part, in making up
The calm existence that is mine when I
Am worthy of myself! (I, ll. 340–50)

Along with moments of joy and spontaneous child-pleasure, his most evolved self comes from his most frightening experiences, remembered as sustenance for the development of his creative spirit and sympathetic imagination. One such spot of time, around which haunting images cluster, involves a summer evening when, as a young boy, he stole a boat and took it for a row, "[p]roud of his skill, to reach a chosen point/ With an unswerving line." But his guilt rose up in the shape of

> a huge peak, black and huge,
> As if with voluntary power instinct
> Upreared its head . . .
> And growing still in stature the grim shape
> Towered up between me and the stars, and still
> For so it seemed, with purpose of its own .
> And measured motion, like a living thing,
> Strode after me. (I, ll. 378–85)

In terror he fled, and records, subtly, how the experience sifted down into the unconscious where "huge and mighty forms, that do not live/ Like living men, moved slowly through the mind/ By day, and were a trouble to my dreams" (I, ll. 398–400). Wordsworth offers this story as an exemplar of how feeling and thought are bound together by "[b]oth pain and fear, until we recognise/ A grandeur in the beatings of the heart" (I, ll. 413–5). Like Nature, the human heart is infinitely complex, resonant with "all forms the characters of danger or desire: and thus . . . make[s]/ The surface of the universal earth/ With triumph and delight, with hope and fear,/ Work like a sea" (I, ll. 471–5).

In the first Book of *The Prelude*, Wordsworth has "endeavored to retrace/ The simple ways in which my childhood walked." Childhood, the time of connection, generates the creative vision of the poet:

> Those recollected hours that have the charm
> Of visionary things, those lovely forms
> And sweet sensations that throw back our life,
> And almost make remotest infancy
> A visible scene, on which the sun is shining. (I, ll. 634–6)

In her highly autobiographical novel of childhood, *The Mill on the Floss* (1860), George Eliot echoes and captures Wordsworth's insistence upon the images of childhood as the wellspring of the imagination. She writes,

The wood I walk in on this mild May day, with the young yellow-brown foliage of the oaks between me and the blue sky, the white star-flowers and the blue-eyed speedwell and the ground ivy at my feet—what grove of tropic palms, what strange

ferns or splendid broad-petalled blossoms, could ever thrill such deep and delicate
fibres within me as this home-scene? . . . Such things as these are the mother tongue
of our imagination, the language that is laden with all the subtle inextricable association the fleeting hours of our childhood left behind them. Our delight in the sunshine on the deep bladed grass today, might be no more than the faint perception of
wearied souls, if it were not for the sunshine and the grass in the far-off years, which
still live in us and transform our perception into love.[16]

It is imperative, then, that we remember. Memory stores the richness of the natural world and its connection with all living things. Before he could even remember, Wordsworth says, "I held unconscious intercourse with beauty." Even when
he stands outside of nature, observing its grandeur as if from a distance,

A stranger, linking with the spectacle
No conscious memory of a kindred sight . . .
Even while mine eye hath moved o'er many a league
Of shining water, gathering as it seemed
Through every hair-breadth in that field of light
New pleasure like a bee among the flowers
. . . even then I felt
Gleams like the flashing of a shield;—the earth
And common face of Nature spake to me
Rememberable things. (I, ll. 573–88)

At the heart of these memories he finds the primal source, the child/mother
dyad. In Book I, he gets a "foretaste, a dim earnest, of the calm/ That Nature
breathes among the hills and groves" when "a babe in arms" he found the sound
of the river, its "murmurs" blended "with my nurse's song." Memories of himself
at five years old, "[b]ask[ing] in the sun/ . . . leaping through flowery
groves . . . [t]he woods . . . bronzed with deepest radiance" (I, ll. 291–6), fore-
shadow the fully disclosed "infant Babe . . . who sinks to sleep/ Rocked on his
Mother's breast; who with his soul/ Drinks in the feelings of his Mother's Eye!"
(II, ll. 233–6). Here is Wordsworth's emblem for the genesis of the sympathetic
imagination, inherited through the mother, as basic as food. The world becomes
infused with her perceptions, her sensibility, the lens through which she sees the
world. He finds his place in the world through her, and "[a]long his infant veins
are interfused/ The gravitation and the filial bond/ Of nature that connect him
with the world." He goes on to ask:

Is there a flower, to which he points with hand
Too weak to gather it, already love
Drawn from love's purest earthly fount for him

Hath beautified that flower; already shades
Of pity cast from inward tenderness
Do fall around him upon aught that bears
Unsightly marks of violence or harm. . . .
For feeling has to him imparted power
That through the growing faculties of sense
Doth like an agent of the one great Mind
Create, creator and receiver both,
Working but in alliance with the works
Which it beholds. (II, ll. 245–60)

Another image of the mother/child dyad, based on his early loss of mother, is transformed in Book V to "the parent hen amid her brood." Although the time of childhood has past, she still functions as "[a] centre to the circle which they make;/ . . . She scratches, ransacks up the earth for food/ Which they partake at pleasure" (V, ll. 246–55). Like the mother hen, Wordsworth's own mother "was the heart/ And hinge of all our learnings and our loves." She left him and his siblings "[u]nder His [God's] great correction and control," delivering them, in their innocence, into God's hands. To trace the source of "the first poetic spirit of our human life," which, according to Wordsworth, informs our moral and spiritual sense of the world—that is his declared purpose. He notes that "[t]he props of [our] affections [in our socialization] were removed/ And yet the building stood, as if sustained/ By its own spirit!" (II, ll. 279–81). We need to recover the house in which our early sentiments are stored, and from which our tastes and deepest desires are generated. We need to become porous, so that we may absorb "[t]he ghostly language of the ancient earth" brought to us by "distant winds," much like the "correspondent breeze," though not as gentle. These winds are harbingers of "a coming storm," one of Nature's darker, more intense faces, similar to our passions and predilections, unknown or unrecognized by most of us who "live as if those [early] hours had never been." And when Wordsworth asks, "How shall I seek the origin? Where find/ Faith in the marvelous things which then I felt?"— he refers to a larger sense of our origin, the childhood of the human race, the legacy of knowledge we might receive from the "ancient earth." Wordsworth imbues the sea, the enlarged and primal symbol of the river of his childhood, with the force of Nature "overflowing in my soul," another source that "steep[s]" all his thoughts in feeling.

. . . I was only then
Contented, when with bliss ineffable
I felt the sentiment of Being spread
O'er all that moves and all that seemeth still;
O'er all that, lost beyond the reach of thought

And human knowledge, to the human eye
Invisible, yet liveth to the heart;
O'er all that leaps and runs, and shouts and sings,
Or beats the gladsome air; o'er all that glides
Beneath the wave, yea, in the wave itself,
And mighty depth of waters. (II, ll. 399–409)

In the vastness of the archetypal sea and "in the wave itself," a smaller rendition of the same movement, Wordsworth finds "[a] never-failing principle of joy/ And purest passion" (II, ll. 450–1).

Throughout *The Prelude*, water connotes various states of consciousness. Its fluidity suggests the vacillation of clear and shadowy elements, the varying levels of the intensity of our memories and the various fluctuations in time in which they occurred. Are they layered in earliest memories embedded in the images of our more recent past? How can we find the lenses through which we originally viewed the world? How can we separate the things we saw from the projections of our early propensities? The sounds of the River Durwent, steady and mellifluous as it flowed along, are mingled with the songs his nurse sang to him and are identified with the harmony of his infancy.

Perhaps the most startling body of water in *The Prelude* is the metaphorical lake through which one moves in a boat, slowly, "solacing himself/ With such discoveries as his eye can make/ Beneath him in the bottom of the deep." Here consciousness is a lake in which shapes appear as bits of memory, glimpsed but difficult to discern. There reflected in the deep waters of the unconscious, it is difficult to distinguish "rocks and sky,/ Mountains and clouds . . . / from things which there abide/ In their true dwelling," like the "weeds, fishes, flowers,/ Grots, pebbles, roots of trees" (IV, ll. 261–7). Consciousness is layered with memories of the past, which appear to us—some as the still life of a whole scene, or even years, a sweep of years distilled into one dense and detailed tableau. Some pieces of memory seem always in motion, a series of lights and shadows that, over time, either fade away or sharpen into focus to form another such tableau. And over these layers of images "now is crossed by gleam/ Of his own image, by a sunbeam now,/ And wavering motions sent he knows not whence" (IV, ll. 268–70)— another layer, the self reflected in the water as well.

This passage is one of the deep moments of reflection that pauses the narrative. It is not a memory, a spot of time, but functions similarly as a dream does, often in stillness. It began with the poet's search for "[a]n auxiliar light/ . . . from my mind, which on the setting sun/ Bestowed new splendour . . . / [Then] the midnight storm/ Grew darker in the presence of my eye:/ Hence my obeisance, my devotion hence,/ And hence my transport" (II, ll. 368–74). Ever after, the poet's journey, whether still and reflective or propelled forward as he walks among the streets of Cambridge in his young adulthood, is steeped in deep imagery. About the objects around him he says, "I was the Dreamer, they the Dream." The world is now infused and heightened with the inward images of his consciousness. "To every natural form," he tells us, "rock, fruit or flower . . . / I gave a moral life . . . and all/ That I beheld respired with inward meaning" (III, ll. 130–5). "Not of outward things," he speaks, "but of my own heart," the private world in which the imagination attunes the things of the outer world. "I had a world about me—'twas my own;/ I made it, for it only lived to me,/ And to the God who sees into the heart" (III, ll. 144–6).

As a child of nature, he was a free spirit, "rambling like the wind," unsuited for "captivity." He has learned to recollect in "solitude," to retreat from the world, "[w]hen from our better selves we have too long/ Been parted by the hurrying world." From his better self, he reaches out to a "companionless" old soldier, whom he comes upon, and restores him to a cottage where he is taken in, in an act of community.

He finds a kindred spirit, an analogue of his better self, in the Winander Boy, a child he remembers and calls on the "cliffs and islands" to remember—this boy who was so responsive to Nature, this boy who

> Blew mimic hootings to the silent owls,
> That they might answer him; and they would shout
> Across the watery vale, and shout again,
> Responsive to his call. (V, ll. 372–6)

This boy becomes an icon of natural childhood, since he died before he was twelve, and will therefore remain always "in childhood." As Wordsworth comes upon his grave, he pays homage to the natural child, in opposition to the dwarf-child, who has been steeped in reason, and therefore has been severed from his natural self. As a lover of books, Wordsworth is not against book learning. He is not advocating that children be educated solely in nature, that the natural world is the only source of spontaneity and truth, as Rousseau believed when he wrote *Émile*. Wordsworth's section on "Books" in *The Prelude* contains a most intense image that reconciles nature and literature. In an apocalyptic dream, generated by reading *Don Quixote*, he constructs a vision. In his dream, an Arab "of the desert," who was also "the knight/ Whose tale Cervantes tells; yet not the knight . . . / Of these was neither, and was both at once," offers him two books:

> The one that held acquaintance with the stars,
> And wedded soul to soul in purest bond
> Of reason, undisturbed by space or time;
> The other that was a god, yea many gods,
> Had voices more than all the winds, with power

To exhilarate the spirit, and to soothe,
Through every clime, the heart of human kind. (V, ll. 103–9)

True to the language and imagery of dreams, he recognizes the stone as "Euclid's Elements," and the shell as poetry, "something of more worth" than reason. The Arab urges him to hold the shell to his ear as it prophesies the coming flood "now at hand," " 'the waters of the deep/ Gathering upon us.' " This dream, with its mad Arab questor, whom Wordsworth understands as himself and not himself, as other as well as self, becomes a cluster of images, a landscape he calls up from his consciousness. And the knowledge it brings nurtures him as do the natural images he has culled from his childhood. These images serve him, throughout the poem, as spots of time to restore his imagination—humankind's informing and sacred gift.

The loss of the self schooled through nature, as it becomes buried in the worldliness of the world, is described in Books VI through XI, when he travels to Cambridge, the Alps, London, and throughout France. This child-self, truer to his spirit and to that of his imagination, is recalled to him in Book XII by the "breezes and soft airs," "the green hills," the brooks ("a busy noise/ By day, a quiet sound in silent night"), the waves (calm and "fearing no storm"), the groves that create a buffer, "[e]ven as a sleep, between the heart of man/ And outward troubles, between man himself,/ . . . and his own uneasy heart" (XII, ll. 26–27). Nature's ability to soothe the pain of "human ignorance and guilt . . . sorrow, disappointment . . . [c]onfusion . . . / And, lastly, utter loss of hope itself" leads Wordworth out of despair into reverence: "O Soul of Nature!" he apostrophizes, "that, by laws divine/ Sustained and governed, still dost overflow/ With an impassioned life" (XII, ll. 102–4). But immersion in nature with all the senses acutely responsive in childhood's spontaneity can also thwart the imagination in adulthood. He remarks that the senses, particularly "the bodily eye . . . gained/ Such strength in *me* as often held my mind/ In absolute dominion" (XII, ll. 127–31). He warns that the senses also can "lay the inner faculties asleep." So that although as a child he actively and passionately loved "whate'er I saw: nor lightly loved,/ But most intensely; never dreamt of aught/ More grand, more fair, more exquisitely framed," what the adult needs to foster the imagination, and through this a deep moral sense, is "the imaginative union of natural scene with human emotion and moral feeling," so that he can stand before us, "[a] sensitive being, a *creative* soul" (XII, l. 207). *The Prelude* is the story of how that happens.

Central to this process is recollection, reflection, and meaning of the "spots of time" which point to "how,/ The mind is lord and master—outward sense/ The obedient servant of her will" (XII, ll. 222–3). These are "scattered everywhere, taking their date/ From our first childhood," he informs us, but in Book XII he selects two such moments to explore fully and convey poetically, that is, feelingly, so that we understand them as paradigms for our own process of recollection and reflection. Herbert Lindenberger describes Wordsworth's method of returning to "the deep well of the personal past" again and again "so that he 'might fetch/ Invigorating thoughts from former years . . . whose power/ May spur me on, in manhood now mature,/ To honorable toil.' "[17] Here they "retain/ A renovating virtue . . . / [by which] our minds/ Are nourished and invisibly repaired;/ . . . [and which] lifts us up when fallen" (XII, ll. 211–18). Each narrates one central event and its associations from his past. Each is marked by the familiar "once," which signals the separation of the one from the many. This is the poet's task: to select, through memory and the imagination, including the spontaneous emergence of images from the landscape of the dream and the unconscious, those moments that shed light, like M. H. Abrams's "lamp," on the mirror of our lives.[18]

Wordsworth demonstrates that memory comes to us through a nexus of images clustered around a moment, which become fixed in association with that moment in time thereafter. In childhood, we are most open to such experiences, indeed have little choice in the infiltration or bombardment of images that accompany our experiences. In adulthood, our most powerful moments gather images in that way, in particular the unprecedented, often traumatic or turning points of our lives. For example, I will never forget where I was when the World Trade Center was attacked, and how I felt driving to school that morning, listening to the reports of first one plane crashing into the first building, followed twenty minutes later by the second one, which I knew by then, indisputably, although I could not and maybe still can not take it in, was a terrorist attack. Nor can I detach from this moment the accompanying images I saw flashed again and again on television in the days that followed of the second plane moving through the WTC and coming out the other side in flames. I continue to see this image, as if I were there and, at the same time, driving in my car listening to the reports of this event over the radio. Also I am, in that same spot of time, sitting in my office on the phone, while my partner, who is watching television at home, reports that the first building is collapsing and then the second. I hear myself screaming and I feel my chest bent over to my knees—the Pentagon has been hit, that's in there, too, and my student as she sits before me, eyes wide in fear, and then crumbling into tears while I hold her—time has disappeared, and what has taken its place is a spot that holds the images in a gel of consciousness.

Wordsworth understood the power of even the seemingly ordinary moment around which early memories coalesce and point toward "future restoration" of the spirit. The first spot of time in Book XII seems at first archetypally heroic. He remembers as a child being led by "[a]n ancient servant of my father's house/ . . . my encourager and guide," when he loses his way and alone comes upon the place where a murderer had been hung, his name inscribed by "[s]ome unknown hand." His "ignorance of the road" and the mysterious nature of the murder and the unknown scribe coalesce with the images that follow: "[a] naked pool," a "beacon on the summit," and "[a] girl who bore a pitcher on her head,/ And seemed with difficult steps to force her way/ Against the blowing wind" (XII, ll. 249–53). Wordsworth is aware of the ordinariness of the scene, although it produces an intense "visionary dreariness," evoked by his solitary state when he saw the girl battling the harshness of the natural world—an emblem, he intuits, of the human condition in its struggle against adversity. The bleakness with which he associates these images is mitigated when he comes upon the same pool and "the melancholy beacon" in later years "in the blessed hours/ Of early love, the loved one at my side" (XII, l. 262). Furthermore, he draws for solace on an earlier memory of "youth's golden gleam," so that he is able most significantly to conclude that "feeling comes in aid/ Of feeling, and diversity of strength/ Attends us, if but once we have been strong" (XII, ll. 269–71).

Lindenberger notes that "the three objects—the pool, the beacon, [and] the girl—which form the center of the vision . . . are not drawn from any recognizable tradition of symbols" (Lindenberger, 84). This idiosyncratic aggregate suggests the very personal nature of image forming and directs us to an exploration of our own imaginations. The way in which Wordsworth "fuse[s] together concrete perception and a statement of its significance . . . [creates a] poetry [that] assert[s] and celebrate[s] at the same time it describes and analyzes" (Lindenberger, 87). Assertion, celebration, meaning making are all tools of the adult, most clearly articulated by the poet. They suggest a consciousness infused with and articulated through meaning. This then "evolves into its own inner frame of reference" (Lindenberger, 87); it "evokes the former self which coexists with the altered present self in a multiple awareness that Wordsworth calls 'two consciousnesses' " (Abrams 90). These spots of time illuminate, like the deliberate revised structure of the poem Abrams points to, "the design inherent in . . . life, which has become apparent only . . . [in] mature awareness, [and] may stand revealed as a principle which was invisibly operative from the beginning" (Abrams, 91). This is evident in the second spot of time when he associates a single sheep and a "blasted hawthorn" tree with his father's death, which occurred ten days later. The single sheep and the hawthorn tree were situated one on each side of him while he waited "[o]ne Christmas-time,/ On the glad eve of its dear holidays" for "the palfreys that should bear us home;/ My brothers and myself." Somehow in memory a transformation occurs wherein

> The single sheep, and the one blasted tree,
> And the bleak music from that old stone wall,
> The noise of wood and water, and the mist
> That on the line of each of those two roads
> Advanced in such indisputable shapes;
> All these were kindred spectacles and sounds
> To which I oft repaired, and thence would drink,
> As at a fountain. (XII, ll. 319–26)

It is almost as if memory itself offers solace in its concrete singularity of focus. Perhaps it is just the alignment of the two consciousnesses, the past returned to the present and the present infused with the meaning of the past, that we, along with Wordsworth, find so imaginatively gratifying.

## III. THE CHILD POET: *THE DIARY OF OPAL WHITELEY*

Opal Whiteley was the spiritual child of Blake and Wordsworth, attuned to the natural world and to her own nature. Her oppression by both family and school is a dramatic representation of everything Blake resisted in the process of socialization. She grew up in a logging camp in Oregon at the turn of the century. The written record of the sixth and seventh years of her childhood, preserved in her diary, was pieced together in the offices of *The Atlantic Monthly* when she was twenty-three years old. Ellery Sedgwick, its publisher, tells the story of meeting Opal when she offered him her children's nature book, *The Fairyland Around Us*, to publish. He turned it down, but was fascinated by her. When he discovered that she had kept a diary, he said, " 'Then it is not the book I want, but the diary.' "[19]

Her story is extraordinary in many ways. According to Opal, she lost her French parents around her fifth year, was adopted by the Whiteleys, who changed her name from Françoise to Opal, the name of their daughter who had died in childhood. Opal's extraordinary knowledge of French, British, and classical history and literature, she claims, is her legacy from her original parents. They left a record of their education and knowledge in the two books Opal treasured and refers to throughout *The Diary*. When Opal was twelve, her foster sister found the diary and tore it to pieces. Opal retrieved it and stored it in the trunk of a tree for many years. It took her months to reconstruct the diary for the 1920 publication. At first it was "[h]ailed as a work of genius . . . [and] became a national bestseller" (*Diary*, back cover). Ten months later it was out of print. Doubting that a child could have written something so brilliant, people returned their copies and Opal was accused of literary fraud. Over the years, her bouts with the mental illness she might have always struggled with worsened, and in 1948 she was found rummaging through "the rubble of bombed-out buildings" (*Diary*, back cover). She was institutionalized in a public mental hospital, where she remained for over forty years until her death in 1992.

The September Productions edition tells the story of the story. It contains three introductions, one by Nan Gurley, a brilliant researcher, who captures a quality of childhood herself, as she recounts the story of her search for the person behind the fragments of the diary she came across in a creative writing class. She was struck by the writer's "acute sense of observation." Gurley remarks, "She missed nothing, and was in love with all she saw. I felt I knew Opal's heart. As a child, I remember saying 'good night' to all my cherished treasures in my room before going to sleep. I dared not leave anything out, lest its feelings be hurt" (*Diary*, i–ii).

When I read this remarkable passage from Gurley's introduction aloud in my seminar on "The Literature of Victorian Childhood," I heard the deep sighs of my students who served as witnesses to what I assumed was a singular personal experience of my own childhood, when I would prepare my bed before going to sleep so that each of my twenty or so stuffed animals had a place around me. The deeply felt animism of childhood, replete with a record of the inner life of a child, is captured in this book with a kind of specificity and immediacy I have never come across before reading *The Diary*, or since. And the need for the testimony expressed here, the need to be believed, feels close to the early experience of the developing human imagination. The introductions and preface, Gurley's as well as those by Ellery Sedgwick, Viscount Grey of Fallodon, and by the adult Opal Whiteley herself, serve this purpose. It is particularly important that this internal narrative of a child prodigy be reconstructed and documented here by the prefatory material, by photographs of Opal and fragments of her diary, and her concluding postscript, all of which attest to Opal's truthfulness.

The question of the *Diary*'s authenticity is still hotly debated, as can be seen in the websites devoted to her.[20] But whether or not Opal was six or seven when she wrote this profound inspirational book actually matters less to me than the fact that it stands as an exquisite narrative of interiority. Here Opal serves as the child-poet of childhood. In her ability to capture the concerns and observations of childhood in the voice and language of a child, regardless of the age at which she did so, she establishes the validity of her vision. Often it takes the bizarre to capture as it heightens the story of ordinary life. Through her personal and idiosyncratic account of rural life, Opal Whiteley illuminates the wisdom of the child. This story of childhood resonates with authenticity perhaps because it is told through the metaphoric language and with the intensity that ordinary children may feel but be unable to articulate about feelings with which they imbue their world.

And it is in her deep connection to the natural world around her and in her keen powers of observation that Opal is so clearly Wordsworth's child, the "seer blest," as Juliet McMasters noted in her brilliant talk at the Australasian Victorian Studies Conference on Victorian Childhood in 1999, where I first heard about Opal. I sat riveted as McMasters quoted from the diary. She so profoundly understood the power of the child, as Blake noted, to see not just with the eye but through the eye into the eternal nature of things. In that talk, McMasters enumerated the ways in which Opal, as child-poet, sees. She sees with the feelings of the world, with the "lowly potato, even the pieces of potato." As she describes what she assumes the eyes of the potato must see, her expression expands into a kind of immersion, a spiritual meditation. Opal says,

> Potatoes are very interesting folks. I think they must see a lot of what is going on in the earth; they have so many eyes. And after I did look those looks as I did go along, I did count the eyes that every potato did have, and their numbers were in blessings. . . . And all the times I was picking up potatoes I did have conversations with

them. Too, I did have thinks of all their growing days there in the ground, and all the things they did hear. Earth-voices are glad voices, and earth-songs come up from the ground through the plants; and in their flowering and in the days before these days are come, they do tell the earth-songs to the wind. And the wind in her goings does whisper them to folks . . . [s]o other folks do have knowing of earth's songs. . . . I have thinks those potatoes growing here did have knowings of the star-songs. I have kept watch in the fields at night and I have seen the stars look kindness down upon them. And I have walked between the rows of potatoes, and I have watched the star-gleams on their leaves, and I have heard the wind ask of them the star-songs the star-gleams did tell in shadows on their leaves; and as the wind did go walking in the field talking to the earth-voices there, I did follow her down the rows, I did have feels of her presence near. (*Diary*, 34–6)

As Opal imbues the natural world with feelings, she expresses a spirituality inherent in the vitality of living things. Her appreciation is wide and deep. In addition to the potato and its defining eyes, she feels with living vegetation, naming each tree as she offers it a particular personality. Her favorite tree is William Wordsworth, for she intuits a Wordsworthian grandeur and comfort in its branches. She even feels "the feels" of the sticks from the wood pile she carries to "the mamma." She says,

I did pick up all the sticks my arms could hold. While I was picking them up, I looked long looks at them. . . . I did have thinks about the tree they all were before they got chopped up. I did wonder how I would feel if I was a very little piece of wood that got chopped out of a very big tree. I did think it would have hurt my feelings. I felt of the feelings of the wood. They did have a very sad feel. (*Diary*, 62)

What is most extraordinary is Opal's ability to move from observation to reflection and to capture both in a kind of epiphany. One of Opal's epiphanic moments serves as a model for the extraordinary connection she feels between herself and all living creatures. She comes upon "a silken cradle in a hazel branch. . . . It was cream, with a hazel leaf half-way round it. I put it to my ear and I did listen. It had a little voice. It was not a tone voice. It was a heart voice. While I did listen, I did feel its feels. It has lovely ones" (*Diary*, 64). This synaesthesia runs throughout the *Diary* and expresses the ways in which the child, porous to the sensory variation of the natural world, moves comfortably in and out of ways of experiencing the senses.

Opal's most intense expression of synaesthesia comes through in her friendship with "the girl who has no seeing," a blind girl who lives near her and whom Opal teaches to "see" through the fine tuning of her other senses. She brings the crysalis to the blind girl who comes to know "its feels and hear its heart voice." Opal concludes, "She has seeing by feels. Often I do carry things to her when I find them. . . . One day I told her about the trees talking. Then she did want to know about the voices, and now I do help her to hear them" (*Diary*, 64–5). As she leads the blind girl through the woods, she touches the "finger-tips" of "that grand fir tree, Good King Louis VI" to her cheeks. "The girl who has no seeing" is one of the few people who is attuned to the child and with whom she shares her inner world. To her, Opal reveals her sense of "a gray shadow walking along and touching the faces of people. Shadows do have such velvety fingers" (*Diary*, 66), she reflects.

Most striking is the depth of her emotions, the sweeping vacillations and breadth of her states of feeling. As Opal connects the two realms of experience— the bodily and the spiritual—the humblest creatures or diminutive aspects of nature are most fully revealed. The yellow jackets are both "chubby youngsters," who greedily share her slice of bread and jam, and "wasp fairies." Opal finds poetry in the tracks of the calf, whom she names Elizabeth Barrett Browning, and music in her mooings—the earthly and the ethereal finely attuned. The shifts in nature are most keenly observed and reflected on. Opal says,

> Now are come the days of brown leaves. They fall from the trees. . . . When the brown leaves flutter, they are saying little things. They talk with the wind. I hear them tell of their borning days when they did come into the world as leaves. . . . Today they were talking of the time before their borning days of this springtime. . . . They told how they were a part of earth and air before their tree-borning days. And now they are going back. In gray days of winter they go back to the earth again. But they do not die. (*Diary*, 57–8)

It is with the animals who accompany her on her "explores" that her deepest feelings lie and in whom she observes the most vital expression.[21] With Thomas Chatterton Jupiter Zeus, her wood rat, she observes his "cheese squeak" after "the mamma" has forbidden her to "carry any more cheese out to that rat," an order she subverts by carrying him into the kitchen to the cheese. She says, "I let him sniff long sniffs at it. Then I push his nose back and I cut from the big piece of cheese delicate slices. . . . This I do when the mamma isn't at home" (*Diary*, 43).

Opal remains remarkably true to her own sense of things, regardless of the increasing warnings and violent punishments by "the mamma." In fact, she seems to bypass or at least transform the cruel beatings inflicted on her, even as she noticeably represses the anger she is too terrified to allow to surface, by focusing on the beauty of the natural world. After one such beating, she says, "The back part of me feels a little bit sore, but I am happy listening to the twilight music of God's good world. I'm real glad I'm alive" (*Diary*, 12). After another spanking "most hard with the hair-brush," Opal goes "from the house we do live in to where do dwell King Edward III and Queen Philippa of Hainault. They are grand trees. . . . Today I did stay long with them and I did talk long with them. . . . And the wind was talking too" (*Diary*, 102). And after the harshest one, when she suffered some internal bleeding and dizziness after being tied up and left in the sun, she winds up singing "Sanctus, sanctus, sanctus, Dominus, Deus, Te Deum laudamus" (*Diary*, 226).

Throughout, Opal remains grounded, observant, always connecting the spiritual with the earthly. About her favorite pig, Peter Paul Rubens, her closest companion, she notes, "I have thinks the trees and the ferns and the singing brook all have gladness when Peter Paul Rubens comes a while to walk in the woods. He does carry so much joy with him everywhere he goes" (*Diary*, 73). Opal's relationship with the pig began when, as she says, "He was little . . . a very plump young pig with a little red ribbon squeal" (*Diary*, 20). A deep affinity and responsiveness develops between them, so that she is able to discriminate between his "red ribbon squeal," which expresses his urgency, and, for example, the grunts with which he punctuates her prayers and songs. In one of the clearest examples of the disparity between the child's inner world and the world outside her, Opal brings her pet pig to school. The teacher is far from pleased. As Opal says, "She did look long looks at me. She did look those looks for a long time. I made pleats in my apron with my fingers. I made nine on one side and three on the other side" (*Diary*, 21)—counting here suggesting a strategy with which the young child orders her world, particularly when she feels, as she says, "screwtineyes[ed]." Opal vividly recreates the scene in which Peter Paul Rubens "did make such a sweet picture as he did stand there in the doorway looking looks about. And the grunts he gave, they were such nice ones . . . saying: 'I have come to your school. What class are you going to put me in?' . . . But I guess our teacher doesn't have understanding of pig-talk. She just came at him in such a hurry with a stick of wood. And when I made interferes, she did send us both home in a quick way" (*Diary*, 22).

There are many passages in which the disparity between the outer world and Opal's inner world evoke this comic quality. However, there are also many dark passages of cruelty and grief. There are devastating passages that are threaded throughout the book and organized with an increasing narrative intensity. Two of the most gripping involve the loss of a cherished animal. They serve to identify the child's alienation from what the adults around her assume as the natural life cycle. The first is the heartbreaking scene when Opal comes upon the dying Peter Paul Rubens on "butchering day." She recalls,

> We had not gone far when we heard an awful squeal—so different from the way pigs squeal when they want their supper. I felt cold all over. Then I did have knowings why the mamma had let me start away to the woods without scolding. And I ran a quick run to save my dear Peter Paul Rubens, but already he was dying—and he died with his head in my lap. I sat there feeling dead, too, until my knees were all wet with blood from the throat of my dear Peter Paul Rubens. After I changed my

clothes and put the bloody ones in the rain-barrel, I did go to the woods to look for the soul of Peter Paul Rubens. I didn't find it, but I think when comes the spring I will find it among the flowers. (*Diary*, 80)

As with her punishments, Opal transforms her pain over these losses into some spiritual connection with the eternal in nature. But her worst devastation comes about as a result of the careless cruelty of a "chore boy," who shoots down her pet crow, Lars Porsena of Clusium. Butchering day is harsh enough, but the pointless killing, and the boy's response—"he just laughed a laugh, and he said—he did— that Lars Porsena was nothing but a crow"—is beyond her understanding. It is with great poignancy that she recounts the way in which she wraps the dying crow in her apron so, as she says, "he would not have cold feels. There was much wet- ness upon my apron. . . . It was wetness of blood. The sky was more gray, and before I was come to the house we live in, the raindrops were coming down in a slow, sad way. I have thinks the sky was crying tears for the hurts of Lars Porsena of Clusium. And I was too" (*Diary*, 249). Still, Opal, a true Wordsworthian child, is able to find comfort in "[t]he waters of the brook [which] lap and lap. They come in little ripples over gray stones. They are rippling a song. It is a gentle song. It is a good-bye song to Lars Porsena of Clusium" (*Diary*, 248). Opal intuitively understands that healing is possible in nature, that one must prepare for this care- fully, as she carves out a place of worship in nature, her cathedral where all sacred rituals take place. She leads a choir in spiritual songs and the animals that accom- pany her there bear witness to the meaning of all those things that are neglected or denied by the adults around her. Healing is given primary importance, and the cathedral doubles at times as a hospital when animals need her care.

Opal is a most innovative child who knows how to provide for the satisfac- tion of her own needs. Of the resources she possesses, her imagination and her ability to articulate her deepest feelings offer her the release and transformation of poetic expression. The way in which she learns that "the girl with no seeing" has died a cruel and painful death by fire—I myself had to engage in a kind of deep breathing to keep from sinking into despair—is recorded with rare immediacy and presentness. As we listen to two loggers speaking about the accident, we come upon the knowledge of the blind girl's death before Opal does, and this delay is articulated through the young child's senses. In other words, Opal sees before she understands what she is seeing and this suspension of time adds an emotional intensity, and gives voice to the unspoken, unacknowledged loss of the young child who cannot take it into the present moment. She records,

And I had hears of the other [of the two men] say, 'Probably the smell of the smoke caused her worry about the fire coming to the house, and probably she was trying to find out where it was when she walked right into it.' And the other man did have asks if she was con chus after. And the other one did say, 'Yes.' . . . Another man did

come in the gate . . . to where they was. . . . There was a green caterpillar close by
him on a bush, but he had not seeing of it. . . . First thing he said was, 'When Jim
went by here last even, that child was sitting on the gate-post. She was waiting for
her to come back. . . .' Then I had understanding. I had knows then it was the girl
that has no seeing they was having talks about. . . . I felt queerness in my throat and
I couldn't see either. I couldn't see the green caterpillar on the leaf. . . . And Thomas
Chatterton Jupiter Zeus had looks like a gray cloud in my arms. (*Diary*, 207–8)

What saves Opal from the brutality around her is her ability to feel and to
communicate her feelings, particularly to those tender-hearted adults who
respond to her soulful questioning. There are several; they include Sadie
McKibben, whose freckles and "smiles in her eyes" identify her as comforting.
Sadie is responsive, sees "the hurrys in [Opal's] eyes," kisses Opal "two on the
cheeks and one on the nose"; "the man that wears gray neckties and is kind to
mice" provides her with writing utensils with which to record her experiences
with the fairies he allows her to believe put them in the tree hollow for her. And
there is Dear Love and Dear Love's husband, and Larry and Jean and their baby
whose hand they let her pat. There are several others whose relationships Opal
observes, those who seem loving to each other as well as to her. She notices how
Jean was crying and Larry comforted her with a "bit of poetry," which she
remembers as: "There, little girl, don't cry,/ I'll come back and marry you by-and-
by." To Opal, who misses the implications of the early pregnancy, these words
connect them with "the angels looking down from heaven [who] saw their happiness and brought a baby real soon . . . for a baby is such a comfort and twins are a
multiplication table of blessings" (*Diary*, 17). Sometimes she projects herself into
the scene, so that although "the pensée girl with the far-away look in her eyes and
the man of the long step that whistles most all of the time," as Opal says, "had not
knows of my reaching out my arms above them. Only God had knows. They did
just have sees for one another" (*Diary*, 261), she feels connected to them in
nature, along with the chipmunk she sees on a stump and the "green caterpillar
having sleeps under the green hazel leaf" (*Diary*, 261).

As Opal observes subtlety in human relationships, her innocence serves as a
balance, her acuteness held in check, as with extremely bright children, and noted
in terms of what she doesn't observe, what is obvious to a more sophisticated
reader. This disparity often provides a kind of sweet and tender humor, similar to
that of the schoolroom scene with Peter Paul Rubens. However, Opal's ability to
love and to accept love both from the creatures and those humans around her also
provides an order to her otherwise fractured world. When she speaks of the creatures, animal and human, she uses the full name with which she identifies them.
Only the complete epithet offers, as it did in the classical epic, a full sense of control. "The man that wears gray neckties and is kind to mice" is never referred to
with less than his full title; the blind girl is always "the girl who has no seeing";

change is only acceptable, and then must be adhered to, when a change comes into Opal's world. After Peter Paul Rubens dies, for example, he is always referred to as "Peter Paul Rubens who is no more."

Certainly, children need to learn how to subvert the powerlessness of their lives. In her talk on child-writers, McMasters explored this lack of control in terms of the child-writer and her narrative position as outsider and spy, as she observes from the corners. This perspective carries a particularly acute awareness, as is often true of the vision of other marginalized people. Opal's language, too, is heightened with a peculiar sense of urgency, an innovation of expression, constructed from this powerless stance, which exposes the intense need for control of the world distilled through its only channel, that of thinking and imagining. Opal's originality is most clearly observed in her use of words. Laura Cappello points to Opal's "fully realised and carefully rendered subplots,"[22] her "strong sense of narrative cadence" (Cappello, xix), and her "self-conscious artistry" (Cappello, xxi). Certainly, Opal is in love with all kinds of words, most notably names. As noted in the Introduction to *Peter Paul Rubens and Other Friendly Folk*, "Like Adam in the Garden of Eden, she takes it upon herself to name and identify the beasts of her world" (Cappello, iv). She is almost constantly talking, to herself and to the creatures and people of her world with whom she is in harmony. Her words and phrases are constructed out of her urgent sense of the present and the presentness of the past. She says, for example, "before I was come to the house we live in," rather than "before I came to the house we live in," or "[a]ll these potatoes I did lay in two rows," rather than "all these potatoes I lay in two rows." What she imagines and remembers is so immediate, the events so concrete that she converts verbs into nouns. She says, "And as I had seeing of them all there, I did have thinks to have a choir" (*Diary*, 37). She "has seeing, "has thinks" and "hears" and "knows" and "feels." What we, as readers, have before us is her voice, which illuminates the inner workings of her mind. We watch her thoughts and feelings align with words as they occur to her.

She gives no voice to "the mamma" or to "the papa," nor are they named, nor owned, as in "my mamma" or just "mamma." As readers of the *Diary*, we are witnesses to the beatings that Opal receives at the hands of "the mamma" and to Opal's desperate need for recognition from her mother, which within these pages she never gets. In one early passage, she tells of her attempt to help her mother by cleaning the kitchen in her own childish way. She notes:

> When the mamma was come, she did look not glad looks at the water on the floor. She did only look looks for the switches over the kitchen window. After I did have many sore feels, she put me out the door to stay out. I did have sorry feels for her. I did so try hard to be helps. (*Diary*, 41)

The beatings become more violent as the story progresses. Certainly their frequency and inexplicable nature are enough to provide the split in Opal's story of her lineage. It is not clear whether the story of her adopted parents, "the mamma" and "the papa," and her original parents, "Angel Mother" and "Angel Father," is the "truth." Was she adopted or are the origins of the extreme disparity between the double set of parents, the bad set and the good set, evidence of the splitting common in childhood? When severe, is this splitting symptomatic of schizophrenia, the disease from which Opal seems to have suffered? It is clear, however, that this fracture transformed in fairy tales into the dead but good mother or the fairy godmother and the cruel stepmother attests to the inability of the young child, as narrated in childhood stories, to integrate the cruelty of the mother with the child's dependency on her.

Opal has a highly developed sense of justice and of the way things should be, though barely articulated in terms of her family. Instead, she relies on Angel Mother and Angel Father to provide the needed lens through which frames her vision. She does, however, express a kind of ethical understanding from early on in the *Diary*. She refers to a particularly meaningful place as "our lane," acknowledging that,

> Of course, it doesn't belong to Brave Horatius and Lars Porsena of Clusium and Thomas Chatterton Jupiter Zeus and I and all the rest of us. It belongs to a big man that lives in a big house, but it is our lane more than it is his lane, because he doesn't know the grass and flowers that grow there, and the birds that nest there, and the lizards that run along the fence, and the caterpillars and beetles that go walking along the roads made by the wagon wheels. And he doesn't stop to talk to the trees that grow all along the lane. (*Diary*, 18)

Opal's sense of justice is linked to her vision of connection, out of which evolves her sense of responsibility to the things and creatures she loves. She is aware of the voice of all things in and out of nature; she locates herself inside, in feeling with all things. And, therefore, when she is told she will be moving, she provides with great care for all her creatures. She says, "Moving is a big amount of problem. But mostly now I do have my prepares done" (*Diary*, 282), and goes on to provide the proper, nurturing homes for each of her beloved creatures. Each gift, each precious bit of landscape is mentioned in the litany that begins, "And in the hollow log there is the old logging boot of the husband of Dear Love, that he has given me to keep some of my rock collections in. And there is the bath-towel of Thomas Chatterton Jupiter Zeus that Dear Love has made for him. And then there is . . ." each object associated closely with its benefactor that comprises the sacred world of Opal. Four pages of poetic prose incrementally fill the stage for the finale, when Opal says, "These things I have now in the log" (*Diary*, 287). Next comes the list of homes for each of her beloved animals, who will feed whom, until Opal can rest in a time frame large enough to include past, present, and future. She says, "And often it is I am going to come comes back again here . . ." (*Diary*, 289). She ends with the future, anticipating the baby Dear Love will have, and with a prayer in the cathedral between "Brave Horatius and me and Thomas Chatterton Jupiter Zeus." Opal announces, "The great pine tree is saying a poem, and there is a song in the tree-tops" (290). She is the teller of her tale here, Blake's piper/poet who pipes with "the reeds" she finds alongside "the creek and out across the field and in along the lane" (*Diary*, 219). And although "the mamma" forbids her from "piping the song of the forest," Opal tells us, "it didn't go out of my heart" (*Diary*, 219).

If I didn't know that Opal spent her last forty years in a mental institution, I would feel hopeful from her final words and from the postscript in which she tells us how she went on to record many other years in diaries where she lived in other lumber camps, where "there were new people and new animal friends and new nurseries and other cathedrals" (*Diary*, 291). She went on in her young adult life to do research in natural science. She taught nature classes and published her first nature book, "paying for it by taking orders for it in advance" (*Diary*, 291). It is painful and difficult to imagine this extremely resourceful, adventurous, and creative soul incarcerated for at least four decades, useless to herself and society.

# 2

# Carroll and Grahame:
# Two Versions of Pastoral

## 1.

With the birth of children's literature in the nineteenth century, representations of various states of desire and fear became associated with childhood in imaginative literature written for and about childhood. The two imaginative uses of the child, in Blake's lyrics and in Wordsworth's *Prelude* and "Immortality Ode," suggest early representations of two paradigms, later reconfigured by two of the great nineteenth-century writers of fiction for children, Lewis Carroll and Kenneth Grahame. Blake's ironic use of the child's voice in his lyrics is echoed in Carroll's satiric mode. And Grahame was highly influenced by Wordsworth's association of childhood with the pastoral imagery of nature and as the source of inspiration for creativity. From the Romantics, Carroll inherited the idea that, as Carroll's most prominent biographer Morton N. Cohen points out, "a child can teach an adult repentance and the way to salvation."[1] As with Blake and Wordsworth, the child was his spiritual leader, sent from heaven.

In Carroll's work, however, the natural world is relegated to his sentimental verses. In his stories, the landscape is unnatural. The roses are painted red, the things run amuck in their animated state, and instead of beautifying the world, or submitting to nature's higher claim, they dominate and render nature impotent. This reflection of Victorian industrialization—with its dehumanizing potential and privileging of objects, money, even progress over people—darkens as we move into *Through the Looking Glass* "darkly." Indeed, the "natural" state is nonexistent in both the Wonderland and Looking Glass worlds. In the Looking Glass vision of the garden, the later and darker Eden suggested by the unnatural Wonderland garden, the flowers are cruel and mocking. Alice begins, as the polite and reverent child she has been raised to be: " 'O Tiger-lily! . . . I *wish* you could talk!' "[2] The acerbic response, " 'We *can* talk ... when there's anybody worth talking to,' " provokes Alice's conflict with the flowers and recalls her endless attempts to retain her good manners and to have them acknowledged by the creatures throughout both worlds. The flowers constantly criticize her, as she tries again and again to begin over. She offers, " 'How is it you can all talk so nicely,' " but no matter how hard she tries to compliment them, she winds up with insults: from the Rose—" 'It's *my* opinion that you never think *at all*' " and from the Violet—" 'I never saw anybody that looked stupider' " (*Looking Glass*, 122).

For Carroll, as for Blake, the child was the touchstone that measured goodness and evil. Blake, in his attacks on social injustice like child labor (in the "Chimney Sweep" and "The Little Black Boy" paired lyrics from *Songs of Innocence and of Experience*); on the corruption of the Church, and on all kinds of oppression and poverty, is satirical. But he is overtly critical, his anger affixed to specific institutions—and certainly not humorous. Carroll's vision is wed to nonsense humor, in which he can remain, like the Cheshire Cat, relatively detached, unpitying and unfeeling. But for both, the child exposes the corruption of the world. Clearly, Alice is the disrupter of the Edenic myth of Victorian morality. Although Carroll does suggest that the Church can be restrictive, that manners cloak feeling, that education is essentially meaningless, that the forces that govern our ordering of our world—all measurement and time, in particular—are false and uncertain, he does not offer any alternative vision; in fact, there is no suggestion that there is one.

Both Carroll and Grahame felt enormous affinity with childhood and longed intensely to return to childhood—and it is this yearning that generated two opposite visions: two versions of pastoral. Both authors defend against fears associated with childhood embedded in the longing: fears of obliteration, of being devoured, of the felt self as invisible. At the heart of these fantasies lie hints of sexual danger, intuited in the taboos of society. At the same time, in these adult authors consciousness resided like a weight, a potential of paralysis, harboring a fear that the lost moments of innocence would not be restored, that there would emerge from experience no higher innocence. What is expressed by these two poles is a primary ambivalence that contains the longing to remember, the desire to forget, and the need to reimagine.

Both *The Wind in the Willows* and the *Alice* books exist in a liminal place, somewhere between childhood and adulthood. They are about the behavior, pleasures, and fears that are childlike and about how they've been made conscious and adult; they contain the insights associated with childhood, but are recollected, part of a meditative state of mind located in adult consciousness.

Carroll's nostalgia for childhood is contained in his poetic prefaces. "[T]he golden afternoon," "the dream-child moving through a land of wonders wild and new,"[3] the "child of the pure unclouded brow" (*Looking Glass*, 103) precede the stories. But the stories themselves are darkly comic, ironic, and distanced. Interestingly, in their humor, they radicalized the direction of children's literature. Instead of being seen as didactic and moralistic, writing for children became characterized as entertaining. Carroll reversed assumptions about writing for children. Rather than condescending to the child reader, he evoked an irreverence toward the adult preaching that was common in writing for children (Dusinberre, xvi).

As a poet of childhood, Carroll may be thought of as the voice of the shadow childhood, that which is hidden behind Victorian mores and expectations of innocence. Aligned with his child protagonist and his child readers, he reveals a fractured adult world of nonsensical rules and conventions. Alice is alienated from the other creatures, from herself, and from us. Her conversations with the creatures are disjunctures, representations of crossed signals that serve as points of alienation. She speaks in two voices, both to herself and about herself. Her body parts are similarly fragmented—neck too long, head too large. Her soliloquy to her feet satirizes her dissociation: " 'Oh, my poor little feet, I wonder who will put on your shoes and stockings for you now, dears? . . . I shall be a great deal too far off to trouble myself about you . . . but I must be kind to them,' thought Alice, 'or perhaps they won't walk the way I want to go' " (*Wonderland*, 14–5). Emotionally, she is also detached, unmoved by her own tears, which quickly become part of the grotesque landscape of objects. If she can swim in her own tears, if the proverbial wisdom of "drowning in your tears" is transformed literally into a pool, how seriously can we take her feelings?

The childhood landscape here, then, is unnatural, reflecting the world Alice sees and experiences. In *Wonderland*, she keeps trying to get into the "lovely" garden she views through the keyhole, when she is too big to fit in, after her "fall" (down the rabbit hole) from innocence. From that postlapsarian perspective, the garden is remembered as unfallen. Perhaps, as Dusinberre claims, "For each child the discovery of Nature is a rediscovery of the parable of Eden" (Dusinberre, 7). But Carroll's perspective here is unromantic, a satiric antipastoral vision. Once Alice is small enough to get inside, what she actually observes is an artificial and hostile landscape. She is pecked at by the pigeon who claims, according to the laws of logic, that if she has eaten eggs, which little girls do quite as much as serpents, then she is " 'a kind of serpent.' " And as serpent in the garden, she is interrogator of the Victorian world even as she is its spokesperson—serving, as children often do, as a signifier of those disparities between what we say we mean and what we really mean.

The characters, other than Alice, belong to the realm of dreams; they are not quite people and not quite things, but rather unconscious recollections and transformations of childhood. Alice herself is either too big or too small, herself and not herself. She is continuously frustrated by the inability of the creatures to connect with each other or with her. No matter how hard she tries, she alienates herself, as she talks about Dinah her cat to the mouse, who flees in fear and anger: " 'Not like cats,' " the mouse says. " 'Would you like cats if you were me?' "

(*Wonderland*, 19). The Caterpillar, who begins a dialogue with Alice with the defining question of Wonderland, " 'You, who are you,' " remains utterly unyielding to Alice's pleas: " 'I don't know who I am sir, because I'm not myself, you see.' " He retorts: " 'I don't see,' " and ends the dialogue having come full circle with " 'You, who are you?' " (*Wonderland*, 35–6). When she asks the Cheshire Cat, "which way ought I to go from here," it ambiguously responds, " 'That way lives the March Hare and that way lives the Mad Hatter; go either way you like, we're all mad here' " (*Wonderland*, 51).

The Cat is Carroll's god figure, positioned above the world, free to disappear at will, and as such establishes Carroll's dominant vision of chaos, with its divine knowledge that, whatever the direction, " 'we're all mad here.' " In the beginning chapters, Alice attempts to locate herself in time and space. She says, " 'I wonder how many miles I've fallen . . . that would be four thousand miles down I think' " and " 'I wonder what Latitude or Longitude I've got to' " (*Wonderland*, 8). Her efforts to position language so that it reflects logic and sequence are inverted again and again throughout her journeys. She wonders, " 'Do cats eat bats' and sometimes 'Do bats eat cats?' " (*Wonderland*, 9). Everything she learned in school is revealed as uncertain. All is in flux, no connection sure and solid.

There is only one scene in which Alice actually has a moment of harmony with another creature and it takes place in The Wood with No Names. There she walks with her arms around a fawn, until they reach the end of the wood, where they spring apart in remembrance of the alienating adult world of language: " 'You're a fawn,' " Alice says, and it replies, " 'oh dear, you're a human child' " (*Looking Glass*, 137). Perhaps Carroll is asserting here the paradoxical nature of language, as he does in so many *Wonderland* and *Looking Glass* scenes: the hilarious puns in the Mock Turtle's Song, the creation of nonsense language in "The Jabberwocky," Humpty Dumpty's attempt to control his words. That we trust language to define, identify, and connect us with the outside world places us in danger, Carroll suggests, as words also indicate the discrete and separate nature of things. Further, Carroll implies that, like Alice who uses the word "cat" to denote comfort while it means danger to the Mouse, we are limited by our own singular perceptions and experiences, and therefore doomed to a kind of absurd alienation. But here, in the woods where things have no names, Alice can enter that preoedipal Edenic state of boundarilessness, only to be severed from her connection with the fawn once language intervenes, and the things regain their borders.

In *Some Versions of Pastoral*, William Empson underscored the unsentimental lack of all "sense of glory"[4] in the *Alice* stories. Even the White Knight, Carroll's most human character and potentially most evocative of nostalgia, fails to bring a tear to Alice's eye. He appears to us, as well as to Alice, pedantic and annoying, tediously insisting on the precision of his song's name (which prevents his ever naming it) and foolishly falling off his horse, like his chess-prototype, first to one side, then to the other. Although Carroll does suggest that "[y]ears afterwards" Alice would remember "the mild blue eyes and kindly smile of the Knight—the setting sun gleaming, through his hair, and shining on his armour in a blaze of light that quite dazzled her" (*Looking Glass*, 187), as a child in the story, she remains essentially unmoved. Reminiscence is adult, and the potential closeness between Alice and the White Knight is never actualized.

Carroll's Alice, as child-challenger to Victorian culture, further reveals that things are more valued than people. This antipastoral landscape belongs to industrialized England where its instrument, the train, is more important than the humans it transports: the tickets are larger than Alice, and " 'the smoke alone is worth a thousand pounds a puff' " (*Looking Glass*, 130). Alice further challenges what Victorian culture most cherishes, an idealized notion of Motherhood. In *Wonderland*, the hideous Duchess, joined in cacophony by the cook, shrieks, " 'Speak roughly to your little boy and beat him when he sneezes' " (*Wonderland*, 48), and with her constant moralizing, digs her sharp chin into Alice's shoulder. The image of Mother, as chaste upholder of the values of hearth and home, is further gothicized by the Queen's cries, " 'Off with her head.' " Even for Alice, as she takes up the mantle of motherhood, the child is essentially a pig. She warns, " 'If you're going to turn into a pig, my dear . . . I'll have nothing more to do with you." She rationalizes, " 'If it had grown up . . . it would have made a dreadfully ugly child: but it makes rather a handsome pig, I think'. . . . And she began thinking over other children she knew, who might do very well as pigs . . . 'if she only knew the right way to change them' " (*Wonderland*, 50).

When Alice does finally claim her right "to grow" during the Trial Scene, her defiant cry—" 'Who cares for you . . . you're nothing but a pack of cards' " (*Wonderland*, 97)—ends the *Wonderland* story of the child's identity in crisis. In *Looking Glass*, the two Queens are equally impotent to serve as mothers (of the country or otherwise). Alice must pin together the clothing of the White Queen, the childish adult who lives "backwards," and remembers best "things that happened the week after next." She is mirrored by the equally inept Red Queen, who responds to Alice's question about losing her way: " 'your way. . . . All the ways around here belong to me' " (124), but who must run twice as fast to stay in the same place. By the end of *Looking Glass*, Alice is left with the two queens leaning on her, "as first one round head, and then the other, rolled down from her shoulder, and lay like a heavy lump in her lap" (*Looking Glass*, 197)—the child-supporter of two mothers. If Alice's body is stabilized in *Looking Glass*, what is unsteady is the world of adults around her. As we grow into a more secure identity, Carroll suggests, what we see reflected back to us is the shakiness of the world: the *un*temporal queens, the perpetually unstable White Knight, and Humpty Dumpty's irreparable fall, which underscores again the untrustworthiness of language. As poet of "The Jabberwocky," Humpty Dumpty proudly claims, " 'When *I* use a word . . . it means just what I choose it to mean—neither more nor less' " (*Looking Glass*, 163), but he belongs to the child's world of the nursery rhyme which subverts meaning and positions sound over sense.

In his *Alice* books, Carroll moves toward the ultimate absurdity: from "who am I" to "am I"? His representation of the meaninglessness of the world is dramatically portrayed in Alice's attempts to find certainty, more humorously in *Wonderland*, more seriously in *Looking Glass*. In *Wonderland*, she begins her proof of her identity with her body—her physical self will establish her as Alice. Since her hair doesn't go in curls like Ada's, she can't be Ada, she reasons. Obviously, this doesn't work by implication: (if she curled her hair, would she then be Ada?). Her mind, then, her thoughts and her knowledge, must distinguish her and secure her individuality. She says, " 'I know all sorts of things and she [Mabel] knows such a very little' " (*Wonderland*, 16). She begins a series of proofs of her knowledge, all of which fail, with the multiplication table. " 'Let me see: four times five is twelve, and four times six is thirteen, and four times seven is—oh, dear! I shall never get to twenty at that rate' " (*Wonderland*, 16). However wrong this appears, Carroll as mathematician—and this has been pointed out by Martin Gardner, knows that in another base system, four times five *is* twelve, four times six *is* thirteen, and that you can never reach twenty because, in this system, four times thirteen doesn't equal twenty.[5] Perplexed, Alice goes on to try geography. She comes up with London as the capital of Paris, and Paris as the capital of Rome, a confusion that suggests a basic truth about British ethnocentricism and about the association of Paris with debauchery and the Anglican view of the Pope. As the last proof that she is indeed Alice, she recites poetry she learned in school, but unknowingly she transforms the sententious "How doth the little busy bee," Sir Isaac Watts's assertion of the Victorian work ethic, in which the "busy bee" endlessly gathers honey to avoid "Satan find[ing] some mischief still/ For idle hands to do."[6] In Alice's recitation it becomes "How doth the little crocodile," in which the crocodile "cheerfully welcomes little fishes in,/ With gently smiling jaws" (*Wonderland*, 17), indeed a more accurate view of the world that governed Victorian culture. And, although by this time Alice assumes she must have been changed for Mabel, we notice the authenticity of Carroll's Darwinian representation of eroding Victorian certainty. So Alice cannot be certain that she is Alice, nor that she is not Alice—nor of anything really. Although she is unaware of it, her truthful parodies have a kind of coded, dreamlike meaning.

This construction, where first the body fails to establish identity, then the mind likewise fails, leaving only a prevailing sense of uncertainty, is repeated in the Cheshire Cat's disappearance. First his body disappears, then his head follows, leaving only that grin—the objective correlative of the nonsense world, and the best defense against the intolerable unknowingness we all must live with. This is further affirmed by the Cat's insistence that it is the converse of a dog, which wags its tail when it is pleased and growls when it is angry. " 'Now I growl when I'm pleased, and wag my tail when I'm angry,' " it asserts. And when Alice declares, " 'I call it purring, not growling,' " the Cat, with ultimate ambiguity, concludes, " 'Call it what you like' " (*Wonderland*, 51–2)—confirming only that the meaning of its grin is essentially unknowable. Again, in *Through the Looking Glass*, this pattern is extended, so that the inscrutability of meaning in life is established and finalized. When Alice comes across the Red King who is dreaming Alice (although, of course, Alice is dreaming the Red King who is dreaming Alice *ad infinitum*), she attempts to prove that she exists independently of the Red King's dream by her tears, the physical manifestation of her feelings and thoughts. When Tweedledee remarks, " 'You won't make yourself a bit realer by crying,' " Alice asserts, " 'If I wasn't real . . . I shouldn't be able to cry.' " But when Tweedledum persists, " 'I hope you don't suppose those are *real* tears' " (*Looking Glass*, 145), Alice is truly stymied. Is she real or only a thing in the Red King's dream, as Tweedledee and Tweedledum assert, likely to be extinguished if he awakes? And how will she know the difference? Here Carroll anticipates the modern absurdists, who profess that in this world there is no certainty, and that the world is essentially nonsensical.

Carroll must have been as obsessed by this tenuous and hollow vision of his culture, as he was haunted by the imminence of the child's loss of innocence. Evident in his life's explorations of relationships with children are his own longings to return to a world that he, like so many writers of children's literature, intensely desired but could not locate or could glimpse only fleetingly. For Alice, there is no way out of Wonderland or of Looking Glass but to wake up and treat them as dreams. But Carroll must have known that the dreams themselves were representations of knowledge. We know from his letters and diaries how he suffered great shame over his unspecified temptations. As Cohen, his biographer, admits, "Underscoring his faith and his philosophy was his belief that life is but a dream. But what were the dreams within that dream? Were they an escape from the larger dream into fantasy, where, like the unchaste knight, he took his imaginary pleasure? Were they infractions of his faith that led to self-contempt and the desperate prayers for change and renewal?" (Cohen, 225). Even though the *Wonderland* and *Looking Glass* dream worlds are apparently presexual, they contain, as many critics have noted, representations of repressed sexuality.[7] More to the point here is that they are comprised of what was socially taboo for Carroll—at least the surface of cultural injunctions against knowledge, whether it be about sex or other aspects of the Victorian world.

The predominant irony of Carroll's work is close to Blake's, when the child, in its innocence, speaks against itself, and takes the side of the very world that will expel it from what it envisions as paradise. Not that any of us has really ever known paradise in any sustained way. But we may remember a rapture, proffered to us as a lure, by a parent, a teacher, the culture. And forever after we search for that, recast imaginatively in terms of one object, one person, one image or another. Alice is attracted by the promise of pleasing authority (the parade of figures "in charge" of the country, like the queens, duchess, kings, knights; those in charge of lessons, like those of the mock turtle, the caterpillar, the Cheshire Cat, Humpty Dumpty). She continually looks for the right path, until the paths disappear entirely, infused into chessboard patterns so that there is no stability in space or size or time or any of the objects and concepts on which we base our sense of order. It takes her the entire *Wonderland* journey to assert her own vision, in contradistinction to everything else she has been told. But in *Looking Glass*, as in *Wonderland*, her subversive act—to pull the table cloth off at the banquet that disrupts that entire world—is deceptive. *Wonderland*, with its bossy, defensive, and incoherent adults, *is* reality for Carroll. Alice's self-affirmations may still be heroic, and I am sure children (as well as many critics) see her as a kind of conquering hero.[8] But what Carroll knows is embedded in the text that follows Alice's awakening in both stories.

At the end of *Wonderland*, when Alice awakes, Carroll turns the dream *qua* dream upside down, when Alice's sister dreams Alice's dream, so that "she too began dreaming . . . about little Alice herself . . . and . . . the whole place around her became alive with the strange creatures of her little sister's dream." As Alwin L. Baum noted, "This is a supreme paradox that characterizes the constant occlusion of boundaries between the two worlds [the waking and dream worlds]."[9] There is no real waking from this dream, Carroll suggests here; that whether in or out of Wonderland, Alice will sexually mature; even as rich and layered a dream world as *Wonderland* can't halt time. Alice's innocence protects her from the knowledge of her dreams, but, in a sense, she is a little like Hopkins's child Margaret, who unconsciously mourns the inevitable passing of her youth and eventual death, allegorized in the falling leaves in his poem "Spring and Fall."

In *Looking Glass*, this ontological questioning is extended from the reflexive Red King's dream to Alice's waking where she considers " 'who it was that dreamt it all.' " Carroll further goes on to address the reader in his last prose sentence, "Which do *you* think it was" (*Looking Glass*, 208), calling our attention to the potential universality of the dream state, and the almost arbitrary identity of the dreamer (even of the dreamed). In his closing verse, Carroll ends with, "Life, what is it but a dream?" (*Looking Glass*, 209), suggesting, beyond the question's clichéd meaning, or reinvigorating the basic truth of the cliché, that the knowledge of both *Wonderland* and *Looking Glass* is inescapable. There is an irony in the fact that Lewis Carroll established the field of children's literature as writing *for* children, discrete from adult writing about children. His work, although read by (and certainly dramatized for) children, is at least equally adult. Its depiction of childhood as dark renders it adult, or a marginalized view of childhood. As literature of the absurd, the sensibility here, although close to the nonsense world of children, is also essentially adult. Carroll did write his stories for children, for a particular child, Alice Liddell, who was immortalized in his work. And although Carroll may not, like Hans Christian Andersen, have consciously envisioned a double audience, what he created was a double world that would entice both the child and the adult, responsive to different aspects, or sensitive in different ways to the same elegiac mood implicit in pastoral, and the fear behind it of the passing of all living things. The tragedy of Carroll's longing is the reality of this inherent loss, the darkness of "bedtime," the "voice of dread,/With bitter tidings laden" (*Looking Glass*, 103). The passing of childhood is the ultimate metaphor for this loss, which is, as Hopkins said, "the blight man was born for," the "bedtime" Carroll dreaded.

## 2.

In his focus on the child and in his longings for childhood, Carroll paved the way for many other children's authors, notably Kenneth Grahame. Grahame's idyll contains significant passages and narrative elements that echo Carroll's sense of the darkness and pain of the child's journey through the adult world, of the socialization process through which we all pass. But the pastoral imagery here is reaffirmed and reestablished in nature. Here is the green world, still green, though at times brooding for the troubling or lost innocence depicted in the characters' quests. The shadow that passes over Grahame's wild woods is reflected in the various landscapes and by the various creatures. And where the longings become too hard to bear, to the point of being shattering, art replaces nature. This vision is close to Wordsworth's where the child comes to us "trailing clouds of glory," then grows into the consciousness of time and loss. The experience is then "recollected in tranquility." In Grahame, the experience is reflected through the growing consciousness of Mole and noted in Rat's poetic process.

As Lois R. Kuznets points out, Grahame's craving for the protection of a childhood space strikingly unlike his own "physically and psychically rugged" childhood[10] is represented as a vision of merging, of unity and harmony of the green world of *The Wind in the Willows*. This world is buoyant, inclusive, large enough to contain the playful spontaneity of the child, and safe enough to distinguish between destructive childish impulse and the wonder and awe of the child in nature. It contains sadness, a sense of loss, and threatening images of chaos and despair. It depicts the struggle inherent in the task of the adult, driven and nourished by the imagination of childhood, to negotiate desire and, through the imagination, to pass in and out of those dark states. While *Wind*, like the *Alice* stories, is propelled by what's not resolvable in adulthood, here what remains haunting from childhood memory is granted respite in the liminal borders of childhood and its accompanying states of dream and trance.

It is clear that Grahame understood a duality to innocence, evidenced by his portrayal of his two "childish" characters, Mole and Toad, as polar opposites. While Mole and Toad are similar in their quests for a kind of spontaneity and playfulness associated with childhood, Mole's calling to find "the delight of spring without its cleaning" is rooted in the natural world, what Grahame presents as the positive pole of childhood. Toad's calling is for the open road, the flight of fancy embodied in the motor car, "that swan, that sunbeam, that Thunderbolt!"[11] The car is a symbol of what Grahame saw threatening the "natural" world, represented as childhood lost. While Mole is porous, vulnerable, receptive, Toad is escapist and narcissistic. Toad's "fits" are rigid suspensions of the self; he is immobilized, rendered inanimate, transfixed by technology, a trickster, associated with the "unnatural" and with the movement out of the agrarian past into the commercialist present.

Mole's state of longing, on the other hand, initiates him into spring "moving in the air above and in the earth below and around him, penetrating even his dark and lowly little house with its spirit of divine discontent and longing. . . . [He believed] something up above was calling him imperiously . . . [to] the joy of living" (*Wind*, 1–2). The green world of "birds building, flowers budding, leaves thrusting—everything happy, and progressive and occupied" (*Wind*, 3)—reflects his childish responsiveness and the state of grace suggested by the harmony of the landscape. This egalitarian order is quite opposed to Toad's snobbishness and selfishness. Grahame suggests here a connection between Toad's infantile imperiousness and the autocratic and arbitrary world of money and power.

In Grahame's pastoral vision, the elegiac tone sounds throughout but is incorporated gently into his green world. The landscape is breathtakingly beautiful, if temporal, spatial, and therefore essentially ephemeral. But it is this fleeting quality of life that the idyll works to subvert and to have us forget. Grahame's pastoral poses a double narrative and establishes a series of doublings as the dominant paradigm of the work. And this has everything to do with his attempt to juggle innocence and experience, to situate childhood and adulthood on a continuum. To the extent that he excludes adult concerns like sex and death that threaten his animal pastoral, as Poss and Kuznets point out, he suppresses what is basic to adult experience. However, in the shadows of the idyll hints of such consciousness reside, which essentially generate the overall doubling. As adults our most difficult task, I believe, is to live on two levels of experience: one encompasses the temporal/spatial world of consciousness, modulated by memory. What we don't remember or do not recognize is contained in the other plane of experience—our deepest knowledge of pain, forbidden desire, and of death—which often appears in dreams and bits of unlocatable memory, or recedes into the darkest corners of the unconscious. This process is dynamic, ever in flux, but reimagined in this pastoral in fluctuating states of remembering and forgetting, and epitomized in the epiphanic experience of Mole and Rat in "The Piper at the Gates of Dawn."

As in the archetypal hero's quest, Mole is first called and guided by the Water Rat, who appears to him as "something bright . . . [that] seemed to twinkle . . . like a tiny star" (*Wind*, 5). The River Bank, Rat's safe and secure land-

scape, is utterly pristine for Mole, as he gasps " 'O My, O My' at each fresh revelation" (*Wind*, 13). Balancing strangeness and familiarity is essential to the
adult's negotiation of the civilized world, which Grahame presents here as man-
nered and inhibiting. There are many comments about "animal etiquette," which
determines what one can and cannot say. The narrator cautions against
"dwell[ing] on possible trouble ahead, or even allud[ing] to it" (*Wind*, 11), or "any
sort of comment on the sudden disappearance of one's friends at any moment, for
any reason or no reason whatever" (*Wind*, 17). But here Mole makes the usual for-
givable mistakes and is forgiven (and, in turn, learns to be forgiving) for his "fool-
ishness." Grahame tell us, "He learnt to swim and to row, and entered into the joy
of running water; and with his ear to the reed-stems he caught, at intervals, something of what the wind went whispering so constantly among them" (*Wind*, 22).

What the wind has to say is at the heart of Mole's education (and of the
book). Mole must learn to listen to the voices of nature carried by the wind. As he
journeys through the Wild Wood, in which nature evokes a range of meditative
states, he sorts through experience toward a balance of security and risk-taking. In
winter, he sees how "The country lay bare and entirely leafless around him, and
he thought that he had never seen so far and so intimately into the insides of
things . . . [into] the country undecorated, hard, and stripped of its finery. He had
got down to the bare bones of it, and they were fine and strong and simple" (*Wind*,
47). It is this feeling of safety mingled with his curiosity that leads him into the
Wild Wood, alone, where, in his terror, he at first sees "the faces," and then hears
"the whistling" and then "the pattering" that leave him "panting and trembling."
He "knew at last in all its fullness, that dread thing which other little dwellers in
field and hedgerow had encountered here, and known as their darkest moment—
that thing which Rat had vainly tried to shield him from—the Terror of the Wild
Wood!" (*Wind*, 50). But his fear opens him up so that he internally resonates with
the natural world in one dangerous correspondence that Wordsworth captured in
the opening of *The Prelude*. Wordsworth "gives thanks" to the doubleness embedded in Nature, as he says, "I grew up/Fostered alike by beauty and by fear," the
pole of fear suggested in the Wild Wood, the bare beauty of the wood in winter
that inspired Mole's journey.

The beauty and fear, their interconnection and their reflexivity, are embodied
in the inevitable struggle inherent in the quest. For Mole, the peak experience
occurs in that extraordinary chapter, "The Piper at the Gates of Dawn." There, for
Mole and Rat, their search for baby otter, for their own infancy, and for the
promise of harmony that drives the pastoral vision is illuminated by the nature
god Pan. There "suddenly Mole felt a great awe fall upon him, an awe that turned
his muscles to water . . . that . . . held him and, without seeing, he knew it could
only mean that some August Presence was very, very near" (*Wind*, 134–5). There
the tension between action and thought is resolved, all movement brought
momentarily to a halt, as Mole and Rat together move beyond temporality to lis-

ten, at first in silence, to the wind in the willows, and glean, from its music, its full
meaning. Here, Mole's perceptions are broadened; here he becomes most fully
porous. At first, he hears nothing "but the wind playing in the reeds and rushes
and osiers" (*Wind*, 132). The transcendent moment depends on clarity, discrete
boundaries, specific sound, or vision. And, in that moment, what one hears and
sees becomes more enunciated so that the "distant piping" is " '[c]learer and
nearer still.' " "The creeping tide of light gained and gained, and now they could
see the colour of the flowers that gemmed the water's edge . . . the rich meadow
grass . . . of a freshness and a greenness unsurpassable. Never had they noticed
the roses so vivid . . . the meadow-sweet so odorous (*Wind*, 133). And then,
Grahame reminds us, we must forget; we are graced with "the gift of forgetfulness," which is the price we pay for being "happy and light-hearted" (*Wind*, 136).
What follows is "less of the richness and blaze of colour than they seemed to
remember seeing quite recently somewhere—they wondered where" (*Wind*, 139).
The words they heard, the articulation of the meaning of "the wind playing in the
reeds," becomes for them music. And the sounds of the wind recall the spiritual,
but now inarticulately and intuitively, as they are located in time and spatially des-
ignated in the willows. This, it seems to me, is the meaning of the title, which suggests the openness of liminality that we in our adult lives lose but mediate through
childhood memory. Paradoxically, what can't be vocalized, the words of the
wind, is, of course, articulated by Grahame in his story, and by his spokesperson,
the Water Rat.

Mole's movement from innocence to experience in "The Piper" chapter
echoes an earlier journey implied in Rat's intermittent acknowledgment of familiarity along the way. Rat is first to grasp the significance of the wind's call. Mole
observes Rat's tears before his initiation into experience, when Rat, "transported,
trembling," professes: " '[s]uch music I never dreamed of [that] the call must be
for us' " (*Wind*, 131). While at first Mole hears nothing " 'but the wind,' " finally,
he sees Rat's tears and "bowed his head and understood" the sacred space they
have entered, " 'the place of my song-dream, the place the music played to me,'
whispered Rat, as if in a trance. 'Here, in this holy place, here if anywhere, surely
we shall find Him!' " (*Wind*, 135). It is fitting that the great spiritual presence take
this pantheistic form; Pan, associated with nature's music, offers a preoedipal
image of the unity of all living things, culminating for Mole and Rat in the
moment that brings them together with the infant otter curled up at the feet of the
Nature god.[12] But this vision, as Grahame points out, lies at the heart of longing,
and, therefore, to proceed forward, it must be forgotten. Of course, as Grahame
knows, it can never be fully forgotten but, rather, is echoed and reimagined as
another kind of call which lies "dormant and unsuspected" (*Wind*, 170) by Rat.

As doubleness suggests reciprocity, now it is Rat's turn to be summoned to
the liminal edge in his relative maturity, while Mole offers support and perspective. In his role as mentor to Mole, Rat had professed the River as " 'brother and

sister . . . and aunts, and company, and food and drink. . . . It's my world and I don't want any other,' " he told Mole. " 'What it hasn't got is not worth having, and what it doesn't know is not worth knowing' " (*Wind*, 10). This is clearly a denial of the vastness of nature (human included), and his desire to make the world smaller, his urges and fantasies more controllable, does not augur well for the Water Rat. He becomes tormented by his conflict between his need for safety in familiarity and desire for freshness and change. "[T]he clear sky . . . seemed to pulsate with promise; today, the unseen was everything, the unknown the only real fact of life" (*Wind*, 171), until the desire for adventure is severed, split off, and "out there, beyond—beyond" (*Wind*, 172) he sees the "dusty" wayfarer, a projection of the longing he cannot conquer. Much like Toad, Water Rat becomes transfixed and inert, will-lessly hypnotized by the Seafarer into "going South with the rest of them." "[H]is body [is] shaken by a violent shivering, passing in time into an hysterical fit of dry sobbing" (*Wind*, 189). This seafaring Rat harkens back to Coleridge's Ancient Mariner, not only in his haunting and haunted character but also in his relationship to the Water Rat, who is held, transfixed, and left glazed-eyed before he can return "to himself," his eyes "clear and dark and brown again" (*Wind*, 187). For a while, he loses "all interest . . . in the things that went to make up his daily life" (*Wind*, 187), before his healing can begin. The Wayfarer disappears, taking with him Rat's consciousness of the narrowness of his world, as he says, " 'I never stick too long to one ship; one gets narrow-minded and prejudiced' " (*Wind*, 177). So Rat escapes the threat of alienation, of becoming a foreigner everywhere, in his choice of safety, but at great cost to his spirit. This expense of spirit demanded of us by civilization is what must be, for Grahame, for Wordsworth, transformed into language.

What saves Rat, then, what restores him to the harmony of his riverbank home, is not forgetfulness, but art, which bears witness to his experience. Mole finds him, after all, writing a poem, "alternatively scribbling and sucking the top of his pencil" (*Wind*, 188). Here is the healing power of the imagination, the primal sucking of the body of the mother replaced and transformed by the potential of language to contain the unresolved complexities of felt experience and the demands of civilization.

While Toad's narrative reveals how uncivilized civilization can be, Mole's quest to integrate the outer world of the flowing river and its banks with his private internal domestic landscape alternatively interprets civilization as a more inclusive social order. The integration of the communal landscape with the private domestic order is at the heart of civilization and the making of a good citizen. Toad comes to exemplify the unexamined life of adventure "in a world that is retreating further and further from nature,"[13] while Mole and Rat together demonstrate, at various points and in different ways, the struggles, the pain, and the satisfaction at last of maturity. Grahame seems to strike a note of ambiguity at the end. We wonder, is Toad "reformed"? He is stabilized and regains his former position as lord of his manor. But does he return to his indulgent impetuosity and resistance to his friends' wise advice? Certainly he has enough self control to present himself as a new Toad, restrained and responsible at his banquet. "Toad's Last Little Song," the outrageous expression of the braggadocio, is delivered only to the imaginary "enraptured audience" in the privacy and safety of his bedroom. Grahame says, "He sang this very loud, with great unction and expression . . . then he heaved a deep sigh" (*Wind*, 256). An altered Toad? He seems resigned. But reform is not what is at stake here. Again, as with Rat, it is the imagination that will sustain him, though his poem is a comic heroic rendering, suggestive of broad farce, at opposite ends of the poetics we imagine Rat creating in the void generated by his unfulfilled longing. We are further told, "The four animals continued to lead their lives . . . in great joy and contentment" (*Wind*, 258), transformed into myth as "the great Mr. Toad," the "gallant Water Rat," "the famous Mr. Mole," and "the terrible, grey Badger," as the mother weasel points out to her children. Although she uses Badger to warn their children against misbehavior, clearly Badger, Grahame's most balanced "adult," who "cared little about society" and "was rather fond of children" (*Wind*, 259), is on the side of domesticity and the green world of childhood.

# 3

# The Body of the Mother

## I. IN LITERATURE FOR CHILDREN

Concerning that stage of my childhood, scented, warm, and soft to the touch,
I have only a spatial memory. No time at all. Fragrance of honey, roundness
of forms, silk and velvet under my fingers, on my cheeks. Mummy.

—JULIA KRISTEVA, "STABAT MATER"[1]

What Grahame left out, particularly in his location of the most primal place of
unity—the preoedipal image of the infant otter at the feet of the father-nature-
god, Pan—is where this chapter begins—with the body of the mother. Kristeva
speaks of her early memory of her mother as "[a]lmost no sight—a shadow that
darkens, soaks me up or vanishes amid flashes" (*"Stabat Mater"*, 180). For pro-
ponents of social attachment theory, like John Bowlby and Mary Ainsworth, the
link with the mother's body is "emotional in nature";[2] but Winifred Gallagher,
building on the work of environmental psychologists and psychobiologists,
claims a further substantiality of the primal bond between mother and infant.[3]
She quotes Thomas Insel, who says, "the mother not only provides a relationship
but also forms an environmental unit with her infant" (Gallagher, 123), and
Myron Hofer, who further claims, " 'For a baby, the environment *is* the mother"
(Gallagher, 120). This leap into metaphor most closely reflects the experience of
the infant, and illustrates a relatively unacknowledged truth about metaphor.
According to Mark Johnson, all thought begins with and includes the body. He
claims that what has been "ignored or undervalued in Objectivist accounts of
meaning and rationality [is] the *human body* . . . especially those structures of
imagination and understanding that emerge from our embodied thinking."[4] This

removal of the body from the mind mirrors the way in which the body of the mother has been withheld in Western culture, noted by Kristeva and other French feminist psychoanalysts.

When I speak of the mother's body, then, I mean to restore it to what I believe is its original place in the imagination—the real body, palpable and incarnate, complete with the metaphors generated by it and standing in for it. And when we look at the imagination of childhood, the poetics, we find Christopher Bollas, a British psychoanalyst, also building on the work of other psychoanalysts, to develop a theory of aesthetic experience as originating with the body of the mother. According to Bollas, the aesthetic "moment" predates consciousness and cognition. It begins with the "spell that holds self and other in symmetry . . . providing a rendezvous of self and other . . . that actualizes deep rapport between subject and object . . . a generative illusion of fitting . . . [that] evok[es] an existential memory. . . . Such moments feel familiar, uncanny, sacred, reverential, and outside cognitive coherence."[5] The aesthetic "moment" articulates the experience of rapport with the mother, "the essence of being . . . recollection of a time when communicating took place solely through the illusion of deep rapport of subject and object . . . of the infant with the mother, where the mother's task is to provide the infant with the experience of continuity of being" (Bollas, 41).

Before thought/word/language, when the pulse of mother and infant beat reflexively, the infant experiences "the first human aesthetic," that which prefigures and foreshadows all future aesthetics, including the propensity for metaphor and image. According to Bollas, the mother's "idiom of care" in large part determines the formation of self, which is developed and transformed by the environment. He says, "Whenever we desired, despaired, reached toward, played, or were in rage, love, pain, or need, we were met by mother and handled according to her aesthetic" (Bollas, 44). Bollas further claims that "[t]he uncanny pleasure of being held by a poem, a composition, a painting . . . any object rests on those moments . . . when the infant's internal world is partly given form by the mother" (Bollas, 41).

His work is based largely on object relations theory and Winnicott's concept of "potential space," the location of which literary critics claimed as lying somewhere between the text and the reader. Psychoanalytic critics assert that we bring our "texts with us into our lives," that we "mark them, and return to dwell 'within' them" (Bollas, 47), that the model for aesthetic experience is formed in our earliest life, and that the search for the aesthetic object is transformational, a yearning driven by the promise of experience to integrate the parts of the self that have not been integrated, "through the form provided by the transformational object" (Bollas, 41). As the word becomes the new transformational object, as it passes from the mother's tongue to that of the baby, it transforms the personality of the baby-self, as it makes its way outward from the home of mother-self toward society. And as we grow, as our first images gather and build accretively, early images may come from mother substitutes—the father or adoptive mother, for example; therefore, it seems important that we include them in this earliest story of the gestation of the imagination. It feels essential here to question and attempt a balance to Winnicott's assumption of the mother as foundation and the mother-infant as primary dyad. Clare Kahane notes Winnicott's "persistent slippage in his discourse between 'the breast' as metaphor of nurturance and as biological object."[6] She further indicates how Winnicott "ignore[s] the way in which culture mediates, if not constructs, our perception of the 'natural' " (Kahane, 279), and "the ways in which that environment not only holds but *captures* both mother and infant within its prevailing symbolic network of representations constructed according to the norms of a masculine subject" (Kahane, 280).

In contrast, Kahane points to Kristeva's concept of "the semiotic chora," a " 'receptacle of as yet unorganized clusters of desires' " that includes "the infant's experience of the maternal voice," embedded in which is a pattern of "sound that is the paternal precursor of the infant's language" (Kahane, 286). To become a "speaking subject," the infant incorporates into its "primary maternal vortex of corporeal needs and pleasures . . . an idealizing primary identification with the Other, an imaginary site of power and desire located elsewhere, beyond the mother" (Kahane, 287). Those primal clusters of images, utterances, indeed pulses of memory might belong to or even originate with the body of an Other— the primary caretaker, although I will continue to refer to her as mother, for purposes of looking at the literature of early childhood, which is so permeated with her presence.

### 1. *The Runaway Bunny*

Desire for the mother is at the heart of much of the literature of childhood, particularly in books for young children. Often in picture books, image and text, reciprocally, imaginatively offer the child words and images that illuminate and evoke the body of the mother and early states of desire. One such representation of the mother/child dyad, Margaret Wise Brown's *The Runaway Bunny*, astutely illustrated by Clement Hurd,[7] dramatizes the kind of language sharing between mother and child, the mother's body evolved and transformed into a process whereby the mother mirrors the baby, and where the baby's existence is affirmed. Winnicott articulates this state of infancy as, "When I look, I am seen, so I exist."[8] Mirroring in the earliest stages of life, according to Patricia Seator Skorman, "occurs in the bodily relationship with the mother." The responsiveness of the mother allows the infant "to fully inhabit the body from which an authentic sense of self emerges."[9]

The cover of *The Runaway Bunny* depicts the gaze of the baby so utterly absorbed in the mother, as to obliterate everything else—the flowers bent in the breeze, the nearby water, as mother and child sit close together in a field. While the mother is focused on her baby, her look is less open, less innocent than her baby's, and on the inner title page, only the bunny is drawn, with that same rapt expression. This is the story of the child's desire for separation, or the impulse toward individuation, which can not be fully realized at this early stage in child development, so it is shown in process, requiring expression and held in the imagination.

The bunny begins by proclaiming, " 'I am running away,' " to which the mother replies, then " 'I will run after you. For you are my little bunny.' " The tale builds intensity in the images of nature, as the bunny recites, " 'If you run after me . . . I will become a fish in a trout stream and I will swim away from you.' " To which the mother replies, " 'If you become a fish in a trout stream . . . I will become a fisherman and I will fish for you.' " This is followed by a double-page wordless spread in color, with baby on one page about to grab the carrot that the mother, shown on the opposite page, uses as bait. It is a dreamlike sequence that prefigures and sets the form for the cluster of images that contain both the separation and the connection between mother and baby: Each appears on a separate page, but they are connected by the river that flows across the pages. Mother and child are also connected linguistically, as each repeats the words of the other in the "if" clause, followed by the new words and images of the implied "then" clause. This provides mirroring, the affirmation of self for the baby rabbit and also for the mother, in a bond of true reciprocity.

This tale builds incrementally as the baby wishes first to become a rock on a mountain, then "a crocus in a hidden garden," then "a bird," a sailboat, a flying trapeze artist—while the mother responds that then she will be, respectively, a mountain climber, a gardener, "a tree that you come home to," the wind "and blow you where I want you to go," a tightrope walker, walking "across the air to you." After each black and white illustration of mother and baby on separate pages follows the dreamlike wordless double-page color transformation. In one haunting image, the baby rabbit has large beautiful wings, while the mother, although transformed into green leaves of a tree, retains her shape. In another, the mother bunny, always safely recognizable, is the wind in the sky while the baby with sailboat ears floats in the sea. Finally, this tale, like most accumulative and early nursery stories, comes full circle as the baby announces, after all his imaginative travels, " 'I will become a little boy and run into a house' "—to which his mother replies, then " 'I will become your mother and catch you in my arms and hug you.' "

In the final two double pages of full color, mother and baby are together, even closer than on the title page—he on her lap in the first, and both at the foot of the tree in a hovel, in the second, where she offers him a carrot, both mutually gazing and resolved. Between these two full color illustrations is the bunny's statement, " 'I might just as well stay where I am and be your little bunny.' "

In fantasy, then, spoken by the child and responded to at every moment of the way by the mother, the bunny will get to be wild, to leave his mother—in

Figure 2. Illustration by Clement Hurd, from *The Runaway Bunny* by Margaret Wise Brown, 1972. By permission of HarperCollins Publishers.

words, in the imagination. Brown approves the play; Hurd makes it voluptuous. But clearly the mother is not ready to let her child go into nature, that holding environment situated between childhood and adulthood. This stasis, a pause in the process of readiness, is most interestingly contained in the two visions provided in the final two double-page spreads: in each, the two are on one page, together at home entwined in the first; together in their den at the foot of the tree in the second, close but separate, in nature. This movement from home to a kind of protected nature demonstrates a stage of the baby's development—an early rapprochement, wherein he might have been caught in the ambivalence of wanting to leave the mother and be reassured at the same time that she is still there; but here, he is free to explore his desire, without fear of reprisal and without actually having to leave.

### 2. *Little Bear*

The gaze between mother and child, placed at the center of Maurice Sendak's illustration of Else Holmelund Minarik's *Little Bear*,[10] the first of the series, suggests its primary importance. Like *The Runaway Bunny*, this is a story of child desire both for separation from and affirmation of connection with the body of the mother. As this is an "I Can Read" book, the child-reader here supposedly will be on her own to a larger extent than with *The Runaway Bunny* and other such picture books. This format serves as a bridge into chapter books. It contains four stories, which are, most ingeniously, pulled together, accumulatively, in the last story, as "Little Bear's Wish," the story of all sorts of impossible and wondrous imaginings.

Here, Little Bear's developmental task is to express desire, and to wander alone into the interiority of the imagination. His mother, steady and at the same time flexible, is there to stabilize him, and to provide boundaries between the real and the imaginary. Like the mother of *The Runaway Bunny*, her connection to her child is revealed in her mirroring, so that as he proclaims his various wishes—to "sit on a cloud and fly all around" (*Little Bear*, 52), "to find a Viking boat . . . [a]nd the Vikings would say, 'Come along, come along! Here we go. Away! Away!' " (*Little Bear*, 53), to "find a tunnel. . . . Going all the way to China" (*Little Bear*, 54), to go "fast, fast" in a "big red car . . . [and] come to a big castle [where] [a] princess would come out and say, 'Have some cake, Little Bear,' and I would have some" (*Little Bear*, 55–6), and so on—she says, " 'You can't have that wish, my Little Bear' " (*Little Bear*, 56). But when he wishes, at last, for something he can have—a story about " 'things I once did' " (*Little Bear*, 57), she grants him that wish, which provides a summary of all the preceding stories—about playing in the snow, about pretending to go to the moon in his space helmet, and about his birthday party. Little Bear's wishes are fully realized in the illustrations and are placed on the top of each page, above the text for each. Having fully responded to her child's desire to " 'Tell me more about me' " (*Little*

*Bear*, 57), the mother then urges her child to go to bed, asserting her own unspoken need for separation when she says, " 'And now . . . you can make me happy,
too. . . . You can go to sleep' " (*Little Bear*, 60). Finally, she is shown in the last
two pages separately, on a page which faces Little Bear, as he leads his three animal friends off to play.


### 3. *Tar Beach*

Another wonderful picture book, radically different in tone and image, but suggestive of the mother's body submerged here as the story of a slightly older
child's imagination, is Faith Ringgold's *Tar Beach*,[11] which she both wrote and
illustrated. It begins, "My first book is for my mother, Mme. Willi Posey, who
took me to Tar Beach. And everywhere else." Her mother has described watching
her grandmother, "boil flour sacks to line the quilts she sewed." Susie Shannon,
Ringgold's great-grandmother, was a slave who made quilts.[12] This book is a
transformation of Ringgold's childhood memories, beginning with the opening
quilt landscape in which the young girl, Carrie, flies over tar beach, her rooftop,
which is empty, ready for her creation. Landscape here includes this element of
transformation from the darkness and despair of economic hardship and racial
discrimination: Her rooftop, the ordinary fare of urban living, becomes "tar
beach," a lush cityscape. The beauty of the rooftop, with the plants around its
edges, is recreated as regenerative and pastoral. Here the city is contained, a fes-
tive, nurturing environment where the family, extended into a community by the
inclusion of friendly neighbors, socialize as they eat together, while Carrie's baby
brother witnesses her night flight, "his eyes like huge floodlights tracing me
through the sky."

The story is a lyrical one, told with the grace of a folk storyteller, beginning
with, "I will always remember when the stars fell down around me and lifted me
up above the George Washington Bridge." The entry into the poetic moment
occurs here with the word "always," with the evocation of memory, and with the
magic of the stars that lift her above the city, above the bridge her father helped to
build, but from which he was excluded by the steelworkers' union, a discrimination recorded in history. This painful memory is transformed in Cassie's fantasy
of her owning the bridge simply by flying over it. She will then give it to her
father, so that "it won't matter that he's not in their old union, or whether he's colored or a half-breed Indian, like they say."

Ostensibly, this story reimagines her father's oppression and the sorrowful
shadow it cast on her childhood. However, it is contained, page by page, by the
body of the mother, creatively depicted in the colorful strips of quilt that run
across the bottom of each page, bordering and supporting each scene with their
vitality. At the top of several of the double-page spreads, Carrie flies above the
George Washington Bridge, with which she closely identifies, as "it opened in

Figure 3. Title page of *Tar Beach* by Faith Ringgold, 1991. By permission of Crown Children's Books, a division of Random House, Inc.

1931, on the very day I was born." As she claims the bridge, she transforms it—she "can wear it like a giant necklace or just fly above it and marvel at its sparkling beauty. I can fly—yes, fly. . . . That means I am free to go wherever I want for the rest of my life." In Carrie's transformation of her own and her family's powerlessness, she will own the bridge, her father will be rich, and her mother "won't cry all winter when he goes to look for work and doesn't come home." Her wishes will all come true—her mother, laughing and sleeping late, and the entire family joined at night for dessert from the ice cream factory, which she will fly over, "just to make sure."

At the end, as an extension of her creativity, she decides to take her little brother with her. She will pass her vision on to him, as he serves as witness to her extraordinary act, which is also ordinary. She says, "I have told him it's very easy, anyone can fly. All you need is somewhere to go that you can't get to any other way"—an invitation to children to imagine their own escape from the trials they are born into. The last illustration is of the entire quilt, which borders and frames the illustrations of the two children and the four adults, a happy community eating on the rooftop with the George Washington Bridge in the background. The word/text is the story of the father (and its effect on the mother), but the image/text, the heart and vitality of the narrative, is the story of the body of the mother(s) who held the family together from the days of slavery, a history of creativity and survival.

### 4. *In the Night Kitchen*

In Maurice Sendak's *In the Night Kitchen*,[13] the mother's body is recast metonymically as milk. The landscape of desire is a projection of mother with a huge bottle of milk protruding into the Milky Way. Mickey's story of the night kitchen is a transformation of his separation from the mother, depicted, in the fluidity of milk and his access to it, as a flexible bond, capable of differentiation and re-entry. The landscape of desire here is also the world from which he is excluded, the night world of adult sounds, which serve as entrance into the story, as Mickey falls out of his clothes, freely, "into the light of the night kitchen."

The story begins with the title page depicting Mickey fondly holding a bottle of milk, which is large, but not as large as he is—certainly not as large as it will become in the night kitchen, where he discovers the three identical father/bakers who threaten to drown him in the cake batter, as they chant, "Milk in the batter! Milk in the batter? Stir it! Scrape it! Make it! Bake it!"—oblivious to the fact that all that can be seen is Mickey's hand, as they put up the cake to bake, a delicious Mickey-cake. But this child is feisty, resourceful, and creates out of the dough a plane with which he will escape the bakers clamoring for milk. Mickey, cool as ever, says, " 'What's all the fuss? I'm Mickey the pilot! I get milk the Mickey way!" one of his many assertions of freedom and individuation. The double-page spread, wordless, and therefore, primal, depicts Mickey in the sky, in his airplane, hovering above a huge bottle of milk, while the bakers below, all three now in miniature, await his return—on which he exclaims, " 'I'm in the milk and the milk's in me. God bless milk and God bless me!' " He is the hero of his own story, self-generating and self-sufficient, survivor of the baking, provider of the milk—he does things his way. At the end, he returns to his bed, sleepy and satisfied, depicted on the last page, as on the first, with his arm fondly around the bottle of milk at peace—the body of the mother transformed, the father surpassed.

## 5. *The Bat-Poet*

The theme of Randall Jarrell's *The Bat-Poet*, illustrated by Sendak,[14] grows out of early individuation of infant from mother. It is about the need for the child to express difference and, at the same time, closeness, even sameness. As adults, we continue to struggle in this recognizable, pervasive, seemingly paradoxical state. In this individualistic culture, we seem to fear loneliness, as inextricably linked to the expression of difference, while we also fear being subsumed, with the same kind of inevitability, by our need (or what we may project as others' need) for intimacy. While it is about childhood that Jarrell writes in *The Bat-Poet*, it is also about the origin of such needs and fears, which he locates in childhood, and about their persistence in adulthood. Thus, it is not surprising that *The Bat-Poet* has been hailed, according to Jerome Griswold, as an allegory of poetics, "half for children and half for grown-ups."[15] Leo Zanderer wrote that Robert Lowell considered Jarrell "the poet of childhood," that the subject of childhood was for him "a governing and transcendent vision," as it was for Jarrell's two favorite poets, Rilke and Wordsworth.[16] James Dickey saw Jarrell's poems as "one long look . . . into a child's face, as the Things of the modern life happen around it, happen to it" (Zanderer 73)—all of which points to Jarrell's vulnerability. Sendak acknowledged Jarrell's childhood longings when he spoke of wanting to provide as a mother for Jarrell the image of his own mother in his illustrations of Jarrell's last children's book, *Fly By Night*;[17] Jarrell didn't have a mother and Sendak felt that deep void in Jarrell's emotional life.[18]

For Jarrell, the poet and the child shared this vulnerability. While *The Bat-Poet* chronicles the process of the poet—writing through mimesis, observation, moving through blocks, and searching for an audience for the poems—it is also about the growing child. The story begins in harmony and moves to isolation, as a necessary but painful state. It then becomes a search for community, albeit one that can tolerate the idiosyncratic poetic nature, the creativity that generates the need for self expression, every human's need for creative expression, which may, at times, produce the deaf ear turned on the little bat. The community of bats functions much like a classical dramatic chorus, defining conventionality and asserting social expectations, which, in this case, are determined in great part by nature. Bats are nocturnal creatures and therefore wish to sleep during daylight hours, but the little bat-poet loves the daytime when the squirrels and the chipmunk "ate nuts and acorns and seeds, and ran after each other playing. And all the birds hopped and sang and flew; at night they had been asleep, except for the mockingbird" (*Bat-Poet*, 2–3), with whom he is most fascinated. He tries to tell the other bats "about all the things you could see and hear in the daytime," but they have no interest in his alternative vision. They hang "in a bunch, all snuggled together with their wings folded, fast asleep" and when one wakes, the others all move in unison, "as if a fur wave went over them" (*Bat-Poet*, 1).

So the bat-poet searches for a witness, a pursuit similar to the child's for mirroring beyond the mother, for a reflexive community. He discovers a range of quality in his listeners, from the narcissistic mockingbird to the receptive chipmunk, although in his search for his own authentic voice, he discovers he needs to write about what he truly knows and is moved with an urgency to tell. Where he turns is to the primal source of energy, the body of the mother. He writes,

A bat is born
Naked and blind and pale.
His mother makes a pocket of her tail
And catches him. He clings to her long fur
By his thumbs and toes and teeth. (*Bat-Poet*, 36)

As he moves the poem out into the bat's natural world—the mother's journey into the night, "her high sharp cries . . . [that] [g]o out into the night" her eating "[i]n full flight," the pond "she skims across"—he comes to a full stop before the epiphanic moment when, "[i]n moonlight or starlight, in mid-air," we see "[t]heir single shadow, printed on the moon . . ." Here is the mother as environment, the central image toward which the poem moves and on which it resolves, the mother "fold[ing] her wings about her sleeping child" (*Bat-Poet*, 37). All sound stops, as we enter the double-page spread that follows, wordlessly, Sendak's cross-hatchings suggesting the richness of nature by moonlight. The imprint of the mother flying above echoes the mother and the baby lion, who, in its innocence, looks out at us from the grasses below.

While the bat's poem is appreciated by the chipmunk, what he really seeks is the mirroring that only comes from empathic likeness. As the chipmunk says, " 'You ought to say the poem to the other bats. . . . They'll like it just the way I liked the one about me.' " But as the bat-poet snuggles up to the other bats, he begins to get sleepy and to lose his memory of the lines. He goes "back to the beginning," as he recites, " 'A bat is born/Naked and blind—' " The book ends with this dash, the bat-poet cut off from the mother's body, literally, and from his inability to remember the final lines, as he yawns and "snuggles closer to the others" (*Bat-Poet*, 43)—which leaves the following questions: Does the bat need to sacrifice his poetic voice to find community, after all? Is this just a "natural" state, as the hibernation of bats in winter suggests? If so, what does this mean?

Jarrell leaves us with these ambiguities, perhaps in overarching ambivalence toward separateness, much the way childhood is expressed and depicted in his other works, both for children and adults, with a powerful and haunting longing.

## II. IN ADULT LITERATURE

### 1. *Annie John*

> The loss of a mother is profound. You will feel deprived and unprotected, of course, but something even deeper is lost to you. This body that is gone, her body, was the first body you belonged to, your very existence, flesh and bone, inseparable from hers. And thus when this trust is broken, connection itself suffers. She is point zero, the place where the geography of the heart begins.
>
> —SUSAN GRIFFIN, *WHAT HER BODY THOUGHT*[19]

In later years, according to psychoanalysts and child psychologists, a second individuation emerges. As a time of striving for autonomy, adolescence often evokes a regressive longing for that original, preoedipal state of merging, where the child lived in symbiosis with the mother. Nancy Chodorow and American feminist psychoanalysts, whose work relies heavily on object-relations theory, assert that the preoedipal period remains important throughout adult life, though the infant gradually internalizes the mother's early mirroring and nurturing, and becomes more independent of her. Chodorow also pointed out that the preoedipal longings are particularly intense for girls; that, in identification with the mother, girls experience the world as fluid and without boundaries, and themselves as inextricably linked to, defined, and completed by this connection. The struggle to separate from the mother, then, can be particularly wrenching for girls, can feel like a denial of some part of the self.[20]

Lacan and his followers as interpreters of Freud believe that the appearance of the father forces the child to separate from the mother to enter the social world of law and language. There the child learns to repress the desire for the mother. Lacanian feminists, like Kristeva and Irigaray, offer an essentially theoretical perspective that focuses on the language used to depict this state. In their experimental writings, they attempt to restore the repressed body of the mother. The language of the Symbolic Order, or the domain of the father and the extended outside world, distances and transforms desire into the linear and hierarchical structures of discourse. By contrast, preoedipal language or the semiotic realm is the articulation of a continuum; as Irigaray said of woman's body, "these streams are without fixed banks, this body without fixed boundaries."[21] For Kristeva, the semiotic is the creation of meaning through preverbal modalities—rhythm, into-nation, gesture, melody,[22] and is associated with the infant's intense attachment to and experience of the world through the mother's body.

Jamaica Kincaid's *Annie John* is a story told through the body of the mother. As a preoedipal narrative in which the mother is the central source of all conflict and movement,[23] its language powerfully suggests merging with the mother's body. It is metaphoric and metonymic, essentially organized and defined by shift-ing constellations that suggest shading, nuance, and resonance. The narrative unfolds through natural, organic images that cluster around the mother's body—her hands, her neck, her mouth, and her hair.

In the first two sections of the novel, the dominant image is of the mother's hand, which metonymically evokes the infant's primary sensation of the mother. The first section, "Figures in the Distance," begins with a loss of innocence: the dead people Annie has heard about come closer and more sharply into focus when, at the age of ten, she learns that a girl younger than she has died in her mother's arms. "Until then," she says, "I had not known that children died."[24] Death is associated with her mother, particularly with her mother's hands, which she avoids once she discovers that they have helped prepare the dead girl for bur-ial. The death of her own child-self is prefigured here in the separation to come, which for her is like a death in its severity.

*Annie John* begins with the image of a child dying in a mother's arms and ends with the image of a "vessel filled with liquid . . . placed on its side . . . slowly emptying out" (*Annie John*, 148)—both invoking a connection between birth and death, between childhood and loss. In her close attention to the severing of this most primal bond between mother and daughter, Kincaid offers a chronicle of the child's psychological journey away from the mother toward adulthood. The novel builds like a poem as the images gather and intensify. The first images of the mother's and child's bodies together, bathing in the rich scents of various barks, flowers, and oils, suggest the amniotic waters that once connected mother and child and the final image of the vessel "slowly emptying out." Bathing—the ritu-alistic washing of body parts—forms part of the mysteries associated with the obeah women who, in the Antiguan culture of Annie's home, embody the femi-nine principle. This act of spiritual bonding represents Annie's entry into an exclusive, female world and affirms her primal intimacy with her mother.

Annie is completely immersed in her mother's world as she follows her through her day, observing the way she shops and cooks, eats and laughs. Her sense of self is created through the reminiscences her mother stores away for her along with her childhood belongings. Annie remembers looking through her mother's trunk of keepsakes with her, and "as she held each thing in her hand she would tell me a story about myself" (*Annie John*, 21).

> As she told me the stories, I sometimes sat at her side, learning against her, or I
> would crouch on my knees behind her back and lean over her shoulder. As I did this,

> I would occasionally sniff at her neck, or behind her ears, or at her hair. She smelled sometimes of lemons, sometimes of sage, sometimes of roses, sometimes of bay leaf. At times I would no longer hear what it was she was saying; I just liked to look at her mouth as it opened and closed over words, or as she laughed. (*Annie John*, 22)

So closely does she identify with her mother that the necessary separation, when it comes, feels like a fall from grace.[25] Although there are hints of imperfection in their relationship during Annie's earlier years, whenever there was a rift between them there was always a way back, a reunification that felt like a return to paradise. The garden where her mother grew the herbs that Annie picked is her Eden. Annie says, "Sometimes when I gave her the herbs, she might stoop down and kiss me on my lips and then on my neck. It was in such a paradise that I lived" (*Annie John*, 25). Annie's love for her mother, charged with the narcissism of childhood and early infatuation, is the erotic adoration associated with first love. In her intimacy with her mother, Annie's sense of self is submerged, and like an infant, she experiences no boundaries between her body and her mother's. They are like animals, instinctually and mutually responsive and, from Annie's perspective, self-enclosed. This preoedipal world, of course, excludes the father, whom Annie experiences peripherally.

> When my eyes rested on my father, I didn't think very much of the way he looked. But when my eyes rested on my mother, I found her beautiful. Her head looked as if it should be on a six-pence. What a beautiful long neck, and long plaited hair, which she pinned up around the crown of her head because when her hair hung down it made her too hot. Her nose was the shape of a flower on the brink of opening. Her mouth, moving up and down as she ate and talked at the same time, was such a beautiful mouth I could have looked at it forever. . . . Her lips were wide and almost thin, and when she said certain words I could see parts of big white teeth—so big, and pearly, like some nice buttons on one of my dresses. I didn't much care about what she said when she was in this mood with my father. She made him laugh so. She could hardly say a word before he would burst out laughing. We ate our food, I cleared the table, we said goodbye to my father as he went back to work, I helped my mother with the dishes, and then we settled into the afternoon. (*Annie John*, 18–9)

This story is told exclusively from Annie's point of view, although we never lose sight of her mother. Our sympathies go out to her as well as to Annie, even as she appears at times cruel and rejecting through Annie's eyes. With the onset of puberty, Annie is forbidden to dress like her mother, and when she asks to engage in their special play with the objects in the trunk, "a person I did not recognize answered in a voice I did not recognize, 'Absolutely not! You and I don't have time for that anymore' " (*Annie John*, 27). The sense of betrayal grows, a deep rage festers, and the severing of such strong bonds is inevitably brutal—as is the shift from her mother to her school friends as the primary objects of her affection. What speeds up this process, what transforms her mother-love into erotic bonding with her peers, is something Annie perceives as the ultimate betrayal, portrayed again through the image of her mother's hands. When Annie comes home one afternoon to find her parents in bed together, she sees only her mother's hand circling on her father's back. The hand that fed and bathed her, that symbolized comfort and utter security, now seems unfamiliar and beyond her reach:

> It was white and bony, as if it had long been dead and had been left out in the elements. It seemed not to be her hand, and yet it could only be her hand, so well did I know it. It went around and around in the same circular motion, and I looked at it as if I would never see anything else in my life again. If I were to forget everything else in the world, I could not forget her hand as it looked then. (*Annie John*, 30–31)

The hand that "had to prepare the little girl to be buried" (*Annie John*, 6) now prepares her for witnessing the exclusive circle in which her mother and father are enclosed and from which she is shut out, and for the bitter knowledge that her father, her rival, has replaced her in her mother's affections.

Longing to recapture her closeness to her mother, at school she writes about a childhood memory of swimming on her mother's back, united with her as if they were one creature:

> When we swam around in this way, I would think how much we were like the pictures of sea mammals I had seen, my mother and I, naked in the sea water. . . . I would place my ear against her neck, and it was as if I were listening to a giant shell, for all the sounds around me—the sea, the wind, the birds screeching—would seem as if they came from inside her, the way the sounds of the sea are in a seashell. (*Annie John*, 42–3)

Annie is the listener, her mother the interpreter of the world and the source of entry into it. The image of bathing recurs here, although the waters are less enclosed, oceanic rather than amniotic. The boundaries here are still porous and the sea element connects the mother and child, yet Annie, as an older child, tells a story of separation. Unable to swim alone, she recounts watching her mother from an island as she swims. A ship comes between them, cutting off her mother from her view, and she panics, like an infant who experiences the loss of the mother if she is not within sight. When the ship has passed, Annie is devastated to discover that her mother had not been paying any attention to her. In the last part of her story, she tells of a recurring dream in which her mother deserts her. Sometimes in the dream her father replaces her; her parents, in exclusive intimacy, "sit tracing patterns on the rock" (*Annie John*, 46). Annie creates an alternative ending to this story, a wishful resolution in which her mother's empathic tears heal her. In reality, however, she is "greeted with a turned back and a warning against eating certain kinds of fruit in an unripe state just before going to bed" (*Annie John*, 45).

As her mother shares less and less of her vision, Annie is forced to create a secret world with her friends. The second section, "The Circling Hand," leads to the third and fourth, entitled "Gwen" and "The Red Girl," the names of the two girls who function as transitional objects in her journey toward separateness and individuation. Gwen and the Red Girl are her light and dark sides. Gwen is neat, clean, serious—all that is acceptable and familiar to her mother. Like her mother, she smells of lavender. While she speaks, Annie watches her mouth "as it moved up and down" (*Annie John*, 52), oblivious to the words, just as she used to watch her mother's mouth create meaning in the preverbal language of the semiotic. While her mother recedes into the distance, Annie finds a new paradise with her friends in a world they "hoped forever to occupy [where] boys were banished" (*Annie John*, 50). But she never really forgets her original loss as she sits on the tombstones at the back of the churchyard, listening to the tolling of the school bell. School becomes tainted for her—restrictive and punitive, associated as it is with her mother's wishes and with her former childhood innocence. Annie rebels against all that is considered respectable, as she leads the other girls in singing "bad songs," using "forbidden words, and, of course, show[ing] each other various parts of our bodies . . . walk[ing] up and down on the large tombstones" (*Annie John*, 81).

Annie, who is essentially spirited, becomes increasingly irreverent and iconoclastic, most defiant in transferring her love from Gwen to the Red Girl. The Red Girl embodies Annie's notions of impropriety. She never bathes, never attends Sunday School, and represents all that is untamed and free. She is associated with Annie's sexuality—with the menstrual blood that precipitated the distance between her and her mother. With the Red Girl, Annie enacts the dark and forbidden sides of erotic love, love mingled with guilt and rage, redirected in the fusion of pain and pleasure:

> Then, still without saying a word, the Red Girl began to pinch me. She pinched hard, picking up pieces of my almost nonexistent flesh and twisting it around. At first, I vowed not to cry, but it went on for so long that tears I could not control streamed down my face. I cried so much that my chest began to heave, and then, as if my heaving chest caused her to have some pity on me, she stopped pinching and began to kiss me on the same spots where shortly before I had felt the pain of her pinch. Oh, the sensation was delicious-the combination of pinches and kisses. And so wonderful we found it that, almost every time we met, pinching by her, followed by tears from me, followed by kisses from her were the order of the day. (*Annie John*, 63)

For Annie, everything becomes tinged with ambivalence, with the arousal of both longing for and aversion to her mother. In the marbles she plays with the Red

Girl, first introduced but now forbidden to her by her mother, Annie sees a reflection of the whole world, land masses and sea. But now her world must be hidden from her mother and the marbles stored under the house. Here she moves about in darkness, the underground girl, secretive and deceptive, stealing from her mother to buy gifts for the Red Girl. Whereas the early sections of the book focus on the upper part of the mother's body—her hands, arms, neck—in this section Annie experiences her mother as two enormous feet which she views from her hiding place. Once seen as "beautifully arched, pink-soled" (*Annie John*, 69) and identical to her own and her grandmother's, Annie's mother's feet now loom large and threatening before her. Once elevated in worship and trust, her gaze toward her mother is now lowered in perspective and suggests the fallen state in which she feels trapped with her mother.

Annie discovers how to be treacherous, two-faced. Although her mother forces her to give up the Red Girl, in her dreams she creates a tale of heroism and revenge in which she rescues the Red Girl from shipwreck, and, secluded together on the island, they cause ships to crash by sending them confusing signals—all of which recalls the early scene where a ship separated her and her mother. This primal severing generates the arc of ambivalence under which the rest of the novel sits.

If the first half of the novel is dominated by oceanic imagery, expansive and lush, in the second half the imagery becomes increasingly constricted. The governing metaphor is "a black ball . . . no bigger than a thimble, even though it weighed worlds" (*Annie John*, 85), lodged inside her and associated with her secretive self and with her self-doubt. The "thimble that weighed worlds" is her defense against her mother's barbs; along with her anger, which weighs so heavily on her, is her repressed love. Her world becomes increasingly airless, a "dark cloud that was like an envelope in which my mother and I were sealed" (*Annie John*, 91). In her dreams, she walks down a sunless road where the leaves of the trees are so thickly enmeshed that they block out the sky entirely. This is the psychic space in which she and her mother live. They are enemies; so intense is the rage that connects them that in these dreams, she chants: "My mother would kill me if she got the chance. I would kill my mother if I had the courage." It is either "her chance or . . . my courage" (*Annie John*, 89). Each is reduced to the "frightening black thing" that lives within them both.

The split between mothers and daughters that often grows with the recognition of the sexuality of both women creates a rivalry. The sexual attention shifts to the father, and with this movement, the younger woman seeks relief outside the home. What retards this expansion in *Annie John* and intensifies the connection between the two females is the association of male sexuality with danger and fear. Although Annie's father is kind, nurturing, and nonthreatening, the obeah women have warned Annie's mother about the harmful spells cast on them by her father's previous lovers, several of whom have borne his children. Annie remembers as a child being swept into the protection of her mother's skirts when they passed one of these women on the streets. In addition, Annie has little contact with boys of her own age. One childhood memory is of a boy laughing sadistically when he tricked her into sitting in a nest of stinging ants. As an adolescent, when she meets this same boy and again he humiliates her, her mother turns on Annie by telling her she has acted like a slut—a final assault on her sexuality, which increases the gulf between them, until her mother becomes a shadow on a wall that stands between her and the rest of the world.

Annie finally retreats into illness, a world of silence and darkness, regressing into the preverbal pulsations, where sounds "rocked back and forth" (*Annie John*, 111), which is also paradoxically a movement toward healing. She returns to the preoedipal world that predated her fall from grace to restore herself. She does not speak, since words, as part of the Symbolic Order of the Father, are substitutes for the desired object. She recounts that during her illness, "my mother and father . . . stood at the foot of my bed and looked down at me. They spoke to each other. I couldn't hear what it was that they said, but I could see the words leave their mouths. The words traveled through the air toward me, but just as they reached my ears they would fall to the floor, suddenly dead" (*Annie John*, 109). Language, the medium through which the child mediates her needs in the world, has broken down along with her faith in that world. She is weightless like an infant in the dark safety of the womb; she has relinquished all mobility and with it all separateness. But the call of the mother, as Kristeva has pointed out, can generate madness. "After the superego," she writes, "the ego founders and sinks. It is a fragile envelope, incapable of staving off the eruption of this conflict, of this love which had bound the little girl to the mother and which then, like black lava, had lain in wait for her."[26] Kristeva's personification of desire for the mother as some kind of predator can also be said to capture Annie's deep sense of distrust. In her weakened condition, she now relies on her father's back, reminiscent of the way she once swam on her mother's back. As Annie remains removed from her mother, the waters associated with the maternal come in the form of rain pounding outside on her roof at a distance, while inside, in her head, she sees the "black thing . . . lying down" (*Annie John*, 111). She tries to cleanse herself of all impure feelings by literally washing some family photographs she finds during her illness. In a photograph of her aunt's wedding, she tries to wash away the creases from her aunt's wedding veil, the dirt from her father's trousers, all the faces of her family. In another, she washes away every part of herself except for her confirmation shoes, the symbol of her rebellion against her mother, who thought them unlady-like. Most telling of all, she washes away her parents from the waist down in an attempt to restore the imaginary presexual world of her girlhood innocence. In her own eyes, she is reduced to a distorted remnant of her childhood, small and mechanical, a "toy Brownie" (*Annie John*, 114), dissociated from the world of adults. "Settling back in my bed," she reports, "I looked up at the beams in the ceiling. I then sat on one of them and looked down at my mother and me" (*Annie John*, 116).

In her dreams, she takes in the maternal waters of the sea, but in her desperate longing she drinks the sea dry and cannot contain it. She cracks and splits open, and wakes to find that she has wet her bed. For Annie, as for most adolescents, the world is polarized; she seems caught between childhood and adulthood, and in identifying with either position there is danger and loss. As she snuggles against her father, she is a child who has wet her bed, but on his lap she feels the stirrings of sexuality, the surfacing of oedipal feelings.

> Through the folds of my nightie, I could feel the hair on his legs, and as I moved my own legs back and forth against his the hair on his legs made a swoosh, swoosh sound, like a brush being rubbed against wood. A funny feeling went through me that I liked and was frightened of at the same time, and I shuddered. (*Annie John*, 112–3)

Her retreat from these feelings, from sexuality altogether, is a return to her original source of sustenance, the body of her mother. Through the maternal world of the obeah women and of her grandmother, who is steeped in spiritualism and magic, she reenters the prerational world associated with the preoedipal. She experiences her grandmother semiotically through her smells and the "sound of her breath as it went in and out of her body. . . . I would lie on my side, curled up like a little comma, and Ma Chess would lie next to me, curled up like a bigger comma, into which I fit" (*Annie John*, 125–6).

Interestingly, Kincaid says that of all the sections in this essentially autobiographical piece, only the long rain and the illness are fictional.[27] Periods of rain are rare in Antigua; the deluge here is clearly metaphorical and her breakdown, an emblem for the dark night of the soul through which she must pass. When she emerges, however, it is not with a sense of wholeness, but rather with a fragmented vision and a deep sense of loss. For her that loss echoes everywhere; everything around her is charged with associations of her father and mother. Her house, bed, chair, and porridge spoon were all carved by her father's hands; the sheets on her bed, the curtains on the windows of her room, and the nightgown she wears through her illness were all made by her mother's hands. She concludes, "I suppose I should say that the two of them made me with their own hands" (*Annie John*, 133), which elicits in her a claustrophobic need to escape from everything familiar, from both her parents and her school friends. What was founded in light for her now, through her young and bitter vision, appears tainted. Her own integrity is suspect, as it is inextricably linked with her family, and particularly with that paradigm of betrayal—her mother's body. She says, "So now I, too, have hypocrisy, and breasts (small ones), and hair growing in the appropriate places, and sharp eyes, and I have made a vow never to be fooled again" (*Annie John*, 133). Now, through a kind of Swiftean vision, her mother's mouth appears "like a donkey's" (*Annie John*, 136); her father's false teeth make a "clop-clop sound like a horse." Even her friends are repulsive to her.

Annie maintains this dark double vision even on her last morning at home before her departure for England.

> I was looking at them with a smile on my face but disgust in my heart when my mother said, "Of course, you are a young lady now, and we won't be surprised if in due time you write to say that one day soon you are to be married." Without thinking, I said, with bad feeling that I didn't hide very well, "How absurd!" My parents immediately stopped eating and looked at me as if they had not seen me before. (*Annie John*, 136)

Feeling invisible in her family and dissociated from all that is familiar, she walks the jetty toward the boat like a ghost, the familiar scenes of her childhood passing before her eyes, "as if I were in a dream. . . . I didn't feel my feet touch ground. I didn't even feel my own body—I just saw these places as if they were hanging in the air, not having top or bottom, and as if I had gone in and out of them all in the same moment" (*Annie John*, 143).

Annie's struggle to separate is not completed by the end of this novel; at sixteen this kind of resolution is rarely achieved. Annie grips her parents' hands at the dock, terrified that they will scorn her for her need. They respond with love, which in turn propels her toward them, and then just as quickly sends her away. At the scene of her departure we feel her ambivalence, as she both desires and fears her mother's love and protection; she vacillates between vulnerability and defensiveness:

> My mother said, "Well," and then she threw her arms around me. Big tears streamed down her face, and it must have been that—for I could not bear to see my mother cry—which started me crying, too. She then tightened her arms around me and held me to her close, so that I felt I couldn't breathe. With that, my tears dried up and I was suddenly on my guard. "What does she want now?" I said to myself. Still holding me close to her, she said, in a voice that raked across my skin, "It doesn't matter what you do or where you go, I'll always be your mother and this will always be your home." I dragged myself away from her and backed off a little, and then I shook myself, as if to wake myself out of a stupor. (*Annie John*, 147)

Annie is not ready to integrate the good and bad mother she sees before her, nor does she feel free of her. Even at the end, when she looks back from the deck, she sees only her mother, watching until she becomes "just a dot in the matchbox-size launch swallowed up in the big blue sea" (*Annie John*, 148).

Although there is a promise of new life as Annie sails for England, the last image of the amniotic waters "emptying out" recalls the broken membrane—the first separation of the infant from the body of the mother—and foreshadows the new independent self Annie will birth. But the tone is somber and suggests weariness, depletion. For Annie, the old world is dying, but the new one has yet to be born. With great acuity, Kincaid portrays this terror of stasis, of being frozen between childhood and adulthood.

Although Kincaid emphasizes the pain of the connection between mother and daughter in *Annie John*, a framework for resolution beyond the end of the novel is provided by her mother's parting words, which assert the continuous and primary nature of the preoedipal bond: " 'I'll always be your mother and this will always be your home.' " The potential reunification of mother and daughter, foreshadowed in *Annie John*, is explored in *At the Bottom of the River*, which invites a more exclusively adult viewpoint:

> My mother and I walk through the rooms of her house. . . . The rooms are large and empty, opening on to each other, waiting for people and things to fill them up. Our white muslin skirts billow up around our ankles, our hair hangs straight down our backs as our arms hang straight at our sides. I fit perfectly in the crook of my mother's arm, on the curve of her back, in the hollow of her stomach. We eat from the same bowl, drink from the same cup; when we sleep our heads rest on the same pillow. As we walk through the rooms, we merge and separate, merge and separate; soon we shall enter the final stage of our evolution.[28]

Kincaid suggests here the fluidity of this most primal bond; complete separation is never fully achieved (and perhaps this is not even desirable). However, she confirms when asked about her own life the possibility of an evolution from the drastic swings of adolescence—between feeling totally merged and just as dangerously dissociated from the mother. She speaks of her own experiences as an adolescent, which closely followed Annie's: her rift with her mother, her need to escape her family by flying to New York at age sixteen. And she speaks of the closeness she feels now as an adult with her mother. The fact that both her mother and her daughter are named Annie attests to her identification with them (Clifton), the three Annies as three selves on a continuum—her mother as one part of herself and her daughter as another—linked through time, gender, and culture.

Like the writings of other contemporary black women, particularly the work of Paule Marshall and Alice Walker, Jamaica Kincaid's fiction focuses on the importance of continuity and community as they are preserved and kept alive by mothers, through their stories and through their connection with their daughters.[29] Even though the intimacy between mother and daughter threatens at times to devour the newly developing spirit of the adolescent girl, it is an essential and integral source of nourishment, based as it is on connection, fluidity and mutuality. *Annie John* is the deeply embodied story of the passion and power of that bond.

## 2. *The Autobiography of My Mother*

If Annie John tells her story through the body of her mother, if the connection with the mother is most visceral to the developing self, particularly for Jamaica Kincaid, who claims, "My mother wrote my life and gave it to me"[30]—then what would happen, imaginatively, if there were no mother (and no nurturing substitute)? How would the young self construct itself? This is the question out of which her novel, *The Autobiography of My Mother*, grew. It is the story of Xuela, a girl whose mother died "at the moment I was born," the determining event of the novel on which every other event turns. It concludes with, "This account of my life has been an account of my mother's life as much as it has been an account of mine, and even so, again it is an account of the life of the children I did not have, as it is their account of me. In me is the voice I never heard, the face I never saw, the being I came from. . . . This account is an account of the person who was never allowed to be and an account of the person I did not allow myself to become."[31] Her repetitions are so powerful—of the word "account," and the phrases which follow, "account of my life," "account of my mother's life," "account of the life of the children I did not have"—which build incrementally to an intense embodiment of voice and face, established paradoxically through negativity, through absence. When Xuela recites the recurring motif, "my mother died at the moment I was born," she acknowledges it as the defining and "central motif" of her life, as it gathers, poetically, the clusters of images of her felt experience. Nowhere do we lose her in disembodied meditation, though she repeats and philosophizes and even contradicts herself. In this poetic novel, Kincaid creates an anatomy of the construction of self, which proclaims the power of the body of the mother to form the young woman even, and particularly, because it cannot be obtained, in absence.

The story opens with two dominant images of being without a body in which to locate and contain the self. Both suggest the lack of sanctuary, the sense of being without boundaries, "nothing standing between myself and eternity; at my back . . . always a bleak, black wind . . . no one between me and the black room of the world" (*Autobiography*, 3). In the other image, the body is effaced, reduced and likened to "soiled clothes," as Xuela is placed by her father in the care of the woman he paid to wash his clothes. As she says, [My father] would have handled one [bundle] more gently than the other, he would have given more careful instructions for the care of one over the other . . . but which one I do not know, because he was a very vain man, his appearance was very important to him. That I was a burden to him, I know; that his soiled clothes were a burden to him, I know; that he did not know how to take care of me by himself, or how to clean his own clothes himself, I know" (*Autobiography*, 4). This is her legacy. From her mother, she constructs her self as "a black wind"; from her father, "soiled clothes."

Her world at four years old is "a series of soft lines joined together, a sketch in charcoal" from which her father appears and disappears. The things that matter to people in this story are bodiless, without human qualities, objects onto which are projected qualities both human and embodied. For example, there is the plate she breaks, over which such sadness is expressed, "so thick with grief, so overwhelming, so deep, as if the death of a loved one had occurred" (*Autobiography*,

8). The body of Eunice, the laundress-caretaker, suddenly appears in focus as "[s]he grabbed the thick pouch that was her stomach, she pulled at her hair, she pounded her bosom; large tears rolled out of her eyes and down her cheeks, and they came in such profusion that if a new source of water had sprung up from them, as in a myth or a fairy tale, my small self would not have been surprised" (*Autobiography*, 8). Myths, the containers of cultural meaning, are generated here by reversal, by revoking the human, or rather the humane. Eunice heaps abuse on Xuela, who is already, at her young years, beyond vulnerability, because, as she explains, "I did not love her. And she did not love me" (*Autobiography*, 9). She is forced to kneel with her hands raised above her head, until she apologizes, but, as Xuela says, "I could not say [the words 'I am sorry']. . . . It was beyond my own will; those words could not pass my lips" (*Autobiography*, 10). Resistance is her survival; it is her source of strength and knowledge. And as we read her story, she serves as mediator for us, the reader, between the colonized and the colonizer. She notices, with whatever remains of her innocence, how the world is divided, between conqueror and conquered. The plate she unconsciously breaks, with its mythic pattern of English country life as "heaven," delicately delineating the idyll to which Eunice, like all good Dominicans, aspires, suggests and parallels Xuela's role as iconoclast. She has been cast, by birth and the lack of birthright, by her early outcast state, as a seer, one who sees beyond the socialization that has defined individuals, one who brings us, therefore, closer to the truth behind the socially created myths of British-dominated Dominican culture.

The education of Xuela is one of bringing the world into the world—restoring what was previously denied to her in the congenital moment of her existence, the body of the world. As she journeys "down the path on the way to my school," the world around her grows from a series of lines and shadows into "sensations of seeing, smelling, and hearing" (*Autobiography*, 13). Covering the wall of the schoolroom is a map, she tells us, on which "were the words 'THE BRITISH EMPIRE.' These were the first words I learned to read" (*Autobiography*, 14). How Xuela retains her own sensory experience of the world as she takes in the world is the story told here, through her own body, which she keeps to herself and for herself. By discovering and embracing her self autoerotically, she refuses to allow her body to be colonized. Whether she takes on lovers in or out of wedlock she will keep her body, not allowing it to bear the children who might take it from her. She learns in her early school days to keep "each thing as it took place in my mind [sharp which] I now take for granted. . . . I did not yet know the history of events, I did not know their antecedents" (*Autobiography*, 15).

Being without antecedents permits an originality, a vital source of knowing, which she learns to speak to herself in her own voice. Her mother and her low descent are what bring her closest to a knowledge denied those who are not set apart, as she is, those whose gifts might promote them, while her ability "to retain information, to retrieve the tiniest detail . . . was regarded as . . . so unusual that my teacher, who was trained to think only of good and evil . . . said I was evil . . . possessed—and to establish that there could be no doubt of this, she pointed again to the fact that my mother was of the Carib people" (*Autobiography*, 17).

As schooling becomes more humiliating for her, as her own vision is increasingly denied, as she is continually punished for that vision, she then turns to nature, to educate and contain her, as if it were the body of the mother herself—which she comes to see, in recurring dreams, descending a staircase from heaven, dressed in white, down to her bare heels—the only body part illuminated to her. Nature first generates and then replaces the face of the mother. And as the child's body replaces the image of the mother's in development, Xuela finds her reflection here in the intensity of the natural world: "I loved the face of a gray sky, porous, grainy, wet . . . the face of that same sky when it was a hard, unsheltering blue, a backdrop for a cruel sun; the harsh heat that eventually became a part of me, like my blood" (*Autobiography*, 17–18). The mother's body and the body of the people, of the nation, become linked as the two great sources of vitality and knowledge that are submerged. She learns to be self-generating, to judge reality, by trusting herself; through her own senses she would know the truth of things, regardless of the words of others. In fact, her own words, her ability to articulate her experience, she claims, "saved my life. To speak of my own situation, to myself or to others, is something I would always do thereafter" (*Autobiography*, 22). Language serves to solidify her experience and completes the early childhood journey from the mother, to natural world, to the social world of language—only here she is the touchstone for validity.

The world is not to be trusted. Her father, whose skin "looks as if it is waiting for another skin, a real skin, to come and cover it up" (*Autobiography*, 49), is not to be trusted. He is identified with his clothes, from his early treatment of her as a bundle of soiled clothes to his "jailor's uniform." His face "was like a map of the world. . . . I did not know this world, I had only met some of its people" (*Autobiography*, 91–2). As her father remains unknown to her, the only body part she identifies with him is his stiff and strong back, "a large land mass arising unexpectedly out of what had been flat; around it, underneath it, above it I could not go . . . so many times had [this back] been turned to me" (*Autobiography*, 92). When he speaks, he does so as representative of the patriarchy, the conqueror of black people, although he is a mixture of Scots and African blood. As a cruel man who enjoys lording his power over those less powerful, he represents the world and the language of the oppressor, his words betraying the real meaning they try to hide. For example, "The word 'love' was spoken with such frequency that it became a clue to my seven-year-old heart and my seven-year-old mind that this thing did not exist . . . —that behind everything I heard lay another story altogether, the real story" (*Autobiography*, 24). At this young age, Xuela learns that nothing "would have the same power it once had over me—the power to make me feel helpless and ashamed at my own helplessness" (*Autobiography*, 25). This is the quest of the child; this is what it must negotiate for itself as it passes through life, to prevent what will kill it—nullify or make foreign its spirit, for that is what shame and powerlessness do, what they are there to do.

Her mother, whose body cannot be known, becomes embodied in a lamp, which sheds little light, though it comes from "a beautiful glass . . . fueled by a clear liquid that I could see through the base of the lamp, which was embossed with the heads of animals unfamiliar to me . . . the shelf [on which it stood] was made of mahogany, its brackets ended in the shape of two tightly closed paws" (*Autobiography*, 27)—images of primal and natural bodily strength. And she learns again and again to use her own body to test the truth of a situation, the truth beyond words; she looks into the faces of those around her. In her stepmother's face, she sees evil, that she will try to kill Xuela. And instead of turning against herself, as her stepmother takes every "opportunity to heap scorn on me"—she embraces her own body. She says, "whatever I was told to hate I loved and loved the most. I loved the smell of the thin dirt behind my ears, the smell of my unwashed mouth, the smell that came from between my legs, the smell in the pit of my arm, the smell of my unwashed feet. Whatever about me caused offense, whatever was native to me, whatever I could not help and was not a moral failing—those things about me I loved with the fervor of the devoted" (*Autobiography*, 32–3).

There are many images of treacherous maternal bodies, aside from Eunice and the stepmother. There is the vision that appears to the children when walking to school one day—"a woman in the part of the river where the mouth met the sea . . . a beautiful woman . . . in a way that made sense to us, not a European way: she was dark brown in skin, her hair was black and shiny and twisted into small coils all around her head. Her face was like a moon, a soft, brown, glistening moon. She opened her mouth and a strange yet sweet sound came out. . . . She was surrounded by fruit . . . all ripe. . . . She beckoned to us to come to her" (*Autobiography*, 35–6). A boy who succumbs to this Cyclopean image drowns, his death denied along with the entire experience, so that "it became a myth," a further source of suppression, and suggests the potential genesis of myth as embedded in cultural denial. Xuela, here speaking with conviction and I believe with Kincaid's sanction, declares:

Everything about us is held in doubt and we the defeated define all that is unreal, all that is not human, all that is without love, all that is without mercy. Our experience cannot be interpreted by us; we do not know the truth of it. Our God was not the correct one, our understanding of heaven and hell was not a respectable one. Belief in that apparition of a naked woman with outstretched arms beckoning a small boy to his death was the belief of the illegitimate, the poor, the low. I believed in that apparition then and I believe in it now. (*Autobiography*, 37–8)

Discouraged from making friends, discouraged from any bond that might chance the discovery of the potential power of the powerless, she recedes from the world and returns to her only source of trust—the pleasure of her own body. Along with and in keeping with the denial of the body of the mother, is, of course, denial of the body itself, and in particular the female body, and again in particular, the girl's body, already by school age, "a source of anxiety and shame" (80)—so that it won't threaten the pleasure of the body of the man, or by extension, the nation. Here, in the pleasure of her own body, she escapes the sounds of the world, of the hunter and the hunted, which come to her in the stillness and blackness of the night. Those "who were hunted, the pitiful cry of the small ones who were about to be devoured, followed by the temporary satisfaction of the ones doing the devouring: all this I heard night after night, again and again. And it ended only after my hands had traveled up and down all over my own body in a loving caress, finally coming to the soft, moist spot between my legs, and a gasp of pleasure had escaped my lips which I would allow no one to hear" (*Autobiography*, 43).

Isolation is to be the governing state of Xuela's life, when she takes lovers, when she marries, when she loses her husband (whom, of course, she cannot love, as he is English, conqueror, like most men, and she the disinherited, like most women), with and without siblings, eternally separated by the governing event of her life, her mother's death, and the denial of the body of the mother, which is also the body of women, and the body of the colored peoples of the nation. What might have been shared, the sisterhood and linking experience of women, is left as disembodied, disconnected fragments of history—her sister's abortion, her caretaker's care of her during her own abortion, friends she might have made at school. Men who might have grown into caring men—Lazarus, a gravedigger, or her brother, who dies mysteriously at eleven, trying, Xuela suspects, to be like his father—are paralyzed by oppressors, such as her father, who escape their own oppression by taking on the role of oppressor with their own people, much like the church, "built, inch by inch, by enslaved people" (*Autobiography*, 133). Kincaid suggests that when separated from others, our only recourse is to be true to ourselves. This is illustrated in Xuela's story.

The personal tragedy of Xuela's life is that what was denied her in her mother's body will render her unable to fulfill. She remains frozen in a state wherein "the child in me would never be stilled enough to allow me to have a child of my own" (*Autobiography*, 57). She acknowledges that

the opening into a bloom, the life of that bloom, must be something wonderful to behold; to see experience collect in the eyes, around the corners of the mouth . . . [t]he pleasure for the observer, the beholder, is an invisible current between the two, observed and observer, beheld and beholder, and I believe that no life is complete, no life is really whole, without this invisible current, which is in many ways a definition of love. No one observed and beheld me, I observed and beheld myself; the invisible current went out and it came back to me. I came to love myself in defiance (*Autobiography*, 56).

She is her own mirror, "found in an old piece of broken looking glass" (*Autobiography*, 58) and she retains her own sense of self through resistance to anybody or anything "to make a pawn of me" (*Autobiography*, 65). Even the woman who shows love to Xuela, who mothers her when she is pregnant, caring for her body, as if it were her own, is a source of danger. As an older woman, and by definition one of the powerless, she tries to use Xuela's youth and fertility to service her own husband. When she tells Xuela "to regard her as if she were my own mother, to feel safe whenever she was near," Xuela, again, resists, though the words mean so much to her. Xuela admits that perhaps Madame LaBatte was the only friend she ever had, but although she does become her husband's lover, she escapes as always into nature and into her own bodily pleasure. Beyond pleasure, her body serves as a testimony to her self, as the sight of her own face comforts her. She notes, worshipfully, the features on her own face, as she imbues them with beauty, and declares that "no matter how swept away I would become by anyone or anything, in the end I allowed nothing to replace my own being in my own mind" (*Autobiography*, 100). In this way Xuela, through all odds, remains true to herself.

Her quest to locate her mother generates meditative passages that circle around the fact that at birth, her mother's life was already a thing of the past, and that her mother's people are also of the past. She says, "she was of the Carib people. . . . Who were the Carib people? For they were no more, they were extinct, a few hundred of them still living . . . they were the last survivors" (*Autobiography*, 197). Her litanies focus on the attempt to locate her mother—"she was tall . . . her fingers were long, her legs were long, her feet were long and narrow with a high instep" and so on, interspersed with the staccato utterances, her mantra—"I did not know her, she died at the moment I was born" (*Autobiography*, 198).

At the end of the book, there are two meditations that reenforce the continual, persistent, and unfinished nature of her quest. One is about the primal and generative nature of this attachment—"spiritual and physical, that a mother is said to have for her child, that confusion of who is who, flesh and flesh, that inseparableness which is said to exist between mother and child—all this was absent between my mother and her own mother" (*Autobiography*, 199). The second focuses on the pastness of the past, on what has gone before us, what has been lost to us—and the desire to transcend history, for a story beyond that of the victor and the vanquished. Xuela says, "Each morning the great mountains covered in everlasting green faced us on one side, the great swath of gray seawater faced us on the other. The sky, the moon and stars and sun in that same sky—none of these things were under the spell of history" (*Autobiography*, 218). Only nature is beyond such vulnerability. For the human race, Xuela asks, "who can really forget the past? Not the victor, and not the vanquished, for even when words become forbidden, there are other ways to betray memory: the unmet eye; the wave of a hand that signifies the goodbye . . . this truth registers on the face, in the arrangement of the body itself" (*Autobiography*, 221).

The text of *The Autobiography of My Mother* is accompanied by a single illustration of a Caribbean woman that covers the cover of the book, suggesting the mother. Obviously, the autobiography of my mother is a term of impossibility or of paradox, and here, in this story of the woman whose mother remains forever unknown to her, but whom she continually seeks to tell her life story, is revealed both the mother's story and the daughter's, their stories linked bodily, though each has been denied the mother's body. The book is divided into seven sections, each preceded by a piece of the mother's picture from the cover. With each part of the story, beginning with the top of the page, the picture of the mother is progressively revealed, until, at the end preceding the seventh section, the full picture of the Caribbean woman is complete. Xuela has constructed her mother as she imagines her, from the shards of history left to her, from the stories she reads in the faces of her father and the survivors of her childhood—and from her belief in her own body to reveal its truths to her.

# 4

# Childhood and the Green World

> Out beyond ideas of wrongdoing and rightdoing,
> there is a field. I'll meet you there.
> When the soul lies down in that grass,
> The world is too full to talk about.
>
> —RUMI[1]

As in all literary pastoral, the green world in the literature of childhood is a response to the worldliness of the world. Whether it represents a retreat from the world's injustices—parental or the extended social world—it offers a natural critique of civilization and stands in contradistinction to the "unnatural"—machines, laws and customs, all that runs contrary to children's sense of freedom. And the pastoral, when coupled with the literature of childhood, often elicits a nostalgia for the past—both personal and historical. Memory is moved into the present, as if it were a series of tableaux happening before our eyes. Time shifts in ways that evoke the timelessness or the lack of consciousness of time associated with childhood, however filtered through the postlapsarian perspective of the adult writer. The green world suggests loss, and the longing for a return to an earlier state, real or imagined. What Bachelard said about the redolence of coming upon nests in nature, as adults, suggests the truth about all pastoral landscape, that "it takes us back to our childhood, or, rather . . . to the childhoods we should have had. For not many of us have been endowed by life with the full measure of its cosmic implications" (*The Poetics of Space*, 93).

The movement associated with pastoral, a retreat from and a return to the world, may be actualized in this literature of childhood, or the retreat may turn out to be a place of resolution itself, and not require a return at all. The literature of childhood offers this possibility; in fact, the retreat may have occurred before the story opens. The child begins in innocence; the story of her maturation may be seen as a retreat from its origins, and the movement to the green world may represent the return, the resting place of the story, where the child retrieves something that had been taken away, and finally is restored to a sense of harmony.

In the literature of childhood, the green world may serve to expose the cruelty and waste of our society. In revealing the various ways we are ruptured from our nature, these stories can be as deeply critical as the literature for adults. They may, therefore, insist on a return from the pastoral, so that the discovery that took place in nature can be integrated into our world in an offering of hope and renewal. Whether a progressive perspective is presented, one I associate with Rousseau's *Emile* and the belief in the natural goodness and rightness of the child, or whether it turns on a conservative view that works to fix us in a sense of the rightness of the past, the pastoral impulse in the literature of childhood has generated a wide variety of deeply imaginative books, some that are quite visionary. What Terry Gifford claimed for literary pastoral, its "versatility . . . to both contain and appear to evade tensions and contradictions—between country and city, art and nature, the human and the non-human, our social and our inner selves, our masculine and our feminine selves—that made the form so durable and so fascinating . . . [what] Lawrence Buell calls . . . 'pastoral's multiple frames' "[2]—is also true of the green world in children's literature. Gifford further notes that pastoral is " 'carnivalesque' in Bakhtin's sense of playfully subverting . . . the hegemony of the urban establishment" (Gifford, 23). The literature of childhood can sustain that sense of play and maintain its idyllic qualities, perhaps without the necessary accompanying ironies that rescue the adult vision from potential bathos. This does not mean that children's literature rarely succumbs to sentimentality. In fact, to create and sustain a vision of innocence, wherever its location, requires remarkable skill: How does one breathe life into such a world? In recollecting one's earliest most natural desires and sensory experiences, what gets lost and distorted? What gets transformed and how?

Critics such as William Empson claimed that all pastoral is allegorical. In the literature of childhood, the child actually can serve as the green world itself. In such an allegory, where childhood is the green world, the retreat from the worldly world is the child himself, the figure of escape, renewal, and possibility. The child may lead us into the garden, but also may become the garden, that which blooms, is cultivated, and nurtured. The landscape of childhood, like the best of literary pastoral, is integrative, rather than escapist. It involves a quest for something undegraded, something that resists the pollution, both moral and physical, of the world. It also involves a quest for something larger than the self, but complementary and congruent with it, a place of harmony and grace.

## 1. *The Secret Garden*

Frances Hodgson Burnett's *The Secret Garden*[3] is a classic rendering of childhood pastoral. It followed on the heels of Grahame's *The Wind in the Willows* and explores similar concepts of home in nature and sacred spaces and time. Like *The Wind in the Willows*, *The Secret Garden* is conscious and critical of the class system, as it splits us apart, severing us each from the other. Here the central characters are children, located in the real world with its unjust political systems, from which a retreat becomes necessary. There are two child-heroes: one of the mythic world, one of the time-bound social world. The integration of the two worlds, typical of much childhood fantasy, is effected by this dual child figure. Dickon is the guide into the green world that is forever waiting for us, the child who comes to us "trailing clouds of glory," a Pan variant, offering a renewal of the spiritual and natural, from which we have become estranged. We enter this world with Mary, the other hero, a selfish, ignorant, unloved and unloving orphaned child of British colonialists. In India, she survives the plague that has destroyed her parents and their entire world, and is left wondering: " 'Why was I forgotten . . . Why does nobody come. . . .' " (*Secret Garden*, 70). Alienated since early childhood, she had noticed, "Other children seemed to belong to their fathers and mothers, but she had never seemed to really be anyone's little girl" (*Secret Garden*, 12). Mary, child of time and of change, will journey to rural England where she will discover both her rich cousin, Colin, who is similarly but even more damaged than she, and the peasant child, Dickon, who has been privileged to be nurtured by his mother in the natural world where he is at home.

Mary journeys from the darkness of her isolation into the bright light of the green world, which is entered here, as in all good fantasy, by degrees, so that its authenticity is established. This book is about the healing power of the green world in which the darkest secrets, what has been driven underground, can emerge and begin the restoration of unity to all the fractures created by civilization: the fragmentation of children from each other, parents from children, children and adults from nature and other living things, and from themselves—from their pasts and therefore from knowledge for their future. In the garden, healing takes place through time for Mary; Dickon enters her world sometime after she has already discovered the garden and its two inhabitants, the gardener and the robin, with whom she forms a trio, an affinity among those who have been lonely.

When we first meet Mary she is nine years old, unaware of the disaster that has hit India, as she plays alone pretending "that she was making a flowerbed . . . sticking big scarlet hibiscus blossoms into little heaps of earth" (*Secret Garden*, 3), foreshadowing the gardener that she will become. She is "Mistress Mary, quite contrary" of the nursery rhyme, her emotional growth charted by the landscapes through which she passes, what Heather Murray called "the correlation of landscape to mindscape."[4] She will grow to know and appreciate the moors which surround the house, "[m]iles and miles and miles of wild land that nothing grows on but heather and gorse and broom, and nothing lives on but wild ponies and sheep" (*Secret Garden*, 24). Their untamed nature suggests her own,

which has been suppressed and kept hidden from her. The drive to her uncle's
house through "the trees (which nearly met overhead) . . . [and the] long, dark
vault" (*Secret Garden*, 22) mirrors the darkness of her soul and of her own consciousness, buried in her arrogance and sense of privilege and, paradoxically, of
deprivation. Susan Sowerby, Dickon's wise and natural mother, notes, " 'the two
worst things as can happen to a child is never to have his own way—or always to
have it' " (*Secret Garden*, 183).

When Mary first comes to England and enters her uncle's house, she is
asked, " 'What do you think of it? . . . You're like an old woman. Don't you
care?' " Her response—" 'It doesn't matter . . . whether I care or not' " (*Secret
Garden*, 15)—establishes her as a frozen child, closely aligned with the ancient
house with its many locked and closed off rooms. Her journey is one of coming
into consciousness, discovering her own inner life and forming a connection with
nature and with others. At Misselthwaite, Mary discovers in the tapestry "a forest
scene with hunters and horses and dogs and ladies" in her room, and feels as if
"she were in the forest with them" (*Secret Garden*, 24), a prelude to the bonds she
will form in nature and with other people. This tapestry, a frieze of an earlier time,
depicts a kind of aristocratic domination of nature, a paradigm that stands in
opposition to the circle of inclusion in the garden toward which this allegory
moves. Mary, as the hero who moves between house and garden, the explorer of
both inner and outer world, illuminates the process of how we get from one world
to the other.

The story begins in denial, the enemy of true progress. When Mary hears a
cry in the corridor, she is told, " 'You heard nothing of the sort. . . . You stay
where you're told to stay or you'll find yourself locked up' " (*Secret Garden*, 58).
At the heart of this story is the denial of childhood pain, of childhood itself, the
birthplace of all human feeling and of natural connection with the body. Feelings
are disavowed in this family, particularly feelings of loss, of the mother, here
Colin's mother, also Mary's dead, vain, cold mother, and of mothering itself.
What Mary discovers at the interior of the house, the heart of her quest, is the suffering child, crippled by fear and anger, Colin, her cousin, who is also her own
cruel and terrified self. Her task is to bring him out of his cloistered, breathless,
tomb of a world, away from the self-loathing and fear of his body, the weak back
and paralyzed limbs assigned to him by the family myths that generated his
prison. Mary brings him into the newly discovered garden, where they both can
be healed by nature's creatures and ultimately by the "natural child," Dickon.
Mary recognizes Colin as an earlier self, intemperate and unhealthy, what she has
moved away from. She stands between Colin, her past, whom she brings along
with her, and Dickon, that which is before her, entry into the timeless green
world. In the house, Mary finds ivory elephants, figures of the exploitation of the
natural world, reminiscent of the exploitation of India by England. She also discovers the natural world of animal mothers, a gray mouse and her babies, nesting
in the velvet chairs. Her journey is twofold: she unlocks the interior rooms of the

house as well as the door to the secret garden, the sacred space in which her own feelings are awakened. In the garden, she says, " 'No wonder it is still; I'm the first person who has spoken in here for ten years' " (*Secret Garden*, 77). Her task is to break the silence, to speak the truth, and in so doing, she rescues Colin, imprisoned in his father's past, negatively suspended in time, the underside of Dickon's bright timelessness.

In *The Secret Garden*, nature is the holding environment for all children, those who have been mothered as well as the motherless, the adult children and their children, in its regenerative and mythic circle. The children who play freely on the moors—Dickon and his many siblings—are the natural children, who live beyond the sculpted gardens that surround the house. In a pantheistic vision, the community recovers, together, a lost paradise, and the book ends with two prayers. One invokes Magic as the pagan center of Edenic images, chanted by the Christian child, Colin, "as high priest": " 'The sun is shining—the sun is shining. That is the Magic. The flowers are growing—the roots are stirring. That is the Magic. Being alive is the Magic—being strong is the Magic. The Magic is in me—the Magic is in me. It is in me—it is in me. It's in every one of us' " (*Secret Garden*, 242). Dickon, the pagan child, offers the other, Christian prayer: " 'Praise God from whom all blessings flow,/ Praise Him all creatures here below,/ Praise Him above ye Heavenly Host,/ Praise Father, Son, and Holy Ghost.' " Colin concludes, " 'Perhaps it means just what I mean when I want to shout out that I am thankful to the Magic. . . . Perhaps they are both the same thing' " (*Secret Garden*, 273–4), an articulation of the lost Eden, which provides a harmony for the disparate elements familiar to the pastoral world—the mythic and the linear, the natural and the civilized, children and adults, and humans and creatures—an utterly inclusive vision. The story resolves, however, somewhat enigmatically:

> In each century since the beginning of the world wonderful things have been dis-covered. . . . At first people refuse to believe that a strange new thing can be done, then they begin to hope it can be done, then they see it can be done—then it is done and all the world wonders why it was not done centuries ago. (*Secret Garden*, 281)

There is no return from the pastoral here. Here is an idyll in which time is inclu-sive and cyclical; yet, there is the suggestion of change, of human evolution, set in time, a paradoxical place of shift and rest, and of infinite possibility.

## 2. *Tom's Midnight Garden*

Philippa Pearce's *Tom's Midnight Garden*,[5] published seventeen years after *The Secret Garden*, strongly bears its influence in terms of imagery and effect. Although Philippa Pearce's vision is not overwhelmingly Christian, it shares the sense of pastoral, the garden illuminated as a heightened reality in contrast with daily life and its limitations. Like Burnett, Pearce distrusts the British upper classes and believes in children's ability to reach deep emotional states, particularly in the green world. But *Tom's Midnight Garden* is a time-travel fantasy and the garden here is linked inextricably to the past, to a rural life, and not one that is especially glorified. The garden is lush and bountiful but cultivated and guarded. It includes all the aristocratic Melbournes and is the chosen site of the cruel as well as the more innocent children. What is exalted in Pearce's pastoral is the bond formed between two alienated children, Tom and Hatty, and the freedom they find in each other's company in the garden.

*Tom's Midnight Garden* begins in "tears of anger." Tom is "in exile," where he is sent by his parents to live with his aunt and uncle, two singularly dense though well-meaning adults, to protect him from his brother's measles. As his mother looking past him bids him good-bye, he is dropped out of a relatively idyllic childhood into a fallen state of anger and isolation. Not that his mother intends to cut him off; not that his relatives don't try to please him. His is the ordinary and all too common isolation of childhood; he is Everychild, tyrannized by adult "reason," as when he is forbidden to get out of bed or put the light on because, as Uncle Alan insists, children need 10 hours of sleep each night. When Tom pleads, " 'But, Uncle Alan, I don't sleep!' " he shouts, " 'Will you be quiet Tom! . . . I'm trying to reason with you!' " (*Midnight Garden*, 13). Aunt Gwen, similarly out of sync with her nephew and the world of children, has chosen a nursery with bars on the windows as his bedroom, complete with her former "girls' schoolbooks."

The familiar pain of childhood—how children's hopes are betrayed by the impenetrability and tediousness of adults—drives Tom to discover the magnificent "midnight garden." What Tom misses is the companionship of his brother Peter, and the simple, small garden where they can play freely. Aunt Gwen and Uncle Alan live in a flat, "with no garden"—at least during the day. But at night, Tom discovers a secret garden at the back of the house that existed in late-Victorian times. And it is there, in that pastoral space, that he reconstructs the lost harmony of his childhood. There he meets the extraordinary child, Hatty, who emerges as a child in Tom's life, we learn at the end, out of her intense longing as an old woman to relive her childhood memories. It is Tom's need for affirmation and for imaginative expression that propels him into the distilled childhood memories of old Mrs. Bartholomew's dreams. Here in this garden the ordinary and the extraordinary meet. The darker potentially threatening side of the typical, though nonetheless painful, heartaches of childhood is mirrored in the pastoral fantasy. Tom's feeling that his mother doesn't really see him, for example, is actualized in the garden where he is literally invisible to those who are like his rather obtuse family. Here Tom meets the orphan Hatty, who has been left in the care of her cruel aunt, who is reminiscent of the wicked stepmother of the fairy tale. This fantasy functions like the fairy tale, where the magic at the center reflects and comments on the mundane world, intensified and enhanced to allow a recognition necessary for healing and restoring a sense of harmony.

This is a story about the development of consciousness in childhood. The awareness of more complex and alternative states of mind comes about through Tom's desperate need for freedom. As he is confined to his bed for ten hours each night, sleep or no sleep, another realm of time opens up for him, one that allows him to live in two orders of reality—the mythic and the linear.[6] Tom can live out his daily life during "regular" time, where "Time was marching steadily onwards . . . from minute to minute, from hour to hour, from day to day" (*Midnight Garden*, 98). At night he lives in the poetic time of the garden, where Time moves "forward to a tree's falling, and then back to before the fall; and then still farther back again . . . and then forward again" (*Midnight Garden*, 98), all without losing a single minute in the "real" world. This aspect of time travel expresses the two states in which we psychologically reside: the conscious and the unconscious. The growing awareness of the tension between the two is reflected in the two alternative landscapes, the "flat" and the garden, and is dramatized by a split into two Toms—one Tom who "would never let the sleepy Tom go to sleep" (*Midnight Garden*, 16)—right before he discovers the garden. This more imaginative and potentially darker self grows out of a longing for the larger world he discovers: "a great lawn where flower-beds bloomed; a towering fir-tree, and thick, beetle-browed yews that humped their shapes . . . from each corner of the lawn, a path that twisted away to some other depths of garden, with other trees" (*Midnight Garden*, 20). Here "[w]hen [the thickly interlacing branches] came calling him, he would hide, silent and safe as a bird, among this richness of leaf and bough and tree-trunk" (*Midnight Garden*, 20).

In this garden, the invisibility from which his suffering originated becomes a gift. He can move about freely, unseen except for those closest to his sensibility. As a relatively innocent child in harmony with the green world, he is recognized by its creatures—cows, geese, birds—and by Hatty, the poor relation of the aristocratic Melbournes. As in *The Secret Garden*, here privilege and class are a corrupting influence on the human spirit; only Hatty, who has experienced early trauma and loss, is "privileged" to see Tom. In this story, the pastoral is where consciousness expands for the child Tom; what begins in longing deepens and is transformed into empathy. About halfway through the novel, at a turning point marking the beginning of the most intense series of scenes that resolve only at the very end, Tom comes upon "the littlest Hatty," and witnesses her in her earliest state of loss.

> Turning the corner into the sundial path, he saw at the end of it a tiny little figure, all in black: a little girl, half Hatty's size, in a black dress, black stockings, black shoes. Even her hair was black, and had been tied with a black hair-ribbon. . . . [S]he was sobbing into her hands.
>
> Tom had never seen a grief like this. He was going to tiptoe away, but there was something in the child's loneliness and littleness that made him change his mind. . . . [H]e could not say this was none of his business. . . .

He never saw the little Hatty again. He saw the other, older Hatty as usual, on his next visit to the garden. Neither then nor ever after did he tease her with questions about her parents. (*Midnight Garden*, 95–6)

As a child, Tom is still porous, receptive, ignorant and innocent of tragedy. At first he is unable to recognize Hatty, but as his consciousness deepens, he comes to understand through sympathy all of Hatty's selves: Hatty when he first meets her, at a similar age—about nine or ten; Hatty at four in the above passage soon after she has lost her parents; Hatty as she grows into a young woman, and finally, Hatty as old Mrs. Bartholomew at the end. Hatty is able to come to Tom, fully and with all her experiences, only in her dreams where she is in touch with the child selves of her memories.

In addition, time travel serves as a metaphor for the way we need to travel, fluidly, reflexively between our own childhood selves, held together in our consciousness, or recalled from our unconscious through dreams and recognized by the conscious self upon waking. This occurs in a kind of mythic time, similar to Wordsworth's "spots of time," where poetic moments of our childhood function as landscapes we return to to reflect on our daily lives.

Developing consciousness, Pearce suggests, is the growing ability to recognize and to empathize with others. It means learning to respect "otherness," that there is more than one reality, that neither the self nor the other is, as Pearce metaphorically asserts, a "ghost," but rather that both are real. Tom and Hatty's only "real quarrel" comes about as they each assert that they are "real" and that the other is only a "ghost," until "[t]hey were glaring at each other" (*Midnight Garden*, 106), challenging each other's very existence. Tom shouts, " 'You're a ghost, and I've proved it! You're dead and gone and a ghost!' . . . and then [he hears] the sound of Hatty's . . . weep[ing] 'I'm not dead—oh, please, Tom I'm not dead!' " (*Midnight Garden*, 107). But once Tom has seen into Hatty's feelings, he can no longer remain detached in his stance. Pearce seems to be saying here that once we have seen the child-fear or most vulnerable part of another person, she becomes "real" to us. We see past our own vision or at least tolerate the possibility that ours is a reality others might not share. But this requires a lifetime of practice, as Pearce seems to understand when she begins the chapter following Tom and Hatty's reconciliation: "And yet, in spite of his assurance to Hatty, Tom continued secretly to consider the possibility of her being a ghost, for two reasons: first, that there seemed no other possibility; and second—and Tom ought to have seen that this was the worst kind of reason—that if Hatty weren't a ghost, then perhaps that meant he was. Tom shied away from that idea" (*Midnight Garden*, 109). Pearce seems to understand the self-protective thrust of defenses that generate such marginalizing. And, of course, she also portrays the potentially heightened awareness that can come from such marginalization. For example, Abel, the gardener, disenfranchised as part of the lower class, is also protector of the garden

and of innocence. As such he comes to see Tom and accept him for what he is—
an innocent child, rather than a creature of the devil, as he first believed.

Time travel becomes possible for Peter, Tom's older brother, only after he
becomes increasingly involved with the world of Tom's letters, when his intense
desire to see what Tom sees intersects with Tom's own desperate longing for a
witness—without which children can not possibly rest firmly grounded in their
own perceptions. As the older brother, Peter is not traditionally slated for the
role of "hero." In the fairy tale world, the youngest and least worldly is the one
who stumbles on the quest. But Peter's desire propels him onto the landscape of
Tom's skating adventure with Hatty, although he does not see what Tom sees—
or rather he sees Hatty as she is at that moment of intersection—a young
woman. This shift from Tom's vision of Hatty as a younger child reveals Tom's
desire to remain a child with the child Hatty, who has become, by the end Tom's
midnight journey—the point at which Peter comes to see him—a figment of
Tom's denial.

In one particularly poignant scene, Tom and Hatty skate together, both with
the same pair of skates, the shared symbol of their time travel, foreshadowing the
reconciliation scene at the end, which brings the two worlds together. Until that
time, Tom wanders between the two, attempting to make sense of it all. Despite
Uncle Alan's "blazing, angelic certitude" (*Midnight Garden*, 169) that anything
beyond his sense of the reasonable is nonsense, Tom reasons, " 'You might say
that different people have different times, although of course, they're really all
bits of the same big, Time . . . '—he saw it all, suddenly and for the first time,
from Hatty's point of view—'she might step forward into my Time, which would
seem the Future to her, although to me it seems the Present. . . . Whichever way it
is, she would be no more a ghost from the Past than I would be a ghost from the
Future. We're neither of us ghosts; and the garden isn't either' " (*Midnight Garden*, 172). From here, Tom decides to remain forever in the fluctuating, timeless
garden, while his parents forever await his return "next Saturday." But for Hatty,
Tom is progressively "thinning out." Earlier, Tom had become aware "of something going on furtively and silently about him" in the beginning shifts in his
travel between the two worlds. He would catch "the hall in the act of emptying
itself of furniture and rugs and pictures. They were not positively going, perhaps,
but rather beginning to fail to be there" (*Midnight Garden*, 23). Now as Hatty
grows older, Tom is "beginning to fail to be there," along with her own child self.
While Tom is most desperate to get back to her, she only wants him to watch her
skate. Her natural young adult worldliness is creeping in, as she moves from
childhood into sexual desire for young Barty, which takes over her childhood
imagination for so many years—until this late season of her life, where it is recaptured in her dreams.

*Tom's Midnight Garden* invokes two central metaphors—time and the garden. At the center is the grandfather clock, a source of inspiration for both worlds, at the heart of which, inside the clock, is the angel of the Book of Revelation, who stands with one foot on land and one on sea. Tom and Hatty read the biblical passage together: " 'And I saw another mighty angel come down from heaven, clothed with a cloud: and a rainbow was upon his head, and his face was as it were the sun, and his feet as pillars of fire: and he had in his hand a little book open: and he set his right foot upon the sea, and his left foot on the earth' " (*Midnight Garden*, 164–5). As the last book of the Bible, it prophesies "Time no longer," an apocalyptic vision that makes "Tom's head, when he had finished reading, whirl . . . with cloud and rainbow and fire and thunder and the majesty of it all—perhaps like the head of the unknown dial-painter of long ago" (*Midnight Garden*, 165)—connecting him with the imagination of the past. Imagination infused with feeling is the source, Pearce suggests, that can link cloud, rainbow, sun, fire, land, and sea. "Time no longer" suggests a final unifying vision "in the end," one that can reconcile opposites and provide the sacred space for a reunion of elements that have become fractured—past from present, child from adult, male from female, inner from outer self—the parts from the whole.

In the last recognition scene, Hatty as old Mrs. Bartholomew says to Tom, " 'Oh, Tom . . . don't you understand? You called me: I'm Hatty' " (*Midnight Garden*, 217). This moment is sure to bring tears, chills, or perhaps deep sighs to readers young and old. It expresses the ultimate wish, an embodiment or projection of desire for harmony, the impulse behind all pastoral, to restore unlike things to their place, to see them as part of the whole. It contains both expectation and surprise—what Tom was prepared for, an old woman, "small and wrinkled, with white hair," and what he was not "prepared for . . . her eyes." Their familiar blackness in an unfamiliar context creates in him a feeling similar to Freud's uncanny. Hatty, too, "stretched out a hand and touched his arm with the tips of her fingers, pressing with them so that she might feel the fabric of his shirt and the flesh under the fabric and the bone beneath the flesh" (*Midnight Garden*, 217)—to reach the deepest and most enduring part, the bare bones, the real person.

Pearce ends by asserting the power of feeling that makes this connection possible. Tom "had longed for someone to play with and for somewhere to play; and that great longing, beating about unhappily in the big house, must have made its entry into Mrs. Bartholomew's dreaming mind and brought back to her the little Hatty of long ago" (*Midnight Garden*, 225). In the end, we are left with Aunt Gwen trying to explain to Uncle Alan what she, as outsider, saw: " 'He ran up to her, and they hugged each other as if they had known each other for years and years . . . [and] he put his arms right round her and he hugged her good-bye as if she were a little girl' " (*Midnight Garden*, 229). We who have been witness to the internal emotional life here recognize it without the "as ifs." We understand that they have known each other "for years and years" and that she is, in fact, "a little girl." The freedom to make these connections function like alternative landscapes makes it possible for Tom to return to "normal" life, to his family, and to the progressive world of time, to which he also needs to be restored.

### 3. *The Amazing Bone*

*The Amazing Bone*,[7] like much of William Steig's work for children, is about living "the unarmored life."[8] Here the green world turns inevitably on the central question of much of children's literature: How can we grow up without losing the spontaneity of our natural responses? Steig, the urbane and sophisticated *New Yorker* cartoonist and student of psychoanalysis and Reichian orgone therapy, turned to writing children's books in his sixties to explore "the primal energy of early desire and impulse . . . [the] raw creativity he feared could be lost by the social defenses acquired in the civilizing process."[9] In *The Amazing Bone*, he depicts the child/pig, Pearl, caught developmentally between the socializing world of education, the child's early venture outside of family, and the early childhood world of wonder and awe. The green world here is located liminally between school and family, portrayed in a forest set in gentle pastel tones, a place of peace and harmony, the mythical first home of childhood.

Pearl's journey begins on "a brilliant day," where she leisurely "dawdle[s]" on her way home from school, watching grownups doing "things she might someday be doing" with the curiosity and sense of timelessness associated with childhood. Steig's illustration on the title page depicts Pearl walking through the forest with an expression I can only describe as blissful—eyes glazed over in awe, oblivious to the fox who awaits her. Here is the pivotal moment toward which the book moves, which suggests the question behind much Romantic literature: Can innocence be retained in the face of evil? Here we are not really talking about the full higher innocence of Blake; it is not wisdom that will take the place of that initial loss. What Steig depicts is the process of how innocence is lost, and what can help along the way to sustain the unarmored vitality of childhood.

Certainly the sense of bliss depicted in the first illustrations that precede the story—Pearl standing with her schoolbooks next to a lovely single flower, Pearl walking through a garden of colorful flowers, a huge butterfly and bee drawing honey from a huge flower—is sustained into the first few pages of the story. Pearl moves through the streets, into the forest, where all movement stops in an epiphanic and timeless moment. Sitting on the ground, dressed in the colors of the flowering trees and plants, set against the greens and grays of the forest, where "spring was so bright and beautiful [and] the warm air touched her so tenderly, Pearl could almost feel herself changing into a flower. Her light dress felt like petals." Here, in this place of absolute harmony, she gives voice to a "spontaneous overflow of feeling." " 'I love everything,' she heard herself say," a subtle indication of the intuitive nature of this utterance—which is answered by the Bone, a further representation of this unconscious and untutored self. " 'So do I,' " it affirms.

Figure 4. Illustration from *The Amazing Bone* by William Steig, 1976. By permission of Farrar, Straus, & Giroux, LLC.

The Bone that can speak "in any language," beyond language or before language, the early language of pure sound serves as her witness. It "can imitate any sound there is": it makes the cultivated sounds of "a trumpet calling soldiers to arms," the natural sounds of wind blowing and the pattering of rain, and the human sounds of snoring and sneezing. When asked, " 'You're a bone. . . . How come you can sneeze?'," it replies, " 'I don't know . . . I didn't make the world' "—a response that locates it in a most primal place, before schooling, before reason—a creation of nature, the bare bones of life, the most elemental of things.

The state of bliss continues as Pearl walks through an intensely buoyant pastoral scene of lake and bordering flowers, accompanied by the bone seen in her open purse, until she is confronted with costumed robbers. Pearl is alarmed, but the robbers can be easily frightened off by the bone who speaks words, "hisses like a snake and roars like a lion." This farcical drama is not the real menace. But the fox she meets next, who threatens to devour her in a kind of desexualized Red Riding Hood scenario, is also a part of the instinctual world. Shameless and acting according to his nature, he represents the other side of impulse. However, the most creative parts of the self are intuitive, and can, Steig suggests, overcome such evil, particularly a foppish creature suggestive of the deceptions and affectations of civilization. The bone makes the sounds that transform the fox into a harmless mouse that crawls into a hole—nature raw but tiny, harmless in the face of such affirmation: " 'I know how you feel,' the bone whisper[s]," mirroring Pearl's feelings. " 'You are very dear to me! . . . Be brave.' " The magical words the Bone uses on the fox are as bewildering to the Bone as they are to Pearl. The intuitive power of the child, the calling up of the uneducated, spontaneous self, remains mysterious to her, perhaps in some sense as it does to adults, who in a moment of spontaneity may discover what they didn't know they knew. " '[W]hat made you say those words,' " Pearl asks the Bone, who replies, " 'I wish I knew. . . . They just came to me, I *had* to say them.' "

The resolution of *The Amazing Bone* hangs on the following question: How can the pastoral impulse, a private and idiosyncratic sense of wonder and awe, be integrated into the socialized world of family? How can parents accept what is, for them, unimaginable—a talking bone? How does the child's imaginative world become part of the larger community? Steig doesn't "answer" these questions. More dramatically, he depicts Pearl's parents recovering from the shock of a talking bone, and leaves his readers with the image of Pearl, sharing both her daytime world and her world of bedtime and sleep with the Bone, the remnant of pastoral, a transformational object that functions to comfort the child while she can mitigate separateness, a most basic and early component of socialization.

## 4. *The World Is Round*

Gertrude Stein wrote *The World Is Round* for children, but like much adult writing for children, it contains the dominant preoccupations of her life. Throughout her writings, her desire, according to William H. Gass, was to "rid ourselves of the old titles and properties, recover a tutored innocence, and then, fresh as a new-scrubbed Adam, reword the world."[10] The story is set in childhood, which offered Stein an inquiry into the process of socialization, particularly the ways in which language and identity are constructed. *The World Is Round* is an accumulative nursery tale, whose form and meaning comes through the incremental repetition of sounds and the accretion of word and image. For Stein, as DeKoven points out with regard to her adult poetry, "Repetition this intense has the effect of cutting the verbal signifier loose, entirely, from lexical meaning."[11] Here Stein employs the simplest words, strung together in a series of coordinating conjunctions, undifferentiated by clauses—an attempt to get back to their original meaning. In these simplest of sentences, everything exists in itself; nothing is subordinated to anything else. In her work, according to DeKoven, Stein revealed "the signifier in its utter arbitrariness, totally divorced from the signified—shattering, as Derrida does in *Of Grammatology*, the notion of an 'organic' or 'natural' or 'necessary' connection between signifier and signified" (DeKoven, 174). Stein has said,

> I began to wonder . . . just what one saw when one looked at anything really looked at anything. Did one see sound, and what was the relation between color and sound, did it make itself by description by a word that meant it or did it make itself by a word in itself. . . . I became more and more excited about how words which were the words that made whatever I looked at look like itself were not the words that had in them any quality of description. (Gass, 147)

Stein uses the nursery rhyme to explore basic connections between sound and meaning, much as Carroll and Lear did in their nonsense poems. She noted how meaning can come through sound, how "Rose" contains a round "oh" sound—in keeping with her primal and intuitive nature. And her story is created from rose-colored pages, designed and illustrated by Clement Hurd, with Stein's approval and input. Each page contains a large circle of white on which blue text or illustrations are set in blue type, Rose's favorite color.[12]

This is the story of Rose's journey to the top of a mountain, where she discovers a green meadow, a pastoral space in which to place her blue chair, where she can take respite; as Stein says, "And Rose was there" (*World*, 106). The structure of pastoral is also suggested in the title, the roundness of the world, repeated in shifting meanings—now comforting, now threatening. It is an inclusive vision of circular patterning, the outer world reflected in the roundness of everything: in the shapes of the animals, in the eyes of the owl, in Rose's mouth, in the lakes, and in objects. The cover of the book and the title page are designed with the names of author and illustrator encircling the title, which itself circles around the continuous circle of the words: "A Rose is a Rose is a Rose," at the center of which is a round blue globe of the world, suggesting areas of land and water in wavy white lines. The first illustration facing the first page of Chapter 1, "Rose is a Rose," depicts an idyllic vision of tails, necks, and trunks of animals circled around Rose, holding a rose, a dog on either side of her.

The tale, then, begins in unity: "Once upon a time the world was round and you could go on it around and around. Everywhere there was somewhere and everywhere there they were men women children dogs cows wild pigs little rabbits cats lizards and animals. That is the way it was" (*World*, 7). Roundness suggests the wonder and connection of all that it includes—good and evil. So it is not surprising that very soon this Edenic vision begins to break down. Paradise, Stein suggests, becomes infected through intellect, with the need "to tell everybody all about it and they wanted to tell about themselves," with the civilizing impulse toward language, the need for language to mirror experience. Furthermore, once you name something, you limit what it can be and imply what it isn't. The desire for naming, differentiating person from person, thing from thing, also leads into issues of identity, as Rose wonders, "would she have been Rose if her name had not been Rose" (*World*, 7). The more socialized, Stein knew, the further we become from the source of the word, the further the thing from itself, the name from the thing, as the one becomes distinguished from the many. Again Carroll comes to mind, as Alice, much like the child Rose here, tries to make sense of the White Knight's assertion that the name of his song is not the same as what the name is called, nor is it what the song actually is. Before Rose begins to think, Rose is a Rose, in perfect symmetry and solipsism; once she comes into consciousness, everything, and her identity in particular, is called into question.

With her questions about self, she begins to observe otherness. There are the two dogs who are split into good and bad, mine and not-mine. With Pepe, the little black dog, who is not really her dog, she comes to understand otherness, that she can't control or possess Pepe. With her white dog, Love, there is perfect harmony. With Love, she sings her identity song:

Why am I a little girl
And why is my name Rose
And when am I a little girl
And when is my name Rose
And where am I a little girl
And where is my name Rose
And which little girl am I am I I the little girl named Rose which little girl named Rose. (*World*, 10)

She locates herself narratively, in her story—why, when, where, which—singing and crying. "And all this time the world just continued to be round," a testament

Figure 5. Illustration by Clement Hurd, from *The World Is Round* by Gertrude Stein, 1939. By permission of Arion Press, San Francisco.

to its wholeness, and at the same time to its lack of beginnings and endings, to its disregard of Rose's emotional state, as it also paradoxically reflects her sadness and her pleasure and comfort in her tears.

The more complex differentiation occurs with Willie, her cousin, separate from her by gender and nature. Willie's name establishes him as the male principle associated with will, a kind of consciousness that defines him as the guiding intellectual force of the Jungian animus. Rose, on the other hand, is all anima, instinctual feeling and song, which come up from the unconscious. Willie knows who he is, and defines himself in opposition to Rose: "My name is Willie I am not like Rose" (*World*, 15). He further is identified by his actions, the fact that "Twice he was almost drowned" (*World*, 11). Action is associated with the danger that exists in the world, even in the lake, which is round. The water lilies found there are "pretty to see," the children discover, but "they are not pretty to feel not at all" (*World*, 13). Two little boys get caught in them and are rescued, not by the unresponsive adult men, but by other children. Willie's song about "Drowning/ Forgetting/ Remembering/ I am thinking" (*World*, 16) does not make him cry, but rather excites him, propels him into further action. The song of the hoot owl, which echoes back to Willie his name-song, identifies his name with his nature. "You are a little boy," it affirms, "And that is your stature." Willie is born into difference, preceded by danger and denial, remembering and thinking—the mind in silence, giving way to the primal instinct of song and tears, where in sleep he murmurs, "Round drowned" (*World*, 17), the utterance of a fallen world.

There are many other images and bits of narrative that suggest socialization. There is the the rabbit held in the headlights of cars, which Rose's dog Love releases into motion. There is the song Rose sings, which includes "a glass pen," a movement from the oral to the written record of experience. There is school, where she is taught that the world is round; also that the sun, moon, and stars are around. "And that they were all going around and around" (*World*, 22), which makes her sad. Rose, still singing and crying, "remembered when she had been young." With memory and reflection, the beginning of adult retrospection, Rose looks into a "looking-glass" and notices her mouth "was round and was going around and around," like the world, which now includes the "mountains [that] were so high they could stop anything," about which she can sing and "of course she could cry"—her primal response to the world of edges and boundaries.

Willie's story further develops the theme of socialization and otherness. Bothered by contradiction "that when there was no wind blowing/ A twig in a bush would get going/ Just as if the wind was blowing" (*World*, 25), he determines to go out into the world. To alleviate his discomfort, he finds creatures to master. His song becomes a litany of imperatives: "Bring me bread/ Bring me butter/ Bring me cheese/ And bring me jam," and concludes with his assertion of conquest: "Believe me because I tell you so/ When I know yes when I know/ Then I am Willie and Willie oh/ Oh Willie needs Willie to tell them so" (*World*, 28). Willie's stance clearly keeps him from facing himself, as he sings, "Once upon a time I met myself and ran." Fear of himself transforms the self into other. In denial, he asserts his right, as a young colonialist, to "do as I please/ Run around the world just as I please./ I Willie" (*World*, 29). He becomes more of a capitalist, at first buying a wild animal since, "Everybody had one so of course Willie would come to have one, any wild animal will do, if it belongs to you" (*World*, 32). And although the lion he selects is terrifying, he tries to hide his fear, much like he denied his tears, by proclaiming "it was exciting" (*World*, 33). But as he begins to cry, his fear comes sharply into focus as he worries that now he is "just like my cousin Rose . . . [and] Oh will he again be Willie" (*World*, 34). He decides to give away his lion, the apparent cause of his terror, cheering himself up, like a true capitalist, because "there were only two baskets of yellow peaches . . . and Willie had them both" (*World*, 35). Stein clearly implies that possession, power, and control, used to cover fear of the feminine, the emotions, and vulnerability, are the signs of male socialization.

On the other hand, Rose tries to confront what she sees and feels—contradictory fragments of conjunctive phrases of "either or"—inclusive and incorporating the disparate sounds, words, and feelings into her soliloquy:

> Oh Willie Willie yes there is a lion for you, a brown lion for you a real lion for you
> neither will you nor will you ever know how little I wanted to take away the lion
> from you dear Willie sweet Willie take back oh take back your lion to you, because,
> and she began to whisper to herself as if she herself was Willie, because if a lion
> could be blue I would like a lion to come from you either from you or to you dear
> Willie sweet Willie there is no blue no lion in blue no blue in lion, neither nor,
> wailed Rose neither nor, and as she said neither nor, there there was a door, and
> filled with sobs Rose went through the door and never any more never any more
> would she remember that it had been a lion that she saw, either or. (*World*, 51)

The resolution comes in the form of mythic narrative, which transforms the story of wildness into a fairy tale in which the lion is named Billie, connecting him through rhyming with Willie, transforming him into a familiar form. Willie asserts that "Billie was not a lion when he was back," and the story ends, after much rationalization, rhyming, and free association, with, "Billie the lion never was anywhere. The end of Billie the lion" (*World*, 54). Stein was acutely aware of the power of sound to connect and transform unlike things, one into the other, to assuage children's fears, as well as those of adults, who may turn a phrase in similar however more sophisticated ways, to suppress the knowledge that threatens their sense of comfort in the world.

It is at this point that Stein turns toward Rose's journey up the mountain with her chair. As child of feeling, Rose's task is to move into nature, away from the repressive forces of civilization into the pastoral where one finds both fear and joy in wilderness. Climbing into the night, Rose uses the same techniques to assuage her fears as Willie used to deny his, essential for calming the self along its journey without either appropriation or denial. Rose rhymes, she counts, she repeats words and whole phrases until they form recognizable associative patterns. Like the ancients imploring the favor of the gods, she addresses the mountains, coloring them blue—her favorite—to "relieve her hearing her thinking":

> Dear mountain tall mountain real mountain blue mountain yes mountain high
> mountain all mountain my mountain, I will with my chair come climbing and once
> there mountain once there I will be thinking, mountain so high, who cares for the
> sky yes mountain no mountain yes I will be there. (*World*, 58)

Memory, a return to what we know and hold dear, helps Rose "to get there," as she "remember[s] that the world is round no matter how it does sound" (*World*, 63). She loses distinction between waking and dreaming, as she thinks she hears

Willie scream, because "Anything can happen while you are going up here" (*World*, 73), but whether it is her projections of her "alarms" onto Willie or her acceptance of the double-edged sword of the pastoral world, she is propelled into action—she continues to walk up the mountain, pushing her chair. Where Rose once associated her self with state of being verbs, "Rose is a rose," now she sees herself reflected in a flurry of action verbs that accompany her on her journey: "Rose did go on smelling and breathing and pushing and shoving and rolling" (*World*, 74). And she is affirmed even in the transitory realm of time, the "many minutes [that] go around to make a second how many hours go round to make a minute how many days go around to make an hour how many nights go round to make a day and was Rose found. She never had been lost and so how could she be found even if everything did go around and around" (*World*, 74).

Distinctions get blurred as Rose ascends higher and deeper into the complexity of things. She wonders how the same thing can be at times "a delight" at times "an awful warning"; she finds that she can't distinguish between a pen, a cage, a hut; is what she sees before her a dwarf or a little boy? What she finds, "What did Rose see close," behind the waterfall, "written three times just how it looked as if it was done with a hair on a chair . . . *Devil, Devil, Devil* . . . right there," and wonders, "was the Devil round"—like Pepe and her cousin Willie, "who could go around and around"? But even in the face of evil, Rose gains clarity in the morning light, as she affirms: "Rose was a rose, she was not a dahlia" nor a buttercup, fuchsia, oleander. And she continues on her journey, into the "cosy" shelter of woods, which are also frightening—"if you hear your own voice singing or even just talking well hearing anything even if it is all your own like your own voice is and you are all alone and you hear your own voice" (*World*, 90), she admits. There is where she places her chair, stands on it, and cuts "Rose is a Rose is a Rose" in a circle into a tree, which makes her feel "funny." This affirmation, Stein suggests, may be necessary, but as it involves the imposition of humanity on nature, it cannot take place without feelings of ambivalence. Staking out one's claim is, Stein understands, how "Rose forgot the dawn the rosy dawn forgot the sun forgot she was only one and all alone there she had to carve and carve with care the corners of the Os and Rs and Ss and Es in *a Rose is a Rose is a Rose is a Rose*" (*World*, 93). Rose, of course, is not the first to defile the green world in such a way: she finds that "some one had been there and had carved a name and the name dear me the name was the same it was Rose and under Rose was Willie and under Willie was Billie" (*World*, 94), which makes her "feel very funny it really did."

When Rose finally arrives at the top of everything, "her eyes round with fright," she sees a rainbow—a mélange of all colors, a paradigm of difference and harmony, through which she moves from a questioning of the nature of things: "Is the chair a bed or is it a chair. Who is where," to an assertion of identity in the face of diversity: "I am Rose my eyes are blue/ I am Rose and who are you/ I am Rose and when I sing/ I am Rose like anything" (*World*, 222).

As night descends, Rose sings of Willie, while "she cried and cried and the search light went round and round," connecting singing, crying, and roundness—a prelude to the destined marriage, inscribed in the pastoral forest in the mountains, of Rose and Willie on which this story ends. The world goes on being round, illustrated by the last wordless page that depicts two blue round circles set off within the large white circle, set off against the rose-colored page. One is the world, with its white, wavy demarcations of land and water, the other a small blue solid globe, the sphere of Rose and Willie, separate from but connected to the large blue world within the largest white circle. Here is where Stein's pastoral vision rests—the unity of all things, civilization, humanity, and nature—joined, however unequal, each in its separate sphere.

### 5. *Linnea in Monet's Garden*

In the preceding pastorals, the green world is located in fantasy, a timeless realm, an inner landscape, apart from the transitory world. *Linnea in Monet's Garden*, jointly created by Christina Björk, the writer, and Lena Anderson, the illustrator,[13] is a realistic story, a collage, constructed from photographs and drawings of people, landscapes, and paintings. It is also a verbal montage of fictional and historical characters, based on stories gathered from a variety of sources: historical narratives, written by artists and family members, as well as memoirs told by family members. This is the story of Linnea, who was "named after a flower [and] interested in everything that grows" (*Linnea*, 7), "a nature-loving city girl" from Stockholm.[14] She and Mr. Bloom, her elderly neighbor, a retired gardener who has studied Monet's work, journey to Monet's house and gardens, the source of his paintings.

What Linnea discovers is how to construct her own pastoral. In the post-Impressionistic time-bound world, in the face of such a constantly shifting series of moments, what can we savor, reflect on, hold in stillness for reverie? As a city girl, Linnea needs to find spots of nature from which to transform and relocate the green world. She will visit the gardens she has seen in books about Monet's paintings. The mythic, timeless world she discovers will be of her own creation.

In this story, Art will serve as a kind of Wordsworthian "recollection" of the experience in nature. Linnea constructs her own story of the story of Monet's work and life, which she will capture in a collage of her own. Her postcards, tickets, a pigeon feather, a photo of Jean-Marie, Monet's step-great-grandson, and other memorabilia of her trip, arranged tastefully and idiosyncratically on her bulletin board, serve as a testimony to her trip. The chronology of her journey reflects her portrayal of the creative process, as an individual—the one rather than the many, a singular vision. In this story, the many does not cohere or fold into one communal vision but, rather, keeps shifting—a realistic vision made up of many single moments, like an individual's life, like the many blobs of paint on Monet's canvas which give the illusion of a single poppy, a single landscape of a whole field of poppies.

Wholeness here is in the human connection with art, a representation of the bond with nature. Linnea's search for origins, like the search for the original creator and the original creation, mythically and spiritually figured in God and Eden, here is found in representations of beautifully cultivated gardens created by the fallen, all too human Monet, a selfish, moody man whose "views and moods ruled the house" (*Linnea*, 46). " 'Imagine having such a famous father,' " Linnea says reverently. The words of Jean-Marie puncture whatever illusions she might harbor: " 'Think of poor Michel [one of Monet's sons], the one who wanted to be an inventor. He was a good painter, too, but he never dared show his paintings to anyone as long as he lived' " (*Linnea*, 47). Even the beautiful garden, Jean-Marie tells her, was a "nuisance . . . [for the] children . . . because it was their job to weed and water it every evening" (*Linnea*, 44). So much for the real thing. And yet, Linnea's story is told with the vitality and excitement of the process of discovery—what is really left for us to reconstruct, the beauty that art can shape out of the many ordinary moments of our lives.

This book reveals the truly subjective nature of learning, how we know things in very personal and particular ways; how we sift through, order, and incorporate new learning, as we hang particles of information on so many little hooks in the mind. Linnea notes the steps of her journey with the emotional and intellectual force of a child, responding appropriately to those things most familiar and relevant to her own sense of reality. The daily tasks, interests, and pictures of Monet's children are most prominent in her narrative. Her story also underscores the idea of history and presentation of information as interpretive and subjective, reinforcing the notion that each individual, like Linnea, has a personal way of experiencing history, and that history is made up of the stories of the lives of individuals. Thus, Monet is presented as a real person, damaged despite his genius, living in a specific era with a specific family.

Every aspect of this journey toward knowledge is recorded in detail, through the reflections of this particular child, as she travels with Mr. Bloom, closer to the source of knowledge, from Paris to Monet's home at Giverny. At their first stop, Linnea looks through the window of their hotel into a park, where she observes with careful attention, the specific trees, the genus of the leaves (like her namesake, Linnaeus)[15]—an artist or historian or gatherer or recorder of information, in training for the human creative task. At the Marmottan Museum, she reflects on a painting of two water lilies: "I stepped a little closer to the picture and looked at it. It was then I noticed that the lilies were nothing but blobs and blotches of paint. But when I stepped away again, they turned into real water lilies floating in a pond—magic!" (*Linnea*, 14–5). And later, transforming her perception into her own artistic activity, she takes pictures of the lily pond from many angles, while she records, "This is the impression the water lilies made on my camera" (*Linnea*, 33). This distinction between modes of expression, that a photograph is created from the viewer's vision, sifted through the mechanism of the camera, suggests her developing aesthetic awareness, as she uses both camera and sketchbook to record her experience. She goes on to note, "It was hard to decide if we should look or take pictures" (*Linnea*, 23). The central philosophical epiphany of the book rests in her perception about the spontaneity of the experience itself, of being in the moment, when she reaches the Japanese Bridge, and exclaims, " 'And now we're really here. . . . It could never be more now than right now' " (*Linnea*, 26).

Linnea has understood the essentially fleeting nature of time, and of the promise of art to capture the moment and still its urgency. She begins to understand the implications of Impressionism, that life is a series of shifting moments and of shifting perspectives of a given moment. But capturing the moments aren't easy, and she learns that it wasn't easy for Monet when he painted water, with its shifts in color. "One moment it looks blue, the next moment it's white. Those . . . little moments that Monet tried to capture in paint . . . disappear so quickly, and it takes so many of them to paint a picture" (*Linnea*, 16). Art is a practiced activity. It may come from inspiration, but, as Linnea notes, "Monet *practiced* capturing impressions" (*Linnea*, 28).

Although the journey is utterly engaging and rejuvenating for both Linnea and Mr. Bloom, there are many hassles along the way: they aren't allowed to picnic in the real garden on Monet's bench; they take their civilized meal of paté, goat cheese, and apple cider, by the River Ru, outside the garden. In the modern, civilized world, the pastoral is removed from the original source, recorded and held in frames of the past. But this book ends with an assertion of the importance of Linnea's creation, what she has retrieved from her memories of her journey, set in contrast to the Eiffel Tower, an "unnatural" creation, which she has neglected to see. Unlike most other tourists in Paris, she asserts, "we had far more important things to see than that" (*Linnea*, 51). The green world, though transformed in a limited, cultivated version, remains primary for her. The pastoral prevails in a vision of creativity, the green world reconstructed out of the objects—found, grown, and created—by those of us, like Linnea, who live in urban landscapes.

### 6. *Julie of the Wolves*

If we look for pastoral in today's world, where do we find it? For the most part, as we have seen, writers of childhood seem to locate the green world in the realm of the imagination—with the exception of landscapes relatively untouched by civilization, and these are becoming increasingly harder to find or, rather, they have been found and plundered by our global and corporate economy. The impulse to

Mr. Bloom told me that Monet bought the land where the lily pond is when he was fifty-three years old. Three years earlier, he had been able to afford the house. People had *finally* started to like his paintings and to buy them. I took pictures of the pond from lots of different angles. Mr. Bloom was afraid that I would fall in when I was taking the water-lily pictures.

*This is the impression the water lilies made on my camera*

Figure 6. Illustration from *Linnea in Monet's Garden* by Christina Björk and Lena Anderson, 1987. By permission of Farrar, Straus, & Giroux, LLC.

escape the world of technology, to find safety in the natural world, has become coupled with an interest in indigenous peoples and culture, and with ecology. Naturalist writing has engendered a literature of spirituality, a quest for the sacred, for something untutored and unspoiled, in tune with natural rhythms and cycles. Jean Craighead George's *Julie of the Wolves*,[16] winner of the Newbery Medal for 1972, became a model for other stories of minority children and their experience in nature, often, as in *Julie of the Wolves*, by way of a retreat from a most uncivilized civilization. Often the child, who represents here as elsewhere the green world itself, finds her natural state threatened by what is demanded of her by her society. At the heart of the story is a search for authenticity, one that questions our treatment of the earth and all creatures, human and animal.

In *Julie of the Wolves*, the pastoral is a vision of wholeness and harmony; the natural world imposes this unity as all nature is inherently interdependent. Not one of us would survive without others of our genus and without other forms of life. However, rather than the individual given primary significance, here, as in the natural world, the individual's place is in the cycle of nature. Here nature is "red in tooth and claw,"[17] exacting and unsentimentalized. The natural pattern of things may appear as a kind of cruel chaos, but it is really an intricate and interdependent vision of all of nature working toward its survival. This is illustrated in the phenomenon of the lemming, who grow "nervous at the sight of each other" if there are too many. "They become restless, then crazy. They run in a frenzy until they die" (*Julie*, 13), Julie is told by her teacher. But if, as her father said, " 'The hour of the lemming is over for four years,'" then, "[u]nfortunately for Miyax [Julie's Eskimo name], the hour of the animals that prey on the lemming was also over" (*Julie*, 14), which include the snowy owl, the weasel, the jaeger. Without food, they "bore few or no young." But then, the grasses grow high again, because the lemmings and other creatures have gone, "and the hour of the caribou," the richest source of food for Miyax, "was upon the land" (*Julie*, 14).

Here the pastoral world is the tundra, the "barren slope" which stretches for hundreds of miles. "No roads cross it. . . . Winds scream across it, and the view in every direction is exactly the same. Somewhere in this cosmos was Miyax" (*Julie*, 6). This is the story of Miyax's journey to find herself and to survive out on the tundra, away from her arranged marriage to a feeble-minded son of her father's friend. There "[n]ot a tree grew anywhere to break the monotony of the gold-green plain, for the soils of the tundra are permanently frozen. Only moss, grass, lichens, and a few hardy flowers take root in the thin upper layer that thaws briefly in summer. Nor do many species of animals live in this rigorous land, but those creatures that do dwell here exist in bountiful numbers" (*Julie*, 9). At first, the tundra appears to her as "an ocean of grass on which she was circling around and around" (*Julie*, 11); however, she learns to find her way in this landscape, to know it, to survive it, and to love it.

For Miyax, the source of all her knowing is her father, Kapugen, the Eskimo hunter, whose teachings are the double-edged sword she must grapple with. From him, she learns how to create and use tools out on the tundra, to understand the wolves who are her brothers, to have "[patience] with the ways of nature" (*Julie*, 18), and to blend "into the plants, still as stone" (*Julie*, 29). Miyax/Julie is bilingual. "She spoke half in Eskimo and half in English," we are told, "as if the instincts of her father and the science of the *gussaks*, the white-faced, might evoke some magical combination that would help her get her message through to the wolf" (*Julie*, 8–9). But to survive out here she must learn a third language, the language of the wolves. And although she has learned much from her father the hunter, that, for example, she must tell the wolves she is hungry and ask for food, she has not been told how to do that. She does learn to speak with the wolves in "this language of jumps and tumbles . . . breaking the wolf code" (*Julie*, 23), to carefully observe their social customs, and to find her way into the pack. She also learns to communicate with Tornait, her spirit bird, whose life she saves and who becomes her companion. All of this learning means going back to an earlier knowledge of how animals and all of nature talk, give signals, make meaning.

*Julie of the Wolves* is divided into three sections. The first, entitled "Amaroq, the wolf," represents the present, her immediate need to survive with the help of Amaroq, who will protect her, become her adoptive father, and for whom she writes: "My feet shall run because of you./ My heart shall beat because of you./ And I shall love because of you" (*Julie*, 60). Part two, "Miyax, the girl," the story in retrospect, begins in the past and illuminates the present retreat into the tundra. It opens with "the wind, the empty sky, the deserted earth"—the story of her abandonment, first by her mother who died when she was four. She is nurtured by Kapugen, warmed by his sealskin parka, encouraged to remember her Eskimo identity, for, as he says, " 'We live as no other people can, for we truly understand the earth' " (*Julie*, 82). From him most of the "color spots in her memory" (*Julie*, 76) originate. Then, after being raised by her father away from gussak culture at seal camp, she is suddenly taken into the custody of Aunt Martha, where Eskimos spoke English almost all the time, where she goes to school, and where finally her father disappears. Again she is abandoned and finds the earth "empty and bleak" (*Julie*, 84). When she escapes at thirteen into the home of her father's friend, Naka, into the marriage her father arranged to protect her from gussak ways, she must again escape—this time from the sexual attack of Daniel, her feeble-minded husband.

Jean Craighead George is a true naturalist, and, as such, describes unflinchingly the natural ways of human beings as well as those of the natural world. Daniel is not shown to be evil. He is humiliated by his peers who mock him because he can't get his wife "to mate." George shows us that "[h]e was as frightened as she" (*Julie*, 102). In fact Julie's way of understanding Naka's drinking and violence is to say, " 'Naka is evil again. . . . His spirit has fled' " (*Julie*, 99). What she can't understand is the senseless killing of Amaroq. She is horrified, not only at his magnificent spirit stilled by shots from the airplane, but at the hunters' desertion of him; they leave his body out there. Then why was he killed? For her, you kill out of need to feed yourself, and, as is often shown in literature of indigenous people who live by the laws of nature, never without paying tribute to the animal's spirit, as she lifts "her arms to the sun" (*Julie*, 59)—even though she laughs at herself "for being such an old-fashioned Eskimo" (*Julie*, 59), even though she is deeply ambivalent about the old ways. There is no denial of the cruelty of nature: Jello, as the weakest of the wolf pack, is destroyed by the "wolves [who] take the old and the sick," the weakest. But the story of Miyax, the girl, becomes the story of Julie of the wolves in part three, which represents the future. It is what lies before her and what she must come to terms with.

When she leaves the tundra, she is acutely aware that her earlier dream of going to San Francisco to live with Amy, her pen pal, where a beautiful pink room is waiting for her, is impossible—now that " 'the pink room is red with [Amaroq's] blood' " (*Julie*, 148). She becomes the hunter Kapugen was, living "as her ancestors had, in rhythm with the animals and the climate" (*Julie*, 156). "[T]ime in the Arctic was the rhythm of life" (*Julie*, 27), we are told, where there is a place for silence, out of which she learns to listen for the ways of the natural world. Here is a vision of the mythic, preindustrial pastoral as it exists in the "real" world. But Julie watches as it is pillaged and ravaged by oil drum after oil drum:

> The air exploded . . . the plane flashed before her eyes. . . . In that instant she saw great cities, bridges, radios, school books. She saw the pink room, long highways, TV sets, telephones, and electric lights. Black exhaust enveloped her, and civilization became this monster that snarled across the sky. (*Julie*, 141)

The tundra and her memory of the wolves, where the spirit of Kapugen the hunter lives, retains its spirituality in her, where it is rendered sacred.

In the last section, she is briefly reunited with Kapugen, no longer the hunter, married to a gussak. His message to her—" 'I now own an airplane, Miyax' "—represents the future. " 'It's the only way to hunt today,' " he tells her. " 'The seals are scarce and the whales are almost gone' " (*Julie*, 169). This sends her back to the tundra. Her last note is mournful, an elegy to both Amaroq, the wolf, and Tornait, her spirit bird. She sings "in her best English": "Amaroq . . . [m]y mind thinks because of you. And it thinks, on this thundering night,/ That the hour of the wolf and the Eskimo is over" (*Julie*, 170). As she "pointed her boots toward Kapugen," we are left with the mournful passing of a way of life, a pastoral which has been destroyed by the modern world. Miyax will become Julie, but, as the title suggests, she is Julie of the wolves, remembered and retained in spirit.

There are two sequels to *Julie of the Wolves*, and in both, *Julie*[18] and *Julie's Wolf Pack*,[19] George remains true to what she knows: that Julie could not live out on the tundra with the wolves in present time; that there needed to be the separation between Julie and the wolves; and that the wolves that children loved to read about can have their own story, a pastoral from which humans are essentially excluded. This fracture of the human world from the natural world is the final elegy for the passing of pastoral out of realism and into the realm of romance.

# 5

# The Dark Pastoral

## I. THE FAIRY TALES

> the fairy realm of glorious wonders, whose mighty strokes summon
> up both supreme bliss and extreme horror . . .
>
> —E. T. A. HOFFMANN, *THE GOLDEN POT*[1]

The dark pastoral depicts the nightmare world of childhood. It is, essentially, the other side of the green world, and as natural in its shadows as is the light and sun of the pastoral. This relationship between the light and dark sides of the green world is not simply dichotomous; it is not a matter of good and evil. The power to survive and ultimately to create is layered into both worlds, as are danger and destruction. Both are part of the imagination and function, at their best, reflexively and by integrating the dark and the light. The nightmares of children, like all our dreams, serve significant functions: they tell us what we are afraid of, what we need to know about our fears, how to locate them, and how to transform them into a source of energy and light.

In the literature of childhood, we find the dark pastoral most frequently imagined as a primeval forest. In Grimms's "Hansel and Gretel," for example, the forest is marked by its density; there are no paths and there are wild beasts. At its center, the children find the perilous witch's house, which mirrors the potential destruction from which they have fled. In the dark pastoral landscape, the stepmother has been recast as nonhuman and bestial, with her red eyes and keen sense of smell. Removed from the realism that might evoke guilt, the child is free to enjoy Gretel's pushing the witch into the oven to burn to a crisp, The source of liberation from poverty, from the weakness of the father and the cruelty of the stepmother, is to be found here: the witch's jewels will release the children from poverty in this magical transformation of the original scene of horror. In other tales of childhood, such as the Red Riding Hood tales, the forest does contain paths, but the girl does not know which to take and can be easily tempted off the right one. Always there is more than one road and confusion. Sometimes, as in an early variant, "The Story of Grandmother," it is at a crossroads where the girl meets the wolf. But always she is sent into the forest by her kindly mother to care for her sick grandmother, a task she must accomplish as a burgeoning young woman. There is no way of maturing, the tales repeatedly tell us, without entering the dark wood, whether we locate it in the outside world or the inner world of dreams and the unconscious.

Often the child finds refuge, as well as danger, in the forest—particularly when the greatest source of destruction comes from within the home. In "Thousandfurs," for example, the girl runs from the incestuous demands of her father, the king. The forces of civilization and its microcosmic center, the home, are sometimes most dangerous of all. The tales in which human is transformed into beast also take place in the forest where the hero, most often a man but sometimes a woman, must live in an animal state to emerge full-bodied with instincts intact but tempered. A most popular transformation tale, "Beauty and the Beast," can be read as a story of the bestial and the beautiful in which, as Maria Tatar notes, the "antithetical allegorical figures resolve their difference to be joined in wedlock."[2] It also has been seen as a model for "expressing a woman's anxieties about marriage" (Tatar, 29). In any case, the transformation symbolizes the integration of the dark and the light aspects of human personality and of natural forces. However configured, the dark pastoral is associated with the creative energy and the imagination of childhood. It is constructed to resolve the tensions and bifurcations associated with civilization, whether demarcated as bestial and spiritual, male and female, or social and natural.

In the nightmares of children, we can locate the socially unacceptable, that which has been split off from the conscious imagination of children. Sendak's modern fairy tale, *Where the Wild Things Are*,[3] serves as an excellent example, with its deliberate attempt to integrate Max's "wild thing" self with the more socialized self approved by his mother. At first we see his wild self contained in a framed picture of Max in his wolf suit, which reads "by Max." But when he acts out in his wolf suit, he is punished. Here begins his dream journey into the dark pastoral land of the wild things where, alternating between states of fear and triumph, he will become king and tame his own wild self. But first he must immerse himself in a wordless, primitive state, which he initiates by announcing, "Let the wild rumpus start"—and which he terminates by saying, "now stop." In other words, his wildness is within his control and part of his imagination. When he returns, his dinner is waiting for him, still hot; he is reconciled with his mother, and he has learned the power of transformation. Rather than being stripped of his primal energy, he knows now how to negotiate with it and to find its place. In the "civilized" world this energy, associated with play and with childhood, is stored in the imagination and can be retrieved there from its darkened place.

In his article on "Blake's Treatment of the Archetype," Northrop Frye described the forest as "the 'natural' or unworked form of the vegetable world . . . its human or intelligible form . . . that of the garden, or grove, or the park" (Frye, 515). The archetypes of our collectively imagined civilized world are refinements of the wild. They represent nature as a projection of civilization—what can be tolerated and contained by the conscious self. The fairy tales with the forest at their center have been seen collectively by writers, translators, and collectors as "maps for coping with personal anxieties, family conflicts, social frictions, and the myriad frustrations of everyday life" (Tatar, xi).

Literary fairy tales grapple with the complexity and depth of human feeling more simply imagined in the folktale. In their attempt to convey that complexity, they address what threatens the socialized personality. The landscape in which those risks are imagined is the dark pastoral of the fairy tale. And among the literary tales that develop and explore most fully the heightened states of feeling that art works to contain are those by E. T. A. Hoffmann. In his tales, Hoffmann constructs two opposing worlds, the quotidian and often bourgeois world of society and the world of the imagination. Through much of the story, his heroes live liminally, on the borders, spanning both realms. Hoffmann is interested in this liminal state: Who is its hero and what is its nature? Who is most open to the imagination? Who can survive this struggle and how? The conclusion resolves the conflict, often by force, when the hero finds herself in one or the other realm, sometimes at the cost of her life.

## 1. *The Golden Pot*

E. T. A. Hoffmann added the perspective of childhood to the literary fairy tale, "observed and formed by sophisticated artistry . . . [its] wisdom and beauty comparable to that of the primeval world."[4] The hero is often a child or a student, a creative spirit struggling to live in harmony with the imagination intact. In Hoffmann's own life, he worked both realms. He was a musician, composer, conductor, theater director, visual artist, and writer; he also worked as a lawyer, an official of the Prussian judiciary, a music teacher, a music critic, and a satirist. He understood and was able brilliantly to convey the intensity of the struggle to survive in both realms. About his first fairy tale, *The Golden Pot*, Hoffmann wrote that he "intended it to be 'fairy-like and wondrous, but stepping boldly into ordinary everyday life.' "[5] His tales are about the fragmentation of the human personality when the social world collides with the creative spirit. And they are about the attempt to restore a primordial wholeness. In the primeval world, the mythical time before division, before gender and morality, darkness and light were connected. And although Hoffmann's world is clearly postlapsarian, its children socialized, the resistance to the world is embodied in its child-artist heroes. They perceive a wholeness and strive toward inclusion. But the world, in its worldliness, whether represented by family or state, disrupts the hero's attempts because they threaten the social order. As the interior world breaks through the too rigid boundaries set by the outside world, the hero becomes increasingly isolated. A blurring of boundaries is generated, often mirrored by stories within stories and characters whose identities merge and fracture—all of which lends itself to interpretation. Is the hero mad? Is he living in the real world? Is she living at all?

The hero of Hoffmann's earliest and most complex fairy tale, *The Golden Pot*, introduced the child's point of view into the literary fairy tale by implication. He is a student, socially between childhood and adulthood and, as Kenneth Negus noted, "child-like in his directness, naiveté, and naturalness" (Negus, 119). His initiation into the interior world of the imagination is unintentional; he collides with the apple cart of an old woman/witch who curses him: " 'Yes, run—run your hardest, child of Satan—into glass you'll soon pass—into glass!' " (*Golden Pot*, 1). His clumsiness signals a dysfunction in his bourgeois aspirations. Although he does not understand what is happening, he gives "an involuntary shudder" at her words. Like the child who knows before she understands, he intuits the danger and prophesy of this seemingly simple accident.

This initiation into the proper sphere of the fairy tale, the alternative world of dream and imagination, takes place on Ascension Day at three in the afternoon in Dresden, locating it in time and space. It is most realistically narrated, so that the veracity of the external world is concretely imagined, as Hoffmann thrusts us, along with the hero, into the realm of the fantastic. On this holiday, Anselmus is expelled from the community of celebratory drinking because the apple woman has taken all his money. This leads to his first scene of isolation, near the River Elbe. Here "the magnificent city of Dresden stretched its gleaming spires boldly and proudly into the translucent expanse of the sky which hung over the flowery meadows and fresh green forests, and the jagged peaks half-hidden by twilight announced the far land of Bohemia" (*Golden Pot*, 2–3). This first vision connecting far and near comes to him aurally and visually, establishing him as the creative spirit with the potential to behold the prelapsarian world. "At one moment it sounded as though the evening breeze were shaking the leaves; at another moment it sounded like birds billing and cooing in the branches, playfully fluttering their little wings. Then a whispering and lisping began, and the flowers seemed to tinkle like tiny crystal bells" (*Golden Pot*, 4), which become the voices of three little snakes "gleaming in green and gold, coiled round the branches and stretching their heads towards the evening sun" (*Golden Pot*, 5). The "whispering" and the "slithering and caressing" movement of the snakes "made it seem as though the elder-tree were scattering a thousand sparkling emeralds amid its dark foliage" (*Golden Pot*, 5). These images suggest the fluctuations of the dark pastoral, the darkness illuminated and suggestive of Anselmus's "inexpressible yearning" and "mixture of supreme happiness and intense pain" (*Golden Pot*, 5). The state of desire in which Anselmus is now immersed is expressed by the elder-tree, who says " 'You lay in my shade, surrounded by my fragrance, but you did not understand me. The fragrance is my language, when it is kindled by love.' " And the wind says, " 'I stroked your temples, but you did not understand me; the breeze is my language, when it is kindled by love.' " And the rays of sunshine that "broke through the clouds and their burning light seemed to say: 'I poured my blazing gold upon you, but you did not understand me; the blaze is my language, when it is kindled by love' " (*Golden Pot*, 5).

Anselmus is awakened to the numinous vitality of the natural world; he now sees all nature as infused with his longing. Here are the first glimmers of the harmony into which he will escape, no matter how the tale's ending is interpreted, as he notes, "Then everything around him began to stir, as though waking into joyful life" (*Golden Pot*, 6). But the vision ends "in a jangling discord." From Anselmus's subjective interior perspective, we are confronted with the conventional view of a "worthy townswoman," who announces, "That gentleman doesn't seem to be right in the head" (*Golden Pot*, 7). And Anselmus, flung out of his newly found paradise, "was deeply ashamed" (*Golden Pot*, 8).

This immersion into the poetic realm recurs visually in clusters of bright light glimpsed in the waves and in the verdant landscape, and aurally in the voices that emanate from the gold and green snakes who implore: " 'Don't you see us always swimming ahead of you . . . believe—believe—believe in us' " (*Golden Pot*, 9). The recurring pattern involves disruption of the visions by their counterpart in the bureaucratic world, expressed in the harsh tones of the townswoman. Her voice is echoed by the boatman—" 'Are you crazy, sir?' " and by Anselmus's bureaucrat friend, Sub-Rector Paulmann—" 'Are you all right, my dear fellow' " (*Golden Pot*, 9). Paulmann offers an application of leeches "to the backside" for Anselmus's "fits," when Anselmus sees the snakes in "the sparkling, crackling flames reflected in the water" and croons, " 'Oh, have you returned, you golden snakes? Sing, please sing! Your song will bring back those lovely dark-blue eyes!' " (*Golden Pot*, 9).

The dark-blue eyes belong both to Serpentina, one of the green snakes, and Veronica, the Sub-Rector's daughter, whose more worldly vision parallels Anselmus's spiritual one. Veronica projects her passion for upward mobility onto Anselmus, although she is also touched by his dreamy, meditative side. This suggests her potentially questing nature. But her journey involves a descent into the underground with the apple woman/witch as her guide. Early in the story Veronica seems to offer a middle ground between the two worlds. Her father, horrified by Anselmus's bizarre behavior, cautions, " 'Come now, my dear fellow . . . I always took you for a thoroughly respectable young man, but to dream while wide awake . . . nobody would do that except a madman or a fool!' " (*Golden Pot*, 10). Less harsh but still on the side of convention, Registrary Heerbrand ponders, " 'is it not possible to fall into a certain digestion dream-like state while one is awake?' " (*Golden Pot*, 10). But, rather than anything spiritual or poetic, his vision is associated with "the meditative state required for physical and mental digestion" and, ultimately, with being drunk. Veronica, on the other hand, objects, " 'Anselmus must have met with something remarkable, and perhaps he just imagines that he was awake, when in reality he fell asleep under the elder-tree and had all sorts of foolish fancies which he is still thinking about' " (*Golden Pot*, 10). She dreams of becoming "a Counsellor's lady, living in a handsome residence in Castle Lane, or on the New Market, or in Moritz Street; her fashionable hat, her new Turkish shawl suited her perfectly; she took her breakfast in the window alcove, wearing an elegant morning gown and giving the cook instructions for the day" (*Golden Pot*, 27–8). Her extensive fantasy includes such details as the lace cap she will wear and the gift her husband will give her upon his return from work—"a pair of magnificent ear-rings in the latest style, which he puts in her ears to replace those she was wearing before. 'Oh, what lovely dainty ear-rings,' cries Veronica out loud, throwing away her work and jumping up out of her chair to look at the ear-rings in the mirror" (*Golden Pot*, 28). Veronica can not comprehend Anselmus's poetic nature nor his passion for her spiritual counterpart, Serpentina, daughter of the Archivist Lindhorst.

Lindhorst, the most liminal figure of the tale, is the protagonist of both realms. He is an experimental chemist, engaged with alchemical elements, and an archivist, "a scholarly antiquary" connected by ancient lineage to primeval myths. In the creation myth, he appears as a salamander, a fire spirit, the creative element in the story within the story of *The Golden Pot*. He and the apple woman function in both realms, as they vie for the soul of Anselmus—Lindhorst through his daughter Serpentina, and the apple-woman through her childhood charge Veronica. Under Lindhorst's guidance, Anselmus must copy manuscripts "in Arabic and Coptic and even in strange characters which belong to no known language" (*Golden Pot*, 12). Anselmus's quest involves, then, reconnecting with a past, both in and beyond time, through languages, ancient, legendary, and yet to be discovered. It is located in Atlantis, "the name given to man's harmony with nature" (*Golden Pot*, xiii, n. 11), from which we, like Anselmus and Lindhorst, are estranged and which, we, like Anselmus, do not remember. Both Lindhorst and the apple-woman exist in various shapes as they move in and out of the realistic and fantastic landscapes. The apple woman/witch is also a projection of Veronica's childhood, in which she appeared as Lizzie, the nurse who encouraged the girl in her feistiness. From there, she has shapeshifted into a door knob, a coffee pot, a creaking stove door "which would not shut properly" (*Golden Pot*, 30)—all figures of domesticity. In contrast, Lindhorst's shapes all suggest the intensity of the dark pastoral. In addition to the salamander fire spirit, he is a white kite that disappears into the air at twilight. He is also an orange lily. And he can descend into an intoxicating "punch-bowl" and retreat into the Sub-Rector's burning pipe, all images associated with fire.

The story of the primeval world is narrated by Lindhorst in Vigil Four and is completed by Serpentina in Vigil Eight. It is a creation myth that tells of seeds emerging "like smiling children in a green cradle" and the "excess of delight [which] gave birth to a fiery lily, opening its petal like lovely lips to receive sweet kisses from its mother" (*Golden Pot*, 15). The pastoral imagery here suggests a Blakean connection between innocence and sexuality, in keeping with the fiery lily's passion for the youth Phosphorus. The impetuous consummation of this passion fractures the primordial harmony. From the union of Phosphorus and the fiery lily "thought" escapes, which separates the lily from her father, mother, and "playfellows." Lindhorst's consummation of his passion for the green snake, which ends in destruction of the garden, reenacts this pattern and recalls the Eden myth. Consciousness creates individuation and differentiation in the postlapsarian world. Thereafter, the quest of the artist involves a struggle against alienation to restore harmony. The story of Anselmus continues to be punctuated by voices of "reason," which culminate in the new voice of social order, that of the up and coming bureaucrat, Registrary Heerbrand. Heerbrand responds to Lindhorst's story, amid choral laughter and derision—" 'Forgive me, my dear Archivist, but that's a lot of Oriental bombast' " (*Golden Pot,* 16), in contrast to Anselmus's silent "uncanny feeling," which "shook [him] to the core" (*Golden Pot*, 18). The "orientalism" here reveals the racism of the Western European rational world. It suggests the ways in which the spiritual realm has been marginalized and projected in a vision of "otherness," from which all good bureaucrats are exempt.[6]

As Anselmus grows increasingly absorbed in the fantasy world of the green snake and her "lovely blue eyes" and "the wonderful sound of crystal bells," we are told that he "sank into a dreamy, brooding state which made him insensible to all contact with ordinary life" (*Golden Pot*, 21). Suddenly, at the beginning of Vigil Four, following Lindhorst's creation narrative, an omniscient narrator directly addresses us: "Let me ask you outright, gentle reader, if there have not been hours, indeed whole days and weeks of your life, during which all your usual activities were painfully repugnant, and everything you believed in and valued seemed foolish and worthless?" (*Golden Pot*, 20). As Anselmus's visions become more heightened and extreme, it becomes imperative that we imagine along with Anselmus, so that the symbol of a "higher vision, the golden pot" (*Golden Pot*, xv) is truly grounded and translatable. In this way, Hoffmann imagines that our original receptivity can be retained and recovered from childhood, the time before consciousness, when we were whole. How can Hoffmann transport us, his readers, from our comfortable daily lives of property and material things into an ephemeral poetic realm, without pushing us into actively imagining the journey ourselves? Hoffmann assumes that we, like Anselmus, can intuit our "primal harmony with nature, in the form of a child-like poetic spirit" (*Golden Pot,* xv). He implores,

> You are now, kind reader, in the fairy realm of glorious wonders, whose mighty strokes summon up both supreme bliss and extreme horror. . . . In this realm, which our spirit so often reveals to us, at least in our dreams, try kind reader, to recognize

the well-known shapes that, as the saying goes, cross your path every day. You will then believe that this magnificent realm is much nearer at hand than you had previously thought; and that is what I heartily wish you to believe, and what the strange story of Anselmus is supposed to convey. (*Golden Pot*, 20–1)

Perhaps it is necessary to render the familiar unfamiliar, transformed into a bizarre state, to release us from recognizing and acknowledging it, as Freud notes in his essay on Hoffmann's *The Sandman*, "The Uncanny."[7] In this way, we can approach the forbidden material more comfortably, be drawn back into proximity with it again and again, until we are ready to reclaim it as part of our familiar world. In the meantime, it remains in the imagination, the realm most intimately and deeply associated with childhood, and breaks through into dream patterns, often in nightmarish configurations.

Anselmus's journey into the interior of Lindhorst's home suggests the interiority of childhood memory. It involves a series of primordial images of nature, magical and numinous. He is enchanted by "a gigantic bush of glowing orange lilies," sweet intoxicating perfumes, azure walls from which "bronze-coloured trunks of lofty palm-trees" emerged "whose colossal leaves, gleaming like sparkling emeralds, formed an arch just below the ceiling. In the middle of the room, three Egyptian lions made of dark bronze supported a porphyry slab on which stood the simple golden pot. As soon as he saw it," we are told, "Anselmus could not take his eyes away from the pot" (*Golden Pot*, 38). This is nature's mythical alchemy—a fusion of natural and precious metallic substances. Here, in this landscape, which is also "an ordinary library and study," the voices are mocking as well as enchanting. Unlike Eden, this pastoral is unstable, erratic, constantly shifting. Anselmus perceives

that many of the strange flowers hanging on the dark bushes were in fact insects resplendent in gleaming colours, flapping their little wings and dancing and flitting in a swarm as though caressing one another with their probosces. . . . [The] murmuring of the lofty trees and shrubs . . . form[ed] mysterious chords that uttered a deep, sorrowful yearning, [and the] mocking birds which had teased and tormented him before now fluttered round . . . incessantly crying . . . : "Not so fast, my scholarly friend—don't keep staring into the clouds, you might fall flat on your face! Hee, hee!" (*Golden Pot*, 51)

This yearning, like that of romantic love, is double-edged. It can intoxicate but also plunge you into despair. When Serpentina holds him "so close that he [can] feel the breath from her lips and the electric warmth of her body . . . it seemed as though her sweet and lovely form were embracing and enfolding him so completely that he could only live, move, and have his being in her, and as though it were only the beat of her pulse that sent tremors through all his fibres and nerves" (*Golden Pot*, 53). Sexual desire, Hoffmann tells us, is embedded in the spiritual; both are really part of the harmonious world from which we have been expelled. It both empowers and weakens the human spirit. Anselmus, like Lindhorst, like the fiery lily before him, and like all of humankind, will be confused, tempted by desire, and fall. Torn between his desire for Veronica and Serpentina, he errs. And his imperfection is echoed in his clumsy copying of Lindhorst's manuscript, his "blot on the original" sacred tomes of ancient myth. He is cast out of paradise and, like a child, finds in Lindhorst both the punishing and rewarding father—sometimes comforting and whimsical, at other times intolerant and forbidding. Anselmus finds himself "sitting in a tightly stopped crystal bottle on a shelf in Archivist Lindhorst's library" (*Golden Pot*, 66), as prophesied by the witch.

His liberation, and that of humankind, is also prophesied. In Vigil Eight, Serpentina tells how the salamander recast as Lindhorst will restore to the "degenerate race of men" their ability to "understand the language of nature" (*Golden Pot*, 55). We are told, "not only will he retain the memory of his primal state; he will again live in holy harmony with all of nature, he will understand its marvels, and the power of his brothers among the spirits will once more be at his command" (*Golden Pot*, 55). The prophecy describes how this will occur through Serpentina's marriage to Anselmus. In other words, Serpentina, like all enchanted beasts of the transformation tale, must evoke trust in a fallen but regenerative " 'child-like poetic spirit . . . often found in youths who are mocked by the rabble because of the lofty simplicity of their behavior and because they lack what people call world manners' " (*Golden Pot*, 56). But for Hoffmann, the enchanted creature, Serpentina, does not transform into a human shape, her marriage to be culminated in the "real" world. This marriage can only take place in Atlantis where the fiery lily of the golden pot and "its lustre will reveal a splendid and dazzling reflection of our wondrous realm, as it now exists in harmony with all of nature. . . . [Here the youth, Anselmus] will learn its language and understand the wonders of our realm, and himself dwell with his beloved in Atlantis" (*Golden Pot*, 56). But not before he is tempted and imprisoned in the crystal bottle.

Again the omniscient voice of the narrator speaks directly to us, as the images get denser and more bizarre. He insists on our feeling with Anselmus, by referring to dreams in which we have experienced such strangeness. Again he implores:

> I may be permitted, kind reader, to doubt whether you have ever been enclosed in a glass bottle, unless some vivid dream has teased you with such magical mishaps . . . but if you have never had such dreams, then you will do me and Anselmus a favour by letting your active imagination enclose you in the crystal for a few minutes. (*Golden Pot*, 67)

And through meticulous delineation of sensuous experience, he propels the reader into a kind of hypnotic trance in which "the shimmering light makes everything quiver . . . you are floating, unable to move a muscle . . . a frozen ether [seems to be] squeezing you so tightly that it is in vain for your spirit to issue commands to your lifeless body" (*Golden Pot*, 67). Anselmus's glass prison, the objective correlative for our own severance—from our imagination and from nature, comes sharply into focus. In language modulated from the numinous illumination of the imaginative realm into that of the everyday world, we are told that Anselmus "could not lift a finger, but his thoughts knocked against the glass with a discordant sound that dulled his senses, and instead of the clear voice of his inner spirit, he could apprehend only the muffled roaring of madness" (*Golden Pot*, 67). Madness, then, has come to be equated with the ordinary world, while clarity is aligned with the poetic and the realm of the imagination.

When we return to the bourgeois world, Veronica stands before a mirror, "examining the effect of the ear-rings" she has received as the lady of the newly promoted Counsellor Heerbrand. Veronica's fantasy has been fulfilled, her desire for Anselmus dismissed as "a silly dream." As spokesperson for this world, Heerbrand proclaims that "Anselmus's attachment to the green snake can be no more than a poetic allegory" (*Golden Pot*, 77). Anselmus has been freed, united with Serpentina in Atlantis, his precarious position between the two worlds resolved. However, the narrator, in the conclusive Twelfth Vigil, becomes the liminal figure, suggesting our own struggle, if we are attuned to the imagination, to balance the two realms. He, as the teller of the tale, including, ultimately, all the tales within the tale, is terrified to complete the story. He sees himself in a mirror, "pale and melancholy from lack of sleep, like Registrary Heerbrand after getting drunk on punch" (*Golden Pot*, 79). He looks to his dreams for inspiration. Finally, he tells us, he receives a note from Lindhorst—a document that conveys the veracity of his "strange spiritual existence revealed in print" (*Golden Pot*, 80), which enables him to finish his tale. Again, the tone is direct, the language concrete. Lindhorst writes,

> I am willing to assist you, Sir, in the completion of your work, since it contains many complimentary references to myself and my dear married daughter. . . . [L]eave your garret, come down your damned five flights of stairs, and pay me a visit. In the blue room with the palm-trees, with which you are already familiar, you will find suitable writing materials, and you may then acquaint your readers, in a few words with what you have beheld. That will please them better than a lengthy account of a way of life which you yourself know only from heresay. (*Golden Pot*, 80)

In the conclusion, the narrator tells us, "For the vision in which I had seen Anselmus in bodily form on his estate in Atlantis I was indebted to the arts of the salamander" (*Golden Pot*, 83). It is a vision of eternal bliss, and although it dissolves into mist, it has been transferred into eternal knowledge through the narrator's tale. Hoffman suggests that the realm of the poetic can be substantiated only briefly in the temporal world; but in poetry, in art, it is captured eternally. However, the narrator wistfully longs for an existence modeled on that of Anselmus, "who has cast off the burden of daily life!" (*Golden Pot*, 83). He moans, " 'But as for poor me, in a few minutes I shall have left this fine room, which is far from being an estate in Atlantis, to return to my garret; the petty cares of my poverty-stricken life will absorb my thoughts, and my gaze is obscured by a thousand ills as though by thick mist, so that I doubt if I shall ever behold the lily' " (*Golden Pot*, 83). But the Archivist Lindhorst has the last world. He cautions the narrator not " 'to complain like that! Weren't you in Atlantis yourself a moment ago, and haven't you at least got a pretty farm there, as the poetic property of your mind? Indeed, is Anselmus's happiness anything other than life in poetry, where the holy harmony of all things is revealed as the deepest secret of nature?' " (*Golden Pot*, 83).

Critics such as James McGlathery and Tatar believe that Anselmus commits suicide, thus "releasing a divided self." His body "may remain trapped in the waters of the Elbe, but his soul soars into an empyrean realm of art."[8] For me, the narrator's pull is too strong; Hoffmann's thrust toward the precarious balancing of the two worlds resists this interpretation. I am left with a desire to embrace the two worlds of our human estate. No matter how difficult to decode, *The Golden Pot*, in the end, is a template for treading the waters of everyday life while we explore and reclaim the internal child-spirit who will guide us into the substantive imaginative realm.

### 2. *Nutcracker and the King of Mice*

Two other of Hoffmann's best-known fairy tales, *Nutcracker and the King of Mice*[9] and *The Sandman*,[10] focus more directly on the nursery and on the nightmare world of childhood. Both contain the two worlds, the social and the imaginative, established in *The Golden Pot*. In both there is an older figure who spans both worlds and a child hero who struggles to live in and integrate the two realms.

*Nutcracker and the King of Mice* begins with the familiar holiday. Here it is Christmas Eve, a time of ritual. Although the tale is grounded in time and space, the particular setting is heightened, liminally situated between the ordinary and the extraordinary. Here the role of ritual—to connect the two and to link the one with the many—finds the two children, Fritz and Marie, "cowering together" at twilight. Immediately we are introduced to the forbidden, a secret the hero must discover and in some way betray to overcome some unfair or otherwise constricting sacrament. The children are not "on any pretext whatever at any time that day to go into the small drawing-room, much less into the best drawing-room"—but

Fritz has seen "a little dark-looking man . . . slipping and creeping across the floor with a big box under his arm" (*Nutcracker*, 130), whom he immediately recognizes as Godpapa Drosselmeier, Hoffmann's borderline figure here, reminiscent of Lindhorst in his ambiguity.

As this is a tale of childhood, Godpapa Drosselmeier holds even more weight, liminally placed between family and friend, and is, therefore, more threatening as well as more inventive. Ugly and disturbing as he is, he also represents a potential source of liberation for the children from their somewhat confined and refined existence—a link to the world outside family and to the inner world of the imagination. He is described as, "anything but a nice-looking man . . . small and lean, with a great many wrinkles on his face, a big patch of black plaster where his right eye ought to have been, and not a hair on his head; which was why he wore a fine white wig, made of glass, and a very beautiful work of art" (*Nutcracker*, 130). This marks him as an artist with a different if slightly askew vision. He is a clockmaker, an arcanist, we are told, someone who has made toys for the children. We are also told that Marie is "quite miserable" watching him "proceed to stick sharp-pointed instruments into the inside of the clock" to fix it; and although we are told, "this didn't really hurt the poor clock, which, on the contrary, would come to life again" (*Nutcracker*, 130), Hoffmann persists in Marie's vision of him as the story unfolds.

Marie is the youngest child, most susceptible to imaginings or at least to the combination of imagination and feeling. Early in the tale the children are separated by gender. Fritz imagines Godpapa Drosselmeier's Christmas gift as "a great castle . . . where all sorts of pretty soldiers would be drilling and marching about; and then that other soldiers would come and try to get into the fortress, upon which the soldiers inside would fire away at them, as pluckily as you please, with cannon, till everything banged and thundered like anything" (*Nutcracker*, 131). Marie, on the other hand, envisions " 'a beautiful garden with a great lake in it, and beautiful swans swimming about with great gold collars, singing lovely music. And then a lovely little girl comes down through the garden to the lake, and calls the swans and feeds them with shortbread and cake' " (*Nutcracker*, 131). The gendered differentiation is marked, as Fritz replies "(with masculine superiority) . . . 'Swans don't eat cake and shortbread,' " asserting the rational order, even as he insists on his own imaginative vision.

The children do sit together in the darkness and share a vision of "fluttering . . . gentle, invisible wings . . . [and] unutterably beautiful . . . music"—an annunciation that the "Christ Child had sped away on shining wings to other happy children" (*Nutcracker*, 132). Although Fritz will continue to move in and out of the imaginative realm, Marie becomes increasingly isolated as the hero who believes in its veracity. It is Marie who sees the nutcracker doll, the one among the many toys, candies, and decorations of the "wonder-tree," which, in keeping with the dark pastoral, contains "in all the recesses of its spreading branches hundreds of little tapers glitter[ing] like stars, inviting the children to pluck its flowers and fruit" (*Nutcracker*, 132). Marie is impressed by its beauty and by the elegant castle Drosselmeier makes for the children. In addition to miniature automata, "beautiful ladies and gentlemen with plumbed hats and long robes down to their heels walking up and down . . . and children in little short doublets . . . dancing to the chimes of the bells," the castle contains a miniature Drosselmeier, perhaps suggesting his presence, though diminutive, in the imaginative realm.

Like Archivist Lindhorst, Drosselmeier plays many roles in this story. He is the inventor of the extraordinary toys, and, later, the teller of the interpolated tale and its questor. But his pride and interest in machinery that, he tells the children, "must work as it's doing now; it can't be altered, you know' " (*Nutcracker*, 134), reveal the limitations of his imagination and separate him from them. Fritz, as hunter and solider, is initiated, in play, into the world of order. But Marie becomes the caretaker of the wounded nutcracker. Her faith, her singular purpose combined with an open heart, distinguish her as worthy and capable of penetrating the two worlds, while Fritz focuses increasingly on the destruction and war paraphernalia associated with his gender. He almost destroys the nutcracker, the figure who can extract the life-giving kernel, repeatedly giving him the hardest nuts to crack until his jaw is loose. Marie, on the other hand, "wrapped the wounded nutcracker up" (*Nutcracker*, 136) and "rocked him like a child in her arms" (*Nutcracker*, 137). We are told that Marie is "a very good and reasonable child" and we see her as practical and grounded. But she is nature's child. She stays close to the young child's belief in the animation of her toys, all of which marks her for the search for wholeness, the journey into the imaginative realm, set, as is typical of Hoffmann's tales, in her house with its transitional clock warning "louder and louder" but unable to strike. First, Marie sees an owl covering the clock with its wings, which becomes Drosselmeier with his coattails; she hears "thousands of little feet behind the walls" (*Nutcracker*, 140), all of which amuse her. But Hoffmann tells us "that the blood ran cold in her veins" when the seven-headed mouse breaks through the floor of her room. The vision becomes increasingly monstrous, replete with the battle of the mice against the Nutcracker's army, made up of Fritz's hussars as well as all the other toys, including "two Chinese Emperors . . . gardeners, Tyrolese, Tungooses, hairdressers, harlequins, Cupids, lions, tigers, unicorns, and monkeys [who] fought with the utmost courage, coolness, and steady endurance" (*Nutcracker*, 145).

This dark pastoral, like the forest of the folktale, contains destructive as well as nurturing elements. And in keeping with a tale of the nursery, what we fear and desire is transformed in miniature. Hoffmann was criticized in his lifetime for attempting to write a children's story that seemed, at least in parts, inappropriate for children.[11] Clearly, he assumed his readers were children, referring to the dolls for girls, and calling them "Fritz, Theodore, Ernest, or whatsoever your name may be" (*Nutcracker*, 132) for boys, reminding them how they "would have plumped into [their] bed, and drawn the blankets further over [their] head" (*Nutcracker*, 141) at the violent intrusion of the Mouse-King into the nursery. But Marie is the hero of this tale. Only initially does she experience pain at the entry into the fantasy world, which involves breaking a pane of glass from the cupboard. After she enters the fantasy she feels lighter and more comfortable. Instead of hiding under blankets, she saves the Nutcracker from the approaching monster "squeaking in triumph out of all his seven throats," by throwing her shoe "into the thick of the enemy, straight at their king" (*Nutcracker*, 146). Marie's heroic act is juxtaposed with the satirical whimpering of the only other females, her dolls, Clara and Gertrude. Stereotyped as vain, haughty, and useless, Clara says, " 'Must I—the very loveliest doll in all the world—perish miserably in the very flower of my youth?' " And Gertrude adds, " 'Oh! Was it for this . . . that I have taken such pains to *conserver* myself all these years? Must I be shot here in my own drawing-room after all?' " (*Nutcracker*, 144) Perhaps such behavior, along with the Nutcracker's quoting Richard III, as he yells, " 'A horse! A horse! My kingdom for a horse!' " (146), suggests Hoffmann's ambivalence about a strictly child audience. However, the thrust of the tale, and of the interpolated tale of Princess Pirlipat, which sits at the center of *Nutcracker and the Mouseking*, feel childlike. However, as Hoffmann demonstrates, *Nutcracker* in its entirety, including the story of Princess Pirlipat, contains the most intense and darkest images of pastoral and suggests suppressed, less acceptable sides of childhood.

Essentially, the story of the Princess Pirlipat is about the dark side of the nursery. At the heart is an image of the most beautiful and highest born daughter of the king, and her transformation into a creature with "an enormous bloated head (instead of the pretty little golden-haired one) at the top of a diminutive, crumpled-up body, and green, wooden-looking eyes staring where the lovely azure-blue pair had been" (*Nutcracker*, 154). This metamorphosis occurs as a result of the king's refusal to share his chief morsels of delight, the fat with which his sausages and puddings are made, with Dame Mouserink and her entourage, who live under the floor of the kitchen. The queen had agreed to offer tastes of her browned fat, after "a delicate little whispering voice made itself audible, saying, 'Give me some of that, sister! I want some of it too; I am a queen as well as yourself; give me some' " (*Nutcracker*, 151). But when the relatives of the queen of Mousolia swarmed the queen's kitchen, the king, wretched from his discovery that his precious sausages and puddings contained " '[t]oo little fat,' " demands the death of Dame Mouserink and the destruction of her kingdom. Even after his daughter's disfigurement from the bite of the monstrous mouse queen, the king, Hoffmann reminds us, "might have seen then, that it would have been much better to eat his puddings with no fat in them at all, and let Dame Mouserink and her folk stay on under the hearthstone" (*Nutcracker*, 155). Instead, he blames his clockmaker and arcanist, Drosselmeier, and sends him out to find the cure for his daughter's enchantment. It takes Drosselmeier many trials to find the nutcracker who can deshell the hardest nut and extract the healing kernel.

Drosselmeier's journey to find the nutcracker begins with a memory of Pirlipat's "remarkable appetite for nuts, and the circumstance that she had been born with teeth" (*Nutcracker*, 155)—a warning that something is not innocent in this cradle. The teeth signal the "bite" of the nursery, the animal and instinctual nature of early childhood. The child's delicacy recast as this grotesque distortion also suggests the underside of society's feelings about children. Certainly, we have signs of this in the double-sided nursery lore that survives in popular nursery rhymes today. Consider "Rock-a-bye Baby," a familiar lullaby, that conveys a primal fear of infants falling, unprotected, out of the cradle, in a peculiarly sing-song, almost jubilant manner. Or the grotesque cruelty of "Three Blind Mice," and the story of their attempt to escape the blade of the farmer's wife. Or "Lady Bird, Lady Bird," one of the most shocking, that sings cheerfully, "your house is on fire, your children will burn." These were all sung to babies by their mothers and other caretakers, as I did to my child, until I became conscious of their dark messages. And despite the many attempts on the part of folklorists[12] to explain away this disparity between the dark messages and the pleasant sounds of the nursery rhymes, they suggest a hidden hostility and secret fear about childhood, not just about the protection of children from the world, but about our denial of the inner darkness of which we suspect them.

Again, however, the dark pastoral enables transformation. Drosselmeier, as the creator and as questor, must enter this realm to discover how to extract the healing kernel. He knows that imagination, first conceived and developed in childhood through stories like the one he tells Marie in her wounded state about Princess Pirlipat, contains destructive as well as creative impulses. If denied, *Nutcracker and the King of Mice* suggests, the forces of darkness will erupt through the chinks in the walls and floors, as do the mice here. The nutcracker, the one who can crack the shell of the outer world and extract the inner truth, can do battle with the rodent realm, the beast beneath the surface. Again a balance must be struck. Drosselmeier's name suggests this duality. He is both a "thrush," a bird, a symbol of freedom and flight, and "a choking coil," a "throttle valve," that which constricts.[13] And these stories must be passed on by just such a character, one who gathers the familiar tales of his family and those of his community, and integrates them or tells them along with tales from afar.[14] Drosselmeier travels to the city of Nuremberg, his childhood home, for the source of salvation. His job is to find the man who can crack the nut, for he himself is no longer young and innocent. Pirlipat grows more grotesque, [t]he hideousness of the face . . . enhanced by a beard like white cotton, which had grown about the mouth and chin" (*Nutcracker*, 160). Interestingly, the nut must be cracked by one "who had never known a razor, and who had never had on boots" (*Nutcracker*, 156), in other words, by one unspoiled by socialization. Her rescuer must be beardless, the beard suggestive of sexuality and the fall from innocence.

As in the more traditional transformation tale, only love, unsullied by the coarseness of the world, can restore beauty to this monstrosity. However, it is Marie, and not Pirlipat who sees beneath the skin. While Pirlipat rejects the Nutcracker after he releases her from her spell, in so doing he himself becomes enchanted. But Marie will love him for his inner beauty. In this presexual *Beauty and the Beast*, Marie's spiritual nature is demonstrated by her faithful innocence. Her willingness to sacrifice first "her cakes, marzipan and sugar-stick, gingerbread cakes," then her "sugar toys," in offerings to the Mouse-King, demonstrates the courage of the innocent believer.[15] But, unlike the hero of simpler folk tales, Marie does not awaken to her union with a prince. Instead, she wakes to find "Something as cold as ice . . . tripping about on her arm, and something rough . . . on her cheek. . . . The horrible Mouse-King came and sat on her shoulder, foamed a blood-red foam out of all his seven mouths, and . . . hissed into Marie's ear:

> "Hiss, hiss!—keep away—don't go in there—beware of that house—don't you be caught—death to the mouse—hand out your picture books—none of your scornful looks!—Give me your dresses—also your laces—or, if you don't, leave you I won't—Nutcracker I'll bite—drag him out of your sight—his last hour is near—so tremble for fear!—Fee, fa, fo, fum—his last hour is come!—Hee hee, pee pee—squeak—squeak!" (*Nutcracker*, 167)

This incantation suggests the darkest of nursery rhymes, a ritualized invocation of the appetitive, insatiable animal nature at the base of our fears about children and about the "childish" parts of ourselves. Marie asks Drosselmeier, the experienced traveler of the two realms, " 'what can I do. . . . Even if I give that horrid king of the mice all my picture books [and everything else] . . . he's sure to go on asking for me. Soon I shan't have anything more left, and he'll want to eat *me*!' " (*Nutcracker*, 168).

Of course, Marie restores the Nutcracker to his original state as Drosselmeier's nephew, young Drosselmeier, whom she inspired "with knightly valour" to rid the kingdom of the mice. He appears with the seven gold crowns of the Mouse-King, and leads her on a journey, through a beautiful wonderland of sweet delights. They arrive at a "delightful water, which kept broadening and broadening out wider and wider, like a great lake, reminiscent of her first Christmas wish, where the loveliest swans were floating, white as silver, with collars of gold" (*Nutcracker*, 172). They pass through "a mosaic of lozenges of all colours," the Orange Brook, River Lemonade, Almond-milk Sea, Honey River, Bonbonville—this pastoral landscape of sensuous delights into a city of beautifully dressed ladies and gentlemen, Greeks and Armenians, Tyrolese and Jews, officers and soldiers, clergymen, shepherds, jack-pudding, in short, people of every conceivable kind to be found in the world" (*Nutcracker*, 175). This is the new community, inclusive and expansive. Like the witch's jewels in *Hansel and Gretel*, these two landscapes collectively represent the reward, the beauty that can be extracted from the child's nightmare world.

When Marie awakens into her ordinary life, she is at first met with all kinds of denial. Even Godpapa Drosselmeier undermines her dreams as "stupid stuff and nonsense," consistent with his ambiguous nature. Marie is forbidden to talk about it, until Drosselmeier's nephew appears in his restored state, with her childhood toys, "the very same figures as those which the Mouse-King had eaten up" (*Nutcracker*, 181). The final betrothal scene suggests the marriage of various dichotomies. The child self, with its accompanying play and pleasure, is to be united with the adult self, which can be both beautiful and bestial. Hoffmann reassures his child-readers,

> At the marriage there danced two-and-twenty thousand of the most beautiful dolls and other figures, all glittering in pearls and diamonds; and Marie is to this day queen of a realm where all kinds of sparkling Christmas Woods, and transparent Marzipan Castles—in short, the most wonderful and beautiful things of every kind—are to be seen—by those who have the eyes to see them. (*Nutcracker*, 182)

## 3. *The Sandman*

*The Sandman* is driven entirely by a singular, obsessive image of eyes, distilled from a nexus of scenes that coalesce around the nursery. Nathanael, as a child, is traumatized by a bogeyman-like figure, who comes to represent the demonic side of his otherwise pleasant father. It is never entirely clear what is going on in the father's study when his friend, Coppelius the lawyer, makes his periodic visits. But in Nathanael's mind they are associated with his father's silence and his mother's sadness. Also, the children are sent to bed whenever this man, unknown to them, arrives amid much secrecy, though the children hear all kinds of strange sounds coming from the father's room. When Nathanael asks his mother about the visitor, she tells him it is the Sandman, and here begins the first split from which the many splittings and doublings originate in this tale. From his mother, he learns that the Sandman is the figure who puts children to sleep by putting sand in their eyes—although Nathanael understands this to be a myth of denial. When he asks his old nurse, she says:

> "He's a wicked man, who comes to children when they don't want to go to bed and throws handfuls of sand into their eyes; that makes their eyes fill with blood and jump out of their heads, and he throws the eyes into his bag and takes them into the crescent moon to feed to his own children, who are sitting in the nest there; the Sandman's children have crooked beaks, like owls, with which to peck the eyes of naughty human children." (*Sandman*, 87)

This narrative, the tale beneath his mother's polite and comforting story, suggests the side of the nursery that is suppressed.[16] At the age of ten, a transitional time which stands between innocence and sexual awakening, Nathanael spies on his father and visitor. What he sees is forbidden knowledge—his father and another man, whom he now recognizes as Coppelius, a frequent visitor at dinnertime, dressed in "long black smocks," engaged in some kind of alchemy with "all manner of strange instruments" before a fire. As his father bent over the fire, Nathanael tells, "[a] horrible, agonizing convulsion seemed to have contorted his gentle, honest face into the hideous, repulsive mask of a fiend" (*Sandman*, 90). He is horrified when he notices that his father looks like Coppelius. The children had always shrunk instinctively from the touch of Coppelius's "big gnarled hairy hands" and refused to eat anything he touched. Nathanael tells that Coppelius "took delight in finding some pretext for fingering a piece of cake or fruit that our kind mother had surreptitiously put on our plates, so that our loathing and disgust prevented us, with tears in our eyes, from enjoying the tidbit that was supposed to give us pleasure" (*Sandman*, 89). At the moment of recognition, Coppelius is immediately transformed from the bogeyman of Nathanael's childhood, the Sandman who "brings children's eyes to feed his brood in their nest in the crescent moon, . . . [into] a hateful, spectral monster, bringing misery, hardship, and perdition, both temporal and eternal, wherever he went" (*Sandman*, 89).

Nathanael's terror increases until he believes he sees "human faces . . . visible on all sides, but without eyes, and with ghastly, deep black caverns instead" (*Sandman*, 90). When he screams out, he is discovered by Coppelius, who cries, " 'Now we've got the eyes—eyes—a fine pair of children's eyes' . . . thrusting his hands into the flames and pulling out fragments of red-hot coal" which, Nathanael reports, "he was about to strew in my eyes" (*Sandman*, 90). Although Nathanael's father entreats Coppelius to let Nathanael "keep his eyes," and although Nathanael is physically unharmed, his memory of this event is imprinted like a primal scene upon his consciousness. He was forbidden to know what he, as a child, could barely recognize, and in the face of this trauma, he faints. A year later, we are told, his father again locks himself in his room with Coppelius, against the mother's wishes. " 'This is the last time he will visit me, I promise you!' " his father pleads. " 'Go, take the children away!' " (*Sandman*, 92). Nathanael reports, "I felt as though I were being crushed under a heavy, cold stone. . . . I was so tormented by indescribable inner terror and turmoil that I could not sleep a wink. Before me stood the hateful, loathsome Coppelius, his eyes sparkling, laughing at me maliciously, and I strove in vain to rid myself of his image. It must already have been midnight when a frightful crash was heard. . . . I raced to my father's room. . . . On the floor in front of the smoking fireplace my father was lying dead, his face burnt black and hideously contorted" (*Sandman*, 92). Soon after, Coppelius, seriously implicated in his father's death, disappears.

All this is recounted retrospectively in the letter Nathanael writes to his friend, Lothair, which opens the story. This memory of the Sandman had been repressed in Nathanael's childhood, but has reemerged because a man, named Coppola, selling eyeglasses that "brought objects before one's eyes with . . . clarity, sharpness, and distinctness" (*Sandman*, 106) reminds Nathanael of Coppelius. And through this encounter, Nathanael reenvisions the original scene of trauma. Nathanael is a young man at the point of entry here, engaged to be married to Clara, Lothair's rational sister, who, despite Nathanael's insistence, completely rejects the possibility that the eyeglass man, Coppola, is in fact, Coppelius.

Hoffmann has established two realms here. Representing rationality, Clara, Lothair, and his mother urge Nathanael to come home, to give up his desire to avenge his father's death, or even, in fact, to "know." The early scene in which, after fainting, Nathanael as a child wakes to the "warm, gentle breath" of his mother is repeated twice, when he returns home from school to such comfort. But no matter how they try, Nathanael is drawn back into the primal scene, reconstructed with Coppola, as inventor and puppeteer. It is Nathanael whom he manipulates, as well as the automaton, Olimpia, whom he helped invent, and who now takes the place of Clara in Nathanael's heart.

Here the realistic is so infused with horror and the fantastic that it is difficult to know how to read this tale. Hoffmann is extraordinarily skillful at intentional confusion between the two realms, the madness presented as strikingly familiar, as the uncanny, Freud noted in his essay on this tale. Nathanael's narcissism is clearly insane. He responds to his friend Siegmund's observations and warning about Olimpia's lifeless eyes and mechanistic movement, " 'Olimpia may well inspire a weird feeling in cold, prosaic people like you. It is only to the poetic soul that a similarly organized soul reveals itself! . . . [O]nly in Olimpia's love do I recognize myself' " (*Sandman*, 111). And to the automaton's single utterance, " 'Oh! Oh!' " he replies, " 'Oh, you wonderful, profound soul, . . . no one but you understands me perfectly' " (*Sandman*, 112). He accuses Clara of being the cold, lifeless automaton he is blind to in Olimpia. He shrieks, " 'You accursed lifeless automaton' " (*Sandman*, 103), when after listening to many tedious readings of his "gloomy, unintelligible, and formless" compositions and solipsistic verse, Clara urges him to " 'Throw the crazy, senseless, insane story into the fire' " (103).

In this story, as in the folktales of forbidden sight, such as *Cupid and Psyche* and *Bluebeard*, a taboo has been broken. In the folktales, no matter how dangerous, it is ultimately an act of liberation. Here, however, Hoffmann's focus is on the obsessive and driven quality of early trauma, a tale of the return of the repressed, in which the hero self-destructs before the denying voices of the conventional world. However, it is not the trauma, but the denial of this childhood knowledge that sends Nathanael in adulthood over the edge. Repression of the irrational and the unusual drives this knowledge underground, where, without possibility for integration into the lighter, ordinary world, it festers; the vision and the dreamer demonized become demonic. And as Nathanael becomes more demented, an independent narrator, identified as Nathanael's school friend, takes over. Hoffmann's objective narrator, as in *The Golden Pot*, helps connect us with Nathanael's vision. He at once acknowledges the bizarre quality of Nathanael's story, but confesses that "its strange and wondrous character absorbed my entire soul" (*Sandman*, 98). In an attempt to engage us, he says:

> Have you, my kind patron, ever had an experience that entirely absorbed your heart, your mind, and your thoughts, banishing all other concerns? You were seething and boiling inwardly; your fiery blood raced through your veins and gave a richer colour to your cheeks. You had a strange, fixed stare as though you were trying to make out forms, invisible to any other eyes, in empty space, and your words faded into obscure sighs. "What's wrong, my dear fellow?" . . . Inquired your friends. And you, anxious to convey your inner vision with all its glowing colours, its lights and shadows, laboured in vain to find words with which to begin. But you felt as though you must compress the entire wonderful splendid, terrible, hilarious, and hideous experience into your first word, so that it should strike your hearers like an electric shock; yet every word, all the resources of language, seemed faded, frosty, and dead. (*Sandman*, 97)

And because of its strangeness, the story has an intensity, an urgency that it be told from the beginning in such a way as to hook the listener before she or he can dismiss it as beyond the realm of possibility, without significance, purely a disorder of some deranged mind—exactly what the benevolent triumvirate—Clara, Lothair, and Nathanael's mother—has done. The narrator worries about how to begin such a story. He considers "Once upon a time," a frame that immediately signals fantasy; or "In the small provincial town of S.," a spatial frame that situates the narrative in the real world; or a dramatic opening in *medias res*—none of which, he tells us, "seemed to reflect anything of the prismatic radiance of my inner vision" (*Sandman*, 98). He decides not to begin it at all; rather, to offer a selection of letters, documents that introduce a variety of narrators, each with a perspective, to establish the authenticity of the strange tale. Besides, the narrator concludes, "nothing can be stranger or weirder than real life" (*Sandman*, 98–9), a recurring message in Hoffmann's tales, in which he meticulously makes the fantastic realistic and situates the extraordinary in the ordinary.

Resistance to this complexity comes from those who uphold the conventional and limited view of reality. Clara is the most significant of those, her vision affirmed by most of the other characters. She considers how to maintain a "normal state of mind," which, Hoffmann informs us, entails explaining away any experience outside her range, like that of Nathanael's father, as "delusive longing for higher wisdom" (*Sandman*, 94). She claims that his father "must have brought about his death by his own carelessness" and that his obsessive desire for knowledge "estranged [him] from his family" (*Sandman*, 94). She, similarly, assumes Nathanael's responsibility for his own dark state, and chidingly assures him that, "I am determined to appear in your presence like your guardian angel and to drive [the Sandman] away with loud laughter" (*Sandman*, 95).

Nathanael never does get free of his obsession. He comes upon a reenactment of his childhood trauma: the two creators of Olimpia, Dr. Spalanzani, her father, and Coppola, pulling at her arms and legs reminiscent of the way in which his own father and Coppelius had, as Nathanael narrated, "dislocated my hands and feet, and put them back in various sockets" (*Sandman*, 90–1), like an automaton. He sees that "Olimpia's deathly pale wax face had no eyes, just black caverns where eyes should be; [he realizes that] she was a lifeless doll" (*Sandman*, 114). He sees her "bloody eyes lying on the floor, staring at him," and, we are told, as Spalanzani picks up the eyes and throws them at him, "[m]adness seized him with its red-hot claws and entered his heart, tearing his mind to pieces" (*Sandman*, 114). He chants, " 'Hey, hey, hey! Fiery circle! Spin, spin, fiery circle! Spin wooden dolly, hey, spin, pretty wooden dolly'" (*Sandman*, 114). Both men, like their predecessors, disappear.

Nathanael awakes, "as though from a terrible nightmare," to the familiar "mild, heavenly warmth" of Clara, Lothair, and his mother. Clara instantly reclaims possession of him, and at first he is infinitely relieved and grateful. But, Hoffmann seems to reiterate, denial and repression will not dispel such darkness. It is Clara who leads Nathanael, again unwittingly, to the tower from which he will jump to his death. It is Clara who points out the " 'funny little grey bush, which really seems to be walking towards us' "—a vision of Coppelius, beckoning to Nathanael, so that "with hideous laughter," he invokes the incantation from the reenactment of his trauma. " 'Spin, wooden dolly! Spin, wooden dolly,' " he shrieks. And we are told that "with superhuman strength he seized Clara and was about to dash her to the ground below," but she is rescued by Lothair. We are also told that, "As people began to climb the stairs in order to seize the lunatic, Coppelius laughed and said: 'Ha, ha—just wait, he'll soon come down by himself,' and looked up, like the others" (*Sandman*, 118). And Nathanael jumps off the tower, just as predicted.

What are we to make of this? Hoffmann certainly substantiates Nathanael's vision here. Furthermore, the story ends with the triumph of convention. Clara survives to marry "an affectionate husband," has "two merry boys," lives in "a handsome country dwelling"—in other words, attains "the quiet domestic happiness which suited her cheerful, sunny disposition, and which she could never have enjoyed with the tormented, self-divided Nathanael" (*Sandman*, 118). We are to conclude that those who live in the light world, like Clara, with their intolerance for the irrational and the bizarre, drive those sensitive to the darker impulses into a cornered state. Nathanael's "poetic powers enable him to discern these forces, but not to master them" (Robertson, xxi). For Nathanael, seeing was associated with the forbidden; his distorted vision also illuminated something we do not wish to see. But, as in other tales of forbidden sight, what has been suppressed must surface. Psyche must see her husband in his enchanted state in order to release him from his enchantment. Bluebeard's wife must enter the forbidden chamber and see the corpses of his former wives, in order to understand that her own life is in danger. Without acknowledging those darker forces, without including them in nature's bounty, this cycle of destruction will continue. Society will weed out the Nathanaels of the world and leave us with the hopelessly banal vision of Clara.

### 4. Hans Christian Andersen: *The Snow Queen*

> Except ye become as little children, ye
> shall not enter the kingdom of heaven![17]

As a storyteller, Andersen has been acclaimed for the way in which he incorporates realistic everyday elements into the fairy tale. His characters invite psychological analysis and demonstrate complexity in their deep longings. But he has been attacked by many critics for, as Tatar says, promoting "a cult of suffering, death, and transcendence for children rivaled only by what passed for the spiritual edification of children in Puritan cultures" (Tatar, *The Classic Fairy Tales*, 212). Often his heroes embody a passivity, delicacy, and, as John Griffith pointed out, a "harmlessness, that purity which is incapacity for lust" (Tatar, *The Classic Fairy Tales*, 213). Sendak noted that Andersen's children are highly sentimentalized and lack the spunk he affords inanimate objects (Tatar, *The Classic Fairy Tales*, 215). Zipes explains Andersen's penchant for martyr-heroes. He claims that as a youth, Andersen survived "by becoming voiceless . . . by denying one's needs."[18] Andersen's narcissistic adult self seems the outgrowth of his sufferings as a child. The many stories of his flattering the very people he exposed in his stories,[19] of overstaying his welcome,[20] of seeking love as an unrequited lover[21] all attest to this imbalance. However, he certainly became one of the strongest voices of storytelling in the nineteenth century. His voice is still powerful, his stories still loved by the double audience he sought, adults and children, all over the world. Why is this so?

Andersen's characters experience, rather than represent, deep states of feeling. They inhabit his landscapes which combine realistic and fantastic elements, a mixture of Christian and pre-Christian elements. And although, as Wolfgang Lederer noted, the narrators "seem to be piously Christian," the stories "far transcend any single dogmatic frame."[22] *The Snow Queen*[23] begins twice: once in the "real" world and once in fantasy. "All right," the narrator tells us, "we will start the story; when we come to the end we shall know more than we do now"; and we are also told that, "Once upon a time there was a troll, the most evil troll of them all; he was called the devil" (*Snow Queen*, 234). Andersen does not maintain these two realms as separate. Elements of each are incorporated into the story, sometimes in the satirical elements, sometimes in the characters. The story opens on the devil and his trolls carrying a magic mirror to God and the angels, but the devil and his cohorts never reach heaven. Instead, the devil's mirror of derision and perversity splinters into pieces, some of which are so small that they enter people's eyes and hearts. Then they see the world "distorted, and [are] only . . . able to see the faults . . . of everyone . . . since even the tiniest fragment contained all the evil qualities of the whole mirror" (*Snow Queen*, 235). The mirror splinters the world, so that everything that was once united in innocence is fractured. This allegory can be read, as Christian theologian Paul Evdokimov did, as leaving paradise and God's state of perfection. He said, "The devil is he who divides . . . and reduces man to ultimate solitude. . . . [T]he innocent being created by God breaks up, atomizes into isolated fragments" (Lederer, 7).

*The Snow Queen* on one level is an aetiological tale, an explanation of how evil came into the world. Distortion and fragmentation occur as people look through windows made from the devil's splintered mirror; some look through eyeglasses. But the smallest, invisible fragments can penetrate the heart of a child, so that he is plunged prematurely into a state of darkness. *The Snow Queen* is the story of two children, one of whom is lost and the other who rescues him. It begins with a vision of wholeness, a kind of Eden with a little girl and little boy, whose houses are connected by a little garden. Although the children are poor, we are told that their small rose trees, from a simple flower pot, "grew as tall as the windows and joined together, so that they looked like a green triumphal arch" (*Snow Queen*, 236). Here the old Grandmother tells them the story of the Snow Queen. " 'The white bees are swarming,' " she tells them when winter comes; that the Snow Queen " 'always flies right in the center of the swarm . . . [and that] she never lies down to rest as the other snowflakes do. . . . [W]hen the wind dies she returns to the black clouds' " (*Snow Queen*, 236). The landscape here is dark, a pastoral associated with winter and its icy beauty. The Snow Queen appears that night to Kai, "beautiful but all made of . . . cold, blindingly glittering ice; and yet she was alive, for her eyes stared at Kai like two stars, but neither rest nor peace was to be found in her gaze" (*Snow Queen*, 237). And when she beckons to him, he sees a shadow cross his window. But until the glass splinters his vision, he is safe in his innocence.

When a sliver of glass enters Kai's heart, his vision fractures the harmony of the two children. Kai becomes irritable, critical of Gerda, and behaves, as Lederer notes, "like a typical adolescent" (Lederer, 27). He wants to play games the bigger boys play and, in his gendered differentiation, is disgusted by feeling. As a Romantic, Andersen connects distortion and the unnatural with reason and perfection. Now Kai embraces multiplication tables, while he rejects prayer, nature, and the imagination. " 'Aren't they marvelous?' " he says of the snowflakes, not-ing how each is " 'quite perfect . . . much nicer than real flowers . . . as long as they don't melt' " (*Snow Queen*, 239). Here Andersen creates a dark pastoral that contains the vitality of the natural world, with its dazzling light and vividly origi-nal shapes. The snowflakes grow "bigger and bigger" until they become "white hens that were running alongside him" (*Snow Queen*, 239). When the Snow Queen comes for him, he does not resist. "It was as if they knew each other," the narrator tells us.

The seduction of Kai begins with an invitation from the Snow Queen to " '[c]ome, creep inside my bearskin coat' " (*Snow Queen*, 239). Then, we are told, he "felt as if he lay down in a deep snowdrift" (*Snow Queen*, 239). As she begins kissing him with a kiss " 'colder than ice,' [h]e felt as if he were about to die, but it only hurt for a minute, then it was over. Now he seemed stronger and he no longer felt how cold the air was" (*Snow Queen*, 240). He becomes numb to all pain and to all memory of Gerda, his Grandmother, and his home. The Snow Queen says, " 'I shan't give you any more kisses . . . or I might kiss you to death' " (*Snow Queen*, 240). By first offering and then withholding kisses, she suggests the teasing of the temptress that Andersen was to explore more fully in his later and less successful story, *The Ice Maiden*. There, a boy is seduced by a similar figure and then claimed by her in death the night before he is to be mar-ried. The Ice Maiden says,

> "I crush anything that comes within my grasp. . . . A lovely boy was stolen from me. I had kissed him but not so hard that he died from it. Now he is again among human beings. . . . Upward . . . he climbs, away from everyone else, but not from me. He is mine and I claim him."[24]
>
> "Mine! Mine!" The cry came from all about him, and within himself. "I kissed you when you were a child. Kissed your mouth. Now I kiss you on your toe and your heel. Now you are mine!" (*Ice Maiden*, 778)

The Snow Queen, like the Ice Maiden, suggests the potentially dangerous and overwhelming quality of passion. Kai is taken into the dark pastoral, "the great void of night . . . high up in the clouds, above the earth . . . [a]bove oceans, forests, and lakes . . . [while] the cold winter wind whipped the landscape below them" (*Snow Queen*, 240). This snowscape is populated by the cries of wolves and the hoarse voices of crows. Even the moon here is associated with the Snow Queen's seduction and the darkness of "the long winter night. When daytime came [Kai] fell asleep at the feet of the Snow Queen" (*Snow Queen*, 240)—which is where we leave him, psychologically and emotionally insensate. The third, fourth, fifth, and sixth stories belong to Gerda. Only in the last story do we come back to Kai. It is up to Gerda to restore harmony and to retrieve an innocence, which will be transformed, in the face of experience, into the potential higher innocence of adulthood.

As in most of the fairy tales, at stake here is the challenge of retaining in maturity the kindness, openness, and spirituality inherent in innocence. Andersen is interested in the journey toward wisdom, but I'm not sure he ever wrote a tale that embodied the philosophical complexity of his psychological and feeling states. Gerda's quest does explore the various pitfalls of entering the worldly world. For this journey, she puts on her new red shoes, which, for readers familiar with Andersen, immediately signals vanity and selfishness in that relentless story of child suffering, *The Red Shoes.*[25] As in that story, in *The Snow Queen*, Lederer suggests, the red shoes suggest emerging sexuality (Lederer, 37). Gerda, in her innocence, throws the shoes into the water, assuming they are not part of her. And in her innocence, she misinterprets the message of the river. Unlike Kai's, Gerda's initiation into womanhood involves a non-sexual seduction. She is carried beyond the green world, "[b]eyond the banks . . . covered with flowers . . . [and] meadows with cows and sheep grazing upon them" (*Snow Queen*, 241), where an old woman beckons to her. Like the heroes of traditional folktales of childhood, like Hansel and Gretel, Gerda must learn to differentiate between real nurturing and deception. Like other girls of folktales, she is seduced in the third story of "the old woman who knows magic" into forgetting her goal, to reach Kai. The old woman combs Gerda's hair with a gold comb, reminiscent of Snow White's temptation when her stepmother/the witch comes to the forest and offers her poisoned gold combs. Also I am reminded of Rapunzel's golden hair and her stepmother's attempts to keep her from the prince. But Andersen's magical figures often are not exclusively evil or good. In this tale, we are told that the old woman "just liked to do a little magic for her own pleasure" (*Snow Queen*, 242), and that "[s]he wanted little Gerda to stay with her very much." Rather than evil, what children need to fear, or at least be wary of, are the very human and childish traits of adults—their vanities and selfishness. No matter how Gerda questions the flowers in the old woman's postlapsarian garden, where "[e]very flower stood in the warm sunshine and dreamed its own fairy tale" (*Snow Queen*, 243–4), she does not learn anything from them. Their songs only get sadder; they turn into songs about child death and coffins. Gerda needs to move beyond this garden where each flower "only signs its own song" (*Snow Queen*, 245). Out in the world there are seasons, possibilities for change, but, we are told, at times the fruits are "bitter."

As a questing hero, Gerda must journey through a full range of experiences. Andersen brings the archetype into the real world, so that the movement from the highest to the lowest is interpreted through a class structure. Gerda first visits the court, where she meets a princess and her prince, youths like herself, susceptible to dreams. Later she will visit humble folk, who provide the wisdom of the peasant class and of maturity. Her rescue of Kai also involves overcoming each aspect of the Snow Queen's power under which Kai is immobilized. In the third story, the seduction scene paralleled that of Kai. The fourth story suggests the power of the Snow Queen's royal position. Here, the princess "has read all the newspapers in the world and has forgotten what was written in them," suggesting that the world has not yet penetrated, both for good and for bad. She is still somewhat innocent and also somewhat ignorant. Her husband, the prince, came to her, a commoner with boots that squeak, but became prince because he was not intimidated by her stature. But neither has much to tell Gerda about the whereabouts of Kai. The satirical touches in this section dramatize Andersen's attack on royalty and servitude. Representing the lower orders and their upwardly mobile dreams of security, a crow and his fiancée are given a choice between permanent positions in the court and freedom. The crow says, " 'To be secure is better than to fly' " (*Snow Queen*, 251). After a brief stay at court, the crow already has a headache and has eaten too much. Here, among royalty, Gerda learns to differentiate between fantasy and reality. Interestingly, dreams whirl around as strange shadows that "have come to fetch their royal masters" (*Snow Queen*, 250). When Gerda sees a dream of Kai passing by on a sled, she needs to recognize it as a phantom of wish-fulfillment, to keep her feet on the ground and not to get lost in dreams of grandeur.

From royalty and privilege Gerda is thrown into the underworld, unprepared for the violence into which she is about to be initiated. Here Gerda, like bait, is dressed "from head to toe" in the silk and velvet gifts of the princess and the prince, as she enters the great dark forest. Immediately, the coachman, the servant, and the soldiers who have accompanied her from the castle are killed by robbers. The robber woman wants to eat Gerda, but her daughter, the robber girl, bites her mother and demands, " 'she will sleep in my bed with me' " (*Snow Queen*, 252).

The robber girl, with her "sad" eyes, is among Andersen's most complex characters. She is both protective of and threatening to Gerda. A mixture of natural kindness and equally natural aggression, she represents the dark forest in which we find her, uncivilized in her aggression, uncivilized in her generosity. She showers affection on Gerda, as she does with her pet reindeer, although she also tickles its throat with a knife. She sleeps with her arm around Gerda and a knife in her hand. She beats Gerda in the face with her pet pigeon: " 'Kiss it,' demanded the robber girl and shoved the frightened bird right up into Gerda's face" (*Snow Queen*, 253). Utterly innocent of but also taking pleasure in her cruelty, she reassures Gerda: " 'I won't allow them to kill you, so long as you don't make me angry. I won't allow them to kill you even if I do get angry at you, I will do it myself' " (*Snow Queen*, 253)—she says, as she dries Gerda's tears. She represents the dark side of innocence, its oral aggression and instinct. But it is here, among the least civilized, that Gerda hears of Kai. And the robber girl sets her free, providing her with food and with the reindeer who accompanies her toward the old northern lights. " 'Look how they shine!' " (*Snow Queen*, 256), he says.

Here in the dark pastoral, there are many lights. The Snow Queen's palace is lighted by the northern lights' sharp glare. When Gerda first comes upon "the old lady who knows magic," she notices colored glass "which gave a strange light to the room" (*Snow Queen*, 242). The golden sled Gerda receives from the prince and princess glows. There is as much sunshine in the false gardens as in the one at home. Gerda must not be tempted by glitter. She must also enter the "wretched little hovel" of the Lapp woman, where one had to walk "on all fours" (*Snow Queen*, 256). Rather than the useless newspapers of the court, Gerda finds helpful messages written on the codfish skin of the humble Lapp woman, who tells her how to reach the Finnish woman. And in her wisdom, the Finnish woman understands that Gerda needs only her own sweetness to free Kai. Here there is no magic. " 'I can't give her any more power than she already has!' " she tells the reindeer. " 'But she must learn of her power; it is in her heart, for she is a sweet and innocent child' " (*Snow Queen*, 257). When Gerda reaches Kai, her compassionate tears melt the ice of Kai's heart. She kisses him back to life, they pray together, and hand in hand they escape to where the "winds were still" and "the sun broke through the clouds."

Together they come across the robber girl, setting out to see the world, with two pistols—a child outlaw. She is the voice of honesty here, as she scolds Kai: " 'You are a fine one . . . running about as you did. I wonder if you are worth going to the end of the world for?' " This grounded and cynical voice is also part of Andersen's sensibility. He returns the children, no longer children, to their unchanged home, where Grandmother is reading the Bible "in the warm sunshine: 'Except ye become as little children, ye shall not enter the kingdom of heaven.' " We are told that "in their hearts" they are still innocent children. Andersen, however, leaves his readers with the words of the robber girl, and with all the images of narcissism and selfishness that Gerda has experienced in the world. Kai has been "on ice," frozen in a state of passivity; but Gerda has traveled into darkness of the adult world, which certainly casts a shadow on the ending of the story and on their "glorious summer day."

## 5. *The Little Mermaid*

A radiance not quite of this earth bathes the placid landscape,
sharpening its shadows to a preternatural darkness . . .

—NESCA A. ROBB, *FOUR IN EXILE*[26]

*The Little Mermaid*[27] has been criticized as one of Andersen's tales that focuses on, as Nesca A. Robb, an early and brilliant critic, puts it, "the spirit's capacity for self-torture" (Robb, 126). However, unlike *The Red Shoes*, which Robb called "the voice of nightmare with a vengeance" (Robb, 132), *The Little Mermaid* is a tale in which the hero moves through intense suffering into a higher state of eternal joy, which Robb saw as "never far off even from the miasma of horror, and may ever at a touch dispel it, leaving its prisoners free" (Robb, 133), as in Andersen's best tales. The pain in these stories is often true to that of everyday life; they dramatize truths that children recognize—so faithful is he to the suffering of the outcast child, or to the moments of childhood in which each of us was an outsider. Andersen saw life, in its rich array of pleasure and pain, the way a child might see it. The Little Mermaid, in her innocence, curiosity, openness, and vulnerability speaks to and for the child as she ventures out into the world of humans from her protected world under the sea.

In each story, Andersen creates an intricate landscape, a series of images through which his characters move and with which they become associated. In this story, the dark pastoral is a seascape. It begins, "Far out at sea the water's as blue as the petals of the loveliest cornflower, and as clear as the purest glass; but it's very deep, deeper than any anchor can reach" (*Mermaid*, 216). Without anchoring, this seascape suggests the depths of the forest, the untamed world. When the Little Mermaid resides there, she is safe. She has no need of anchors. Her world is one of temperate movement, a kind of stasis, as the "cockle-shells open and shut with the current" (*Mermaid*, 216). But she longs, as real children and adolescents do, for difference, for the world that lies on the other side. Each year, one of her older sisters emerges from the sea to describe what human life looks like. It is striking that Andersen is able so vividly to reimagine a human, familiar world through the fresh and innocent eyes of a sea maiden. In this way, he renders it unfamiliar to us, or, rather, allows us to experience its natural beauty anew. Flowers smell and birds are fishes you see in the branches that sing. The Little Mermaid sees the moon and the stars "through the water [so that] they looked much larger than they do to us" (*Mermaid*, 218). From her sisters' reports, she imagines a "big town where the lights were twinkling like a hundred stars; to listen to the sound of music and the noise and clatter of carts and people; to see all the towers and spires on the churches and hear the bells ringing . . . [—] because she couldn't get there, it was this above everything that she longed for" (*Mermaid*, 218). Another sister tells her about how "just as the sun was setting . . . [t]he whole sky had looked like gold . . . and the clouds . . . [were] beautiful . . . as they sailed, all crimson and violet, over her head. And yet, much faster than they, a flock of wild swans flew like a long white veil across the water where the sun was setting. . . . [And when] the sun sank, . . . its rosy light was swallowed up by sea and cloud" (*Mermaid*, 219). Another sister sees pastures and farms, children "splashing about quite naked in the water," a dog. Another thought that "what was so wonderful [was that] you could see for miles and miles around you, and the sky hung above like a big glass bell . . . and jolly dolphins . . . turning somersaults, and enormous whales . . . spurt[ing] up water from their nostrils, so that they seemed to be surrounded by a hundred fountains" (*Mermaid*, 219). In winter, one of the sisters sees "great icebergs . . . floating about . . . like pearls . . . in the most fantastic shapes, and they glittered like diamonds. . . . [When] it lightened and thundered . . . the dark waves lifted the great blocks of ice right up, so that they flashed in the fierce red lightning . . . [while] she sat calmly on her floating iceberg and watched the blue lightning zigzag into the glittering sea" (*Mermaid*, 219). But all the sisters agree that it is "nicest down below [and] . . . such a comfort to be home" (*Mermaid*, 219).

However, the Little Mermaid, as youngest, is most open to an alternative vision of the world. While the other sisters decorate their gardens "with the most wonderful things they had got from sunken ships" (*Mermaid*, 217), the Little Mermaid creates a bed of "rose-red flowers that were like the sun high above, and a beautiful marble statue . . . of a handsome boy, hewn from the clear white stone" (*Mermaid*, 217) from the bottom of the sea. Next to the statue she plants "a rose-red weeping willow, which grew splendidly and let its fresh foliage droop over the statue [so that] the shadow took on a violet tinge and, like the branches, was never still" (*Mermaid*, 217). The intensity of the image marks her feelings, as she falls in love with the statue, who will become the earthly prince.

The Little Mermaid saves the life of the prince in a shipwreck. He becomes her idol, her love object, her reason for living, and in hopes of gaining his love, she sacrifices her greatest gift, her beautiful singing voice. This is where the tale gets objectionable, particularly for us feminists, who are repelled and horrified by her sacrifice. She had learned all about what she needed to become immortal from the sea witch, whose dark underground world reflects the underside of the beautiful sea. To reach her you must travel to "the far side of roaring whirlpools" to where "[t]here were no flowers growing, no sea grass, nothing but the bare grey sandy bottom . . . [to where] [a]ll trees and bushes were polyps, half animals and half plants . . . like hundred-headed snakes growing out of the earth. . . . They wound themselves tight round everything they could clutch hold of in the sea, and they never let go" (*Mermaid*, 225). The sea witch herself embodies a perversion of nurturing, as she concocts a mixture "scratched [from] her breast [where] her black blood drip[s] down into the kettle" (*Mermaid*, 227).

While the prince turns out to be superficial and unworthy, the Little Mermaid is released into air, doing good deeds for three hundred years—as opposed to dissolving into the foam of the sea into which she jumps. According to mermaid lore, the mermaid can only achieve immortality if she wins the love of a mortal in marriage. In Andersen's tale, the Little Mermaid will become immortal without depending on the love of another. Andersen considered this original addition to this type of fairy tale significant. Certainly, he tempered the pain of her journey and wrote truthfully of unrequited love. Unfortunately, he also tacked on one of his moralistic endings. He says,

> God shortens our time of trial. The child never knows when we fly about the room and, if that makes us smile with joy, then a year is taken away from the three hundred. But if we see a child who is naughty or spiteful, then we have to weep tears of sorrow, and every tear adds one more day to our time of trial. (*Mermaid*, 232)

While the moral is abhorrent to modern readers, the story of romantic love de-romanticized holds up. And the courage and sympathy his heroes discover within themselves allows them their dignity and affords hope to readers.

Andersen told stories about children in their innocence, how they, as Robb notes, "can understand the speech of birds and animals quite as well as that of their father and mother" (Robb, 129). He understood that in this way they are enchanted. And he created a fairy land that they in their enchantment inhabited, a world in which they could move *between* the natural and supernatural. Andersen stands as a poet of fairy land. Robb concludes,

> Not for nothing does the fairy world mingle so intricately with the world of every-day and lay its spell even on the most commonplace objects and events. For imagi-nation is not mere fantasy, though that is included in it; rather it is a mode of love, the understanding that sees things in their true significance. (Robb, 140)

## II. DICKENS: *THE OLD CURIOSITY SHOP* AND THE NIGHTMARE OF CHILDHOOD

> "Who has sent you so far by yourself," said I.
> "Somebody who is very kind to me, sir."
>
> —*THE OLD CURIOSITY SHOP*, CHAPTER THE FIRST[28]

In his preface to "the first cheap edition" of *The Old Curiosity Shop* (1848), writ-ten seven years after his original preface, Dickens made clear his intention to illu-minate the nightmare world of childhood. He wrote, "I had it always in my fancy to surround the lonely figure of the child with grotesque and wild, but not impos-sible companions, and to gather about her innocent face and pure intentions, asso-ciates as strange and uncongenial as the grim objects that are about her when her history is first foreshadowed" (*Curiosity Shop*, 42). As Little Nell lies sleeping, before the start of her story, she is surrounded, not by childhood toys, but by the dark and ugly curios of her grandfather's shop. From the dark imagination of childhood—both hers and Dickens's, they spring into life, transformed into the characters she meets on her journey.

Like other writers of the dark pastoral Dickens has a gift for creating "other" worlds. These landscapes, like those of Hoffmann, Andersen, and other writers of fairy tales, interpret the real world and bring it more sharply into focus. Dickens's world, however, is novelistic—at least more so than the magical ones of the fan-tasy writers. But what he creates is a poetics of childhood, a state of mind that derives from the child's point of view. It is infused with a glow, illuminated with a heightened sense of things as they appear early on in the human imagination, when images are first forming and coalescing. The child's imagination does not fully distinguish between fantasy and reality, daydream and nightmare. Often Dickens's novels are governed by a central metaphor that dominates the landscape so primally as to suggest the imagination of childhood—which, as he so deeply understood, often operates obsessively in adulthood. Consider the fog of Esther's childhood in *Bleak House*[29] or the prison of Amy Dorrit's relationship with her father in *Little Dorrit*.[30]

*The Old Curiosity Shop* is the story of a childless childhood. Without toys or playmates, the life of the child hero, Little Nell, is somber. Briefly, we see her laughing at her only childhood friend, Kit, who appears early in the novel as a huge open mouth, "the comedy of the child's life" (*Curiosity Shop*, 49). But this is before she is separated from him, before she is rendered essentially friendless and squeezed out of her home, such as it is, in her grandfather's curio shop. This is the devastating story of the attempts of an orphaned child to save her only guardian, her grandfather, from addiction, and in so doing, she sacrifices herself.

The orphan state preoccupied the imagination of nineteenth-century novelists.[31] Hochman and Wachs, in their excellent study of the orphan condition in Dickens's work, note that Dickens sees orphaned children as doubly burdened with the rage they feel about their abandonment by their parents—"both to the brutality of the world outside and to the violence of the conflicts that fill their souls" (Hochman, 14). The world of Dickens's orphans is tinged with an intensity that borders on the surreal. According to Hochman and Wachs, for Dickens to have treated his characters realistically "would have been to affirm the possibility of self-realization within the world he knew, and hence, implicitly, to have affirmed the world itself. Dickens's refusal to portray character as other great nineteenth-century novelists did is grounded in the judgment that the world does not permit such self-realization" (Hochman, 28). They assert that Dickens's refusal to "work within the conventions of nineteenth-century novelistic realism . . . [is] the result of identification with humanist values that lead to a revulsion from the world in which it is impossible to realize those values" (Hochman, 28).

*The Old Curiosity Shop*, however, goes beyond the orphan condition. Here Dickens's focus is on that most deeply confusing condition—the nightmare of the parenting child, whose very source of emotional life is also the very source of her deprivation. This is not an unfamiliar scenario. It is recognizable today in the preponderance of stunted and compulsive adults who were psychologically orphaned.[32] Little Nell is orphaned in more ways than one. Her grandfather is a gambler who sees only himself and his need to amass the fortune he deludes himself into believing is for the sake of this child. Even her older brother is a procurer—at fourteen years old she is, unbeknown to her, being sold by her brother into marriage.

The betrayal of Little Nell is prefigured from the very opening of the novel. It opens with an odd, old man, who narrates and participates in the first three chapters, and then disappears, abandoning Nell to her life within these pages. The narrator begins:

> Night is generally my time for walking. . . . The glare and hurry of broad noon are not adapted to idle pursuits like mine; a glimpse of passing faces caught by the light of a street lamp or a shop window is often better for my purpose than their full revelation in the daylight, and, if I must add the truth, night is kinder in this respect than day, which too often destroys an air-built castle at the moment of its completion, without the smallest ceremony or remorse. (*Curiosity Shop*, 43)

This novel dramatically connects the realm of night with that of childhood. Although sentimental portraits of Victorian children envision them surrounded by light, the truth of most Victorian childhoods is dark and dreary. Here we are plunged immediately into the dangerous landscape of childhood abandonment and neglect. The narrator's vision illuminates, like the "glimpse . . . caught by the light of a street lamp," the shadow people—the outcasts, the homeless, those who live in the margins of Victorian society. He reflects on the "constant pacing . . . that never-ending restlessness, that incessant tread of feet . . . the stream of life that will not stop, pouring on, on, on . . ." (*Curiosity Shop*, 43). The crowds crossing to and from bridges where they overlook the water suggest the restlessness of humanity and the relentless demands of the world—a frame to contextualize Little Nell's journey. "Some," the narrator tells us, "halt to rest from heavy loads and think as they look over the parapet that to smoke and lounge away one's life . . . in a dull slow sluggish barge, must be happiness unalloyed—and where some, and a very different class, pause with heavier loads than they, remembering to have heard or read in some old time that drowning was not a hard death, but of all means of suicide the easiest and best" (*Curiosity Shop*, 44).

   This darkly retrospective view of life belongs to this old and solitary man. But what does it say as the beginning of a novel about childhood? In his wisdom, the narrator reinforces the inappropriateness of the child running mysterious errands alone at night, as if she were part of this city night life. And so, when he asks, " 'Who has sent you so far by yourself?' " he raises the pivotal question of the novel. And when she answers, " 'Somebody who is very kind to me,' " the narrator is compelled to follow her home to investigate the answer. There he locates the grandfather, the moving force of the child's life, and urges him to take "more care of your grandchild another time . . ." (*Curiosity Shop*, 47). He states the case clearly and emphatically when he says, " 'It always grieves me to contemplate the initiation of children into the ways of life, when they are scarcely more than infants. It checks their confidence and simplicity—two of the best qualities that Heaven gives them—and demands that they share our sorrows before they are capable of entering into our enjoyments' " (*Curiosity Shop*, 48). He pays a few follow-up visits; he worries about her "Alone! In that gloomy place all the long, dreary night" (*Curiosity Shop*, 53). He even becomes obsessed with "the old dark murky rooms—the gaunt suits of mail with their ghostly silent air—the faces all awry, grinning from wood and stone—the dust and rust, and worm that lives in wood—and alone in the midst of all this lumber and decay, and ugly age . . . the beautiful child in her gentle slumber" (*Curiosity Shop*, 56). But he disappears at the end of the third chapter, saying, "I shall for the convenience of the narrative detach myself from its further course, and leave those who have prominent and necessary parts in it to speak and act for themselves" (*Curiosity Shop*, 72). Dickens explains this abrupt shift in point of view in his discussion of *Master Humphrey's Clock*,[33] the original story on which he based *The Old Curiosity Shop*. Critics have treated the narrator's sudden disappearance as an awkward transition in an early Dickens novel.[34] However, it certainly is in keeping with the theme of childhood betrayal for the sensible, mature narrator to abandon the child, much the way adults observing child neglect often do.

Little Nell has been seen as a mawkish romanticization of the child victim, her goodness inconceivable—much the way Esther Summerson has been received by contemporary critics. However, I always found both heroes believable. The abandoned girl child, slated for a domestic and caretaking role, like Nell or Esther, may deeply and fully deny any anger towards her oppressors. This is particularly true in Nell's case, since she is praised for her goodness and told that her welfare is the cause of the suffering. The rage that we often assume accompanies such beatitude is not always accessible to children or noticeable to others.

In this novel, such rage is projected onto a nightmare landscape of the "other" childhood, embodied by the dwarf Quilp. He is all instinct, without impulse control, a representation of all that we fear about childhood. A splendid incarnation of gallows humor, he is also created out of the ugliest attributes of human nature. He is greed, lust, infantile murderous rage—a Rumpelstiltskin without compassion, he who takes joy in spite, an allegorical imp of the perverse. He epitomizes the surreal figure from the nightmares of childhood—the way a child might conceive of a goblin. He seems to have stepped out of a medieval morality play, but he is drawn with vivid details that are realistically described. Dickens tells us: He "ate hard eggs, shells and all, devoured gigantic prawns with the heads and tails on, chewed tobacco and water-cresses at the same time and with extraordinary greediness, drank boiling tea without winking, bit his fork and spoon till they bent again, and in short performed so many horrifying and uncommon acts that the women . . . began to doubt if he were really a human creature" (*Curiosity Shop*, 86). The ambiguity of his character, the question of whether he is located allegorically or realistically, is suggested by his two domiciles. In one, he resides with his wife in society on Tower Hill; the other is the his rat-infested Wharf, where he dwells most happily, free of civilization. His only companion is his boy-servant, whose pleasure is to stand on his head, a reversal that hints at the perversion of childhood—the dominant theme of the novel. A force rather than a human being, Quilp is "a panting dog," a murderous gnome in the mirror—he appears everywhere, belying human laws of time and gravity.

In this unprotected child's life, Quilp is, in quite another sense, everywhere. He echoes the greed and selfishness of the grandfather, her brother Fred, her brother Fred's friend, Dick Swiveller, who sets his pecuniary hopes on her as his future bride—of all those she meets in her travels who prey on her innocence. Although the grandfather is in earnest when he says to the old man who brings her home, " 'It is true that in many respects I am the child, and she the grown person. . . . But waking or sleeping, by night or day, in sickness or health, she is the one object of my care, and if you knew of how much care, you would look on me with different eyes' " (*Curiosity Shop*, 52). However, as he is more and more driven by his addiction, he becomes the waking nightmare of her life, the worst threat to her very safety. Stripped of any pretense of civility and concern, the grandfather, along with the other male abusers of childhood innocence in this novel, becomes a Quilp, the personification of the malevolence of the dwarfed male. " 'Such a fresh, blooming, modest little bud . . . such a chubby, rosy, cosy, little Nell' " (*Curiosity Shop*, 125), Quilp leers, plotting to marry her, even as his own sweet wife, Nell's only confident, is young, alive, and well. As he takes over Nell's home, he croons, " 'Has she come to sit upon Quilp's knee . . . or is she going to bed in her own little room inside here' " (*Curiosity Shop*, 140). And as she recoils, he stakes out his claim: " 'The bedstead is much about my size. I think I shall make it *my* little room' " (*Curiosity Shop*, 140). He defiles her one sanctuary, "by throwing himself on his back upon the bed with his pipe in his mouth, and then kicking up his legs and smoking violently" (*Curiosity Shop*, 140–1). He represents the "paranoid plot" of the orphan novel.[35] But no matter how frightening, no matter how powerful, Quilp is identifiable—one can locate his cruelty. Nell instinctively repels his advances.

Nell's vision of escape is the utopian dream of the abused or neglected child, that she can save her grandfather from his misery. She pleads with him,

> "Let us be beggars, and be happy. . . . Dear Grandfather," cried the girl, with an energy which shone in her flushed face, trembling voice, and impassioned gesture . . . "oh hear me pray that we may beg, or work in open roads or fields, to earn a scanty living, rather than live as we do now. . . . Let us walk through country places, and sleep in fields and under trees, and never think of money again, or anything that can make you sad, but rest at nights, and have the sun and wind upon our faces in the day, and thank God together." (*Curiosity Shop*, 122–4)

As Nell and her grandfather flee their oppressors, they are two pilgrims in search of safety, which neither the child nor the old man can provide. Neither is a providential questor. The world is corrupt and the grandfather easily tempted. And like all literary pilgrimages, this is a spiritual journey, Nell's education from innocence into the world of experience. What can be salvaged from the world? How can the child, in the face of intrusive experience, maintain goodness and further serve as a source of redemption, the way Dickens envisioned innocence?

The characters on this journey sort out into rogues and benefactors. And this sorting task, associated with coming of age, is prematurely assigned to the child, Nell. The first pair of rogues they come upon, from the Punch and Judy shows popular with both children and adults at that time, grotesquely parody child play. They are the puppeteer conmen who construct their roles to confuse Nell and her grandfather. At first, Short appears optimistic and generous, while Codlin presents himself as melancholy and suspicious. Then they reverse roles, so that Short is the trickster and Codlin, the good guy, and it is up to Nell to untangle the threads of deception, while Codlin repeatedly whispers in her ear, " 'Codlin's the friend, remember—not Short' " (*Curiosity Shop*, 207). Various other street entertainers dramatize the underside of Victorian society.

Dickens uses theater—and in this novel, the streets, the alleys, the public squares all provide theater—like a fantasy landscape, revealing by distorting the real social world. The circus, for example, mirrors the expediency of Victorian society. With its giants, dwarfs, and dancing animals, it serves as a microcosm of the commodification of workers. We are told, " 'Once get a giant shaky on his legs, and the public care no more about him than they do for a dead cabbage-stalk. [Old giants are] usually kept in carawans to wait upon the dwarfs. . . . [I]t's better than letting 'em go upon the parish or about the streets. . . . Once make a giant common and giants will never draw again' " (*Curiosity Shop*, 204). The owner of the dancing dogs exhibits a sadism suggestive of the punishing parent. A particular dog in disgrace is forced to grind the organ, "sometimes in quick time, sometimes in slow, but never leaving off for an instant. . . . [While the others] got an unusually large piece of fat he accompanied the music with a short howl, but immediately checked upon his master looking round" (*Curiosity Shop*, 203). Dickens asserts, "We are all going to the play, or coming home from it" (*Curiosity Shop*, 380), all the protagonists of our own lives, acting various parts, whether deliberately chosen. So that Dickens uses his child characters as a refuge from guise. Distinguished from the hypocritical procurers around them, they remain true to themselves in their innocence, even as they learn to hide or pretend to others. Nell learns to dissemble, at first to protect both her grandfather. She cautions him:

"Grandfather, these men suspect that we have secretly left our friends, and mean to carry us before some gentlemen [for a reward]. . . . If you let your hand tremble so, we can never get away from them, but if you're only quiet now, we shall do so easily. . . . Keep close to me all day. Never mind them, don't look at them, but me. I shall find a time when we can steal away. When I do, mind you come with me, and do not stop or speak a word. Hush! That's all." (*Curiosity Shop*, 211)

However, Nell soon understands that she needs to hide from him as well. She sews a gold coin into her clothing for "an emergency." Once her grandfather discovers a group of gamblers along their way, Nell becomes increasingly invisible to him. She becomes an observer, a helpless onlooker to a diabolical scene in the forest where her grandfather is manipulated by the gamblers, but completely unaware of himself as the victim. She follows two sisters at night, drawing strength from their intimacy from the sidelines, a witness but not a part of any family. The sympathetic adults—such as the schoolmaster, whose job it is to protect children, or Mrs. Jarley, the eccentric owner of the waxworks, or any of the poverty stricken mothers who might understand her plight—cannot protect her from her grandfather's profligacy. Drawn further into his addition, he enacts a scene of horror equal to the most nightmarish in Victorian fiction, which recalls Quilp defiling her bed. Dickens takes us step by step through the feelings of the child, as she lies, frozen in the darkness of her innocence, watching a horror she can't take in all at once, but eventually comes to understand. After falling asleep one night, she wakes

> with a start and in great terror. A deeper slumber followed this—and then—What! That figure in the room! A figure was there. . . . [I]t crouched and slunk along, groping its way with noiseless hands, and stealing round the bed. She had no voice to cry for help, no power to move, but lay still, watching it. On it came . . . [t]he breath so near her pillow, that she shrunk back into it, lest those wandering hands should light upon her face. . . . The dark form was a mere blot upon the lighter darkness of the room, but she saw the turning of the head, and felt and knew how the eyes looked and the ears listened. . . . At length, still keeping the face towards her, it busied its hands in something, and she heard the chink of money. Then, on it came again, silent and stealthy as before. . . . How slowly it seemed to move, now that she could hear but not see it, creeping along the floor! It reached the door at last, and stood upon its feet. . . . [A]nd it was gone. The first impulse of the child was to fly from the terror of being by herself in that room—to have somebody by—not to be alone—and then her power of speech would be restored. (*Curiosity Shop*, 301)

So she enters her grandfather's room to protect him from the creeping stranger, but she discovers him there, "counting the money of which his hands had robbed her" (*Curiosity Shop*, 302). Dickens relates to us the power of this trauma from the perspective of the child: "The grey-headed old man gliding like a ghost into her room and acting the thief while he supposed her fast sleep, then bearing off his prize and hanging over it with the ghastly exultation she had witnessed, was worse—immeasurably worse, and far more dreadful . . . than anything her wildest fancy could have suggested" (*Curiosity Shop*, 303). And like most trauma, like a recurring dream, "in imagination it was always coming, and never went away" (*Curiosity Shop*, 303).

This primal scene of childhood recalls to us our darkest and earliest irrational childhood fears. "There is nothing under the bed, no monster lurking in the shadows"—the reassuring parental voices dominate early picture books. I remember as a child waking in absolute terror to feel what I first thought was a stranger's hand in my bed. I was paralyzed with fear in the few moments it took me to recognize it as my own hand that had fallen asleep. But here, there are no soothing voices, no illusions to sweep away her fears. Again, Dickens, with utmost care, delineates the psychological devices of the child who cannot take in the horror of what she has seen. Nell splits her grandfather in her mind into the good and bad grandfather. Dickens tells us,

> She had no fear of the dear old grandfather, in whose love for her this disease of the brain had been engendered; but the man she had seen that night, wrapt in the game of chance, lurking in her room, and counting the money by the glimmering light, seemed like another creature in his shape, a monstrous distortion of his image, a something to recoil from, and be the more afraid of, because it bore a likeness to him, and kept close about her, as he did. (*Curiosity Shop*, 303)

The split familiar in the fairy tale between the kind, weak father and the ogre or the wicked stepmother and the witch is dramatized here in the two grandfathers. What is most impossible to integrate, the "wandering hands," suggests a molestation Dickens may have been hesitant to write about. Like the carnivorous ogre that displaces the father in the fairy tale, Quilp can enact the lasciviousness forbidden to the grandfather. However, while Nell is concerned with running from Quilp, she becomes increasingly preoccupied with observing her grandfather. Her knowledged now separates the two pilgrims: her grandfather goes off to meet his gamblers in the forest, while she plans another escape for them both. She learns to speak in code, in the language of indirection. She tells him, " 'I've had a dreadful dream of grey-haired men like you, in darkened rooms by night, robbing the sleepers of their gold' " (*Curiosity Shop*, 405). What never should belong to a child becomes, now, her primary mandate: to lead her grandfather "further from [his] guilt and shame" (*Curiosity Shop*, 422). She is conscious now of what has always been true, that she is on her own, unprotected from the shaming taunts of a most vicious class system; she is forced into becoming completely self-reliant. She becomes a most resourceful child, developing talents and evoking favor with the public in her presentation of Mrs. Jarley's wax figures. Mrs. Jarley, one of Dickens's eccentrics, further exposes the pretensions of the proper social world— even as she exhibits her own grandiosity. Nell learns to perform, whether for the Victorian public at the waxworks, or for the rowdy crew of drunken men who terrorize her into singing as they carry her and her grandfather across a river on their raft.

The many characters Nell and her grandfather encounter mark the various stages of her education. Particularly poignant is the lonely firewatcher, who offers Nell and her grandfather a pile of ashes on which to rest. Out of the furnace of a factory, he creates a hearth. He tells her, "it's my memory, that fire, and shows me all my life. . . . Ever since I came to watch it; but there was a while between, and a very cold dreary while it was. It burnt all the time though, and roared and leaped when I came back, as it used to do in our play days. You may guess from looking at me what kind of child I was, but for all the difference between us I was a child, and when I saw you in the street to-night, you put me in mind of myself . . . and made me wish to bring you to the old fire. . . . Lie down again, poor child, lie down again." (*Curiosity Shop*, 420)

The firewatcher suggests the home she will learn to create out of precious little. He serves to remind us that in order to nurture ourselves as well as others, no matter how humbly, childhood memory must be accessible.

In *The Old Curiosity Shop*, childhood innocence rests here, in a heap of ashes near an old factory furnace—so illusory is the pastoral dream of the child safe in nature. Nell's pastoral vision begins in fantasy and ends where Dickens, at last, allows her to rest—in the graveyard of a peaceful church, decorated by the flowers of kindly gardeners and faithful mourners. This is not a typical *bildungsroman*; Little Nell's epiphanies do not inaugurate even the promise of a future. Dickens sentimentalizes her death, dragging it out, as she hovers, angelically, over the ending for many pages. But with it comes the possibility of redemption, if not for Little Nell (who does not need redemption), for her grandfather, whose mourning and eventual death are equally tedious. Dickens is at his worst in such funereal scenes. But in the many child deaths that occur in this novel—some out of illness, most out of poverty, Dickens foreshadows Nell's. And Nell herself prepares us for her death. She becomes a wise child, not only in the ways of the world, but spiritually. She finds peace in the cemetery, and takes her place in history,

in this old, silent place, among the stark figures on the tombs. . . . [S]he thought of the summer days and the bright spring-time that would come—of the rays of sun that would all in aslant upon the sleeping forms—of the leaves that would flutter at the window, and play in the glistening shadows on the pavement—of the songs of birds, and growth of buds and blossoms out of doors—of the sweet air, that would steal in. . . . What if the spot awakened thoughts of death! Die who would, it would still remain the same; these sights and sounds would still go on as happily as ever. It would be no pain to sleep amidst them. (*Curiosity Shop*, 494)

Once outside, she finds her place in pastoral:

Oh! The glory of the sudden burst of light; the freshness of the fields and woods, stretching away on every side and meeting the bright blue sky; the cattle grazing in the pasturage; . . . the children yet at their gambols down below—all, everything, so beautiful and happy. It was like passing from death to life; it was drawing nearer Heaven. (*Curiosity Shop*, 495–6)

Her acceptance of death is markedly different from the resistance of the aged adults around her. She understands that the sexton and his companions, the gravediggers here, who "dwelt upon the uncertainty of human life, seemed both in word and deed to deem themselves immortal. . . . [Nell understands also] "that by a good and merciful adjustment this must be human nature, and that the old sexton, with his plans for next summer, was but a type of all mankind" (*Curiosity Shop*, 493). So, while Nell is the tragic hero here, she does not see herself as such. This is not simply a gesture of martyrdom. It is a representation of Wordsworth's wise passivity and Blake's higher innocence, and, as such, Nell serves Dickens as a source of redemption.

Nell is Dickens's tragic protagonist of childhood, and hers is the tragic plot of the novel. But in *The Old Curiosity Shop* another source of redemption is the Marchioness, the hero of the comic plot. She is the shadow child of this novel; she lives in the basement of Sally and Sampson Brass, two of Quilp's stooges. From her position as underground spy, she learns the secrets that release the imprisoned Kit, that eventually put Quilp out of harm's way, and she redeems Dick Swiveller, the only psychologically dynamic character of this novel from fortune hunter to mentor. Dick finds this child starving under the stairs, where she is kept hostage by the Brasses. Most abused of orphans, she has no name, no history, no knowledge of any kind, except what she sees and hears through her peephole in the basement. Appalled by her conditions, Dick offers her the childhood of which she has been deprived. He nourishes her and teaches her to play, both of which she does with great passion and proficiency. He gives her the name of "Marchioness," to reverse her humblest origins, and then "Sophronia Sphinx," to honor her ingenuity, before sending her off to be educated. Eventually he marries her. But first, she saves him from a life-threatening illness. Most significant of all, she transforms him into a compassionate human being. To Dickens's credit, he never loses his eccentricities. For Dickens, it is the humblest people, replete with their idiosyncrasies, who shall inherit the earth.

*The Old Curiosity Shop* is a testament to childhood innocence. For Dickens childhood was sacred. He deplored its abuse and distortions. Pointing to dotage, he says,

> We call this a state of childishness, but it is the same poor hollow mockery of it, that death is of sleep. Where, in the dull eyes of doating men, are the laughing light and life of childhood, the gaiety that has known no check, the frankness that has felt no chill, the hope that has never withered, the joys that fade in blossoming? Where, in the sharp lineaments of rigid and unsightly death, is the calm beauty of slumber, telling of rest for the waking hours that are past, and the gentle hopes and loves for those which are to come? Lay death and sleep down, side by side, and say who shall find the two akin. Send forth the child and childish man together, and blush for the pride that libels our own old happy state, and gives its title to an ugly and distorted image. (*Curiosity Shop*, 146–7)

The novel does resolve its burning question. Although Nell dies, her spirit of childhood innocence is affirmed. Childhood, for Dickens, is a state of mind; it flourishes in the imaginations of adults as well, in those close to memory and the past, like the old woman who has been visiting the grave of her husband for fifty-five years. As an old woman she carries with her all the aspects of her life: as a young wife and as an old widow, she has moved through time, while her husband has stayed young in death. Nell is at first confused by the apparent discrepancy in their ages: " 'Were you his mother?' said the child. 'I was his wife, my dear,' " the old woman replies. Nell is astonished: "She was the wife of a young man of three-and-twenty!" (*Curiosity Shop*, 188). But she bears witness to the old woman's story:

> [S]he spoke of the dead man as if he had been her son or grandson, with a kind of pity for his youth, growing out of her own old age, and an exalting of his strength and manly beauty as compared with her own weakness and decay; and yet she spoke about him as her husband too, and thinking of herself in connexion with him, as she used to be and not as she was now, talked of their meeting in another world as if he were dead but yesterday, and she, separated from her former self, were thinking of that comely girl who seemed to have died with him. (*Curiosity Shop*, 188–9)

In this way, Nell comes to understand what Dickens so passionately believed—that childhood as a state of mind provides the potential for compassion and for understanding its inherent wisdom. Here we are not speaking of those stunted in childhood—the dwarfed and distorted Quilp or the infantile paralyzed grandfather. We are not speaking of those who abuse the charm of childhood, like Harold Skimpole in *Bleak House*. Even the imagination of Mr. Dick of *David Copperfied*, benignantly arrested in this state, contains an originality, a brilliance, even as it cannot complete a single one of its visions. For Dickens, childhood innocence is his guide and muse. It is the touchstone of all that is valuable in humanity, its very vitality. And in *The Old Curiosity Shop*, he speaks as its bard.

# 6

# The Antipastoral

The antipastoral constructs a landscape of fear, but unlike the dark pastoral, it is a rejection of the possibility of pastoral. It is defensive—sometimes an exploration of the denial of childhood fears and fears of children, sometimes a denial of the fear itself. It is about the dislocation of childhood, children severed from the world of adults, or the child part of the adult from a more acceptable adult self. It is an imaginative disconnection, a landscape of isolation. It may encompass the grotesque, as in the dark pastoral; however, it is approached indirectly and from a distance. Poetically, it relies on humor and irony. Its connection with childhood goes back to Lewis Carroll and Edward Lear and the world of nonsense they created.

In her extraordinary early study, *The Field of Nonsense*, Elizabeth Sewell developed a theory about nonsense poetry. She saw it as antithetical to the basic impetus of poetry, which is "only to connect."[1] Nonsense, literally non-sense, is about disconnection: from emotions and all that they encompass. Rather than the natural world, then, with its beauty, both benign and threatening, artifice is at the center of nonsense images. Food, objects, numbers, letters, nonsense words—these are the playthings of the nonsense poet. Although each of these can cluster around and evoke emotional responses, nonsense uses them almost as mathematical sets, as discrete units. Feeling is cut off, as when Alice's tears become rivers, evoking laughter at how she could "drown in her own tears." So that even as the fear is suggested it is avoided. Disturbing thoughts are expressed—feelings of anger, violence, sadness, profound existential discomfort. However disguised, distorted, and reimagined from a natural to unnatural terrain, they are funny and playful. The poetic stance is absurdist.

In *Alice's Adventures in Wonderland*, for example, Alice recites "You Are Old, Father William" to the Caterpillar, unaware of the disconnection between the characters, father and son, although she understands that " 'some of the words have got altered.' " The Caterpillar concurs, " 'It is wrong from beginning to end,' " and yet, such reversals—old father William standing on his head, turning " 'a back-somersault in at the door,' " or eating " 'the goose, with the bones and the beak' "—permit a reversal of expectations of familial manners. The hostility silenced under a dominant Victorian sense of order breaks through, so that a son who aggressively questions his father and battles between father and mother are permitted expression. The poem ends, not with connection and reconciliation, but rather with the father's antagonistic farewell: " 'I have answered three questions, and that is enough/ . . . Do you think I can listen all day to such stuff?/ Be off, or I'll kick you down stairs!' "

As liberating as gallows humor, a strain of gallows humor itself, nonsense poetry encourages such disconnection. In "The Walrus and the Carpenter," Carroll's hilarious poem from *Through the Looking Glass*, little innocent oysters are tricked into being eaten by this unlikely, more experienced couple. Blithely, they announce: " 'Now if you're ready, Oysters dear,/ We can begin to feed.'/ 'But not on us!' The Oysters cried,/ Turning a little blue./ 'After such kindness, that would be/ A dismal thing to do!'/'The night is fine,' the Walrus said./ 'Do you admire the view?' " While they "weep" for the oysters, we are told that "[w]ith sobs and tears he sorted out/ Those of the largest size." Finally, the Carpenter says, " 'O Oysters, . . . You've had a pleasant run!/ Shall we be trotting home again?'/ But answer came there none/ And this was scarcely odd, because/ They'd eaten every one." So the poem merrily concludes.

Carroll has many examples of emotional states transformed by disconnection into humorous ones. In an ode, a beautiful evening becomes "beautiful soup, soup of the evening" (*Looking Glass*); rather than a twinkling star, "a diamond in the sky," in his parody of the popular song, a twinkling bat is likened to "a tea tray in the sky" (*Wonderland*). Edward Lear's limericks also are based on such moments. In his longer poems, too, he straddles a delicate border, introducing emotions, happiness as well as fear—of falling, of paralysis, of disintegration, but controls their expression. "In Mr. and Mrs. Discobbolos,"[2] the nonsense words dispel continuity. Not quite words in themselves but, rather, syllables that suggest real words, they can appropriate some meaning through sound, but essentially function, as in much of Carroll's work, to resist meaning. Also there are constant intrusions of the last four letters of the alphabet, with which Mr. and/or Mrs. Discobbolos undercut each expression of feeling. As the couple climb to the top of a wall "to watch the sunset sky," and are said to be "as happy as happy could be," Mrs. Discobbolos says, " 'Oh! W! X! Y! Z!' " This nonsense expletive follows Mrs. Discobbolos's fear that, " 'We might never get down again!' " At the end of Part One of the poem, as Mr. and Mrs. Discobbolos together sing, " 'Far away from hurry and strife/ Here we will pass the rest of life,/ Ding a dong, ding dong, ding!'," the nonsense sounds sever feeling. The interjection of the alphabet series further undermines the liberation anthem they sing: " 'We want no knives nor forks nor chairs,/ No tables nor carpets nor household cares,/ From worry of life we've fled' "—from a kind of domestic tyranny, which becomes darker and more terminal in Part Two. After raising many children on "this ancient runcible wall," where the children "have never been at a ball,/ Nor have even seen a bazaar!'," which worries Mrs. Discobbolos, Mr. Discobbolos "lighted a match, and fired the train,/ And the mortified mountain echoed again/ To the sound of an awful fall!/ And all the Discobbolos family flew/ In thousands of bits to the sky so blue,/ And no one was left to have said,/ 'Oh! W! X! Y! Z!' "

In these poems, language, even utterance, disrupts the sense-making propensity of childhood. Instead, the literature that followed in this vein told a story of dislocation—the child as object, as plaything for adults, although, in some of these books, there is little play or any communication between adults and children. Often adults are depicted encased in a narcissism which makes them remote from each other and themselves, as well as from children. And in these stories, the child, like Alice, is left, essentially, on her own, to discover ways of controlling her unwelcoming environment.

## I. THE PICTURE BOOKS

### 1. *The Shrinking of Treehorn*

Florence Parry Heide's *Treehorn* series, which includes *The Shrinking of Treehorn*,[3] *Treehorn's Treasure*,[4] and *Treehorn's Wish*,[5] are stories of the emotional chaos of contemporary childhood. The disengaged and dysfunctional family story gets coherence from the single, grounded perspective of the child, Treehorn. *The Shrinking of Treehorn* is governed by the metaphor of Treehorn's psychological existence: he is shrinking. It begins, "The first thing he noticed was that he couldn't reach the shelf in his closet," and goes on to describe that his clothes are "all stretching or something," that he can't reach the table from his seat anymore. Treehorn's lucid and thoughtful observations are rendered all the more thoughtful as his parents seem completely oblivious to this state of affairs. Their denial, although disturbing, is also portrayed through humor:

"Sit up, dear," said Treehorn's mother.
"I *am* sitting up" said Treehorn. "It's just that I'm shrinking."
"What, dear?" asked his mother.
"I'm shrinking. Getting smaller," said Treehorn.
"If you want to pretend you're shrinking, that's all right," said Treehorn's mother,
"As long as you don't do it at the table."
"But I *am* shrinking," said Treehorn.

Figure 7. Illustration by Edward Gorey, from *The Shrinking of Treehorn* by Florence Parry Heide, 1971. By permission of Holiday House, Inc.

"Don't argue with your mother, Treehorn," said Treehorn's father.
"He does look a little smaller," said Treehorn's mother, looking at Treehorn.
    "Maybe he *is* shrinking."
"Nobody shrinks," said Treehorn's father.
"Well, I'm shrinking," said Treehorn. "Look at me."

At which point, they are depicted, in Edward Gorey's cool, elegant drawings, turning to see Treehorn's eyes barely above the edge of the table.

Treehorn's father looked at Treehorn.
"Why, you're shrinking," said Treehorn's father. "Look, Emily, Treehorn is shrinking. He's much smaller than he used to be."
"Oh, dear," said Treehorn's mother. "First it was the cake, and now it's this. Everything happens at once."
"I *thought* I was shrinking," said Treehorn, and he went into the den to turn on the television set.

In the illustration that follows, Treehorn is at the bottom of the page, lying on a dark spot of rug watching television. The many books in his parents' library are centered on the page, suggesting their significance in the family self-construction. This is a cultured family, one that takes pride in its "enlightenment." In the lower left, all we see of the parents are their legs, crossed. Supposedly they are watching television as well, but there is no connection between them and Treehorn. We hear their voices, worrying, " 'What will people say?' " and wondering, "if he's doing it on purpose. Just to be different.' " Treehorn's mother asks, " 'Why would he want to be different?' " revealing her conventionality, her utter incomprehension, enforcing our sense of Treehorn's isolation.

This is disconcerting enough. But when Treehorn ventures into the world outside, he is met with a similar lack of concern. When he asks for help reaching the mailbox to mail a letter, his friend Moshie says, " 'How come you can't mail it yourself, stupid?' " When Treehorn, in true childhood simplicity replies, " 'Because I'm shrinking,' " Moshie, with more direct hostility than the parents, offers: " 'That's a stupid thing to do. . . . You're *always* doing stupid things, but that's the *stupidest*.' "

The following scene with "his friend, the bus driver," one of the most hilarious in the book, underscores Treehorn's invisibility. " 'It's me, Treehorn,' " Treehorn says to the bus driver, who replies, " 'You do look like Treehorn, at that . . . [o]nly smaller. Treehorn isn't that little.' " Treehorn says,

"I am Treehorn. I'm just getting smaller. . . ."
"Nobody gets smaller," said the bus driver. "You must be Treehorn's kid brother. What's your name?"
"Treehorn," said Treehorn.
"First time I ever heard of a family naming two boys the same name," said the bus driver. "Guess they couldn't think of any other name, once they thought of Treehorn."
Treehorn said nothing.

School presents similar scenarios—the teacher who says, " 'We don't shrink in this class,' " and the principal who insists that he has "solved" Treehorn's problem by (not) listening to him: " 'Shrinking, eh?' said the Principal. 'Well, now, I'm sorry to hear that, Treehorn. You were right to come to me. That's what I'm here for. To guide. Not to punish, but to guide . . . all the members of my team. To solve all their problems.' " When Treehorn, again true to himself, answers, " 'But I don't have any problems . . . I'm just shrinking,' " the Principal insists that he's "right here . . . to help. . . . A team is only as good as its coach.' "

Further isolated from the world of narcissistic adults and cruel, ignorant children, Treehorn finds his own solution. It comes, as does Alice's, with discovering how to modulate size. It involves a game he keeps hidden under his bed, "The Big

Game for Kids To Grow On," which he decides, in the end, is a "pretty boring game."

The story concludes with Treehorn, ever persistent, pointing out his new and correct size. His mother prevails in her narcissism, as if she were capable of any other position: first, " 'Don't put your elbows on the table while you're eating, dear,' " and then, " 'It's a very nice size, I'm sure, and if I were you I wouldn't shrink anymore.' " The book ends with Treehorn turning green as he reaches to change channels on the television. He concludes, " 'I don't think I'll tell any-one . . . If I don't say anything, they won't notice' "—and, indeed, they don't. He is urged to comb his hair, as they are having company for dinner. The mother remains consistently self-absorbed and uncomprehending. Only Treehorn changes. Resigned to being unseen, he will probably, hopefully, learn to use his newfound sense of balance, as Alice does with the mushroom. And hopefully, those children in similar circumstances will turn one day and say, to themselves if not to the authorities of their lives, as Alice does at the end of *Wonderland*: " 'Who cares for you? You're nothing but a pack of cards.' " In the meantime, I hope the expression of such experience, removed from and unacknowledged as the real world by Gorey's cartoonlike drawings, can offer some release through humor. And if children do experience the adults around them as monstrously ego-tistical, it might be helpful to them to know that it is not their fault, and that they are not the only ones who feel that way.

Joseph Zornado, in *Inventing the Child: Culture, Ideology, and the Story of Childhood*, writes about what he calls "detachment parenting," so named in contrast to attachment theory of John Bowlby and those who followed, which places pri-mary value on "strong affectional bonds to a particular other."[6] Detachment parent-ing is "a style of child-rearing . . . [which] encourages the child to repress his own emotional needs in favor of the adult who 'knows better' . . . [and] ignores the rich tapestry of the child's emotional life" (Zornado, 187). Zornado further explains:

> the *emotional reasons* behind the child's behavior are invisible to the parent who is blind to his or her own emotional condition. Attachment parenting, on the other hand, assumes there is a reason for the child's emotional condition, and when the parents discover their own emotional reality, they can then bear witness to the child's emotional reality . . . [which will restore] an emotional balance again. (Zor-nado, 187)

This reconciliation and harmony is exactly what the anti-pastoral resists. Its hero, the "child of detachment," tells his or her story "of adult detachment, aban-donment, and neglect as child-rearing," as Sendak said about his own work (quoted in Zornado, 174). And because we are dealing with child heroes, the story will often be framed in fantasy, removed through the suggestion of illustration, the landscape distorted into some unrecognizable shape, and, most often, dis-tanced through humor. This perspective will shift somewhat when we discuss *Lolita* and *The Fifth Child*, where the narrator is clearly an adult. But for this child to survive he must create an alternative world, in itself an act of discovery. He often develops a rich interiority to provide for the impoverished sense of coherence of his external world.

## 2. *The Zabajaba Jungle*

William Steig's work for children depicts the child-self in the act of discovery. His stories are about the evolution of the self. Unlike his more pastoral stories, such as *The Amazing Bone*, which celebrates the "unarmored" life of childhood, his antipastoral stories restore to the child his eroding sense of empowerment. They speak about inner voices or the internalized drama of childhood at various stages of development. *The Zabajaba Jungle*[7] introduces such a landscape. Distinction and differentiation, a primary development task or rather process of childhood, is complex and somewhat chaotic in this non-sense jungle, where the characters are drawn from the world of humans (the child, Leonard, and his family), the plant world (the flora), and the animal world (the fauna). Here Steig grapples with the role of the unconscious to reflect (and to solve) the child/hero's psychological conflicts along the evolutionary road toward human consciousness. Leonard journeys into the jungle, the uncivilized, instinctual world of the unconscious, its potential danger offset by its nonsensical name. Here, as in most antipastoral literature, distance can be maintained through humor; terror can be removed so we may enter the jungle world more freely.

Leonard enters it defensively. His sharp knife offers protection in the world, "where it is said, no human being has ever penetrated." The noisiness of the jungle, with its "squawking birds and raucous insects," reflects the chaos of the antipastoral landscape. It is a threatening, somewhat paranoid vision of the universe of "staring" birds and "grop[ing]" plants, but he can, Steig assures him, survive it. Here he rescues a butterfly—the metamorphic creature that suggests his own state of psychic flux—from the "jaws of a flower." And here he enters the "gaping mouth of a petrified monster," penetrating deeper and deeper into the "belly" of the unconscious, suggesting the taboo of entering the mother. Steig's imagery also expresses the early oral world of incorporation.

Each stage of psychological development is depicted as Leonard moves through the mouth and through the digestive track, the belly, the intestines, the cloaca—a kind of rebirth taking place at each stage. And in this ancient cave, Leonard discovers "strange writing on the wall," a sign that others were here before him. Language belongs to the world of civilization, the world of the many as opposed to the one, where experience can be organized into patterns and recognized. Words, representations of things, help to universalize the earliest preoedipal strivings of fear and desire suggested by the images of mouth and cave. Leonard can't read the message—he is not old enough, developed enough to shape his experience into abstraction, to recognize its universality—but he is calmed by the suggestion that his journey is not unprecedented.

His fears somewhat allayed, Leonard falls into a deep sleep, floating above the jungle in a hammock, an open but sheltering container, where he awakens to the hissing of snakes beneath. Here are the dangers of the phallic/male world, and the movement from the vegetable to the animal world depicts the awakening of more bestial instincts that surface from the world of sleep. He is carried to the safety of a glade of flowers by the butterfly he rescued earlier. He is not yet ready to confront the unconscious fears of the father. Instead he hears a voice that tells him to drink the nectar of the flower; the nurturing he will receive here will enable his further entry into the jungle, although the movement will be, paradoxically, closer and closer toward civilization.

Leonard's fledgling consciousness is reflected in the voice of Flora, an ungainly bird—tentative, shy, awkward. This voice appears in many of Steig's children's stories at moments of extreme danger, where the child-hero is about to perish from the evil forces that have pursued him throughout the journey. In *The Amazing Bone*, the bone suddenly and for no apparent reason speaks magical jibberish, which shrinks the fox to the size of a mouse. Here Flora utters some untranslatable "magic" words, which are not understood, even by the hero, but that turn the situation around and save Leonard's life. The voice of intuition here is that of a bird, which suggests a nonverbal spirituality. The regenerative power of plants and flowers is also evoked in her name. Leonard says of the nectar Flora offers him, "Somehow he always knew this special sweetness existed." Like the inner voices of dreams, it tells you what you always knew, but didn't know you knew. Part of any creative journey is learning to trust the intuitive. And this creative impulse is deeply connected with the spontaneity of childhood. For Steig, understanding or analysis comes later.

Leonard is carried from the oral stage by mandrills "with blue behinds," a suggestion that he has moved from the oral to the anal stage, into civilization, the world of rules, and the world of the father. Most pressing now are issues of autonomy. He is brought into the jungle court before three judges, each of whom bears the head of one threatening creature of each species: the bird has a dangerous beak, the mammal has a rat's head, and the reptile bears a snake's head. Together they challenge him: " 'Who told you you could drink?' " and " 'Who do you think you are?' " They are the voices of law and order, the restrictive forces in society. Leonard's desire to return to the mother's body, to reclaim desire, sensuality, and creativity repressed in civilized society, is depicted in his attempt to climb into "the bowl" of the yellow flower, the sexual female symbol, where he tasted "the special sweetness." The flower "suddenly rising" suggested Leonard's sexual desire that carried him into the center of the jungle, where he now learns about taboos—where his spirit is in danger of annihilation. However, the inner voice of Flora, the embodiment of his own imaginative powers, helps him escape the forces of repression. Flora, less shy and tentative here, urges: " 'Show them who you are. Do your stuff.' "

Figure 8. Illustration from *The Zabajaba Jungle* by William Steig, 1987. By permission of Farrar, Straus, & Giroux, LLC.

What Leonard creates, what he didn't know he knew how to use, is awesome— a display of fireworks that combines the powers of the primitive and the inventions of civilization. By dazzling his opponents, he escapes, alone, to the end of the jungle, where he finds his parents in an enormous glass bottle. His father is reading the newspaper, embroiled in words, and in the male external world of social order. His mother is knitting, the traditional female associated with connection, creativity, and domesticity. True "detachment" parents, they do not notice his attempts to capture their attention. They suggest, in their self-enclosed self-absorption, the child's worst fears about venturing out on his own: that upon his return, he will be forgotten and closed off from his family by his new knowledge. Leonard has to break through by smashing the bottle with a rock. Reentry in this antipastoral world requires a violence, but now Leonard becomes their guide. They ask: " 'Where are we?' " and " 'How do we get out?' " Leonard, the hero of his own story, says, " 'Follow me.' "

### 3. *Higglety Pigglety Pop! or There Must Be More To Life*

The survival of the spirit of creativity in childhood is clearly the dominant issue of the literature of childhood. It tells the story of how we, as human beings, evolve creatively, how we survive the materialism and repression of adulthood, with the intuitive faculty of childhood intact. This has long been a driving concern in the work of Maurice Sendak as well. Most prominent in *Higglety Pigglety Pop! or There Must Be More To Life*,[8] Sendak brilliantly depicts the necessity of imaginative expression associated with childhood, which for him is as essential if not as primal as the desire for food. His book opens with a black-and-white cross-hatching of Jennie, its dog hero, seated at table, her bowl and vitamins before her. Behind her, on the wall, is a framed picture of the Mona Lisa, smiling mysteriously. This illustration facing the title page suggests two aspects of our instinctual and primal nature—oral aggression and creativity, first located and exemplified in the child.

The story begins with an existential quest for meaning, a search for what might lie beyond "a place of comfort," or, as Sendak proposes, "There must be more to life than having everything." In dialogue with a plant about the meaning of life, Jennie, in true animal fashion, nibbles at the plant until, by the end of the chapter, "her mouth full of leaves . . . snapping off the stem and blossom," she tells the plant, " 'I want something I do not have. There must be more to life than having everything!' " Sendak ends this first chapter.

The plant had nothing to say.
It had nothing left to say it with. (*Higglety*, 5)

Without the sentimentality of the enabling and ennobled tree/mother of Shel Silverstein's *The Giving Tree*, in which the boy takes everything from the tree until it is a stump on which he sits, Sendak portrays Jennie's gluttony as natural—she is after all a dog. Furthermore, Sendak associates her voracious eating with the emptiness of the comfortable life. But in her innocence/ignorance, Jennie has no idea how to fill that need. She continues to eat her way through the world without consciousness, although Sendak's humor provides the sophistication Jennie herself lacks. For example, Jennie meets a pig wearing a sandwich board, advertising the position of "Leading Lady for The World Mother Goose Theatre!" There are many puns, also associated with the antipastoral, where language in its literal and doubling propensity, provides humor. The pig with the sandwich board is giving away free sandwiches. To apply for the job advertised, you need experience; you need to call EX 1-1212, so Jennie yells, " 'EX 1-1212.' " The pig immediately turns around and says, " 'You called?' " (*Higglety*, 7–8).

Jennie's journey is from innocence to experience, but in a reversal here of the pastoral vision, this is a catalogue of food: "anchovy, tomato and egg on toast . . . liverwurst and onion on white bread . . . turkey, bacon and mayonnaise, salami [her favorite]" sandwiches—tasty, civilized food which would never be served to a dog. Thus, we are placed in the world of humans, children, sheltered by "having everything." As Jennie continues to eat: "raspberry yogurt . . . farmer cheese . . . a pint bottle of milk . . . suck[ing] the insides out of half a dozen eggs"—everything in the milk wagon with which she catches a ride, she takes on her first job as Nurse and comes upon her first task: "to make Baby eat" (*Higglety*, 13). Like Hansel and Gretel, she is told that if she fails, she will become food for the lion kept locked in the basement of "the big white house." Under the surface of comfort and domesticity, Sendak warns us, lies a bestiality.

As Jennie meets the parlor maid, she is greeted with, " 'You must be Baby's new nurse,' " to which Jennie responds, " 'I'm certainly not nurse's new baby' " (*Higglety*, 17). Like the punning so basic to nonsense poetry and much of children's literature, this repartée suggests a playful as well as disconnecting principle of language. Puns are part of the game of language play, here meant to confuse rather than to convey message. This distancing quality of language permits Sendak to explore the most subversive aspects of child-rearing. In the big, white house there is a Baby who "used to [have a name], but everyone's forgotten what it is,' " including her mother and father, who are "at the Castle Yonder," Jennie is told. She continues to consume pancakes, syrup, coffee. Even the tall yellow windows "looked buttery in the morning light" to her. As she devours Baby's entire breakfast, she and Baby engage in battle. In opposition to everything Jennie suggests, Baby uproariously asserts: " 'NO YUM! . . . NO EAT! NO GROW! SHOUT! NO BITE! NO EAT!' " (*Higglety*, 24–5). Obviously, Baby's refusal of nourishment, her aggression turned inward as well as outward, is the result of her parents in Castle Yonder who tell Jennie when she calls EX 1-1212, that " 'what with hustling and bustling we forgot our old address and phone number and just didn't know how to get in touch' " (*Higglety*, 28). For the first time, Jennie moves beyond selfishness and self-absorption. She answers, " 'I don't know Hustling or Bustling . . . but whoever they are, they made you forget Baby too' " (*Higglety*, 28). This is a burlesque of child neglect; Baby's parents ask Jennie to send her by lion—the one in the cellar who " 'has eaten up six nurses and I don't know how many babies' " (*Higglety*, 29). Jennie becomes Baby's protector as her journey takes her deeper and deeper into the cellar, where she is confronted with the lion, even to the point of self sacrifice, when nothing will deter the lion from his desire to eat Baby. It is not entirely clear what happens from here. Sendak tells us, "There was only one thing left to do. Jennie sighs and sticks her head into the lion's mouth. 'Please eat me. I need the experience anyway. Otherwise The World Mother Goose Theatre might never—' " (*Higglety*, 36). On the one hand, it seems that the lion is stopped dead in his tracks because Jennie has "guessed" Baby's name and, therefore, the lion cannot eat Baby. On the other hand, it reads, "For a moment [the lion] crouched silently, then leaped high into the night" (*Higglety*, 37). Jennie implores, " 'Wait! Don't eat Baby!' " and receives no answer. At the chapter's end, Jennie "looked up at the sky. The stars were shining. The moon was full" (*Higglety*, 37). Somehow Jennie now has nothing, "nowhere to sleep and nothing to eat," and "beneath an ash tree, her nose between her paws," she sighs: " 'There must be more to life than having nothing' " (*Higglety*, 39). In a dialogue echoing that with the plant, Jennie asks the ash tree why it is complaining when it has everything—" 'a place to live, a very broad top, friends all around, and surely someone loves you' " (*Higglety*, 40). The chapter ends with Jennie buried in leaves.

In an unpublished interview with Sendak, he shocked me when he said that Jennie died at this point and that the rest of the book is her dream, her vision of heaven. Chapters 8 and 9 are framed in a liminality that suggests a continuation of Jennie's dream. We are never exactly told that she died, or that she awoke from her dream of the lion saying, " 'Please eat me up, there's nothing more to life' " (*Higglety*, 43). We see that Jennie is reunited with the other characters of her journey— the cat/milkman, the pig of the sandwich board, and Rhoda, the parlor nurse—who are all players in The World Mother Good Theatre. She is welcomed because she " 'stuck [her] head in the lion's mouth. . . . That was an experience' " (*Higglety*, 46).

The journey from innocence to experience in this story involves leaving the comfort of familiarity and of "having everything." It involves entering the chaos of "having nothing"—a movement beyond the eat-or-be-eaten stage of immediate gratification and oral aggression. The theater group is an inclusive community of artists. Even Baby, grown "big and fat," has joined the company. They perform the nursery rhyme "Higglety Pigglety Pop!"—the sense of which is elusive, hovering around eating, as Jennie is shown eating a mop. But, essentially, like most nursery rhymes, it is nonsensical. It is preceded by a wordless double-page spread, a cross-hatched moonscape of Castle Yonder. In the lower left-hand corner under a tree is a small burial plot. Jennie's grave? The ambiguity of the story, which probably goes unnoticed by children, seems underscored here for adult readers. It creates a hiatus, a silence after which words and images can come together in a unified vision. After briefly setting the stage, twelve pages of stage sets enact the "Higglety Pigglety Pop" rhyme in which all the characters, including the lion, appear. Words, or utterances, which comprise most of the rhyme, are incorporated into the illustrations, a departure from the first two-thirds of the story. The journey to creativity can only develop following "experience," for which, Sendak suggests, one must put one's head in the very jaws of danger. Up to that point, image is severed from text. To integrate the primal visualization and its verbal representation, one must have journeyed to Castle Yonder, to the end of the known world. This is a kind of death, an end to innocence, to instant gratification, and a beginning of artistic innovation—rendered here as theater.

The epilogue returns us to the quotidian world. On the left-hand side of the page is a picture of Jennie holding a map framed in a circle, and on the right-hand side, a conclusion that reads: "Now Jennie has everything." She is the "finest leading lady The World Mother Goose Theatre ever had." She writes to her "old master" informing him of her new life, which involves "eat[ing] a mop . . . of salami . . . [her] favorite." She says that although she can't locate Castle Yonder, suggesting its fantasy status, if he ever "come[s] this way, look for me" (*Higglety*, 69). However Sendak resists being pinned down to one interpretation, one landscape, or one genre, he asserts, playfully and with an accompanying seriousness, the importance of creativity and its kinship with childhood.

## II. THE ADULT NARRATIVES

### 1. *Lolita*

In a sense, we are all crashing to our death from the top story of our birth
to the flat stones of the churchyard and wondering with an immortal Alice in
Wonderland at the patterns of the passing wall. This capacity to wonder at
trifles . . . these asides of the spirit . . . are the highest forms of consciousness.

NABOKOV, *LECTURES ON LITERATURE*[9]

Carroll's *Alice's Adventures in Wonderland* deeply affected Nabokov. In 1923, he became its Russian translator. In *Lolita*,[10] he constructs a twentieth-century, self-reflexive narrative about the longing that informed Carroll's *Alice* stories. Nabokov had the distance that Carroll artificially, though brilliantly, created. *Lolita* is an adult vision of that longing for the ephemeral, eroticized and explored through a madman's confession. In the *Alice* stories, Carroll's desire is buried in the buoyant, aggressive humor of the questioning child. Nabokov's humor, heavily ironic and parodic, is constructed out of that impossible passion which remained unspeakable for Carroll. And the landscape that contains such desire is, inherently, unnatural and antipastoral. The "pubescent park . . . [the] mossy garden" of Humbert's desire is as impossible a terrain to maintain as the prepubescence of early adolescence. "Let them play around me forever. Never grow up" (*Lolita*, 21), he exclaims. Nabokov draws parallels between the distorted sexuality of Humbert Humbert and the ugliness of the world he sees—a landscape of suburban America, motels and tourist landmarks, and youth-hungry popular culture. His quest for forbidden desire is, Nabokov suggests, a convoluted perversion of a search for newness, for original observation and perspective, and, in this way, for innocence. Humbert becomes frozen in a moment of pre-sexual sexuality, of nymphet obsession. He reports that at the age of fourteen, he fell in love with fourteen-year-old "Annabel Lee"; as he was about to consummate his desire, they were discovered and she died soon after of typhus. Thereafter, Humbert goes from the highly idealized desire of *coitus interruptus* to the "sanitary relations with women [in which] I was practical, ironical and brisk" (*Lolita*, 15). By placing nine- to fourteen-year-old girls in a mythic realm, he believed he could "reveal their true nature which is not human, but nymphic (that is, demonic)" (*Lolita*, 16), and their "elusive, shifty, soul-shattering charm" (*Lolita*, 17). The pedophile's projection images girls as either the exquisite "downy limb" of nymphic enchantment or the grotesque, after-image of the child-prostitute. He does not recognize the "monstrously plumb, sallow, repulsively plain girl of at least fifteen with red-ribboned thick black braids who sat on a chair perfunctorily nursing a bald doll" (*Lolita*, 24)—an emblem of the ruination of childhood which prefigures the ravaging of Lolita by Humbert, her mother, and her social world.

What profoundly moved both Carroll and Nabokov was innocence with its power to see the world with fresh eyes. Nabokov wrote in his autobiography, *Speak, Memory*, of his infant son's eyes,

> which seemed still to retain the shadows [they] had absorbed of ancient, fabulous forests . . . where, in some dappled depth, man's mind had been born . . . an infant's first journey into the next dimension the newly established nexus between eye and reachable object . . . the closest reproduction of the mind's birth . . . the stab of wonder that accompanies the precise moment when, gazing at a tangle of twigs and leaves, one suddenly realizes that what had seemed a natural component of that tangle is a marvelously disguised insect or bird. (quoted in *Lolita*, 297–8)

This wonder, this microcosmic vision that hints at the largeness of all creation is precisely what Humbert has lost. And obviously, tragically, that is what he has stolen from the child, Dolly Haze, his love object, Lolita, in depriving her of her childhood. Toward the end of his confession, Humbert concludes, on a serious note,

> We had been everywhere. We had really seen nothing. And I catch myself thinking today that our long journey had only defiled with a sinuous trail of slime the lovely, trustful, dreamy, enormous country that by then, in restrospect, was no more to us than a collection of dog-eared maps, ruined tour books, old tires, and her sobs in the night—every night, every night—the moment I feigned sleep. (*Lolita*, 175–6)

Lolita is the verdant landscape he violates.

Adult erotic longing affixed to girls in preadolescence, a liminal state between childhood and womanhood, represents, in fact, ultimate liminality, where desire is perpetuated by its inherent suspension. So that, even though Humbert and Lolita technically, as he notes, become lovers, Humbert can never freely or reciprocally love or be loved; he can only be her lover by keeping her captive.

He very quickly becomes repulsive to his "partner," his love-making inevitably an unending series of submissions that involve repeated threats he refers to as "the reformatory threat." He succeeds, as he admits, in "terrorizing Lo," with laws

"relating to dependent, neglected, incorrigible and delinquent children . . . of those admirable girls' protectories where you knit things, and sing hymns, and have rancid pancakes on Sundays . . . where you will be analyzed and institutionalized . . . with thirty-nine other dopes in a dirty dormitory . . . under the supervision of hideous matrons. . . . Don't you think that under the circumstances Dolores Haze had better stick to her old man?" (*Lolita*, 151)

Those circumstances include the newly orphaned state of this child and her isolation from everything familiar in her childhood.

Even though technically Lolita is not a virgin when she, as he sees it, "seduces" him, he sets the stage for the play in which he, the aging pervert, is cast as Adam, "helpless . . . miraged in his apple orchard" (*Lolita*, 71), she as Eve, chucking "the core of her abolished apple" (*Lolita*, 59–60). Humbert is unconscious of, oblivious to what Nabokov so deeply understood: that childhood sexuality, no matter how far it goes, is different enough in degree to render it different from adult sexuality in kind. Humbert mechanically reports,

She saw the stark act merely as part of a youngster's furtive world, unknown to adults. What adults did for purposes of procreation was no business of hers. My life was handled by little Lo in an energetic, matter-of-fact manner as if it were an insensate gadget unconnected with me. While eager to impress me with the world of tough kids, she was not quite prepared for certain discrepancies between a kid's life and mine. (*Lolita*, 134)

He goes on to say, "I am not concerned with so-called 'sex' at all. Anybody can imagine those elements of animality. A greater endeavor lures me on: to fix once for all the perilous magic of nymphets" (*Lolita*, 134).

Humbert's desire is, by its very nature, insatiable. It will need to be fed, beyond Lolita, for certainly, as Nabokov points out, as Humbert himself acknowledges, Lolita will imminently become a woman. Thus, Humbert constructs a fantasy of an infinite series of nymphets, in which a daughter begot by him and Lolita takes over where Lolita, as adult woman, leaves off. He imagines marrying Lolita, but then worries that

I would have to get rid somehow of a difficult adolescent whose magic nymphage had evaporated . . . that with patience and luck I might have her produce eventually a nymphet with my blood in her exquisite veins, a Lolita the Second, who would be

eight or nine around 1960, when . . . [in] the telescope of my mind, or un-
mind . . . bizarre, tender, salivating Dr. Humbert, practicing on supremely lovely
Lolita the Third the art of being a grandad. (*Lolita*, 174)

Sexuality, or rather adult sexuality, is exactly what Humbert finds repulsive.
The sexuality of his first wife, whom he married only to protect him from acting
on his nymphet obsession, is, metaphorically, a "bleached curl reveal[ing] its
melanic root; the down turned to prickles on a shaved shin; the mobile moist
mouth, no matter how I stuff it with love, disclosed ignominiously its resemblance
to the corresponding part in a treasured portrait of her toadlike dead
mama. . . . [I]nstead of a pale little gutter girl, Humbert Humbert had on his hands
a large, puffy, short-legged, big-breasted and practically brainless *baba*" (*Lolita*,
26). He refers to his second wife, Lolita's mother Charlotte, as "she of the noble
nipple and massive thigh" (*Lolita*, 76), whom he can only tolerate in bed by imagining her, as he "bayed through the undergrowth of dark decaying forests" (*Lolita*,
77), as Lolita.

One of the challenges of interpreting *Lolita* has to do with tone. I believe
Nabokov is quite serious in his treatment of pedophilia; he is also outrageously
funny. Many critics have written about the parodic and satiric elements of his
humor.[11] What strikes me is his use of the antipastoral mode, in which humor is a
distancing device to foray into such dark material. Iconoclastic and experimental,
Nabokov engages his readers in the intimate details of such taboos. The particulars
are not sexually exploitive but, rather, approximate the interiority of the madman/
pedophile. To do this, Nabokov needed to engage a first-person narrative of a
sharply observant, articulate, acutely self-reflexive narrator. So that, while Charlotte
is pathetic, for example, Humbert's irritation with her generates broad, semifarcical
humor. It is hilarious to watch Charlotte, as viewed by Humbert, "her cheek propped
on her fist . . . star[ing] at me with intolerable tenderness as I consumed my ham and
eggs. Humbert's face might twitch with neuralgia, but in her eyes it vied in beauty
and animation with the sun and shadows of leaves rippling on the white refrigerator"
(*Lolita*, 77). Similarly, Humbert describes "Lolita with her curved spine to Humbert,
Humbert resting his head on his hand and burning with desire and dyspepsia"
(*Lolita*, 130). Not only is the position of the gazer and the object of desire parallel in
these two scenes, but they both liken romantic desire to a bodily function or disease.
Neuralgia and dyspepsia undercut the heightened moments of these obsessed lovers.
Along with others, Humbert is the object of his own satire and self-mockery, which
are a great source of humor throughout the book. Aware of the rapacious aspects of
his desire, Humbert is burlesquely comic, when Nabokov extends this posture to his
appraising Lolita as a vulture would his prey. He declares, "My only grudge against
nature was that I could not turn my Lolita inside out and apply voracious lips to her
young matrix, her unknown heart, her nacreous liver, the sea-grapes of her lungs,
her comely twin kidneys" (*Lolita*, 165). Humor also accentuates the incongruity of

the pair. Humbert attests that with Lolita on his lap in "his massive nakedness [she was] a typical kid picking her nose while engrossed in the later section of a newspaper, as indifferent to my ecstasy as if it were something she sat on, a shoe, a doll, the handle of a tennis racket . . ." (*Lolita*, 165).

The antipastoral creates and sustains humor by combining the uncomfortable emotion with the inanimate, often with the grotesque. At times the disparate nature of the inflated emotion juxtaposed with the thingness of its object—its lack of animation, its discrete nature—creates a dialogue between the two inherently incongruous modes. In *Lolita*, the unnatural nature of the pair produces Bakhtinian dialogic voices.[12] Since the narrative is only Humbert's, however, it is dialogical only through a single perspective. Narcissistic as always, Humbert places Lo's voice, her perspective, in parenthesis. As he describes the landscape, a jarring combination of pristine beauty defiled by other natural activity, including decay, Lo's detached remarks further undercut his litany. He reports from his travelogue:

> A patch of beautifully eroded clay; and yucca blossoms, so pure, so waxy, but lousy with creeping white flies. Independence, Missouri, the starting point of the Old Oregon Trail; and Abilene, Kansas, the home of the Wild Bill Something Rodeo. Distant mountains. Near mountains. More mountains; bluish beauties never attainable, or ever turning into inhabited hill after hill; south-eastern ranges, altitudinal failures as alps go; heart and sky-piercing snow-veined gray colossi of stone, relentless peaks appearing from nowhere at a turn of the highway . . . pink and lilac formations, Pharaonic, phallic, "too prehistoric for words" (blasé Lo). . . . Our twentieth Hell's Canyon. Our fiftieth Gateway to something or other *fide* that tour book. . . . A tick in my groin. . . . A hazy blue view beyond railings on a mountain pass, and the backs of a family enjoying it (with Lo, in a hot, happy, wild, intense, hopeful, hopeless whisper—"Look, the McCrystals please, let's talk to them, please"). (*Lolita*, 156–8)

The directness and spontaneity of the child surface in the various scenes as counterpoint to Humbert's inflated oratory. In opposition to his coyness about their love-making, for example, she says with sarcasm and impatience: " 'You talk like a book, *Dad*' " (*Lolita*, 114). " '*Don't* do that. . . . Don't drool on me. You dirty man' " (*Lolita*, 115). " 'Are we to sleep in *one* room? . . . The word is incest' " (*Lolita*, 119). " 'Can you remember,' she said, 'what was the name of the hotel, *you* know . . . the hotel where you raped me. Okay, skip it' " (*Lolita*, 202). He reports,

> Sometimes . . . while Lolita would be haphazardly preparing her homework, sucking a pencil, lolling sideways in an easy chair with both legs over its arm, I would shed all my pedagogic restraint, dismiss all our quarrels, forget all my masculine pride—and literally crawl on my knees to your chair, my Lolita! You would give me one look—a gray furry question mark of a look: "Oh no, not again" (incredulity, exasperation); for you never deigned to believe that I could, without any specific

designs, ever crave to bury my face in your plaid skirt, my darling! The fragility of those bare arms of yours—how I longed to enfold them, all your four limpid lovely limbs, a folded colt, and take your head between my unworthy hands ... and— "Pulease, leave me alone, will you," you would say, "for Christ's sake leave me alone." (*Lolita*, 192–3)

Nabokov cleverly links the larger natural world with Humbert's reductive concerns all through their journey, so that "somber Yellowstone Park and its colored hot springs, baby geysers, rainbows of bubbling mud" are merely symbols of his passion. "A herd of antelopes in a wildlife refuge [and] [o]ur hundredth cavern" are noted along with the price—"adults one dollar, Lolita fifty cents." His "rows, minor and major" with Lolita mark their journey. No matter where, they are all reduced to an indistinguishable catalogue of places of domestic combat:

The biggest ones we had took place: at Lacework Cabins, Virginia; on Park Avenue, Little Rock, near a school; on Milner Pass, 10,759 feet high, in Colorado; at the corner of Seventh Street and Central Avenue in Phoenix, Arizona; on Third Street Los Angeles, because the tickets to some studio or other were sold out; at a motel called Poplar Shade in Utah, where six pubescent trees were scarcely taller than my Lolita, and where she asked, *a propos de rien*, how long did I think we were going to live in stuffy cabins, doing filthy things together and never behaving like ordinary people? (*Lolita*, 158)

No matter how the subject of child abuse is presented, an important question remains: What prepares Lo for this relationship—for her trying out her nubile sexuality on her stepfather? Lolita is introduced to a world of abuse by her vicious mother; she has already lost her father—(this is as early a glimpse of her life as Nabokov allows us). Humbert captures Charlotte's particular crassness and cruelty toward her daughter in her fervent quest to get rid of her. He reports an "inventory" of her child's personality in which she underlined "the following epithets": "aggressive, boisterous, critical, distrustful, impatient, irritable, inquisitive, listless, negativistic (underlined twice) and obstinate. She had ignored the thirty remaining adjectives, among which were cheerful, co-operative, energetic, and so forth" (*Lolita*, 81). She refers to her as "[t]he dumb child" and clearly resents any attention Humbert pays to her. Charlotte, as a product of the "soap operas, psychoanalysis and cheap novelettes" (*Lolita*, 80) of her culture, further infects her daughter. Both fall for Humbert's suave, European glamour. And the culture is persistently pernicious for young girls. Humbert tells us that Lolita "believed, with a kind of celestial trust, any advertisement or advice that appeared in *Movie Love* or *Screenland*. ... If some café sign proclaimed Icecold Drinks, she was automatically stirred, although all drinks everywhere were ice-cold. She it was to whom ads were dedicated: the ideal consumer, the subject and object of every foul poster" (*Lolita*, 148).

Institutions for girls also come under scrutiny through the double perspective where Humbert is joined by Nabokov. The camp to which Lolita is sent is characterized by "some gaudy moth or butterfly, still alive, safely pinned to the wall" (*Lolita*, 110). Butterflies, those symbols of transformation, are used in *Lolita* to suggest various states of arrested growth, of unnatural stasis. (For example, late in the novel, Humbert notices the "pale moths" that have been "siphoned out of the night by my headlights" (*Lolita*, 293)—as he has siphoned Lo out of her childhood.) The Beardsley School for girls, the expensive day school to where she is sent, focuses, as the headmistress asserts, on "the four D's: Dramatics, Dance, Debating and Dating'" (*Lolita*, 177). Headmistress Pratt, who refers to Dolores Haze alternatively as "Dorothy Humbird" and "Dorothy Hummerson," to Humbert Humbert as "Dr. Humberg and Dr. Hummer" during one interview, reenforces the haze through which people are viewed in the novel, interchangeably, indiscriminately. The names of the characters similarly resonate: Humbert Humbert is the humbug, doubly, self-reflexively; Dolly Haze, seen through the haze of his desire and the erotic projections of American culture, is reduced to an automaton, an empty and outer-directed doll. And her real name, Dolores, by which she is never called, is lost, its meaning, "sorrow," denied.

At the school, as well, the headmistress' attitude toward young girls is reminiscent of Humbert's disease metaphors. Pratt informs him that, " 'To put it briefly, while adopting certain teaching techniques, we are more interested in communication than in composition. . . . We are still groping perhaps, but we grope intelligently, like a gynecologist feeling a tumor'" (*Lolita*, 177). About Dolly, she says, " 'She is still shuttling . . . between the anal and genital zones of development. . . . All I mean is that biologic and psychologic drives . . . are not fused in Dolly, do not fall so to speak into a—into a rounded pattern.' Her hands held for a moment an invisible melon" (*Lolita*, 194). And the school play, "The Hunted Enchanters," for which Dolly was "a perfect little nymph in the try-out" (*Lolita*, 196), is another permutation on the seediness of Humbert's "love," consummated at The Enchanted Hunters hotel. Nabokov extends the spoof on adulthood to Humbert's double, the famous playwright Clare Quilty. Quilty, with whom Dolly escapes, who becomes Lolita/Dolly's lover, and with whom Humbert is obsessed and whom he eventually murders, is known for his plays, *The Little Nymph* and *Fatherly Love*. Of course, Humbert fails to recognize the projective nature of romantic obsession. As the gazer, who projects a nexus of associations onto the object of his gaze, he protects this skewed vision and his self-image as well by a further series of projections. As a projection of Humbert's guilt, Quilty is the pervert, the exploiter of young girls, a dissociated part of Humbert to whom he addresses this poem:

Because you took advantage of my inner
essential innocence

because you cheated me—
Because you cheated me of my redemption
because you took
her at the age when lads
play with erector sets . . .
A little downy girl still wearing poppies
still eating popcorn in the colored gloom . . .
Because of all you did
because of all I did not
you have to die. (*Lolita*, 300)

During the murder scene, Quilty sweeps by Humbert in a purple bathrobe, "very like the one I had" (*Lolita*, 294), Humbert notices. As Quilty and Humbert roll over the floor "in each other's arms like two helpless children," Humbert reports, "He was naked and goatish under his robe, and I felt suffocated as he rolled over me. I rolled over him. We rolled over me. They rolled over him. We rolled over us" (*Lolita*, 299). They form one solipsistic creature. When he accuses Quilty of raping Dolly Haze, Quilty says, " 'I saved her from a beastly pervert. . . . I'm not responsible for the rapes of others' " (*Lolita*, 298). It is only after killing Quilty that Humbert takes any responsibility for his crime against Lolita and the larger green world.

Nabokov repeatedly reminds us of the reductive nature of romantic obsession, how small, how relentless, how the world narrows to its base contention—that all else is minute beside the rush of its urgency. As Humbert admits, his sole reason for the "general circuit," their tour, "was to keep my companion in passable humor from kiss to kiss" (*Lolita*, 154). He and Lolita become outlaws, he as captor, she as captive, hiding out in "clean, neat, safe nooks, ideal places for sleep, argument, reconciliation, insatiable illicit love" (*Lolita*, 145). Humbert invokes *Madame Bovary*, that nineteenth-century exposé of European bourgeois romantic escapist fantasy. Suggesting its tawdry and tedious nature, he writes, "*Nous connûmes* . . . the stone cottages . . . the brick unit, the adobe unit, the stucco court. . . . *Nous connûmes* . . . all those Sunset Motels, U-Bean Cottages, Hillcrest Courts, Pine View Courts. . . . *Nous connûmes* the various types of motor court operators, the reformed criminal, the retired teacher and the business flop, among the males; and the motherly, pseudo-ladylike and madamic variants among the females"—all this nonchanlantly, playfully recited. He continues, "And sometimes trains would cry in the monstrously hot and humid night with heartrending and ominous plangency, mingling power and hysteria in one desperate scream" (*Lolita*, 146)—echoes of Lolita's desperate sobbing "every night, every night." The wide range of emotionality, huge swings from cheerful hilarity to muted but resonant sorrow romp through this extraordinary novel, the humor serving, always, to permit exploration of this otherwise forbidden and sorrowful terrain.

So Nabokov portrays Lolita as pulled further and further into banal escapist fantasy of American popular culture, because she is, literally, a kid trying to escape. While Humbert quotes her mercilessly, vividly depicts her as vulgar and stupid, his condescension exposes himself along with her other perpetrators. Her fascination with, for example, "real singers and dancers who had unreal stage careers in an essentially grief-proof sphere of existence wherefrom death and truth were banned" (*Lolita*, 170) is to a large extent constructed out of the compulsive movie-going she and Humbert engage in and enforced by her isolation. She is forbidden to have girlfriends or boyfriends; she is banned from even participating in a school play, forbidden from playing the part of a nymphet, the only role Humbert has assigned to her in real life. But no matter how Humbert tries to diminish her, her vitality comes through in Nabokov's depiction of the child, her "two deft little hands" over his eyes, barefoot or one-socked, alternately chatty and sullen, her "yelp," her "hiccups of laughter," and the sobbing "every night, every night" after she is informed coldly, matter-of-factly, that her mother is dead. Humbert tells us after her initial withdrawal, "in the middle of the night she came sobbing into [my room], and we made it up very gently. You see, she had absolutely nowhere else to go" (*Lolita*, 142).

America and Lolita both function here as landscapes of potentially wild bucolic beauty. For Humbert, they exist as part of the pastoral world that he, jaded, from an older culture, must defile. While America may be crass, its ugly youth culture tawdry, its landmarks inauthentic, Humbert, it is suggested, has inherited the effeteness of European snobbery. Even as Humbert notes the majesty of the America, it registers for him only as a series of one-night motels, where he hears mostly the toilets of the adjoining rooms flushing.

In contrast, in one pastoral scene in the mountains where Humbert and Lolita have just made love, they come across two staring children, Humbert desperately trying to conceal his nakedness, as "a gradually rising figure of a stout lady [the mother] automatically added a wild lily to her bouquet, while staring over her shoulder at us from behind her lovely carved bluestone children" (*Lolita*, 169). This bucolic medallion, the pastoral defiled, represents the gap in Lolita's childhood. Other images of children safe in the protection of family will follow, leading to the final inclusive sound of all children playing—the collective voice of the green world, the community of childhood from which Lolita has been excluded.

Nabokov claimed he was not anti-American, that he "needed a certain exhilarating milieu. Nothing is more exhilarating," he writes, "than philistine vulgarity. . . . [M]y creature Humbert is a foreigner and an anarchist, and there are many things, besides nymphets, in which I disagree with him" (quoted in *Lolita*, 315). Still, American culture comes across at best as vulgar, exhilarating or not. At worst, it reeks of the racism that transforms children into grotesque "pickaninnies . . . 'tap-danc[ing] for pennies' " (*Lolita*, 156).

Nabokov claimed that "[t]he first little throb of *Lolita* went through me late in 1939 or early 1940, in Paris . . . the inital shiver of inspiration . . . somehow prompted by a newspaper story about an ape in the Jardin des Plates, who, after months of coaxing by a scientist, produced the first drawing ever charcoaled by an animal: this sketch showed the bars of the poor creature's cage" (quoted in *Lolita*, 311). How poignant, how sad this image produced by the wild, innocent spirit trapped by a society that does not recognize its cages. Like the entrapped beast, Lolita's innocence is only glimpsed in moments of mute vulnerability. And regardless of her vulgarity or her charms, her intelligence, or lack thereof, she has been deprived of "the mind's birth" and of "the stab of wonder" Nabokov so valued in the young child.

Nabokov's "monster"[13] is not wholly without feeling, not entirely static. A more compassionate voice is heard, at first, as the mere whisper of his conscience. Following the consummation, he reports feeling "as if I were sitting with the small ghost of somebody I had just killed" (*Lolita*, 140). But it is only after Lolita has lost her nymphet look, when he finds her at the end of the novel, married, pregnant, and in need of money, that he offers her anything without exacting a price. At the end, he comes to understand that he has never really seen her, has never even entertained the idea that she might have an imagination. Two particularly painful scenes emerge from his memory. In one, he remembers her remarking about how dying means " 'that you are completely on your own,' " and he is suddenly aware that he "simply did not know a thing about my darling's mind and that quite possibly, behind the awful juvenile clichés, there was in her a garden and a twilight, and a palace gate—dim and adorable regions which happened to be lucidly and absolutely forbidden to me, in my polluted rags and miserable convulsions" (*Lolita*, 284). Here, the pastoral has been driven underground, and emerges hypothetically, conceived of as the loss of its potential.

The other memory, which follows closely, is most devastating—an image of the ordinary safety and comfort of childhood of which Lolita is made aware by the image of another child, comfortably resting on her father's lap. Humbert recalls,

> Suddenly, as Avis clung to her father's neck and ear . . . I saw Lolita's smile lose all its light and become a frozen little shadow of itself, and the fruit knife slipped off the table and struck her with its silver handle a freak blow on the ankle which made her gasp, and crouch head forward, and then, jumping on one leg, her face awful with the preparatory grimace which children hold till the tears gush, she was gone— to be followed at once and consoled in the kitchen by Avis who had such a wonderful fat pink dad and a small chubby brother, and a brand-new baby sister, and a home, and two grinning dogs, and Lolita had nothing. (*Lolita*, 286)

And it isn't until Humbert is overtaken by police after he has murdered Quilty that he has the epiphany, at the heart of which is the pastoral vision of childhood as community from which Lolita has been excluded:

As I approached the friendly abyss, I grew aware of a melodious unity of sounds rising like vapor from a small mining town that lay at my feet. . . . One could make out the geometry of the streets between blocks of red and gray roofs, and green puffs of trees, and a serpentine stream, and the rich, ore-like glitter of the city dump, and beyond the town, road crisscrossing the crazy quilt of dark and pale fields, and behind it all, great timbered mountains. But even brighter than those quietly rejoicing colors—for there are colors and shades that seem to enjoy themselves in good company—both brighter and dreamer to the ear than they were to the eye, was that vapory vibration of accumulated sounds that never ceased for a moment. . . . And soon I realized that all these sounds were of one nature. . . . Reader! What I heard was but the melody of children at play, nothing but that, and so limpid was the air that within this vapor of blended voices, majestic and minute, remote and magically near, frank and divinely enigmatic—one could hear now and then, as if released, an almost articulate spurt of vivid laughter. . . . I stood listening to that musical vibration from my lofty slope, to those flashes of separate cries . . . and then I knew that the hopelessly poignant thing was not Lolita's absence from my side, but the absence of her voice from that concord. (*Lolita*, 307–8)

Lolita dies at seventeen, still a child, with her stillborn child, in childbirth.

Precluded from this novel are characters who embody a "higher innocence" or wisdom of adulthood. Only the work of art itself seems to contain and carry the wisdom of the author's vision, which he has denied his characters. One critic, in focusing on parody, writes about the novel as a parody of the artist "trying to capture his subject in the act of motion but succeeding only in divesting it of its vitality . . . a potential fictional subject, existing in the unformed flux of the physical world . . . [who] lives in the everyday landscape of suburban America, mediocre and anonymous . . . [whom the artist] decides to build . . . into a work of art."[14] Several critics suggest, at the very least, a mutuality of responsibility for Humbert and Lolita. Appel, for example, claims that "each is captive of the other, imprisoned together in a succession of bedrooms and cars, but so distant from one another that they can share nothing of what they see—making Humbert seem as alone during the first trip West as he will be on the second, when she has left him and the car is an empty cell" (*Lolita*, xlix–l). Pifer notes Leslie Fielder's assertion that *Lolita* is "the final blasphemy against the cult of the child," and, most condemnatory, that "it is the naive child, the female, the American who corrupts the sophisticated adult, the male, the European . . . as nymphomaniac, demonic rapist of the soul" (Pifer, 69). Pifer also notes Appel's claim that *Lolita* puts an end to "the romantic myth of the child, extending from Wordsworth to Salinger" but, as she says, "Rather than sounding a death knell to the romantic myth of the child . . . *Lolita* renews and reinvigorates the myth, rendering the image of childhood with fresh resonance and complexity" (Pifer, 70–1), "[where] . . . the child's image [which] shines like a beacon" (Pifer, 88). Pifer sees *Lolita* as an exploration of how society conspires against children, which is both a "betrayal of human consciousness and its creative potential" (Pifer, 75).

Perhaps, then, the only grounded adult with the wisdom to see beyond the "platinum haze," "the distant amorous mist" (*Lolita*, 152) of Humbert's gaze is Nabokov himself. Although critics, such as Bader, see a "persistent identification with Humbert as lover and Humbert as artist" (Bader, 57) (and Quilty as "pseudo-artist"), it seems to me that Humbert's quest is the false search, the failed aesthetic of American popular culture that mistakes the arrested vision of the psychologically dwarfed Humbert, the humbug of an artist, for the real thing. Decidedly, there are moments of conflation of Nabokov's and Humbert's perspectives. These occur and build toward the end, as Humbert moves from his early flamboyant pseudo-reflexivity toward a more authentic consciousness. Toward the end, Humbert remarks: "Curious: although actually her looks had faded, I definitely realized, so hopelessly late in the day, how much she looked—had always looked—like Botticelli's russet Venus—the same soft nose, the same blurred beauty" (*Lolita*, 270). "Blurred" is the operative word here. An odd combination of close observation and romantic washing over of the subject—this seems to represent Humbert's potential and failure as artist. The fact that he notices his tendency to blur and is aware of his failure to notice her as a source of inspiration or as a work of art in herself is an advancement over his earlier proprietary treatment of her as nymphet. Botticelli's Venus, as a representation of idealized beauty, is an aesthetic construct. And Humbert does become aware of just how inflated his feelings are, as he would be before her "(with my soul actually hanging around her naked body and ready to repent), all at once, ironically, horribly, lust would swell again—and 'oh, *no*,' Lolita would say with a sigh to heaven, and the next moment the tenderness and the azure—all would be shattered" (*Lolita*, 285). Not until the end does he fully recognize Lolita's separateness, the boundary between her self and his, where he sees that her place is not by his side—not now, nor should it have been ever. Her rightful realm is that of childhood and this is what he then mourns in his attempt, as he says, "to save not my head, of course, but my soul" (*Lolita*, 308).

Perhaps, for Nabokov, the only place where innocence and the larger pastoral realm can be sustained is in art. Certainly, this is where Humbert locates a timeless order, a durability, when, in the last sentence of his "memoir," he says: "I am thinking of aurochs and angels, the secret of durable pigments, prophetic sonnets, the refuge of art. And this is the only immortality you and I may share, my Lolita" (*Lolita*, 309).

## 2. The Fifth Child

> What would the mother look like, the one
> who would welcome this—alien?
>
> —DORIS LESSING, *THE FIFTH CHILD*[15]

I have always found Lessing intellectually challenging, a kind of sybil, her vision apocalyptic, unsettling in its power to see through and expose those contemporary cultural myths of which we are barely conscious. Embedded in her fiction are warnings boldly proclaimed through the subversive voices mostly of women, sometimes children, chosen to be conscious or forced into consciousness by their marginality. Often they move from a more centrist position into an underworld— whether it be of madness (*The Golden Notebook*,[16] *The Four-Gated City*,[17] *The Summer Before the Dark*[18]) or some more external form of social disintegration (*The Memoirs of a Survivor*,[19] *Love, Again*[20]). From there, they interrogate the conventions of the world they look back on, and, looking forward, they discover and explore some alternate state of consciousness.

Lessing's *The Fifth Child* works this way. It is a devastating exposé of "family values" and the romance of childhood innocence, told as the interior narrative of the mother. It begins with the emptiness of modern life and a young couple's rebellion against the unconventional conventionality of sixties youth culture. As outcasts and "observers" of their world, Harriet and David find each other and decide to refurbish their culture with their conventionally unconventional family values. The novel opens on their self-righteousness:

> Harriet and David met each other at an office party neither had particularly wanted to go to, and both knew at once that this was what they had been waiting for. . . . They defended a stubbornly held view of themselves, which was that they were ordinary and in the right of it, should not be criticised for emotional fastidiousness, abstemiousness, just because these were un-fashionable qualities. (*Fifth Child*, 3)

They see themselves as building a new race. Out of their alienation, they will reconstruct an inclusive community, a vision of pastoral. They buy a house in the suburbs large enough for the enormous family they envision. But almost immediately there are signs of corruption, which generate the antipastoral counterplot. A subtle fissure in their bond begins with their initial love-making, where Harriet felt "his taking possession of the future in her." She is silenced from mentioning the unprotected sex they were not planning on by the way "his arm tightened around her . . . a grip [that] said, Be quiet" (*Fifth Child*, 10–1). This establishes a pattern of denial on David's part and suppression of what Harriet comes to recognize. With the expense of the oversized house and with Harriet's unplanned pregnancy come the compromises of their values: Harriet will rely on her mother, Dorothy, and David on his father, James, undermining their pride in self-sufficiency. James, the rich father, whose lifestyle David has vehemently rejected, is generous with his money as is Dorothy with her time, but Harriet and David continue to produce babies as they desire, regardless of what they consume in their path. Determined to restore family and community, they provide a series of dinners, ritualized by the holidays of Christmas and Easter, where they attract a range of disparate people—David's split parents, each remarried, his single sister, Harriet's sister and her somewhat estranged husband, even a distant relative/schoolgirl whose own family was in disarray. Although everyone enjoys the family parties, which extend over several days, sometimes weeks, the couple is criticized by the family and remains immune to their warnings. Dorothy's reactions seem most reasonable: " 'You want things both ways,' " she tells them. " 'The aristocracy—yes, they can have children like rabbits, and expect to, but they have the money for it. And poor people can have children, and half of them die, and expect to. But people like us, in the middle, we have to be careful about the children we have so we can look after them' " (*Fifth Child*, 16).

"There was a cloud," Lessing notes, in the harmonious vision of family. Sarah and William, Harriet's sister and brother-in-law, are "unhappily married," and worse, have a baby with Down syndrome. Harriet sees Amy, the baby, as the result of their "quarreling [which] had probably attracted the mongol child—yes, yes, of course she knew one shouldn't call them mongol. But the little girl did look a bit like Genghis Khan, didn't she? A baby Genghis Khan with her squashed little face and her slitty eyes?" (*Fifth Child*, 22). This judgment comes back to haunt Harriet, when her fifth child, Ben, is born "a real little wrestler . . . fighting the whole world . . . not a pretty baby" (*Fifth Child*, 48). Lessing takes great care to describe Ben in detail, as we witness Harriet's perspective, seen but unacknowledged by David. She tells us,

> He did not look like a baby at all. He had a heavy-shouldered hunched look . . . [h]is forehead sloped from his eyebrows to his crown. His hair grew in an unusual pattern from the double crown where started a wedge or triangle that came low on the forehead, the hair lying forward in a thick yellowish stubble, while the side and back hair grew downward. . . . He opened his eyes and looked straight up into his mother's face. They were focussed greeny-yellow eyes, like lumps of soapstone. . . .
>
> But she heard herself say nervously, though she tried to laugh, "He's like a troll, or a globlin or something." And she cuddled him, to make up. But he was stiff and heavy. (*Fifth Child*, 49)

Prior to the birth of the fifth child, there were four children, two complementary pairs of boys and girls to support the two-child figure of their idyll, to wash over the pain of Harriet's prenatal relationship with a fetus that "seemed to be trying to tear its way out of her stomach" (*Fifth Child*, 38). "Sometimes she believed hooves were cutting her tender inside flesh, sometimes claws" (*Fifth Child*, 41). Harriet's fantasy of taking a knife and "cut[ting] open her own stomach" (*Fifth Child*, 48) is not only the desperation of the extreme pain, relieved only by constantly moving and consuming enormous quantities of food, but the expression of her isolation. She thinks, "Alone in her ordeal—and she had to be, she knew that, and did not blame her family for not accepting what she was being slowly forced to accept—she became silent, morose, suspicious of them all and their thoughts about her" (*Fifth Child*, 40). Aware of the change in her social position in the family, Harriet also perceives an internal shift; she is conscious of living in a different time, on a different plane, of being a creature from another realm.

> Time passed. It did pass, though she was held in an order of time different from those around her—and not the pregnant woman's time either, which is slow, a calendar of the growth of the hidden being. Her time was endurance, containing pain. Phantoms and chimeras inhabited her brain. (*Fifth Child*, 41)

Lessing constructs two allegories which layer the narrative. The first begins as a socially acceptable fairy tale in which the archetypal two-child figure, like Hansel and Gretel, is separated as the two children lose each other in the forest. In telling his children the tale, David inverts the main thrust of the story, which is to rejoin the two children after their initial severance from each other, from the family, and from the larger society, in an integrative and regenerative image. Instead of the warning against the forbidden sweets and false nurturing, in David's narrative the children are nourished on "sweet chocolate." The "friendly deer," the spiritual power animal of fairy tales, is peremptorily thanked. And at the center of the tale is the little girl's vision of a girl's face smiling up at her from a pool. As David tells it, " 'it was a face she had never seen in her whole life . . . smiling . . . a nasty smile . . . and the little girl thought this other girl was going to reach up out of the water and pull her down into it' " (*Fifth Child*, 45).

The fairy tale threatens to erupt into the dark denial of David's hostility, which Harriet recognizes. "[S]he was wanting to cry out, 'Stop—stop it! You are talking about me—this is what you are feeling about me!' " (*Fifth Child*, 45). It is framed and contextualized by the outside world, which intrudes with reports from the television in "a professional cool voice . . . about murders in a London suburb" (*Fifth Child*, 44). The children's voices and actions also disrupt the tale, particularly the oldest child's serious question, " 'Do the birds sing to us. . . . When we are in the garden and the birds sing, are they singing to us?' " (*Fifth Child*, 44). This pivotal interrogation by the child of the meaning of pastoral, how literally to understand its ardent promise, is reminiscent of Alice's questions and observations in the garden, and, at the same time, it is strangely singular. It raises issues of inclusiveness, as well, and these notes prefigure the story of Ben's place in or exclusion from the larger social world. The children's eyes, wide with awe, rapt at the telling of the tale, Dorothy's protective "heavy, shocked, indrawn breath" at the frightening nature of this bedtime story, Harriet's "lumbering over" to turn off the TV, the sound of her serving herself "more soup, pil[ing] in the bread"— dialogically indicate the cacophony that is immediately covered over by Dorothy. She concludes, " 'Phyllis [she has named the little girl] decided to leave that nasty pool *at once*. She ran fast along a path until she bumped into her brother. He was looking for her. They held each other's hands and they ran out of the forest and they ran safely home' " (*Fifth Child*, 45). And David concurs. The children's questions continue: " 'Who was that girl in the pool . . . ?' " " 'What's materialised?' " " 'But why, why is it?' " But they go unanswered, the gap filled with food as "Helen took an apple, Luke another, and Jane lifted some bread off her mother's plate" (*Fifth Child*, 46). In this small way, Lessing indicates that Helen and Luke follow the family's adherence to a kind of Edenic pastoral, while Jane, who remained unmoved by the story, is more nourished by her mother's darker sense of things. But not for long.

Harriet is criminalized by the family and by the larger society—first because, in the face of their denial, she acknowledges Ben's difference, his somewhat monstrous nature, as she wonders: "what the mother would look like, the one who would welcome this—alien" (*Fifth Child*, 51). Her plaint to David—" 'I suppose in the old times, in primitive societies, this was how they treated a woman who'd given birth to a freak. As if it was her fault. But we are supposed to be civilised!' "—is greeted with further condemnation. "He said, in the patient, watchful way he now had with her, 'You exaggerate everything' " (*Fifth Child*, 60). Dr. Gilly, a prominent psychiatrist concurs: " 'The problem is not with Ben,' " he tells Harriet, " 'but with you. You don't like him very much' " (*Fifth Child*, 103). Doctors, nurses, teachers—all upholders of our institutions for child-rearing—engage in permutations of denial and blame. And when the family conspires to send Ben into an institutional dungeon where freakish babies are kept drugged and hidden from sight, Harriet goes to rescue him and assume her responsibility for her child along with what all of society denies, the place in the human order of this child, any child, anything human.

As always, Lessing's vision of character is broad and deep. Although Harriet clearly speaks as a strong voice of truth here, each character, in close adherence to a psychological realism, demonstrates a partial sense of justice. Ben *is* dangerous to the other children, his "yellowish white" anger a constant source of disruption. Cruelly and with great strength, he strangles a dog and a cat and threatens serious damage to the other children. Dorothy's reasonable stance supports Ben's removal from the family. " 'You have five children, not one' " (*Fifth Child*, 69), she tells Harriet. But Lessing asserts here and throughout her work the need to go beyond the reasonable, in fact the urgency of being "unreasonable"—of descending into the irrational to the kind of madness necessary for the paradoxes that most challenge our humanness.

As is typical of Lessing, there are no heroes here—only people deeply in struggle. As the afflicted mother, Harriet is not romanticized. She recognizes the horror of her position, of her child about whom, she notes, "Never, not once, did he subside into a loving moment. He resisted, he strove, he fought—and then he turned his head and closed his jaws over her thumb. Not as an ordinary baby will, in the sucking bite that relieves the pain of teething, or explores the possibilities of a mouth, tongue: she felt her bone bend, and she saw his cold triumphant grin" (*Fifth Child*, 56). She is forced to cage Ben so that he cannot destroy either himself or the other children, and finally, to protect them, she is forced to lock the other children into their rooms at night.

Along with their sense of freedom, what Ben succeeds in destroying are the family's illusions represented as pastoral images. No matter how they try to restore their green world, to separate Ben out, images of him "trying to push aside his bars" persist. Ben himself seems somewhat aware of the childhood realm from which he has been banished. Essentially nocturnal, we are told that "[h]e spent most of the night standing on his window-sill, staring into the garden . . . like a little troll or a hobgoblin" (*Fifth Child*, 63). He is only allowed in the garden, "a squat little gnome, poking with a stick at the earth" (*Fifth Child*, 71), when the other children are upstairs. David and Harriet pull back the "heavy curtains" of "the dark winter garden" of their illusions. The light from inside illuminates "a shrub that was starkly black with winter . . . twiggy growths that showed a glitter of water . . . the white trunk of a birch" (*Fifth Child*, 75). Theirs is a dark pastoral. They can only participate in the carefree glow at one remove, through the children "indistinguishably unisex in their many-coloured" clothing. Lessing says,

> For a moment it was the meeting of two alien forms of life: the children had been part of some old savagery, and their blood still pounded with it; but now they had to let their wild selves go away while they rejoined their family. Harriet and David shared this with them, were with them in imagination and in memory, from their own childhoods: they could see themselves clearly, two adults, sitting there, tame, domestic, even pitiable in their distance from wildness and freedom. (*Fifth Child*, 75)

This ability to imagine, to merge through memory is what binds us one to the other, and with our history. And the garden, the natural world tamed, suggests the natural ability of humanity in childhood to be civilized. But this requires an acquired flexibility which Ben does not have. He is not able to connect. His first words are demands, indiscriminate imperatives: " 'I want cake,' " and then later, " 'Give me that. Go for a walk now' " (*Fifth Child*, 68). He never develops the capacity to tell a story, as narrative is built on connection. Ben serves as the mirror for everything we deny, our most uncivilized, least "human" selves.

After Ben is sent to the institution a kind of pastoral is reestablished. Lessing tells us that "the family expanded like paper flowers in water" (*Fifth Child*, 76) in a brief "little festival of kisses and hugs" (*Fifth Child*, 95). But the flowers are paper, insubstantial like their attempt at harmony. Haunted by Ben's cries of rage as he was taken away" (*Fifth Child*, 77), Harriet cannot forget. And she decides to embark on the darkest journey—a descent into the hellish world of institutions where the freaks of society are stowed away. What she sees is a kind of ultimate horror, a vision of the heart of darkness. Its intensity, like an uncanny chill, provides a glimpse, a hint of something we know but cannot tolerate and therefore have buried away. As Harriet arrives at the gates of this hell, she hears "a high thin screaming" (*Fifth Child*, 79). The two guardians at these gates, "a young man" and "a girl," confirm society's denial: " 'You can't be here,' " the young man says. And Harriet, in defiance again of what's "reasonable," asserts, " 'But I am here' " (*Fifth Child*, 80). What she bears witness to is society's criminalization of infants—children, in their innocence, locked away and left to die. Lessing spares us nothing. What society has treated as monstrous is nothing more or less than

> the human template [which] had been wrenched out of pattern, sometimes horribly, sometimes slightly. A baby like a comma, great lolling head on a stalk of a body among stiff fragilities that were limbs . . . a small girl all blurred, her flesh guttering and melting . . . a doll with chalky swollen limbs, its eyes wide and blank, like blue ponds, and its mouth open, showing a swollen little tongue. A lanky boy was skewed, one half of his body sliding from the other. A child seemed at first glance normal, but then Harriet saw there was no back to its head; it was all face, which seemed to scream at her. (*Fifth Child*, 81)

So dark, so relentless is this perspective that it moves into allegory while retaining its realistic position in the narrative. It is an extreme but nonetheless authentic perspective, a revelation of the treatment of "other," of those whose difference is intolerable to the social world. And when Harriet comes upon Ben, covered with feces, lying "like a drowned fish on the slab" (*Fifth Child*, 83), "she was shocked to the point where she felt nothing at all" (82). The muted tones of her horror reenforce this assault on the senses. Lessing allows no turning away. Harriet rescues this child who will continue to siphon off all her vitality and that of the entire family.

For Ben, there is no reentry into the family. There is only a distant and hostile parallelism with Paul, the youngest and most damaged by Ben. "Where was that enchanting, delicious little child," Harriet wonders, who now nags and whines, stares with his soft blue eyes at nothing, is "never appeased," never at rest. Together, each hating the other, he and Ben sit, both soothed by the violence they see on TV. Later, when Ben becomes the mascot of a gang of marginal youth, and in adolescence, the boss of a "bunch of gangly, spotty uncertain adolescents" (*Fifth Child*, 121), these images of violence recur as they are all "fed" by TV "shootings and killings and tortures and fighting" (*Fifth Child*, 122). Harriet observes that "it was more as if they were actually part of the stories on the screen," as they become the perpetrators of crimes, real and imagined.

In her own denial brought on by the horror of her choices, for which she had no choice, Harriet joins the others in condemning herself. She says to David, who immediately exculpates himself, " 'We are being punished. . . . For presuming. For thinking we could be happy. Happy because *we* decided we would be. . . . [W]ho were *we* to decide we were going to be this or that?' " (*Fifth Child*, 117–8). Her strange sense of the hubris, which set them above what Lessing sees as the challenges to human existence, is a modern expression of ancient warning against such grandiosity. Any attempt to separate ourselves from the complexity Lessing sees as the human condition, from our past—any attempt to deny the legacy of the crimes of humanity—the killings and rapes—brings us back to Ben, whose existence is so vividly portrayed in this novel. Towards the end, Harriet says to Dorothy,

> "Ben makes you think . . . all those different people who lived on the earth once—they must be in us somewhere."
>
> "All ready to pop up! But perhaps we simply don't notice them when they do," said Dorothy.
>
> "Because we don't want to," said Harriet.
>
> "I certainly don't want to," said Dorothy. "Not after seeing Ben."
>
> (*Fifth Child*, 114)

Ben is the throw back, the mirror of our crimes against humanity that actually return us to our precivilized selves, which we label, "alien," and banish from consciousness. Harriet tries to imagine him "among a group of his own kind, squatting in the mouth of a cave around roaring flames. Or a settlement of huts in a thick forest? No, Ben's people were at home under the earth, she was sure, deep underground in black caverns lit by torches—that was more like it. Probably those peculiar eyes of his were adapted for quite different conditions of light" (*Fifth Child*, 122). She notices that,

> Compared with the raw and unfinished youths [of the gang], he was a mature being. Finished. Complete. She felt she was looking, through him, at a race that reached its apex thousands and thousands of years before humanity, whatever that meant, took this stage. . . . Did his people rape the females of humanity's forebears? Thus making new races, which had flourished and departed, but perhaps had left their seeds in the human matrix, here and there, to appear again, as Ben had? (*Fifth Child*, 130)

But we don't have to look that far back into our history for the rapes and atrocities. And Lessing's bioanthropological allegory leaves us wondering, with Harriet, if she can start a new life, alone, where one day she would see Ben, on TV, "standing rather apart from the crowd, staring at the camera with his goblin eyes, or searching the faces in the crowd for another of his own kind" (*Fifth Child*, 133). Harriet is left wondering at the end of the novel what will happen to Ben. "Would people always refuse to see him, to recognize what he was?" (*Fifth Child*, 131). Like Frankenstein's monster,[21] he is our creation, Lessing suggests, which we refuse to acknowledge, for which we refuse to accept responsibility.

Several years later, Lessing wrote *Ben, in the World*,[22] her sequel to *The Fifth Child*, in which she explores what happens to Ben after his majority. At the end of *The Fifth Child*, she left us with Harriet wondering how Ben would deal with the world. It is a grim story, told for the most part, through Ben's own consciousness, of the cruelty of the world from which he is relentlessly ostracized. It seems awkwardly narrated, not because its main protagonist is severely limited verbally and socially, but because Lessing's writing is cumbersome, the transitions from scene to scene jarring. At times the characters come to life, but for the most part they seem constricted, emanations of the world around Ben. Some represent an empathic response to his condition; some are detached, and some overtly vicious. But when Ben leaves childhood behind, Lessing attempts to create a vision that remains, essentially, unevolved. *The Fifth Child* leaves us without answers—the family can make no "right" or "appropriately humane" decision. As a character, Ben has little human sympathy, although he has the capacity for suffering and for anger. He stands as an emblem of disconnection itself, a warning against the denial of the past out of which he grew. Lessing is reminiscent of Carroll and the *Alice* stories in this way: she astutely perceives and exposes the incongruity, ambiguity, and irrationality of the world, but is without answers for the questions she raises. In her treatment of the human condition in *The Fifth Child*, she rejects the romance of childhood and its place in the green world. However, even the unrealized vision of *Ben, in the World* is profoundly antipastoral. Ben is able to connect emotionally with a few of the women characters, partially and in an undeveloped way, but the world uses him. It never opens for him. His search to find his own people, people like him, is doomed from the start. He remains the unintegrated—that which cannot be taken in, the world unremitting in its barring what it doesn't want to see from its borders, a vision of its violations.

# 7

# The Contemporary Child
# in Adult Literature

> To the Kathakali Man these stories are his children and his childhood.
> He has grown up within them. They are the house he was raised in, the
> meadows he played in. They are his windows and his way of seeing.
>
> —*THE GOD OF SMALL THINGS*[1]

Like the stories of the Kathakali Man, the stories we grow up with are so integrated into our childhood that they serve as our point of entry into culture. If we
reflect back on them, they also can be seen as critiques of the culture that produced them. Informed by our consciousness of history, our childhood stories
reveal how childhood realizes (or is prohibited from realizing) the seeds of possibility. The books considered here are contemporary representations of childhood;
they struggle to approximate the way one thought and imagined as a child, always
with a sense of the presentness of the past. They represent childhood as a way of
seeing the world—freshly, and viewed almost from outside, as children essentially are outside the agency of the adult world. But they comment on, as children
unconsciously do, the adult contexts of the stories.

## 1. *The God of Small Things*: Language, Childhood, and the Genesis
## of Trauma

Arundhati Roy chose to tell the tragic story of the disintegration of a family
through the perspective of children. The expression of childhood here is an exca-
vation into memory as it lives in the adult. The extraordinary sensuousness of
childhood offers a highly poetic narrative. The book is teeming with images,

sounds, tastes, and tactile impressions that suggest our earliest memories and ways of perceiving the world. At the same time, they bring us close to a world so different from our own. With the fleshiness of Arundhati Roy's metaphors, we are plunged into May in Ayemenem, "a hot, brooding month . . . [when] the river shrinks and black crows gorge on bright mangoes in still, dustgreen trees. . . . Dissolute bluebottles hum vacuously in the fruity air. Then they stun themselves against clear windowpanes and die, fatly baffled in the sun." We are thrust "into early June [when] [t]he countryside turns an immodest green. Boundaries blur as tapioca fences take root and bloom" (*God of Small Things*, 3). The "sharp, glittering sunshine . . . [the] wild creepers that spill across the flooded road . . . [the] small fish [that] appear in the puddles that fill the potholes on the highways" (*God of Small Things*, 3) frame the story the adult Rahel tells in retrospect, as she returns to "[t]he wild, overgrown garden" of her childhood home—a place "full of the whisper and scurry of small lives" (*God of Small Things*, 4)—to retrieve Estha, her twin brother, from whom she has been separated for twenty-three years. As Estha stopped speaking long ago, sometime after their divorced mother "returned" him to his father, Rahel is keeper of his words, his childhood memories and dreams, which are also her own—even those, as Roy says, "she has no right to have" (*God of Small Things*, 5).

The "two-egg" twins here suggest at once sameness and otherness, connection and differentiation. As each evolves distinctly and alone, different in appearance, in gender, each continues to connect primally with the other, so that they share a dream world. Each can read the other's inner thoughts; each undergoes the other's experiences bodily. In this way they are most porous and suggest a potential of the human race to connect deeply physically, emotionally, and spiritually. Like the archetypal brother and sister, Hansel and Gretel, they represent the potential of innocence and of the race to survive, even in the face of abandonment, and, more generally, to evolve in the world as individuals, distinct from but inextricably linked to each other through family, community, and history.

The opening chapter traces the story of their childhood, its end, and their violent separation. The effects of the traumatic sequences are conveyed retrospectively, the events ordered in a backward chronology to parallel the viewpoint of the adult Rahel, as she reclaims her brother, her other self. As she tells the story of the etiology of Estha's silence, retrospectively, she unravels the pivotal incidents that engendered Estha's current restlessness. He roams Kerala, their hometown in southernmost India, a walker in the city. Roy tells us, "It had been quiet in Estha's head until Rahel came. But with her she had brought the sound of passing trains, and the light and shade and light and shade that falls on you if you have a window seat. . . . A dam had burst and savage waters swept everything up in a swirling. Comets, violins, parades, loneliness, clouds, beards, bigots, lists, flags, earthquakes, despair were all swept up in a scrambled swirling" (*God of Small Things*, 16). The mixture of objects and feelings in this series, suggests the chaos of a childhood of arrested growth, and Estha's inability to arrange or reflect on what he sees or feels. We are told that, "Over time he had acquired the ability to blend into the background . . . into bookshelves, gardens, curtains, doorways, streets—to appear inanimate, almost invisible to the untrained eye" (*God of Small Things*, 12), that "Estha, walking on the riverbank, couldn't feel the wetness of the rain" (*God of Small Things*, 16). But Rahel feels it for him. We are told that, "She could feel the rhythm of Estha's rocking, and the wetness of rain on his skin. She could hear the raucous, scrambled world inside his head" (*God of Small Things*, 22).

Estha, without words, is experienced as "a gradual winding down and closing shop. A barely noticeable quietening" (*God of Small Things*, 12). This slow stoppage of time is juxtaposed with the "early amorphous years when memory had only just begun, when life was full of Beginnings and no Ends, and Everything was Forever, [a time when] Esthappen and Rahel thought of themselves together as Me, and separately, individually, as We or Us" (*God of Small Things*, 4). Now Rahel thinks of them as "*Them*, because, separately, the two of them are no longer what *They* were or ever thought *They'd* be" (*God of Small Things*, 5). To capitalize here suggests establishing the thing*ness* of a thing, the transformation of a particular moment into a state of being, a location—a representation or distillation of childhood perception. That preoedipal state of immersion in the life of the twins was abruptly replaced by "Edges, Borders, Boundaries, Brinks and Limits [which] . . . appeared like a team of trolls on their separate horizons" (*God of Small Things*, 5), when their world destructed—when they learned that "Things Can Change in a Day."

So Rahel guides us into the story of their past, though for intimate moments of passion and intense, formative experience we are taken, at times by Estha, at times by each of the family members, inside the imagination so that by the time the novel ends, we understand the inevitability of the destruction of the family. We come to understand the links between the corruption of the family and the caste system that sucks the life out of women, children, and the poor, and that ultimately annihilates the humanity of all its inhabitants.

Perhaps most brilliant is Roy's portrayal of the effects of childhood trauma, the story of the way it takes hold and perpetuates itself, in Estha's narrative. It is described as,

A quiet bubble floating on a sea of noise . . . [a] quietness . . . [that] reached out of his head and enfolded him in its swampy arms. It rocked him to the rhythm of an ancient, fetal heartbeat. It sent its stealthy, suckered tentacles inching along the insides of his skull, hoovering the knolls and dells of his memory, dislodging old sentences, whisking them off the tip of his tongue. It stripped his thoughts of the words that described them and left them pared and naked. Unspeakable. Numb. . . . Slowly, over the years, Estha withdrew from the world. He grew accustomed to the uneasy octopus that lived inside him and spirted its inky tranquilizer on his past. Gradually the reason for his silence was hidden away, entombed somewhere deep in the soothing folds of the fact of it. (*God of Small Things*, 13)

Rather, it is cumulative, this violation of the evolving human spirit, and at once parentally and socially condoned.

Because children are so vulnerable, their perceptions and experiences so little validated, it is rather easy for adults to betray them, sometimes consciously, sometimes without intention. The initial betrayal, Estha's molestation by a stranger, although horrible, would not, in itself, have become the site of atrocity from which Estha runs throughout his childhood. The trauma is aided and abetted unconsciously by Ammu (his mother), and by the adult betrayals that crystallize in Estha's being "returned" to the father he hardly knows. Roy viscerally describes Estha's molestation by the Orangedrink Lemondrink Man in the lobby of the theater when the family goes to see *The Sound of Music*, the favorite musical of the children. So enamored, so identified with the children is Estha that he cannot keep from bursting into song, to the annoyance of all, so that Ammu sends him into the lobby to sing alone. Estha has become Estha Alone just minutes before, when he must go off to the men's bathroom alone, as all the other family members—Rahel, Ammu, and Baby Kochamma—are female. Gender initiates his separateness, his differentiation embodied in the Elvis Puff he fusses over in the bathroom— "Slicked back, then pushed forward and swivelled sideways at the very end" (*God of Small Things*, 92)—the hairstyle that, along with his "beige and pointy shoes" (*God of Small Things*, 100), defines him. But his manipulation by the man selling drinks in the lobby, so cruelly manifested in his deliberate preying on Estha's barely perceived class privilege, propels him into a powerlessness so prevalent in childhood. After maneuvering Estha into masturbating him, he forces him to accept his orange/lemon drink, saying, " 'You mustn't waste it. . . . Think of all the poor people who have nothing to eat or drink. You're a lucky rich boy, with pocketmunny and a grandmother's factory to inherit' " (*God of Small Things*, 100).

The Orangedrink Lemondrink Man is one of the grotesques in the novel who, seen from the child's perspective, fascinates and terrifies. He is depicted as "yellow teeth [which] were magnets. They saw, they smiled, they sang, they smelled, they moved. They mesmerized" (*God of Small Things*, 98). Roy tells us, "Estha went. Drawn by yellow teeth" (*God of Small Things*, 98), and the vulnerability of the little boy is underscored by his helplessness before such grotesque manipulation. The fact that the Orangedrink Lemondrink Man uses Estha's status and privilege against him reflects both his perversion and his rage against the treatment of his class. And the way in which Estha lists his grandmother's produce in columns of "PICKLES SQUASHES JAMS" during the act illustrates his brave attempt to survive intact—to dissociate himself from this heinous perpetration of injustice.

When Estha returns, holding "his sticky Other Hand away from his body," he now views the characters in *The Sound of Music* as an ideal, a norm from which he is forever excluded. They are "Clean children, like a packet of peppermints" (*God of Small Things*, 100), loved by Baron von Clapp-Trapp and Julie Andrews, "clean white children, and their beds were soft with Ei. Der. Downs" (*God of Small Things*, 100). Rahel, who also has been scolded by Ammu for her ebullience, for running up and down stairs two at a time, for the same energy that provoked Estha to burst into song, Rahel who has learned her lesson that "*Excitement Always Leads to Tears*" (*God of Small Things*, 94), joins Estha in thinking about "some questions . . . that needed answers,"

(a) *Did Baron von Clapp-Trapp shiver his leg?* [a further sign of bad behavior]

He did not.

(b) *Did Baron von Clapp-Trapp blow spit bubbles? Did he?*

He did most certainly not.

(c) *Did he gobble?*

He did not. (*God of Small Things*, 101)

And as this event is framed by anticipation of the visit of their nine-year-old cousin, Sophie Mol, who has been raised in England and is only half-Indian, the questions, for Estha, expand to include those he imagines Baron von Trapp might ask:

(a) *Are they clean white children?*

No. (*But Sophie Mol is.*)

(b) *Do they blow spit bubbles?*

Yes. (*But Sophie Mol doesn't.*)

(c) *Do they shiver their legs? Like clerks?*

Yes. (*But Sophie Mol Doesn't.*)

(d) *Have they, either or both, ever held strangers' soo-soos?*

N . . . Nyes. (*But Sophie Mol hasn't.*) (*God of Small Things*, 102)

This leads Baron von Clapp-Trapp, in Estha's imagination, to conclude, " 'Then I'm sorry. . . . It's out of the question. I cannot love them. I cannot be their Baba' " (*God of Small Things*, 102). And when Ammu, flattered by the Orangedrink Lemondrink Man, concludes, "Sweet chap, that Orangedrink

Lemondrink fellow" (*God of Small Things*, 106), Estha feels unsafe and further isolated. Only Rahel, another child, relatively untainted by such indicators as class and position, notices something "hideous" in "the steady gaze in which [the Orangedrink Lemondrink Man] held her," and feels Estha's fear in his "fever-hot fingers whose tips were as cold as death" (*God of Small Things*, 106). As Ammu refers to him as "Uncle," and insists that "he was surprisingly sweet with Estha," Rahel lashes out, " 'So why don't you marry him then?' "

This is one of Roy's many moments of illumination, her sharp insight into the intuitive nature of children revealing how innocence, unmarred by the infected systems of adult society and without full awareness, speaks truth to power. Roy tells us, "Rahel froze. She was desperately sorry for what she had said. She didn't know where those words had come from. . . . But they were out now. . . . They hung about . . . like clerks in a government office. Some stood, some sat and shivered their legs" (*God of Small Things*, 107). In Ammu's response the children's deepest fears are realized: " 'Rahel,' Ammu said, 'do you realize what you have just done? . . . D'you know what happens when you hurt people?' Ammu said. 'When you hurt people, they begin to love you less. That's what careless words do. They make people love you a little less' " (*God of Small Things*, 106–7).

What follows, the emotional trauma suffered by Rahel, begun in the many warnings about her childish behavior, is crystallized into the state most feared by children: that they will lose the love of their beloved protector. Rahel experiences it as "[a] cold moth with unusually dense dorsal tufts" (*God of Small Things*, 107). The moth refers back to the bitter defeat of Pappachi, the children's grandfather, when the particular moth he discovered as "Imperial Entomologist" was named after a junior officer. His resentment at being slighted is transformed into violence against Mammachi, the children's grandmother, then further transformed into the "Unsafe Edge" that Ammu carries, which, in turn, at times transforms their loving, lovely mother into a cruel and lasting source of punishment. This is their inheritance; this along with the ordinary treachery of adult abandonment leaves them vulnerable to similar betrayals.

There are many references to betrayal throughout the novel. The interpolated tale of Karna, the god whose mother betrays him, and the recurring line from *Julius Caesar* that Estha uncomprehendingly repeats—"Et tu Brute?", for example, form the very backdrop of the story against which the family betrayals play themselves out. Roy tell us, "It was as though the window through which their father disappeared had been kept open for anyone to walk in and be welcomed. To Ammu, her twins seemed like a pair of small bewildered frogs engrossed in each other's company, lolloping arm in arm down a highway full of hurtling traffic. Entirely oblivious of what trucks can do to frogs, Ammu watched over them fiercely" (*God of Small Things*, 42). Roy reminds us how even devoted parents, with their own limitations, propelled by the agonies of their own personal struggles to survive in a rigid and malevolent social world, can devastate their children, as the "icy legs" of the moth descend, over and over, on Rahel's heart. "Six goosebumps on her careless heart. A little less her Ammu loved her" (*God of Small Things*, 107).

As with Rahel, the reverberations of the initial trauma recur throughout Estha's life because they concur with other betrayals of the adult world, which confirm that,

(a) *Anything can happen to Anyone.*

   and

(b) *It's best to be prepared. . . .*

> The Orangedrink Lemondrink Man could just walk in through the gauze doors. If he wanted to.
> And Ammu would offer him pineapple juice. With ice. (*God of Small Things*, 186)

Roy's portrayal of the ways in which Ammu loves and yet betrays her children, as seen through their eyes, is subtle. Although Ammu is supportive, she has retained the strict and conventional assumptions of her class and is particularly harsh when Rahel and Estha behave in ways she considers improper. Her ambivalence toward her children is one of the greatest revelations of this story of childhood. Roy demonstrates Ammu's profound love for them as they play with her hair, "with the bare skin of her midriff" (*God of Small Things*, 211). But they are the reason she must stay in her provincial home, rebel though she is, as, out of despair and desperation she tells them, " 'If it wasn't for you I wouldn't be here! None of this would have happened! . . . I would've been free! I should've dumped you in an orphanage the day you were born! You're the millstones around my neck! . . . Just go away and leave me alone!' " (*God of Small Things*, 240). This rage sends them out on the disastrous journey during which Sophie Mol drowns, and that, along with other catastrophes, leads to the torture and murder of Velutha, Ammu's "Untouchable" lover. This last renunciation comes from Ammu's grief at being discovered with Velutha. However, her ambivalence toward her children is prepared for long before this climactic turn.

With compassion for her character, Roy unfolds the story of Ammu's childhood, one of a brutal and rejecting father and a helpless mother. We are told, "As a child, she had learned very quickly to disregard the Father Bear Mother Bear stories she was given to read. In her version, Father Bear beat Mother Bear with brass vases. Mother Bear suffered those beatings with mute resignation" (*God of Small Things*, 171). Even with the brother who gets to go away, to develop his intellect, Roy is careful to depict him as emotionally crippled, severely hampered, as are all the adults, privileged and unprivileged alike, by the sexism and racism of their culture. Roy understands deeply, with a crisp lucidity that no one is healthy in such a society that perverts pleasure and love. The fact that Velutha is the only character that seems to have a strong core, that he alone plays with the children freely, allows them to paint his nails red, allows them to jump into his arms, without recrimination, without impatience, suggests a spirit untainted by his masters.

Velutha spans both a mythic and realistic realm. Roy presents him as palpably human, embodied, down to earth. It is to him that the novel's title refers—he is the God of Small Things, the God of Loss, who persists, like the original Kathakali Man, keeper of the stories, "the most beautiful of men. Because his body *is* his soul" (*God of Small Things*, 219). Unlike Velutha, the Kathakali Man has lost his mythic power in the commercial, industrialization that degrades him. We are told that

> he has become unviable. Unfeasible. Condemned goods. His children deride him. They long to be everything that he is not. He has watched them grow up to become clerks and bus conductors. . . . With unions of their own. But he himself, left dangling somewhere between heaven and earth, cannot do what they do. . . . In despair, he turns to tourism. He enters the market. He hawks the only things he owns. The stories that his body can tell. He becomes a Regional Flavor. . . . He checks his rage and dances for them. He collects his fee. He gets drunk. (*God of Small Things*, 219–20)

But Velutha, with his magic hands and his keen intellect, his courage and his compassion, is a humanized God, the God of Small Things like children, like the small creatures of the natural world, a protector who, in the final moment, cannot protect himself from such a brutal world. In his beauty and vitality, he has the potential like the Kathakali Man of earlier times to "reveal the nugget of sorrow that happiness contains. The hidden fish of shame in a sea of glory. He tells stories of the gods, but his yarn is spun from the ungodly, human heart" (*God of Small Things*, 219). Velutha is the "ungodly" god, god of the "human heart," who will be disappeared by the combined efforts of Comrade Pillai and Inspector Thomas Mathew, leaders of his own Marxist Party, "both men," we are told, "whom childhood had abandoned without a trace. Men without curiosity. Without doubt. Both in their own way truly, terrifyingly adult" (*God of Small Things*, 248).

Adulthood in this society and in this family is tyrannical and indeed terrifying to the children. Baby Kochamma, the infantile adult, who, as the adult Rahel says, is "living her life backwards" (*God of Small Things*, 23), a perversion of childhood, indeed, a child hater, "sw[inging] her tiny, manicured feet, like a small child on a high chair" (*God of Small Things*, 21), provides the ammunition that ignites the rage against Velutha. And the children are tyrannized by Baby Kochamma into lying, into ultimately offering testimony against Velutha, for fear that they, along with Ammu, will go to jail, "three different jails," their great aunt tells them, as she dwells on "[t]he cockroach-crisp food. The *chhi-chhi* piled in the toilets like soft brown mountains. The bedbugs. The beatings. She dwelled on the long years Ammu would be put away because of them. The How she would be an old, sick woman with lice in her hair when she came out—if she didn't die in jail, that was" (*God of Small Things*, 301). And to "Save Ammu," which meant "Save us," Estha is chosen to identify Velutha. Lying on the "scummy, slippery floor. A mangled genie . . . naked, his soiled mundu. . . . His face . . . swollen and his head . . . like a pumpkin with a monstrous upside-down smile" (*God of Small Things*, 303), Velutha has been transformed from a beautiful, sensuous young man into a grotesque.

Roy describes the end of Estha's childhood as, once "Estha's mouth said Yes. Childhood tiptoed out. Silence slid in like a bolt" (*God of Small Things*, 303). She reminds us, in many ways and throughout the book, that

> [t]he twins were too young to know that these were only history's henchmen. Sent to square the books and collect the dues from those who broke its laws. Impelled by feelings that were primal yet paradoxically wholly impersonal. Feelings of contempt born of inchoate, unacknowledged fear—civilization's fear of nature, men's fear of women, power's fear of powerlessness. Man's subliminal urge to destroy what he could neither subdue nor deify. . . . What Esthappen and Rahel witnessed that morning, though they didn't know it then, was a clinical demonstration in controlled conditions . . . of human nature's pursuit of ascendancy. Structure. Order. Complete monopoly. It was human history, masquerading as God's Purpose, revealing herself to an under-age audience. (*God of Small Things*, 292–3)

In *The God of Small Things*, Roy constructs a sense of inevitability, a determinism to the events by revealing the social systems of Kerala—life "Before Independence" and "After Independence," the caste system and the Marxist groups that governed and threatened to govern Kerala—all played out on and by the particular family members: on Mammachi and Pappachi, the grandparents; on Ammua, the mother; on Chako, the uncle; on Baby Kochamma, the great-aunt. As Syrian Christians, they represent the long established hierarchy of Kerala, and although Kerala was the most Marxist of Indian states, the caste system was deeply entrenched there, as was sexism. Roy understands the clash between cultures and the contradictions within each, as she demonstrates the corruption and perversion of innocence in the story of the children as they are betrayed, as is their beloved friend, Velutha. The History House, the abandoned estate of an Englishman, is their playground, and represents their inheritance—an abandonment that echoes everywhere.

As mixed breeds, children of a Syrian Christian and Hindu marriage, of a divorced mother, they were already somewhat separated out from the social world, were already regarded with suspicion even by their own family, particularly by Baby Kochamma. Bedecked in "[w]inking rings, diamond rings, gold bangles"—jewelry she touches to "reassur[e] herself that it was there and that it was hers [l]ike a young bride who couldn't believe her good fortune" (*God of*

*Small Things*, 22), she is the inheritor and the legacy, literally and metaphorically, of the family jewels. After her brief youthful rebellious conversion to Catholicism in hopes of winning the love of a priest, as "young Baby Kochamma's aching heart on a leash . . . lurch[ed] over leaves and small stones. Bruised and almost broken" (*God of Small Things*, 25), she becomes the archetypal betrayer, the force that leads to the murder of Velutha, the destruction of Ammu, the separation of the twins. Roy suggests that, as a girl growing up in Kerala, Baby Kochamma is also a product of its cultural and political institutions. But in embracing the conventions of the very society of which she is a victim, she becomes one of its greatest victimizers. As Roy says, "She viewed ethnic cleansing, famine and genocide as direct threats to [the] furniture" (*God of Small Things*, 29) she inherited "by outliving everybody else" (*God of Small Things*, 28). Viewed by the children, she is the novel's greatest grotesque, the aggressor against innocence. Roy tells us, "Baby Kochamma grudged them their moments of high happiness when a dragonfly they'd caught lifted a small stone off their palms with its legs, or when they had permission to bathe the pigs, or they found an egg hot from a hen. But most of all, she grudged them the comfort they drew from each other" (*God of Small Things*, 45). The image of her "armfat [which] hung down like a fleshy curtain, blocking Estha from Rahel" (*God of Small Things*, 60) suggests her persistent role in both their childhood and later in adulthood.

It is a testament to the power of Roy's writing, the clarity of her vision, that we get enough depth in Baby Kochamma's story, so that we are provided with the genesis of her cruelty, and the dark human story of how sadistic impulses evolve. The children's vision, however, is always the darkest aspect, and Roy never turns away from it. To them, Velutha "left behind a Hole in the Universe [again in capitals] through which darkness poured like liquid tar. Through which their mother followed without even turning to wave good-bye. She left them behind, spinning in the dark, with no moorings (*God of Small Things*, 182).

Interestingly, after the discovery of Velutha as Ammu's lover, which forces Ammu to separate from her children, she degenerates and is similarly transformed into a grotesque, "swollen with cortisone, moonfaced, not the slender mother Rahel knew. Her skin was stretched over her puffy cheeks like shiny scar tissue that covers old vaccination marks. . . . Her curly hair had lost its sheen and hung around her swollen face like a dull curtain. She carried her breath in a glass inhaler in her tattered handbag," constantly coughing up phlegm and to Rahel's disgust, showing it to her, then leaving without saying good-bye. We are told that, "She hated her mother then. *Hated* her" (*God of Small Things*, 153). We are told that that is the last time Rahel saw Ammu, who died "in a grimy room . . . where she had gone for a job interview as someone's secretary. She died alone" (*God of Small Things*, 154) at thirty-one.

In the end, even in the face of such darkness, Roy seems somewhat hopeful, immersed in what survives. We are left with the vitality of little things and of children. Sophie Mol, the child who is loved and respected, given more freedom, more privileged than the twins, has a refreshing original response to things. Although her adventurous spirit leads to her drowning, she displays the trust, the legacy that has been offered her by her mother and stepfather. Sophie Mol, "Loved from the Beginning" (*God of Small Things*, 129), displays the spontaneity that has been suppressed in the twins' expression. The twins' questions about what they see, what they wonder about, what they are forbidden to ask, are aborted, frozen moments. Estha wonders (but knows not to ask) about the "three kinds of hair" on a man who runs naked in the town: "the hair on his head . . . the hair in his windy, armless armpits . . . and the hair in his crotch . . . how that could be" (*God of Small Things*, 62). But when the twins ask Sophie Mol the most burning question, " 'Who d'you love Most in the World?' "—the question they have answered unswervingly, by rote, with the acceptable list, which includes Sophie Mol, she responds, " 'Me? What d'you love me for?' " They inform her that they have to love her next in line after the appropriate family members, " 'Because we're firstcousins' " (*God of Small Things*, 144). Sophie Mol replies, again with her consistent directness, " 'But you don't even know me. . . . And anyway, I don't love you' " (*God of Small Things*, 144). To the surprise of the twins, she loves Joe, her stepfather most, more than her living "real" father, even more, it seems, than her living mother. Sophie Mol has "walked out of the Play," the "Welcome Home, Our Sophie Mol Play," that the twins, "a pair of actors, [are] trapped in . . . with no hint of plot or narrative. Stumbling through their parts, nursing someone else's sorrow. Grieving someone else's grief" (*God of Small Things*, 182)—the unspoken, unacknowledged, perhaps mostly unknown determinism of family dynamics.

The memories Rahel revisits early in the novel as she revisits her childhood home are of Sophie's funeral—and they are rich with humor and energy. In fact, the two inspirational forces in the life of the twins, Sophie Mol and Velutha, are remembered as two stars, one falling, one rising. As a child, Rahel remembers thinking that Sophie Mol "was awake for her funeral [and that s]he showed Rahel Two Things."

> Thing one was the newly painted high dome of the yellow church . . . painted blue like the sky, with drifting clouds and tiny whizzing jet planes with white trails that crisscrossed in the clouds. . . . [She thinks of s]omeone who had taken the trouble to go up there [and paint the sky blue, the clouds white, the jets silver] someone like Velutha, barebodied and shining, sitting on a plank, swinging from the scaffolding in the high dome of the church, painting silver jets in a blue church sky. (*God of Small Things*, 7–8)

"Thing Two" is a baby bat who hides in Baby Kochamma's midriff, and when discovered, "flew up into the sky and turned into a jet plane without a crisscrossed trail" (*God of Small Things*, 8), both things symbols of the spirituality of little things and of those untainted, excluded from this society. Furthermore, what Rahel notices is that Sophie turns a cartwheel in her coffin, and that she wasn't dead, that "Sophie Mol died because she couldn't breathe . . . [that] [h]er funeral killed her" (*God of Small Things*, 9). The "Loss of Sophie Mol" remains a vital force in the lives of the survivors, as Rahel notices that "the Loss of Sohie Mol stepped softly around the Ayemenem House like a quiet thing in socks . . . grew robust and alive. It was always there. Like a fruit in season. Every season . . . [i]t ushered Rahel through childhood (from school to school to school) into woman-hood" (*God of Small Things*, 17). Roy suggests that the vitality of the child sur-vives even in its loss, so devastating and so energizing is her memory for her cousins who felt so implicated in her death.

The children's sense of wonder, a remnant of childhood imagination, does survive the heavy hand of suppression. Rahel continues to wonder about words, how they look and sound—"*Humbling* . . . a nice word, . . . *Humbling along with-out a care in the world . . . twinkle* . . . a word with crinkled, happy edges" (*God of Small Things*, 53). And Estha's wonderful question, which he senses he is per-mitted to ask, seems at the heart of things. He asks, " 'If you're happy in a dream, Ammu, does that count?' " And then " 'If you eat fish in a dream, does it count? Does it mean you've eaten fish?' " (*God of Small Things*, 208).

It certainly counts in Roy's sense of where hope comes from. In such a treacherous world, examples of which echo everywhere in the novel, one turns inward, to the imagination and the landscape of dreams, for inspiration. In her erotic dream of the one-armed man, a foreshadowing of her love affair with Velutha, Ammu finds happiness. And in the small things, one finds hope—in nature, in Beginnings, in children, and in love. The strange love that restores the twins to each other, the incest that marks their banishment from the larger world, underscores both the impossibility of inclusion in the macrocosm and a kind of fulfillment in the microcosm. Roy prepares for this by her early assertion "[t]hat the emptiness in one twin was only a version of the quietness in the other. That the two things fitted together. Like stacked spoons. Like familiar lovers' bodies" (*God of Small Things*, 21). And after they go to see the Kathakali dancers, they are "Quietness and Emptiness, frozen two-egg fossils, with hornbumps that hadn't grown into horns" (*God of Small Things*, 224). The incest, of course, is a regression, but like all regressive acts, has the potential to heal what was imma-nent, gestating, but paralyzed. Their separation, abrupt and violent, forced on them in childhood, created a hiatus, a frozen moment in their development. And so, this natural and at the same time antisocial love suggests here a return to the earlier moment of innocence, and a renewal. Roy tells us,

> There is very little that anyone could say to clarify what happened next. Nothing that (in Mammachi's book) would separate Sex from Love. Or Needs from Feel-ings. . . . Only that Quietness and Emptiness fitted together like stacked spoons. Only that they held each other close, long after it was over. Only that what they shared that night was not happiness, but hideous grief. Only that once again they broke the Love Laws. That lay down who should be loved. And how. And how much. (*God of Small Things*, 310–1)

There is something infinitely healing about finally sharing what they had previously borne alone.

At the end, we are returned through the almost primeval imagery back to the beginning of the novel—the world sensuous and teeming with vitality. As Ammu and Velutha make love at the end of the novel (although this happens many years before the incest scene that precedes it), the world is alive with, "The White termites on their way to work. The White ladybirds on their way home. The White beetles burrowing away from the light. The White grasshopper with whitewood violins. The sad white music. All gone" (*God of Small Things*, 318)—but only because it is day and they are recurring creatures of the night. And against the dangerousness of their love, Roy tells us that Velutha "folded his fear into a perfect rose" (*God of Small Things*, 319), which he offered to Ammu, in love. This on the eve of Sophie Mol's arrival, after which nothing will be the same, after which all their worst fears are actualized.

If these pairs of lovers negate the constructed social order, one that draws on the deep and crippling divisions of the caste system, fracturing the body from the spirit, sex from love, child from parent, Roy has said that "the god of small things is the inversion of God. God's a big thing and God's in control" of a cruel world that mutilates the human spirit. She says,

> The god of small things . . . whether it's the way children see things or whether it's the insect life in the book or the fish or the stars—there is a not accepting of what we think of as adult boundaries. This small activity that goes on is the under life of the book. All sorts of boundaries are transgressed upon. At the end of the first chapter . . . little events and ordinary things are just smashed and reconstituted, imbued with new meaning to become the bleached bones of the story.[2]

The two acts of love, both forbidden, are the only two acts of wholeness in the book, and they form the last two chapters. While the incest suggests regression, arrested growth, the consummation of the love between Ammu and Velutha placed at the every end of the book, so that we end on the word "Tomorrow," suggests the hope that cannot be realized in this world. But there is still tomorrow, "the one small promise" the lovers gave to each other, with its potential to heal and generate less fractured, more gratifying love. At the end, with this love, we are returned to early life forms, to innocence, suggested by the first human pair, the lovers, to begin again, with the promise of tomorrow.

## 2. *The Poisonwood Bible*: Childhood as Site of Colonization

Both Arundhati Roy and Barbara Kingsolver explore the connection between childhood and history, childhood as history of the self. Their stories depict childhood as a microcosmic site of colonization, similar to the colonizing of the less industrialized nations by white imperialist nations. In *The Poisonwood Bible*,[3]

Kingsolver makes manifest her hatred of patriarchal oppression of women, children, and nations. It is the story of Reverend Price, his wife, Orleanna, and four daughters, who leave for the Belgian Congo in 1959 as missionaries. It is a long and often painful read through the various injustices Reverend Price inflicts on everyone, his family and his new community in the Congo, relieved by Kingsolver's hilarious sense of humor and the dramatic and convincing voices of the four girls who tell this story. It is told against a background of biblical movements: from "Genesis," to "Revelation," to "Exodus." It ends with "The Eyes in the Trees," a movement toward insight into the primeval past of our heritage. Kingsolver says in a preface, "I spent nearly thirty years waiting for the wisdom and maturity to write this book" (*Poisonwood*, x), and though she claims this book demonstrates "neither," it seems to contain both, even if it feels at times sprawling and uneven. The vitality of the highly individualized narratives of the four girls transform this story from a treatise on the horrors of colonization or a history of the freeing of the Congo from rule by imperial powers—both of which it is—to a page-turner of depth and insight.

*The Poisonwood Bible* begins with a quote from Genesis about "replenish[ing] the earth, and subdu[ing] it," which assumes mankind's "dominion over every living thing that moveth upon the earth" (Genesis 1:28), a position that, when isolated and uncontextualized, contains a warning. Certainly the unfolding events reveal the destructive ways in which Reverend Price interprets the Bible, as it has been by others who saw themselves as spiritually transforming a primitive society. Reverend Price incessantly cites particular passages as proof of his autocratic right to impose his will over the indigenous Congolese, over his family, over the creatures, and over the landscape itself. He becomes increasingly unyielding and isolated as each daughter, sequentially, speaks her piece. Together their voices reveal the story of the Congo, as they come to know it, intimately, but from their position as outsiders.

The girls relay the story, one picking up where the other left off, moving it along chronologically like a log or diary. It is framed by Orleanna, their mother, in present time in Georgia, told in retrospect. She begins: "Imagine a ruin so strange it must never have happened," and yet, of course, it did, has, and does, repeatedly. She seems to be directly addressing the reader: "First, picture the forest. I want you to be its conscience, the eyes in the trees" (*Poisonwood*, 5). She says, "Maybe I'll even confess the truth, that I rode in with the horsemen and beheld the apocalypse, but still I'll insist I was only a captive witness. What is the conqueror's wife, if not a conquest herself?" (*Poisonwood*, 9). But no matter how hampered by gender and by her provincial southern upbringing, she waits too long before abandoning her cruel, obsessed, and barely sane husband, and, as a result, their youngest child, Ruth May, dies in Africa. The story of the sacrifice of Ruth May and the violation of Africa are part of the same tale of oppression.

The story of the colonization of Africa and its aftermath has been told many times and in many ways. But the story of the Congo's fight for self-rule, the murder of Lumumba by the CIA, and the development of the larger world economic order from which we are still reeling is brought to life here through the eyes of four children with very different perspectives. And the story's poignancy as it is told through the children's perspective, as in *The God of Small Things*, is what distinguishes this novel from many other political and historical critical fictions. Unlike its early prototype *Heart of Darkness*,[4] *The Poisonwood Bible* is a domestic, female view of male colonial domination. The point of entry into the story is that of the mother, while the children serve, as in much of the literature of childhood, to question and reveal the assumptions of their society. After having witnessed "the ruination" of their youngest sister, as well as many African children (and adults), the children come to represent the "story waiting to be told," the hope that they can make use of the knowledge they come to in their adult years. The story of their development into adults represents a challenge to the outsider as it raises the following questions: What does Africa "mean" here? What can come from this experience? Kingsolver asks us to consider these questions when Orleanna calls upon us to judge them. She says, "Later on you'll have to decide what sympathy they deserve" (*Poisonwood*, 5). She seems to mean something beyond this initial assessment, when we discover shortly that, beyond the reader, she is addressing Ruth May, her "uncaptured favorite child" who, having died so young, remains perpetually in a state of innocence, and, therefore, can judge with her childlike truthful eyes her sisters—their choices, who they turned out to be. Orleanna urges Ruth May (and us, as well) to "Look at what happened from every side and consider all the ways it could have gone. Consider, even, an Africa unconquered altogether" (*Poisonwood*, 7). From here we might even imagine a free, unshackled humanity with children at the heart of such a vision.

The stories in the first chapter, "Genesis," are grouped together as "The Things We Carried," literally conceived as the objects and metaphorically as the attitudes and expectations they brought with them—the beginnings, their initiation into their experience. Leah, the daughter most attuned to the father, begins with an honest accounting. She enters "expect[ing] everything: jungle flowers, wild roaring beasts. God's Kingdom in its pure, unenlightened glory" (*Poisonwood*, 17)—which prepares for mythic Africa, the "other" onto which we, as a culture, have projected our primal fears. Kingsolver manages to establish and maintain a real, political context, while exploring the fantasies of the colonizers and the myths they disseminate rooted in Christianity and in the economic policy of white imperialist nations. Leah, at fourteen, says, ironically, "My father, of course, was bringing the Word of God—which fortunately weighs nothing at all" (*Poisonwood*, 19), the full meaning of which she comes to discover when, as a young woman, she decides to stay in Africa and marry Anatole, the black nationalist revolutionary, the antithesis of her father.

Following Leah's narrative is that of Ruth May, the youngest child, but it is primarily used to introduce the twins, Leah and Adah, the way she sees them, as "one person" (*Poisonwood*, 21), but set in opposition, severely differentiated into light and dark, active and passive, believer and critic. This either/or paradigm will be reimagined as the twins evolve into real and complex women. The oldest child, Rachel, is heard from next. Having already entered the American teenage culture of narcissism, she is most alienated from this mission, most worldly, and least likely to change. Her immediate and forthright response establishes her as a credible character. She says, "Man oh man, are we in for it now, was my thinking about the Congo from the instant we first set foot. We are supposed to be calling the shots here, but it doesn't look to me like we're in charge of a thing, not even our own selves" (*Poisonwood*, 22). Rachel unashamedly registers the shock they are all experiencing. She says, for example, "Whenever [the women] bent over, their heavy breasts swung down like balloons full of water. I kept my eyes turned away from them, and from the naked children who clung to their long draped skirts. I kept glancing over at Father, wondering, Am I the only one getting shocked to smithereens here?" (*Poisonwood*, 25).

The narrative of Adah, the disabled twin, is last and most powerful. Her words, spoken only in her head as the family is convinced that she cannot talk, register the "truth told slant." She is the poet and approaches meaning indirectly. She begins her section, "Sunrise tantalize, evil eyes hypnotize: that is the morning, Congo pink. Any morning, every morning" (*Poisonwood*, 30). Her description of the Congo, "sprawl[ed] on the middle of the world," evokes the vitality of this primeval landscape. She says, "Sun rises, sun sets, six o'clock exactly. Everything that comes of morning undoes itself before nightfall: rooster walks back into forest, fires die down, birds coo-coo-coo, sun sinks away, sky bleeds, passes out, goes dark, nothing exists. Ashes to ashes" (*Poisonwood*, 30). Her voice encompasses the widest truth of place, both its dailyness and its mythical quality. She has the largest grasp of the way in which each family member experiences the Congo. She understands that for Leah, " 'It's a place right out of a storybook' "; she records Ruth May's innocent observations: " 'Nobody here's got very many teeth' "; and Rachel's cynicism: " 'Jeez oh man, wake me up when it's over' " (*Poisonwood*, 32).

The children speak in a mixture of realistic, colloquial "kidspeak" and the heightened prose that captures the allegorical quality of this antimissionary story. Some of their insights seem perfectly in line with their experience. At times, however, where the density of language and perception might strain credibility, the story is propelled forward at such a compelling pace, the girls' personalities so funny and inviting, that we embrace the whole epic. As the story progresses, the children record the first stirrings of their resistance and those of their mother. Even the youngest, Ruth May, observes that when the father refers to the Congolese as "living in darkness. Broken in body and soul . . . [unaware] how they could be healed," her mother suggests that " 'maybe they take a different view of their bodies' " (*Poisonwood*, 53). But it is Adah who provides the strongest counterpoint, the potentially transformative power of experience. For Adah, "Living in the Congo shakes open the prison house of my disposition and lets all the wicked hoodoo Adahs run forth" (*Poisonwood*, 55). She is liberated and ultimately healed by her experience there. Her "strong sympathy for Dr. Jekyll's dark desires and for Mr. Hyde's crooked body" (*Poisonwood*, 55) suggests the possibility of integration of her doubleness and her sense of being fractured as a twin. She understands contrariness, perversity, reversal, and the necessity to strip things from their initial positions to see them more fully. First she tells us, "When I finish reading a book from front to back, I read it back to front. It is a different book back to front, and you can learn new things from it" (*Poisonwood*, 57). Then she reverses the order of the words to read, "It from things new learn can you and front to back book different a is it?" Finally, she reverses the order of letters within words, which, rather than cohere in their original meaning, suggests new ways of understanding and approaching meaning. She says, "*Ti morf sgniht wen nrael nac uoy dna tnorf ot kcab koob tnereffid a si ti.* The normal, I understand, can see words my way only if they are adequately poetic" (*Poisonwood*, 57).

Adah notes the connection between the marginal and the poetic, suggests that the truth must be told slant if it is to be told or heard at all. And the palindrome, something that can be read backward or forward, is her objective correlative for a personal sense of order, one that takes her beyond the "drear monosyllabic" language of teasing children who victimized her, when they would chant, "*Ade*, lemonade, Band-Aid, frayed, blockade, switchblade, renegade, call a spade a spade" (*Poisonwood*, 57). She prefers "*Ada*," because, as she says, "it goes either way, like me. I am a perfect palindrome. Damn mad!" (*Poisonwood*, 58). The palindrome she associates with her father's sermonizing, the " 'Amen enema' " (*Poisonwood*, 69), is also particularly apt.

Adah's sections contain the most playful language and the most astute perceptions of childhood. For her, "The Congo is a fine place to learn how to read the same book many times. . . . Everyone else will finish with the singular plowing through, and Ada still has discoveries ahead and behind" (*Poisonwood*, 58). And her discoveries embody a good portion of the book's wisdom. The Congo offers her a different orientation, an opportunity to view her handicap in a neutral or even positive light, as difference. She says, "Here bodily damage is more or less considered to be a by-product of living, not a disgrace. In the way of the body and other people's judgment I enjoy a benign approval in Kilanga that I have never, ever known in Bethlehem, Georgia" (*Poisonwood*, 72). From her marginalized position, from the shadows she is able to perceive the double-sidedness of nature—to appreciate the creativity of the maker of such strange creatures as a parasite "as thin as a hair meandering across the front of a man's startled eyeball." "I was struck through with my own wayward brand of reverence"; she continues, "praise be the lord of all plagues and secret afflictions! If God had amused himself inventing the lilies of the field, he surely knocked His own socks off with the African parasites" (*Poisonwood*, 76). Her irreverence is a consistent source of humor while it also offers an alternative paradigm for assessing life—even living it. Rather than the limited, even destructive polar positions of good/evil, black/ white, normal/abnormal, Adah sees a light side to the dark and, equally impor- tantly, a dark side to the light. She understands that there are many ways to view a single moment or issue. Her reversals tolerate what isn't seen by living in the light, by traveling down the "right" road, by not straying from its path. And through Adah, Kingsolver explores the ways in which children are oppressed by ideas of what is normal, by the roles they are expected to play, and by the dreams and wishes they are conditioned to fulfill that rent and subvert their nature.

It is Adah who observes the ways in which Kilkongo, an inflected language, which is "not exactly spoken but sung"—in which "[t]he same word slanted up or down the scale can have different meanings" (*Poisonwood*, 94), expands possibil- ity and, in fact, offers insight in surprising ways that again remind us of the way poets hear and construct language. Adah quotes from William Carlos Williams, "So much depends on a red wheelbarrow glazed with rain water," and transforms it into a statement about the relativity of culture, when she says, "So much depends on the tone of voice," and "Our Baptist ears from Georgia will never understand the difference" (*Poisonwood*, 175). As an outsider to her own culture, Adah grasps the difficulty in crossing cultural boundaries, of mediating between cultures. Rachel, already inculcated with American teenage preoccupations, such as complexion, hairstyle, clothing, cares little for precision of language or mean- ing, and recites malapropisms, in her smug commentaries: "It's a sheer tapestry of justice," she says, and "your chances are dull and void" (*Poisonwood*, 177).

Adah recognizes the power of language to convey a worldview or way of seeing, and to express the complexity of states of mind. She notes that,

> *Muntu* is the Congolese word for *man*. Or *people*. But it means more than that. Here in the Congo I am pleased to announce there is no special difference between living people, dead people, children not yet born, and gods—these are all *muntu*. . . . All other things are *kintu*: animals, stones, bottles. A place or a time is *hantu*, and a quality of being is *kuntu*: beautiful, hideous, or lame, for example. All these things have in common the stem word *ntu*. "All that is being here, *ntu*," says Nelson with a shrug, as if this is not so difficult to understand. And it would be simple, except that "being here" is not the same as "existing." He explains the difference this way: the principles of *ntu* are asleep, until they are touched by *nommo. Nommo* means *word*. The rabbit has the life it has—not a rat life or mongoose life—because it is named *rabbit, mvundla*. A child is not alive, claims Nelson, until it is named. I told him this helped explain a mystery for me. My sister and I are identical twins, so how is it that from one single seed we have two such different lives? Now I know. Because I am named *Adah* and she is named *Leah*. (*Poisonwood*, 209)

This contextualizing of experience allows Adah to know her own experience more fully, to discover meaning the ways poets do in the act of creating—a reve- lation that begins in Book Two, "The Revelation," and continues throughout the story. Understanding Congolese language brings Adah to a pivotal insight, an epiphany about her father's use of religion. She sees that when Reverend Price declares, " 'Tata Jesus is Bangala!' " he does not understand that the way he pronounces *Bangala*, transforms its meaning from "something precious and dear" to "the poisonwood tree," which "will make you itch like nobody's business" (*Poisonwood*, 276). She observes that "while Our Father was preaching the gospel of poisonwood, his own daughter Ruth May rose from the dead. Our Father did not particularly notice. Perhaps he is unimpressed because he assumed all along this would happen. His confidence in the Lord is exceptional. *Dog ho! Evol's dog!*" (*Poisonwood*, 276). Adah's palindrome here, the reversal of God's love, accentuates her father's neglect of her sister, that his obsession with "the Lord" prevents him from even noticing that his critically ill daughter has been saved, at least for the time being.

Furthermore, Adah notes, "Ruth May is not the same Ruth May she was. Yam Htur. None of us is the same. . . . Only Nahtan remains essentially himself, the same man however you look at him. The others of us have two sides. We go to bed ourselves and like poor Dr. Jekyll we wake up changed" (*Poisonwood*, 276). Such rigidity, such inability to acknowledge, appreciate, or bend in any way in the face of such difference, suggests the fate of Reverend Price. As the story unfolds and the children evolve, Nathan notices "the children less and less." It is dangerous not to notice children, Kingsolver suggests here—not only because they are vulnerable, and need care and protection. But also because they illuminate what the world needs to attend to. As the least powerful beings in our society, they often speak in code, so that we need particularly to note the signs and symbols of their observations and intuitions. Orleanna says, "Their individual laughter he couldn't recognize, nor their anguish. He never saw how Adah chose her own exile; how Rachel was dying for the normal life of slumber parties and record albums . . . [how] Leah followed him like an underpaid waitress hoping for the tip" (*Poisonwood*, 98).

*The Poisonwood Bible* urges us to listen to children, who, like slaves with their masters, watch their parents and those who control their world, so that they often know more about the powerful than the powerful know about them or about themselves. Each of the children reflects some significant aspect of the experience. In "The Things We Learned" section of "The Revelation," Leah articulates the primal quality of any new experience, when she says,

> In the beginning we were just about in the same boat as Adam and Eve. We had to learn the names of everything. *Nkoko, mongo, zulu*—river, mountain, sky—everything must be called out from the void by the word we use to claim it. . . . Our very own backyard resembles the Garden of Eden. I copy down each new word . . . and vow to remember it always, when I am a grown-up American lady with a backyard garden of my own. I shall tell all the world the lessons I learned in Africa. (*Poisonwood*, 101).

To do this, she says, "I look hard at everything and blink ... my eyes ... a Brownie camera taking photographs to carry back" (*Poisonwood*, 102).

But translating difference is not as simple as she, the child, expects it to be. As she becomes more reflective, she notes "It struck me what a wide world of difference there was between our sort of games—'Mother May I?,' 'Hide and Seek,' " and the games of the African children—" 'Find Food,' 'Recognize Poisonwood,' 'Build a House' " (*Poisonwood*, 114). She concludes, "that the whole idea and business of Childhood was ... something more or less invented by white people and stuck onto the front end of grown-up life like a frill on a dress" (*Poisonwood*, 115). Leah begins to perceive the structure of colonization, the oppression of race and gender, that "gifted doesn't count for a hill of beans in the Congo, where even somebody as smart as Nelson [her African friend] isn't allowed to go to college, anymore than us Price girls are" (*Poisonwood*, 143). What she has learned has been so transformative that when she is thinking about writing to her friends back home, she wonders:

> Where do you start? ... "This morning I pulled back the mosquito netting that's tucked in tight around our beds because mosquitoes here give you malaria, a disease that runs in your blood which nearly everyone has anyway but they don't go to the doctor for it because there are worse things like sleeping sickness or the *kakaka* or that someone has put a *kibaazu* on them, and anyway there's really no doctor nor money to pay one, so people just hope for the good luck of getting old because then they'll be treasured, and meanwhile they go on with their business because they have children they love and songs to sing while they work, and ..." You'd have to explain the words, and then the words for the words. (*Poisonwood*, 235)

There is no simple meeting ground for such diverse cultures. Many bridges have to be built. Even the way Leah literally sees has changed. She notices Ruth May's shadow on a swing transform "into the thin, curved legs of an antelope, with small rounded hooves at the bottom instead of feet." And although she understands that "it was only shadow and the angle of the sun, but still," she reports, "it's frightening when things you love appear suddenly changed from what you have always known" (*Poisonwood*, 236). Even Ruth May, youngest and simplest in her observations, records a sense of chaos, a shift in the family's condition, as she wonders: "Where will we be safe? When Mama raises her eyes up to him [Father] they are so cold there isn't even any Mama home inside there" (*Poisonwood*, 238). She reflects, "Bandu is name. ... It means the littlest one on the bottom. And it means the reason for everything," which suggests her belief in an order, a coherent sense of God and of their father, which has collapsed for the others, and which gradually disintegrates for Ruth May as well. They all come to understand that for their father, God equals authority, power, and control. As children, they associated God with their father as a sense of justice or fairness in the world. This is the core of innocence that has shifted.

Their belief in their country has also undergone a change. Even Rachel, who will become an exploiter of Africa in her own way, begins to comprehend the imperialist business of the United States in Africa when she points to a cartoon in an American newspaper, in which "big, fat, bald-headed Nikita Khrushchev in his Communist uniform was holding hands and dancing with a skinny cannibal native with big lips and a bone in his hair . . . singing, 'Bingo Bango Bongo, I don't want to leave the Congo!' " (*Poisonwood*, 161). She also understands that her father is impermeable, that with each new bit of news, he acts like "it's a movie he's already seen" (*Poisonwood*, 162). Adah intuits that the United States is implicated in the plans for Lumumba's assassination, when she says, "The King of America [Eisenhower] wants a tall thin man in the Congo to be dead . . . the smiling bald man with the grandfather face has another face" (*Poisonwood*, 297). She has begun to understand complexity in its many forms by embracing her own darkness. She identifies with Emily Dickinson, when she says,

> She liked herself best in darkness, as do I. . . . *Benduka* is the bent-sideways girl who walks slowly, but *benduka* is also the name of a fast-flying bird, the swallow with curved wings who darts crookedly quick through trees near the river. This bird I can follow. I am the smooth, elegant black cat who slips from the house as a liquid shadow after dark. Night is the time for seeing without being seen. (*Poisonwood*, 295)

She says, "I want to make the shadow pass over all the clean, startled faces, all those who believe in president grandfathers" (*Poisonwood*, 298). To see and know the underside of things is a gift that Adah, the poet, comes to value. Whatever blocks this potential for illumination is dangerous. Denial, rather than seeing in and through the darkness, will obscure the truth. And Reverend Price is the almost too perfect example, in his refusal to see what is perfectly obvious to everyone. Even after his child dies, and his wife and three surviving children leave him alone without any support from the villagers, he resists everything except his idea of Jesus, and goes insane, much like Kurtz does in Conrad's *Heart of Darkness*.

Kingsolver uses two pivotal events in *The Poisonwood Bible* to represent two aspects of nature, both darkly compelling, which lead to the final transforming event of Ruth May's death. The first is a plague of flesh-eating ants that devour everything in their path. This experience, which Rachel describes as being "alive in hell" (*Poisonwood*, 301), serves as a touchstone of survival. A recognition that nature is, indeed, red in tooth and claw, ants doing what ants do to survive, calls into question the basic tenets of humanity: What distinguishes us from the animal kingdom? Leah, who has most fully embraced her father's religious stance, concludes in the face of such ravaging that " 'God hates us' " (*Poisonwood*, 308). But Anatole, the educated Congolese, urges more reflection, when he answers, " 'Don't blame God for what ants have to do. We all get hungry. Congolese people are not so different from Congolese ants. . . . When they are pushed down long enough they will rise up. If they bite you, they are trying to fix things in the only way they know' " (*Poisonwood*, 308). He offers this advice: " 'Don't expect God's protection in places beyond God's dominion' " (*Poisonwood*, 309). To survive, the children must go beyond the example of their father, who tried to plant an American garden in Congolese soil. They must leave behind the sense of fairness that belongs to childhood, which Leah feels as "the breath of God grow[ing] cold on my skin" (*Poisonwood*, 309–10). Adah, on the other hand, adopts a new palindrome, "Live was I ere I saw evil," to underscore her sense of unfairness, of being *left behind* as a state of being rather than a moment or event through which she temporally passes. During the ant plague, when her mother chose to save Ruth May, Adah says, "I should have been devoured in my bed, for all I seemed to be worth" (*Poisonwood*, 305). But in the face of her worst fear of abandonment, Adah has an epiphany. She comes to recognize, "That night marks my life's dark center, the moment when growing up ended and the long downward slope toward death began. The wonder to me now is that *I* thought myself worth saving . . . the crooked girl believed her own life was precious. That is what it means to be a beast in the kingdom" (*Poisonwood*, 306). Perhaps this is the pivotal moment where childhood is left behind, when we realize that we must choose ourselves, that we are responsible for ourselves, that we, as Adah says, are worth saving.

The second pivotal event is the hunt, in which Leah bucks all convention to join the men of the tribe in their hunt for animals. It is a truly harrowing scene with fires startling the innocent creatures into a kind of obeisance. In the face of this horror, Rachel vows,

> that if I lived through the ordeal, I would not touch a single one of those animals they trapped and killed out there on the hillside like innocent children. That's all they were—the baboons and warthogs and antelopes scared crazy by the fire. And the people no different from animals. . . . All of them . . . just dumb animals cursed with the mark of ash on their brow. . . . Poor dumb animals running for their lives. (*Poisonwood*, 351)

The bestiality, the natural behavior of ants hunting down all living things and the equally natural behavior of the hungry humans hunting animals, depicts a dark necessity. But the "melee of screaming and fighting" that followed depicts the horror at the core of the heart of darkness that Kurtz envisioned and embodied. What should have been cause for a celebration—enough meat for the whole village—becomes a scramble of man against man: as Leah comments, "We were all swept up in a greediness we couldn't stop" with a war "already roaring toward us, whites against blacks" (*Poisonwood*, 352). The question is, what do we do in the face of such a vision?

Rachel's vow is short-lived. Leah becomes overtly oppositional to her father, the hunt just the beginnings of her rebellion, as she leads the children in a break with the father to support Nelson, in his fear of "some dark thing out there watching us from the forest" (*Poisonwood*, 358). Leah has come to understand that "whether you call it fear or the dreaming of snakes or false idolatry or what—it's still *something*. It doesn't care what prayers we say at bedtime, or whether we admit we believe in it. Does it believe in us, that's the question" (*Poisonwood*, 357–8). And, indeed, the danger is real, whatever the name. Ruth May dies bitten by a snake positioned right outside the house as an act of revenge. And in the face of this ultimate devastation, the death of the youngest child, each child becomes an outsider to the family, or rather, the family disintegrates, which Adah, in her sense of powerlessness, expresses in one of her "most perfect backward-forward hymns":

> *Lived a tune, rare nut, a devil,*
> > *Lived a devil!*
> > *Lived a devil!*
> *Wets dab noses on bad stew,*
> > *Evil deed live!*
> > *Evil deed live!*
> *Sun! opus! rat! See stars upon us,*
> > *Eye, level eye!*
> > *Eye, level eye!*
> *Warn, rotten Ada, net torn raw:*
> > *Eye did peep did eye.* (*Poisonwood*, 360)

Cryptic, poetic, incantatory, Adah's words suggest meaning beyond sense, meaning that can't be located syntactically. Death, and in particular the unnecessary death of the youngest child, subverts logic. The evil Adah speaks of is inextricably linked to some insight she has had into living, into the horror she has seen: "Ruth May marvel-eyed with a hand cupped over her mouth," as she says, [is what] "I have willed myself to forget, forget, forget, and not forget, for those eyes will see through anything, even my dreams. Ruth May with the eyes of an Easter morning" (*Poisonwood*, 361). Rather than Christ rising, the vision of the dead child, of the death of innocence prevails and will be revisited forever in memory. Adah invokes Emily Dickinson's allegory of death: "Because I could not stop for Death—He kindly stopped for me" (*Poisonwood*, 365), remembering Ruth May's

> final gulp of air as hungry as a baby's first breath. That last howling scream, exactly like the first, and then at the end a fixed, steadfast moving backward out of this world. After the howl, wide-eyed silence without breath. . . . Because I could not stop for death he kindly stopped for me, or paused at least to strike a glancing blow

with his sky-blue mouth as he passed. A lightning that cannot strike twice, our lesson learned in the hateful speed of light. A bite at light at Ruth a truth a sky-blue pre-
sentiment and oh how dear we are to ourselves when it comes, it comes, that long,
long shadow in the grass. (*Poisonwood*, 365)

"After the first death, there is no other," Dylan Thomas said. Accompanied by a
loss of innocence is the knowledge that the natural world goes on, oblivious to our
loss. Leah notes that, "It seemed impossible that an ordinary, bright day should be
proceeding outside our house" that makes her feel "invisible" (*Poisonwood*, 369).
She also notices that "[f]or once" her father "had no words to instruct our minds
and improve our souls, no parable that would turn Ruth May's death by snakebite
into a lesson on the Glory of God" (*Poisonwood*, 368). The world has been utterly
changed; Leah notes how all familiar things "seemed like objects I hadn't seen
before" (*Poisonwood*, 370), and the air "a wet wool blanket you could not take
off" (*Poisonwood*, 371). Rachel, too, recognizes this

strange moment in time . . . [when] [t]he whole world would change then, and
nothing would ever be all right again. Not for our family. All the other people in the
whole wide world might go on about their business, but for us it would never be
normal again. . . . Until that moment I'd always believed I could still go home and
pretend the Congo never happened. The misery, the hunt, the ants, the embarrass-
ments of all we saw and endured—those were just stories I would tell someday
with a laugh and a toss of my hair, when Africa was faraway and make-believe like
the people in history books. The tragedies that happened to Africans were not
mine. We were different, not just because we were white and had our vaccinations,
but because we were simply a much, much luckier kind of person. (*Poisonwood*,
366–7)

The end of childhood also means coming to terms with one's ordinariness, with
the fact that each of us is only one person on the face of this large, multitudinous
earth—a basic tenet of human mortality we all have to bend to.

What use do we make of this knowledge? of our tragedies? our pasts? The
rest of the book, Books Five through Eight, addresses this question. Beginning
with "The Exodus," each of the girls, along with Orleanna their mother, shapes her
destiny in response to that turning point in the chapter, "What We Carried Out."
Indeed, as Leah says, "We only took what we could carry on our back" (*Poisonwood*, 389), their profound insights into the nature of grief, their transition out of
childhood. Orleanna keeps moving, her grief, she tells us, "streamed out behind
me like a swimmer's long hair in water. . . . My body understood there was no safe
place for me to be. A mother's body remembers her babies" (*Poisonwood*, 381).
"*My baby*," she says, "*my blood, my honest truth: entreat me not to leave thee, for
whither thou goest I will go*" (*Poisonwood*, 382). Her primal words, heightened by

Kingsolver's italics, refer to the ancient biblical archetype of loyalty, the creed of blood, family, and tribe, as Naomi and Ruth spoke, beloved to beloved. Orleanna invokes, "My little beast, my eyes, my favorite stolen egg. Listen. To live is to be marked. To live is to change, to acquire the words of a story and that is the only celebration we mortals really know. In perfect stillness, frankly, I've only found sorrow" (*Poisonwood*, 385). And, of course, Reverend Price, who couldn't change, who could not listen, the only character in the family who does not tell his own story, does not survive. He embodies the cautionary plot, his story a reminder that to survive you must allow experience to work its work. "I moved," Orleanna tells us, "and he stood still" (*Poisonwood*, 384).

The story each girl tells of the meaning of her experience in postcolonial Africa crystallizes into a modern exemplar. Rachel tells the survival story. She becomes an entrepreneur, owns her own hotel, exploits and is exploited by several husbands, living as a white women in Johannesburg, South Africa, where, as she says, "I was determined right off the bat to make the best of my situation. . . . When I get out of bed every morning, at least I'm still alive and not dead like Ruth May. So I must have done something right. Sometimes you just have to save your neck and work out the details later." Referring to the ant plague, she concludes, "Stick out your elbows, pick up your feet, and float along with the crowd! The last thing you want to do is get trampled to death" (*Poisonwood*, 405). She lives her life without introspection, without consciousness, without connection to her past, as she says:

> I have put the past behind me and don't even think about it. . . . Do I have a mother, father, and sisters? Did I even *come* from anywhere? I have a little tiny picture of my sisters and me. . . . Sometimes I get it out and stare at those teeny little sad white faces, trying to make out where I am in that picture. . . . But the picture is so small I have to hold it practically at the end of my nose to make out who is who. It hurts my eyes to focus on it, so it mostly stays in the drawer. (*Poisonwood*, 425)

Leah tells the love story. She says, "Love changes everything. I never suspected it would be so. Requited love, I should say, for I've loved my father fiercely my whole life, and it changed nothing" (*Poisonwood*, 399). To love as an adult, with full consciousness, means loving the right person, being loved back. Her love story is one of integration between the white American and the black African, Anatole, who saves her from illness, to whom she is " 'Beene-beene. The truest truth' " (*Poisonwood*, 396). And a basic truth about love is that the loved one is always an "other," similar in some ways to any other kind of "otherness." In other words, naratives of love always represent difference. Whether the pair is from such disparate cultures as they are or simply from the differing cultures of gender, the issue is difference. How, finally, can we reach a point of integration or at least acceptance? Leah's four children represent a balance, an integration of "the colors of silt, loam, dust, and clay, an infinite pallette" and, as her final words assert, "I understand that time erases whiteness altogether" (*Poisonwood*, 526). At least that is her dream, what she has built her life on, embracing black Africa as her homeland. From Angola, Leah writes, "And in our bed, which Anatole calls the New Republic of Connubia, my husband tells me the history of the world" (*Poisonwood*, 520), which suggests a place of peace, a resting place, or at least a domestic narrative of integration. In its political counterplot, the story of Lumumba's assassination, Mobutu's reign, and finally of the forming of Zaire, which runs throughout Leah's love story, it is a story of constant and dangerous struggle.

Adah's narrative is more psychological. It embraces the issue of identity as a story of process, of the synthesis of the various parts of a self in relation to culture. She says, using Dickinson again, "Tell all the truth but tell it slant. . . . And really what choice do I have?" she asks. "I am a crooked little person, obsessed with balance" (*Poisonwood*, 407). The balance Adah seeks seems a profound search for truth. Her most striking palindrome, "Live was I ere I saw evil," is a statement about fracture, or, as she says,

> Alive one moment, dead the next, because that is how my divided brain divined the world . . . room in Adah for nought but pure love and pure hate. Such a life is satisfying and deeply uncomplicated. Since then, my life has become much more difficult. Because later on, she [mother] chose *me*. In the end she could only carry one child alive out of Africa and I was that child. Would she rather have had Ruth May? Was I the booby prize? . . . Am I alive only because Ruth May is dead? What truth can I possibly tell? (*Poisonwood*, 413)

But truth is more complicated, as Adah comes to understand, when she loses her "slant." When she discovers that she is not permanently crippled, but in fact "normal," she has to confront the dark story of her identity. She asks, "Will I lose myself entirely if I lose my limp? . . . Will salvation be the death of me?" (*Poisonwood*, 441). And what Africa has forced her to acknowledge, the floor it "has slipped . . . out from under my righteous house, my Adah moral code . . . [w]hat I carried out of Congo on my crooked little back is a ferocious uncertainty about the worth of a life" (*Poisonwood*, 443). Her terror at this discovery involves acknowledging that "[i]n spite of myself I have loved the world a little and may lose it" (*Poisonwood*, 444). As a child that world was her mother, and her crookedness kept her safe from competing with "Perfect Leah." Her protection against abandonment was to keep her dark identity intact, to assume, to choose being left behind. When her mother finally tells her, " 'After Ruth May, you were my youngest . . . a mother takes care of her children from the bottom up,' " Adah comes to grips with "the bedtime story my mother made up for me. It was not a question of my own worth at all. There is no *worth*. It was a question of position, and a mother's need. After Ruth May, she needs me most. I find this remarkably comforting. I have decided to live with it" (*Poisonwood*, 444). Adah knows that we are all "[t]rying to invent our version of the story. All human odes," she claims, "are essentially one. 'My life: what I stole from history, and how I live with it' " (*Poisonwood*, 492). In the final analysis, the stories we embrace as our life's destiny, rather than the truth of our lives, are actually those truths we are able to live with.

> At the end, Adah asserts, I am still Adah but you would hardly know me now, without my slant. . . . Oddly enough, it has taken me years to accept my new position. . . . Along with my split-body drag I lost my ability to read in the old way. When I open a book the words sort themselves into narrow-minded single file on the page; the mirror-image poems erase themselves half-formed in my mind. (*Poisonwood*, 492)

What Adah refuses to give up is her "privilege" as a marginalized person, the truths she has seen from the shadows. And her African story tells of how, "In Congo I was one-half *benduka* the crooked walker, and one-half *benduka*, the sleek bird that dipped in and out of the banks with a crazy ungrace that took your breath. . . . And how can I invent my version of the story without my crooked vision?" (*Poisonwood*, 493).

*The Poisonwood Bible* becomes the story of the construction of the story of childhood. Only by understanding that she spent most of her "childhood energy" feeling betrayed, "[b]y the world in general, Leah in particular," that "[b]etrayal bent me in one direction while guilt bent her [Leah] the other way," can Adah recast her identity, reclaim parts of herself that she had to discard. "Misunderstanding is my cornerstore," she claims, and understands that "It's everyone's, come to think of it. Illusions mistaken for truth are the pavement under our feet. They are what we call civilization" (*Poisonwood*, 532). Just as different versions of the Bible are flawed and come to be known for their flaw—"In the Sin-On Bible," she tells us, "John 5:14 exhorted the believers not to 'sin no more,' but to 'sin on more!' " (*Poisonwood*, 533), Adah has come, like many of us, to be identified by our mistakes and in limited and mistaken ways. To survive childhood, Kingsolver seems to conclude, you learn to assess the mistakes of your parents and the damage that was done. But this is only half of the story. The rest is an acknowledgement of the tale in retrospect. As an adult, your childhood story includes not only the mistakes of your parents, the damage they did, but your own transgressions. In denying her own failings, in creating the story of their African experience with her father as the single villain, Rachel has constructed a melodrama, a limited and limiting narrative as her destiny. For, as Adah says, "Believe this: the mistakes are part of the story" (*Poisonwood*, 533).

In *The God of Small Things* and *The Poisonwood Bible*, the adults' visions and choices are inevitably flawed. The "mistakes" are the parts of the story that are not told. The suppression of such truths is shown to be dangerous, and the child becomes a way of talking about the truth, a compass that directs us to an alternative vision, one eclipsed by all the oppressive "forces that block children's full emergence as expressive subjects,"[5] from familial to colonial powers. And the discovery of how to overcome these forces, how to begin to envision a more honest and egalitarian society, is revealed by children in their often unconscious questioning of adult authority and in their suffering.

# 8

# The Contemporary Child
# in Children's Literature

It seems that much contemporary writing for children is more explicit about the traumas of children than ever before. The accompanying feelings of grief, terror, loneliness, anger, and anxiety are explored more fully and, I believe, demonstrate the release that such expression often offers to the characters in the stories and to the empathic reader. Freedom from inhibitions about what one can and cannot write can inspire creativity and originality in children. Even in fantasy literature, children's darkest fears and the various taboos implicit in the horror story are portrayed more directly and graphically than in their predecessors. Whether the focus is on sex, death, or a conflation of the two, Kimberly Reynolds[1] offers two different understandings, both from French feminists, Julia Kristeva and Hélène Cixous. She claims that Kristeva sees the entry from the "maternal semiotic realm to the paternal symbolic realm," the basic socializing process, as generating the images of horror. She writes,

> Entering the symbolic is achieved at a cost—the separation from the blissful condition of unity with the mother—and maintained with difficulty. This means that anything which threatens to undermine the self-identity achieved by the transition to the symbolic is construed as fearful, and images associated with the domain of the semiotic come to be regarded as loathsome and repugnant. (Reynolds, 6–7)

She offers such examples as "leaky bodily fluids" and "inarticulate," babyish monsters. It seems to me that infantile parents suggest another frightening and compelling source. Reynolds goes on to state what many psychologists and psychoanalytic critics have noted, that "[t]he images that frighten us are perverted and disguised images of what we long for," particularly in adolescence when "the process of separation begun in infancy is generally reactivated" (Reynolds, 7). Cixous, on the other hand, sees children's fascination with the "bizarre and the uncanny" as "flirting" with the idea of death in that a figure such as a ghost represents both an attempt at adjustment to and an escape from the idea of mortality (in Reynolds, 7). Everything today is more explicit and we seem, as a culture, less protective of children. What Geraldine Brennan says of David Almond's books for children might well be said about popular novels for young adult readers. Brennan points to a tension "between children's legitimate fears, adults' fears for them, and adults' fears for themselves."[2] However fears are conflated, whether treated as fantasy or fiction, books which explore the child's psyche as a dark journey dominate the contemporary scene of children's literature and culture. My concern here is to find in the imaginative expression of childhood a poetics for children. How is their experience captured so that it becomes a landscape where they can turn for solace as well as inspiration?

When we evaluate children's books, those books that engage children, we confront the usual perspectives about aesthetics and excellence: how to tell a story authentically with language, character, and plot details that reflect and contain the truth of that experience. But children's books urge further consideration. The values the story offers, particularly those assumptions embedded in the story and perhaps unrecognized by the author, need to be teased out and explored. What does the work investigate, encourage, and teach? It is my belief that a faithful rendering of the story must not leave the child-reader in despair. And although what evokes hopelessness varies from child to child, this issue compels examination, particularly for the younger age group. A poetics for children requires a delicate rendering of hope and honesty.

In the best recent literature for children, the darker sides of childhood experience are conveyed with a depth of emotional expression. However, the vision at the heart of each story is not exclusive of hope, even in the portrayal of the darkest, often unimaginable pain that is, horrifyingly enough, the truth of some children's lives. Even in writing about incest, poverty, bigotry, and other trauma, the thrust is toward achieving balance. The experience must be recounted with the unflinching honesty that serves to witness and acknowledge the child's experience. As Annie Ernaux says in her recent memoir, *Shame*, "The worst thing about shame is that we imagine we are the only ones to experience it."[3] Children's books that tell these stories can liberate children who have encountered and internalized such experience from a belief that there is something inherently wrong with them, that they themselves are tainted. The story should also include a kind of chronicle of how one survives—and further, an indication of what one retrieves from such painful experience.

Whether the story is written in a realistic or fantastic mode, this is central to a poetics of childhood. Of course, often the richest literature for children moves between the two realms of realism and fantasy. Some fantastic literature for children moves beyond a mere echo of or rootedness in realism into a place quite recognizable in daily life. And the best realistic novels often contain at their core recurring poetic moments and extraordinary, heightened states of feeling.

## I. THE REALISTIC MODE

### 1. *Amber Was Brave, Essie Was Smart*

One such wonderful "realistic" book for children is Vera B. Williams's story of sisters, *Amber Was Brave, Essie Was Smart*, or, as Williams writes, "*The story of Amber and Essie told here in Poems and Pictures.*"[4] In her picture book, she creates portraits of her family[5] in two media: the pictures in color look like they were done with children's crayons (in this sense similar to her earlier *Cherries and Cherry Pits*[6]), and the black-and-white drawings in soft pencil. Each picture reflects a profound emotional moment in the narrative. Told in poems, the story establishes each experience as a poetic moment. Williams introduces the story with full color portraits, one back and one front, of each girl. She ends with an album of full color pictures—a collection of the moments narrated in the stories as still lifes. The stories the children tell, which are illustrated by the black-and-white drawings, place the two sisters at the center of these family sketches, as is so natural to the imagination of children.

What is most impressive about this book is the depth and breadth of emotion it portrays. The relationship between the sisters is loving and complex. They are defined by each other, though it is not a simple competitive dichotomy; nor is their relationship free from such feelings. The story seems more Amber's with its focus on the trials and triumphs of the younger sister, who is always impressed with, at times in awe of, Essie. As older sister, Essie gets to know things first, her character illuminated by that position. Amber tells us, "Essie could write her name in script . . . could tie her own shoes . . . could read hard library books" (*Amber*, 17). Amber is differentiated as brave—unafraid "of the rat/ in the wall under the sink/ or of climbing up in high places" (*Amber*, 17). But immediately after this initial psychological division of labor, their deep reciprocity is established. We are told that although "Essie kept their house key in her little purse . . . the front door to their building wouldn't even open/ unless they both pushed on it hard" (*Amber*, 17), because, as the variations on the following incantation, which run through the story, affirm:

Essie was tall and Amber was small
Essie was smart and Amber was brave
Essie and Amber
Amber and Essie. (*Amber*, 17)

Perhaps the strongest metaphor for their mutuality is what they call "Best Sandwich," a position they take where they lie closely together as one fluid breathing form. Best Sandwich, we are told, "filled them up/ when peanut butter wouldn't/ and jelly couldn't/ (only crackers were on the shelf anyway)" (*Amber*, 18). When their mother was away at her job and their father, we learn, is "far away" in jail for forging a check, when "the house felt dark . . . Best Sandwich . . . turned the room friendly from strange," as they "breathe each other's breath/ in and out and in and out" (*Amber*, 18). The pencil drawing of the two sisters curled together like twin fetuses, with their stuffed bear Wilson "right in the middle/ up against them both," recalls and even substitutes, as it often does in families, for that early preoedipal boundarylessness of mother and child. The mother here feels loving, real, and limited—at times overwhelmed with tiredness, at times with sadness, as her children watch her, "sitting sitting/ just sitting/ on her bed" (*Amber*, 35). The children are enormously comforting to each other in this difficult time.

Figure 9. Illustration from *Amber Was Brave, Essie Was Smart* by Vera B. Williams. By permission of HarperCollins Publishers.

But there are, of course, moments of anger. The sisters' greatest point of separation concerns their differing needs around their father's incarceration. Amber's need to ask "The Question That Always Made [her] Cry," "Where is Daddy?" clashes with Essie's need to put it aside and move on. Their difference is not just one of temperament, but also of development, as Essie yells at Amber, "never to ask that question again," while Amber begs, "Tell me just one more time, Essie." As an older sister, Essie has accepted the situation, but Amber has more trouble understanding it emotionally. "It's not *really* stealing . . . / And Daddy is *not* bad," she pleads, while Essie insists, "It is *too* stealing . . . and it's *very* bad"—and, further, that "*even* if you ask about it a million times more/ that won't change it" (*Amber*, 21–2). In her incapacity to accept this, Amber turns away from Essie toward Wilson, the mute bear, and affirms that

Daddy is *not* bad is he . . .
Daddy is good isn't he . . .
Daddy can't really be bad
because he's *my* daddy . . .
And he'll come back
and everything will be all right
Isn't that right, she said
and she made Wilson nod Yes Yes Yes. (*Amber*, 23)

This is a temporary rift, however. Essie restores Amber with cocoa and toast, wipes her tears away, and Amber easily forgives her, because, as Williams tells us, "it would always be Amber and Essie/ Essie and Amber" (*Amber*, 24). The drawing facing the written text shows the reassuring gaze of the bigger sister, the open responsive gaze of the smaller sister, their fingers linked—even their feet expressive of deep feeling.

There are many moments of deep feeling, as Amber's story takes center stage. One particularly beautiful time focuses on Amber's desire and fear of telling Essie the poem she has written, "a silly poem," she says, entitled "Daddy Song." Aware of Amber's embarrassment, Essie insists, "So? . . . So?" until Amber, exquisitely drawn, small in her father's shoes, arms holding herself, eyes shyly downcast, recites:

Daddy
Sadly
Daddy
Badly
Daddy
Bigly
Daddy
Minely

Figure 10. Illustration from *Amber Was Brave, Essie Was Smart* by Vera B. Williams. By permission of HarperCollins Publishers.

Daddy
Whenly
Daddy
Really
Really
Soonly. (*Amber*, 29)

Their world opens somewhat when a new little girl, Nata-Lee, "two words with a dash," moves in upstairs. Amber, brave, "goes first" to meet her, and she becomes, at times, a substitute for Essie (and also for the inanimate Wilson), when their needs clash, when Essie wants to read and Amber wants to talk. Nata-Lee has lost her mother and her sad face, as Amber tells us, her "poor little hands, my mother said/ You've bitten them bloody" (*Amber*, 48) is contrasted with the spirited sisters, whose mother, though burdened and saddened, plays beauty parlor with them, and whose father, in the end, returns home. His return is narrated in Amber's voice, as she says, "I got to the door first. . . . Daddy was standing right there" (*Amber*, 52). No more words, but such moving soft pencil drawings follow: of Amber swept into her father's arms, then of the two girls encircled in his arms, and then of all four in each other's arms, the mother smiling, eyes open.

Along with the father's return, full color returns to the illustrations of the moments narrated in the story in the album. Family life is once again cohesive, joyous, although the pictures cover a full range of feeling. They are of the pleasure of Amber and Essie jumping on the bed, tickling each other, the mother and the sisters at "beauty parlor time." They are sad and quiet of Nata-Lee sucking on the string to her jacket, hands in pockets, eyes slightly vacant. There are two opposing portraits of Amber's more solitary, emotional life. On one page, there are three pictures of her with Wilson—one in which she looks sad, one in which she is smiling, and one in which she is looking directly at the bear, in a kind of mute dialogue. Facing these is Amber wildly jumping on the bed, arms outstretched, in mid air, ecstatic. There are pictures of arms full of groceries to prepare for the father's homecoming—all of which record this deeply significant period in their lives.

At the end of the book, there are two lovely separate portraits of Amber and Essie, together on one page, which capture the psychological bearing of each sister: Amber, wondrous and still holding onto Wilson; Essie, more confident, gaze directed outward, hands on hips, adorned in a necklace, although still vulnerable in underclothes. The final picture is of the two girls, arms around each other, the swirling colors creating an enclosure for them.

### 2. *A Step From Heaven*

Like Vera B. Williams's story, An Na's recent novel, *A Step From Heaven*,[7] draws largely on her childhood. It is an intimate family portrait told by Young Ju, a sensitive and observant child. Her story is constructed, like the stories of Amber and Essie, around pivotal moments of her early childhood. We enter her story when she is very young living in Korea, and follow her immigration to America as a young girl through her life in America. We leave her when she is entering college. Young Ju tells her stories with the ear and eye of a poet, always attuned to the nuances of her parents' emotional lives. We never lose a sense of her childness, of her real and vibrant personality—although the violence of her father, and her mother's inability to stand up to him, subvert her vitality. Often, while her actions seem timid, her spirit and intensity are revealed to us through her thoughts and in the way she imagines.

The book begins with a joyous spot of time in two voices, those of the young child and her grandmother, Halmoni, playing together in the ocean. This first narrative poem, "Sea Bubble," represents a movement from timidity to exuberance:

> Just to the edge, Young Ju. Only your feet. Stay there.
> Cold. Cold water. Oh. My toes are fish. . . .
> Hold me. Hold me.
> Young Ju, can you be brave? . . . Can you try to be a brave girl for me?
> Good girl. Ready for the wave? Here it comes. Get ready. . . . There, do you still
>     want to go back?
> Again. Do it again. . . .
> *I am a sea bubble floating, floating in a dream. Bhop. (Step From Heaven, 9)*

The closeness and trust between the child and her grandmother, their fluid relationship suggested by the sea, will be sharply contrasted by the second poem, "All This Weight." It begins, "Apa [her father] is not happy. Uhmma [her mother] is not happy" (*Step From Heaven*, 10). This is the misery of the young child—to witness the pain of those on whom she utterly depends. Young Ju tell us, "It sits in my chest, hitting, hitting my heart until my eyes bleed water from the sea" (*Step From Heaven*, 10). In this extremely sexist society, Halmoni has no control over her son's drinking and violence. She expresses her helplessness by addressing her late husband's picture: "Do you see what is happening? How could you leave me with all this weight" (*Step From Heaven*, 10). For the powerless child and grandmother, the resolution of these opposite states of feeling comes in the third movement in a moment of prayer. Halmoni holds the Bible "tight with both hands" up to God for help, as she whispers, "He is the only one who can [help]" (*Step From Heaven*, 12).

Buoyancy and heaviness become the emotional poles that frame Young Ju's childhood. As the family leaves Korea for America, which Young Ju is told is "a step from heaven," the story of her life darkens and becomes more defined by a creeping despair. How and where Young Ju finds hope in this dark story of her childhood is the central concern of the book. Impressed with the magic of America, Young Ju is taught that in "Mi Gook everyone can make lots of money . . . in Mi Gook all the uhmmas are pretty" (*Step From Heaven*, 13). She is forced to curl her hair in an attempt to look more American. Here, with the beginnings of her loss of a sense of self, she tells her first lie. She says, "Even though Uhmma tells me I should always tell the truth, and Halmoni says God will be very angry if you lie, I want Uhmma to smile happy lots of teeth at me. Young Ju, do you like your curly hair? I look at the floor. Yes, I lie, quiet as snow" (*Step From Heaven*, 22). Lying becomes a source of freedom for Young Ju, associated with the early feeling of floating. When her brother Joon is born, he is clearly favored by her father. Joon can grow up to be a doctor, a lawyer, while Apa laughs at her ambitions: " 'You are a girl, Young Ju' " (*Step From Heaven*, 40), he tells her. So the gap widens between her brave self, that jumped in the waves with Halmoni, and her present emptiness. And her lies fill the void. In school, Young Ju gets the attention she craves by telling the teacher that her brother died. When the class makes "warm fuzzies" for her, she says, "today I am special. I play with my fuzzies, scratch and sniff my stickers, and think about how nice it is that my brother is dead" (*Step From Heaven*, 45). However, in her fear of being discovered, she buries them. As she says, "I cover my lies with dirt" (*Step From Heaven*, 46).

Apa continues to tyrannize the family. His sexism extends to humiliating and beating Joon for being weak, which means "whining and crying like a girl" (*Step From Heaven*, 70). He forces Joon into a suppliant position with his demands: " '[L]ook at me when I am talking to you' "; " '[w]ipe that look off your face' " (*Step From Heaven*, 69). These words are familiar to any child who has been the object of such attempts to break the young spirit. With increasing frequency and intensity, Apa's beatings take over the household. These terrifying moments become the daily fare of their lives. In this book, they are truthfully portrayed in all their darkness. And yet Young Ju, like many children, is resilient. The buoyancy that initially defined her persists. She becomes the best student in her class, negotiates her way around the Department of Immigration, learns the culture of American girls, makes a best friend. But this is also threatening to her old fashioned immigrant parents, as she becomes, in their words, "too American." Young Ju is told, "be American/don't be American." The cultural clashes are specific to Asian immigrant families, the reserve, the sense of pride demonstrated here in the mother's shame over Young Ju borrowing money from her best friend, Amanda: " 'How could you do this,' " Uhmma reproaches. This familiar conflict of the immigrant children's story is so powerfully drawn, so faithfully rendered, that it serves as a paradigm of the impossible position of many children who get caught in the double messages of childhood.

Away from his native country, Apa further deteriorates, and Young Ju and Uhmma become increasingly victims of his abuse—until one day, during a brutal beating, Young Ju dials 911 and betrays her family by telling: " 'My father is killing my mother. Please, please . . . Hurry' " (*Step From Heaven*, 141). The police insist that her father be locked up and that her mother go into a hospital. But although "her face [is] so badly bruised and misshapen," even with twelve stitches and taped ribs, she still will not press charges. Once released from prison, her father drives away with another woman, as her mother, "eyes fixed on the road," says to Young Ju, " 'This is all your fault' " (*Step From Heaven*, 142).

This is among the darkest truths of such experience for a child: that after all her pain, which of course includes the trauma of witnessing the suffering of those she most loves, she is told that she is to blame. This is one of the most honest books I've ever read about domestic abuse. It captures the complicated feelings embedded in such experience for children—the deep pockets of guilt, fear, and shame that the child internalizes and carries. It also offers an honest redemption in the understanding, always with the child in mind, of how such things happen to "ordinary" people.

What saves Young Ju, and ultimately her mother and brother, is a vision of freedom, of pleasure and of something natural and lovely, like the sea bubble experience with Halmoni at the ocean. Young Ju observes Uhmma in a rare moment of peace, walking along the beach, singing a song from church, "the one that reached impossibly for the sky. I listen to Uhmma sing," she tells us. "Her voice carries all the high notes" (*Step From Heaven*, 104). The ocean, the green hill with "a clear view of the sky" and "brand-new houses," where she and Joon find a tiny bird they name Harry, "an orphan we had to save," who is, as Young Ju says, "worse off than we were" (*Step From Heaven*, 72)—these are the landscapes of promise. Even the darkest, most horrible image of Young Ju kicked in the stomach by Apa—as she says, even as "[t]he rain of blows on my face, shoulders, and head forces my body to the ground," she escapes into the safe place of the powerless but resourceful child—the imagination. She tells us, "[m]y hands slide into the shag carpet I pretend I am drowning, letting the sea take me under. I close my eyes and the world cannot touch me" (*Step From Heaven*, 139).

Until Young Ju is able to break away from Apa's tyranny, until Uhmma finally leaves him, her vision of freedom persists in her dream world. In a section entitled "Reaching," Young Ju says, "I cling to the branch with one hand and lean out. The wind sings in my ears. If I could just get out a little farther, let the branch go and take one more step, I could almost touch the cloud. But I'm afraid to let go of the branch, so I continue to stretch. It's right there. Almost" (*Step From Heaven*, 92), and then the phone wakes her. But for a moment she felt the freedom in the vision, which often precedes the real thing. When Uhmma finally leaves Apa, whose deterioration has bound them to poverty, the three realize their dream, which takes the form of a house with a green lawn.

In this novel, healing also comes with understanding, portrayed here in beautifully wrought epiphanic moments. Subtly and delicately, An Na depicts Uhmma offering a healing vision to Young Ju in a photograph of her and her father together by the ocean. She tells her, "he taught you to be brave that day. You loved the waves after that. . . . What dreamers you two were! Pretending to be dolphins, then seals, then ships that could sail far across the sea. . . . He was a different man back then" (*Step From Heaven*, 151). As Young Ju holds the picture "close to [her] heart" she recites, "*I am a sea bubble floating, floating in a dream.*

*Bhop*" (*Step From Heaven*, 152). On this note, she leaves for college, her mother and brother safely situated in their new home.

In the epilogue that follows, entitled "Hands," An Na portrays one of the most profound lessons a child needs to learn: that she can not save her parents. Young Ju tells us, "Uhmma said her hands were her life" (*Step From Heaven*, 154), and it is from the harshness of her life, "the lines of history," that she wishes to rescue her. She says, "I tell her, I wish I could erase these scars for you" (*Step From Heaven*, 155). She has come to accept that she could not save Apa from his sorrow when Halmoni died, when in his self-lacerating grief, she observed how he cried, "pounding his fists into his forehead," and she thought, "Who is this man crying like an abandoned child? This is not my Apa who growls instead of talks" (*Step From Heaven*, 96). She has had to learn a most difficult truth, that yes, that too is her Apa, that cruel, self-pitying, infantile, abusive man who is grieving. And with the compassion that is also her source of strength, she reassures him, "Halmoni is already in heaven. She does not need you to fly to Korea to see her. She can see you" (*Step From Heaven*, 96). In response, in a rare moment of connection, she tells us, "He reaches back and holds my hand" (*Step From Heaven*, 96). Although in the final analysis, she is only reconciled with him at a remove, through a photo, although she cannot erase Uhmma's scars from her sad past, she and Uhmma walk along the beach together at the end, Uhmma's arm around her, as she "tucks a wisp of my long, straight black hair behind my ear" (*Step From Heaven*, 156) in a protective and healing gesture.

For all the graphic violence of the beatings, the story is quite quiet really. It is drawn with care and contains many contemplative parts, without sacrificing the powerful plot that drives the reader to find out what happens to Young Ju and her family. We are propelled forward in this story, which gains in intensity as the characters grow—along with our complex feelings about them—because they are so finely drawn, because we really come to know and care about them.

## 3. *Push*

The poet Sapphire's recent brilliant novel, *Push*,[8] perhaps the darkest I've ever read about childhood, has been adopted in some English classrooms in a flurry of controversy.[9] Even though it does not seem as if it were intended for children, a diverse group of young adolescents have embraced it. It is the story of Claireece Precious Jones, whose sixteen years of life have been among the most terrible imaginable—she lives in squalor and poverty, the victim of sexual abuse and violent beatings by both parents—and has given birth to one child and is pregnant with another, both by her father. This child speaks to us as one of society's invisible children, a shadow child who has been deprived of her voice as well in a school system that maintains, whether intentionally or not, the illiteracy associated with racism. Her middle name suggests the sacredness of each child, sometimes buried, between the family and first names which identify us. She takes

Precious as her name, and begins her story to tell the truth, "else," as she says, "what's the fucking use? Ain' enough lies and shit out there already?" (*Push*, 4):

> I was left back when I was twelve because I had a baby for my fahver. That was in 1983. I was out of school for a year. This gonna be my second baby. My daughter got Down Sider. She's retarded. I had got left back in the second grade too, when I was seven, 'cause I couldn't read (and I still peed on myself). . . .
> I got suspended from school 'cause I'm pregnant which I don't think is fair. I ain' did nothin'! (*Push*, 4)

Precious's abuse and neglect, coupled with her obesity, have left her with little self-esteem. But her family's extreme cruelty ironically allows her a modicum of understanding that it is not her fault, and this, in turn, helps to save her.

The title refers to the first positive connection of her life, when, as she gave birth to her first baby, and lay, "bleeding on the kitchen floor," a "coffee-cream-colored man from Spanish talk land . . . put his hand on my forehead again and whisper, 'Push, Precious, you gonna hafta *push*' " (*Push*, 16). This becomes a mantra for her, a location of inspiration retrieved from a moment of compassion. Throughout the novel, she retreats to this landscape for solace and for help coping with her new baby, with whom she breaks the cycle of abuse that has been her legacy. This is the story of what is needed to push through trauma, a chronicle of how a child can actually transform such psychological damage into poetry, the vital language of distilled experience. Even as Precious learns she is HIV positive, and, for her, is almost a certain death sentence, she is saved through the love and teachings of Miss Rain, the teacher at the alternative pre-GED class for girls. The story is built on Sapphire's experience as a literacy teacher in the Bronx and Harlem in New York. She said she wanted to "document the courage and intelligence of the students who I encountered as I was teaching."[10] She quotes from the Talmud in her epigraph, stressing a belief in the vitality of the life force she found in Precious: "Every blade of grass has its Angel that bends over it and whispers, 'Grow, grow.' "

The story is told through several kinds of language. The horror of the traumas almost preclude direct representation, so that only the unrepresentability of it can be captured. How do we create a language to contain such experience? First, through Precious's voice, which reveals the trauma of abuse as well as illiteracy. It is a stunted voice, but oddly infused with a muffled intensity. It is at times direct and angry:

> I is goin' down to the nineteenth floor . . . to the all-tur-nah-TIVE! Reeboks, white!
> Better than Nikes? No, next shits I get be Nikes! Green leather jacket, keys. I is
>     going, got my hand on the doorknob.
> "Where you going?" Mama holler from her room.
> Why ain' her fat ass sleep? I don't say nuffin'. Fuck her!

"You hear me talking to you!" I start undoing locks on the front door. . . .
"Precious!" Fuck you, bitch. Ize gone. (*Push*, 23)

It is also thoughtful, contemplative:

> I wanna say I am somebody. I wanna say it on subway, TV, movie, LOUD. I see the
> pink faces in suits look over top of my head. I watch myself disappear in their
> eyes. . . . I talk loud but still I don't exist. . . .
> Do all white people look like pictures? No, 'cause the white people at school is fat
> and cruel like evil witches from fairy tales but they exist. Is it because they
> white? . . .
> Why can't I see myself, *feel* where I begin and end. . . .
> My fahver don't see me really. If he did he would know I was like a white girl a *real*
> person, inside. . . . Can't he see I am a girl for flowers with thin straw legs and a
> place in the picture. I been out the picture so long I am used to it. But that don't
> mean it don't hurt. (*Push*, 32–3)

Her illiteracy engenders a sense of confusion and self-hate, which are themselves
a form of testimony. Precious's voice seeks to offend, wound, and eventually
move its readers beyond sympathy to some kind of social action.[11]

Sapphire's novel moves between metaphors that can sustain her through
such purgatory, like the place she escapes to in her imagination when, raped by
her father, she becomes the dancing girl on TV. As she says,

> . . . I change stations, change *bodies*, I be dancing in videos! In movies! I be break-
> ing, *fly*, jus' a dancing . . . heating up the stage at the Apollo. . . . They love me! Say
> I'm one of the best dancers ain' no doubt of or about that! . . . (*Push*, 24)

Precious creates a list of heroes who embody for her a vision of hope, and
their names, like her own, represent and serve metaphorically as a place of liberation, such as Farrakhan, "a *real* man, who don't fuck his daughter" (*Push*, 58)
and Harriet Tubman, a real woman.

The challenge for Sapphire, one she embraces continuously in her poetry, is
to connect us with such a realistic representation of abuse that we are helpless to
turn away, and that will inform the way we see the world, influence us in new
ways. How do we understand such experience? Who translates it for us? In this
novel, Precious's teacher, Miss Rain, is the liminal figure who spans both Precious's world and one more familiar to many of us. She is an educated and sensitive black lesbian who serves Precious as both witness and translator of her
experience. And through their communication, through her comments in
Precious's journal, she offers salvation. Precious tells us, "Underneaf what I
wrote Miz Rain write what I said in pencil. . . . li Mg o mi m," Precious writes,
and Miss Rain translates (*Little Mongo on my mind*)." With such reciprocity, she
helps Precious learn the alphabet so that she will be able to teach her child to

read, and, ultimately, break the cycle of abuse. She learns how to save both herself and her child with the nurturing she never got. She says, "Listen baby, I puts my hand on my stomach, breathe deep. Listen baby (I writes in my notebook): A is fr Afrc," followed by Ms. Rain's echo, placed right underneath Precious's words, distinguished by italics, "*(for Africa)*." "B is for u bae," Precious writes, and again, Miss Rain's corrections, translations, "*(you baby)*" (*Push*, 65). Some of the notations are devastating, such as "E is el l/m," translated as "*(evil like mama)*" and some like "X ma mml," translated as "*(main man Malcolm)*," are inspirational. Most touching is Precious's voice when she speaks to her unborn baby: "Listen baby, Muver love you. Muver not dumb. Listen baby: ABCDE-FGHIJKLMNOPQRSTUVWXYZ" (*Push*, 65–6).

By speaking in Precious's voice, the voice of "the barbarian poet," Sapphire refuses to deny the past. She seems to see no advantage in preserving the illusion of civilization and recalls the atrocity for what it is. She resists romanticizing or domesticating the horror. Poverty and child abuse are not new to the literature of childhood. But throughout the nineteenth century, although the picture that writers like Dickens drew might be dark and painful, the children were often charming; they often emitted an inner glow in their innocence. Even contemporary portrayals of children who have been victims of violence and abandonment, such as David Almond's *Heaven Eyes*[12] or Laurie Halse Anderson's wonderful novel, *Speak*,[13] are easily read, even gentle by comparison. But Sapphire tells the story of Precious's fight for self-respect dramatically, graphically, as well as subtly. The incidents themselves become metaphorically enhanced. For example, the elevator of the alternative school charts the beginning of her mobility. She says, " [p]ush the button, stupid, I tell myself. I push the button; I'm not stupid, I tell myself" (*Push*, 25). Her sense of self worth develops out of the intimacy she achieves with Ms. Rain which extends to a companionship with the other girls. And although the odds are that Precious will die from the AIDS virus with which her father infected her, her child is born free of it and of the curse of her life.

The book ends with a collection of the class' "Life Stories"—the testimony of others, like Precious, who have survived unbearable poverty and abuse, and who, in turn, bear witness to her story. Together they affirm that such deprivation and cruelty is not the purview of one child, in one family, but the devastating results of an unjust, uncivilized society. The book ends with an "untitled" poem by Precious, in her poetic and nonstandard, literate and illiterate language:

HOLD FAST TO DREAMS
Langston say.
GET UP OFF YOUR KNEES
Farrakhan say.
CHANGE
Alice Walker

say.
Rain fall down
wheels turn round
DON'T ALWAYS RHYME
Ms Rain say
walk on
go into the poem
the HEART of it
beating
like
a clock
a virus
tick
tock. (*Push*, unpaginated)

*Push* is a story of survival, visionary in that it offers us a chance to look closely and fearlessly into the darkest childhood. It brings visibility to those who have been for the most part invisible. Hopeful, even apocalyptic, *Push* urges us, in Walter Benjamin's apocalyptic visionary formula, to look for the jewels in the ashes, to discover the spirit and resilience of these courageous children who have been utterly discarded, who are, after all, part of the hope for the nation's future. From their experience, in their words, they illuminate the failures of our social world. Without them, there is no chance for salvation.

## II. THE FANTASTIC

### 4. *Skellig*

With *Skellig*, David Almond's recent first novel for children,[14] we enter a realm of wonder and awe. This is an extraordinary story that, organically, insistently, fuses the everyday with the fantastic. Michael, a preadolescent boy, and his family are going through a painful and stressful time. Michael's baby sister has been born prematurely and her fate is delicately positioned between life and death, as she is taken back and forth to the hospital, undergoes heart surgery, and ultimately survives. At the beginning of the novel, Michael discovers an angel, named Skellig, living or rather deteriorating in the garage of the dilapidated house the family has just bought. This is, of course, an unlikely site for a heavenly creature. Skellig is a creature of flesh and feathers. "I found him," Michael begins, "lying there in the darkness . . . in the dust and dirt. . . . He was filthy and pale and dried out and I thought he was dead. I couldn't have been more wrong" (*Skellig*, 1).

Like Michael, we are quite unprepared for this corporeal angel, although he has his predecessors in several literary sources on which Almond seems to draw. The filthy feathers and awkwardness are reminiscent of Gabriel Garcia Marquez's angel in "The Very Old Man With Enormous Wings."[15] At first Michael thinks Skellig is old and infirm. It is also suggested that he is associated in some mysterious way with Ernie, the former owner of the house, an old man who lived there alone. Skellig seems a metaphoric incarnation of Ernie, neglected, as Michael observes him with "[d]ead bluebottles . . . scattered on his hair and shoulders. I shined the flashlight on his white face and his black suit," he tells us. " 'What do you want?' [Skellig] said. . . . His voice squeaked like he hadn't used it in years" (*Skellig*, 8). The real estate agent who sold Michael's family their house (named Stone to suggest his lack of feeling), had told Michael's family that they needed to see the house "in your mind's eye"—the first allusion to Blake. Imbued with the child's sensitivity to discrepancy between adult talk and behavior, Michael notes how Ernie had "been dead nearly a week before they found him under the table in the kitchen. That's what I saw," Michael says, "when Stone told us about seeing with the mind's eye. He even said it when we got to the dining room and there was an old cracked toilet sitting there in the corner behind a plywood screen . . . that toward the end Ernie couldn't manage the stairs. . . . Stone looked at me like he didn't think I should know about such things" (*Skellig*, 2). Such things include the pain and unpleasant smells of the elderly, which make the rest of society uncomfortable, and that are also embodied in Skellig, whose breath stinks from the carrion he eats. Skellig tells Michael, offhandedly, speaking almost into a void, " 'I'm nearly nobody' " (*Skellig*, 31), as a spider crosses his mouth and he gulps it down. As Skellig feeds on dead things and lower forms of life, he recalls Bram Stoker's incarcerated madman, Renfield, of *Dracula*. Like Skellig whose valuable understanding of the world is ignored, Renfield warns against impending disaster, but is written off as a lunatic. He entreats, " 'Can't you hear me, man? . . . Will you never learn? Don't you know that I am sane and earnest now; that I am no lunatic in a mad fit, but a sane man fighting for his soul?' "[16]

Almond suggests throughout this novel that in the voices of the marginalized, whether they come from the unconventional, the "mad," the elderly—those who do not function in the mainstream of society—one can hear and see signs of promise for the future. Skellig represents the human spirit, rotting away, unheeded. Furthermore, the character in *Dracula* who ultimately breaks the spell of the vampire, who represents a synthesis of head and heart, is, like Michael's friend and mentor in this novel, named Mina. With such striking similarity of detail, it seems to me that Almond must be alluding to Stoker's gothic novel, and that *Skellig* is a kind of monster story recast as sadness, the underside of fear. It is a tale of the uncanny, which places it in the realm of fear and longing, frightening in its ability to draw us in, and in our attraction to it. The most recent popular rendition of such experience is the brilliant film, "The Sixth Sense," in which a child, in his openness, sees dead people and discovers what it means to be haunted. What takes possession of us is actually denied experience, particularly unclaimed sorrow and grief. In the film, ghosts reach out to him with their yearning to make their feelings and experience visible. Similarly, *Skellig* illuminates the realm of the uncanny as an imaginative transformation of our longing. Rather than a horror story, Michael's tale portrays a displacement of love and its restoration.

At the heart of this story is Michael's hurt and resentment, the complexity of feeling that accompanies the birth of the new baby, as well as her lingering illness. Because his parents are utterly preoccupied, understandably, with the life of their new child, nothing he was promised with the move to the new house has materialized. He says, "The garden was another place that was supposed to be wonderful," and goes on to list the things that "were going to be" lovely: benches, swings, "a pond with fish and frogs." Instead there are "just nettles and thistles and weeds and half-bricks and lumps of stone," he tells us as he "kick[s] the heads off a million dandelions" (*Skellig*, 6). In fact, the only garden is the one his father constructs out of Ernie's old toilet. Michael's parents are not insensitive to his disappointment. " 'Sorry it's all so rotten and we're all in such rotten moods,' " his mother says.

Almond does not schematize the adults in this novel. One of the most touching and psychologically complex scenes, a testament to his power as a realistic writer, occurs when Michael is fighting with his father:

"No!" I yelled. "I won't go to school! Why should I? Not today!"

"You'll do as you're bloody told! You'll do what's best for your mum and the baby!"

"You just want me out of the way so you don't have to think about me and don't have to worry about me and you can just think about the bloody baby!"

"Don't say bloody!"

"It is bloody! It's bloody bloody bloody! And it isn't fair!"

Dad kicked the leg of the table and the milk bottle toppled over on the table and a jar of jam crashed to the floor.

"See?" he yelled. "See the state you get me in?"

He raised his fists like he wanted to smash something: anything, the table, me.

"Go to bloody school!" he yelled. "Get out of my bloody sight!"

Then he just reached across and grabbed me to him.

"I love you," he whispered. "I love you."

And we cried and cried. (*Skellig*, 142–3)

While Almond is not condescending toward parents, teachers, or families, he does present some interesting radical alternatives to conventional notions of family and education. So while Michael attends the local public school, with its supportive as well as tedious aspects, it takes the home-schooled child, Mina, whom Michael finds in a tree in the garden next door, to heal his wounded heart. Mina helps him to open up, so that rather than denying his feelings about his baby sister or remaining paralyzed with fear that she will die, he finds he can feel her heart beating close to his. Mina helps him to see the world in new ways and to connect the outer world of nature with his inner emotional and spiritual life. She introduces him to Blake who, we are told, "saw angels in his garden" (*Skellig*, 59), who believed in their physicality and presence. Almond's spiritual vision is also located in the natural world. Through Mina, Michael discovers the vitality of the mystical world of spirit and matter. She teaches him to "[l]isten deeper . . . [l]isten harder. Listen for the tiniest sweetest noise" (*Skellig*, 59) of the baby blackbirds. "Once I'd found it," he tells us, "and knew what it was and where it was, I could hear it along with all the other, stronger noises" (*Skellig*, 60).

Michael is a kind of wounded healer here, nurtured by his own nurturing of the wounded angel. He brings Skellig the leftovers from Chinese take-out, numbers "27 and 53," that Skellig calls the "food of the gods" that he has fed himself on out of Ernie's garbage, along with aspirin for his "Arthur Itis." Michael has felt despondent in his powerlessness to do anything about his family's crisis: there is nothing he can do about the baby's critical state and the grief of his family. With Mina's help, he is restored by his usefulness, which in itself lifts his despair. And Skellig, renewed by the love and care of Michael and Mina, is able to heal and nurture in turn, as he mysteriously saves the baby's life.

Skellig in many ways embodies Blake's vision of spirituality. He is the soul of humanity, the link between the earthly and the heavenly, and between life and death. Innocence for Blake was an inclusive state where all forms of life—man, beast, angel; all stages of life—infancy, childhood, adulthood, old age—were on a continuum and part of a whole. Almond's imagery is the connective tissue: Ernie, Skellig, and the baby, a mixture of "[s]pittle, muck, spew, and tears" (30), all exhibit the less attractive evidences of the body—the vulnerability and carnality, the messy business of humanity that the socialized world generally seems to hide and deny. Almond offers a theory of evolution inclusive of our connection to the apes and also, as Mina says, to our " 'rather more beautiful ancestors' " (*Skellig*, 50). The baby blackbirds and owls, diurnal as well as nocturnal creatures, and Mina's beloved and predatory cat, Whisper, all feed on weaker things. Nature is certainly "red in tooth and claw." But, as Michael's mother tells him, " 'They say that shoulder blades are where your wings were, when you were an angel . . . where your wings will grow again one day' " (*Skellig*, 38–9). When he asks whether the baby had wings, she replies, " 'Oh, I'm sure that one had wings. Just got to take one look at her. Sometimes I think she's never quite left Heaven and never quite made it all the way here to Earth. . . . Maybe that's why she has such trouble staying here' " (*Skellig*, 39). "Before she went away," Michael tells us, "I held the baby for a while. I touched her skin and her tiny soft bones. I felt the place where her wings had been" (*Skellig*, 39).

As these vestigial wings signify our fragility and spirituality, the baby is symbolic of our personal childhood and the childhood of the human race. Michael can feel Skellig's "feathers, and beneath them the bones and sinews and muscles that supported them" (*Skellig*, 95), which suggests the way in which the spirit and body are reflexive, each requiring the support of the other. Skellig embodies our early experience that travels with us throughout the various stages of our lives and helps us to remain "innocent." At the heart of such openness is an emerging consciousness of the connection between the natural and the imaginative worlds. In this regard, Michael's dreams serve as psychological maps. He reports an early dream in which "the baby was in the blackbird's nest in Mina's garden. The blackbird fed her on flies and spiders and she got stronger and stronger until she flew out of the tree and over the rooftops and onto the garage roof. When I went closer, Mina whispered, 'Stay away. You're danger!' " (*Skellig*, 27). The experiences of his day are transformed into emotional truths—certainly he feels guilty about the baby in some overarching generalized way. Later, he dreams his bed "was all twigs and leaves and feathers, just like a nest" (*Skellig*, 32). His dreams also reveal his growing awareness of the spiritual connection between the baby, the natural world, and Skellig, recalled here in the flies and spiders—all of which point to the central question of the poetics of childhood: what feeds the "fledgling" spirit? Almond shows us to be deeply connected, our images and dreams accessible to each other. As Mina says, "There's no end to evolution" (*Skellig*, 99). She can "call" Skellig "from somewhere deep inside me," Michael tells us, "like we were looking into the place where each other's dreams came from" (*Skellig*, 100). At this intensely connected moment, they are interrupted by "sniggering" of Leakey and Coot, Michael's school buddies—a reminder of what has become "other" for Michael, the more conventional world that he must learn to integrate into the new order.

How we do this, while on earth, is part of what Michael learns from Mina and her mother, who verify the otherworldly. Mina's mother quotes Blake, " 'Soon my Angel came again;/ I was arm'd, he came in vain" to warn against shutting down. She also tells the story of Persephone to illustrate the fluidity of life, the flux of the seasons, and the courage it takes to be alive. With the spring, she says, "[t]he animals dared to wake, they dared to have their young. Plants dared to send out buds and shoots. Life dared to come back" (*Skellig*, 146).

The novel moves toward the epiphanic moment as Mina, Michael, and Skellig dance in a circle, evidence of a potential for harmony, as Michael describes:

> I felt their breath in rhythm with mine. It was like we had moved into each other, like we had become one thing . . . and for a moment I saw ghostly wings at Mina's back, I felt the feathers and delicate bones rising from my own shoulders. (*Skellig*, 120)

Almond's story challenges notions of what children can learn, what spiritual lessons we can impart to them. It explores how to access the creative and essential part of themselves, whether it be through dreaming, or looking and listening "deeper" in the world. On the wall near Mina's bed is a quotation from Blake that reads, "How can a bird that is born for joy/ Sit in a cage and sing" (*Skellig*, 50). How can we free children from the structures that confine them? How can we educate them to be bold and clear in their vision? How can we move our schools to go beyond misleading and destructive categorizations of children? As Mina says, " 'And where would William Blake fit in? . . . 'Tyger! Tyger! Burning bright/ In the forests of the night.' Is that for the best readers or the worst readers? Does that need a good reading age?' " (*Skellig*, 90).

Almond's book is in itself the story of creating a poetics for children. Michael uses his imagination in new ways as a result of his exposure to Mina's home schooling. He observes closely and draws what he has come to see, and he writes a story about his extraordinary experience with Skellig. From Mina he also learns that

> Sometimes we just have to accept there are things we can't know. Why is your sister ill? Why did my father die. . . . We have to allow ourselves to see what there is to see, and we have to imagine. (*Skellig*, 140)

In his need to be close to the baby, in the empathic location of her heart beating next to his, Michael tries to imagine, "what would I feel when they opened the baby's fragile chest, when they cut into her tiny heart?" (*Skellig*, 141). He asks of one of the less conventional doctors in the book what for him is the most urgent question: " 'Can love help a person to get better?' " The doctor's reply illuminates the heart of Almond's work for children. Quoting Blake, he says, " 'Love is the child that breathes our breath/ Love is the child that scatters death' " (*Skellig*, 161).

## 5. *The Golden Compass*

Like all high fantasy, Philip Pullman's *The Golden Compass*[17] portrays the various struggles between good and evil. It is the story of eleven-year-old Lyra, an orphan who has grown up among the scholars and kitchen help at Jordan College in Oxford, England. Lyra intercepts an attempt to poison Lord Asriel, her uncle, which leads her into many battles and discoveries. The most significant of these involves the recurring disappearance of children and the discovery of her own identity. While traveling to the Arctic North to recover the lost children, she discovers the secret behind particles called Dust, which seem to be at the center of the battles.

*The Golden Compass*, however, goes beyond deciphering and distinguishing between polar opposites such as good and evil. It challenges the very nature of such bifurcation. This becomes clear as the book opens with an epigraph from Book II of Milton's *Paradise Lost*, where Satan "[s]tood on the brink of hell . . . [p]ondering his voyage." The quotation begins,

Into this wild abyss,
The womb of nature and perhaps her grave,
Of neither sea, nor shore, nor air, nor fire,
But all these in their pregnant causes mixed
Confusedly . . .
Unless the almighty maker them ordain
His dark materials to create more worlds.

The realm of the "dark materials" here includes the whole range of experience, "from the cradle to the grave," so to speak, a mixture of all the elements. It suggests a perspective beyond good and evil, or at least of these values redefined, the way Blake reinterpreted Milton as being "of the Devil's party without knowing it."[18] In this first of Pullman's "Dark Materials" trilogy, the darkness is the source of creativity, and dark for being unformed. With the epigraph, Pullman seems to build on Blake's vision of Satan as Los, the artist and rebel. In a recent interview about his "Dark Materials," Pullman said, "this time Satan is understood to be good rather than evil," and the hero, Lyra, is Eve, who must fall: "It's the best thing, the most important thing that ever happened to us, and if we had our heads straight on this issue, we would have churches dedicated to Eve instead of the Virgin Mary."[19]

Goodness and, to some extent, darkness are aligned with creativity, spontaneity, and honesty, embodied first and foremost in the child, Lyra. And as she tends toward the mischievous, rebellious, disruptive, like raw energy itself, she follows Blake's idea of innocence as buoyancy and porousness of spirit. She is an artist too, but rather than purely "imaginative," Pullman sees her as an excellent liar—not a trickster but a seeker of justice. To be a hero in this treacherous world, she must rely on her wits, her ability to discern and deceive, since, as a child, her physical prowess and power are severely limited. Evil, then, by contrast, is all that crushes that spirit. Most pernicious of all are those who destroy children, bodily and spiritually. In this story, children are abandoned, kidnapped, murdered, and exploited by individual and institutional desire and greed.

The story turns on the most extraordinary concept. Each human being has a "daemon," a physical embodiment of the soul, which incorporates the concept of the demonic. The daemon represents and suggests the inner self. It takes the form of an animal and accompanies the individual everywhere. It is always of the opposite gender, which suggests a Jungian vision of wholeness, although Pullman's sense of gender is not divided like Jung's into male/animus (the intellectual, guiding spirit) and female/anima (the unconscious and emotionally inspirational sides of our humanity). While a child, one's daemon is a shape-shifter, suggesting the unformed and dynamic spirit of the child and the unknown quality of its destiny. As the child reaches puberty, the daemon takes a lasting shape that holds throughout the lifetime. Pullman develops the daemons carefully, dramatically engaging them in fascinating ways, so that as we meet each character we come upon an inner expression, and a dynamic tension between the interior and external self. For example, although Lord Asriel is highly civilized and refined, his daemon reveals his dangerous underside in the form of a majestic snow leopard that growls in a way that makes Lyra "suddenly aware of what it would be like to have teeth meeting in her throat" (*The Golden Compass*, 26). The daemon embodies the instinctual, the sensuous, the fundamental nature of our inheritance, prior to and beyond socialization. For children, this conception might speak to a primal longing. Imagine never to be lonely, always to be accompanied in an intimate and reflexive relationship by a liminal being, both "me" and "not me," a brilliant representation of Winnicott's transitional object. The longing addressed here is spiritual, deeply and palpably vital, expressive of the sense of wholeness that children are civilized away from.

In *The Golden Compass*, the forces of evil have captured hundreds of children and are attempting to sever them from their daemons, so that the child either survives as a shadow of its former self or quite literally dies. The church that teaches and supports a false concept of sin and the dangers of expression; the police who turn away from the kidnappings, as long as they occur in working class and "gyptian" neighborhoods; academics, scientists, and teachers who are quite willing to go along with these sacrifices in the name of either "progress" or upholding "traditional" values—all are implicated. Most deadly are Lyra's parents, her father, Lord Asriel, the brilliant scientist, and her mother, Mrs. Coulter, the head of the Oblation Board, nicknamed the "Gobblers"—who are the kidnappers themselves. Not only are they themselves engaged in this action, but also they do not acknowledge Lyra as their daughter until they are forced to, and even then, it is with coldness and a lack of concern for her welfare. Worst of all, they set her up, in her innocence, to be the greatest betrayer of all. As Lyra rescues Roger, her lost friend, from the Gobblers, she delivers him into the hands of her father to be sacrificed. Lord Asriel wants to use the energy released when the child's daemon is split off from his body in his quest for Dust, the particles that the church uses as physical evidence for original sin. So Lyra falls, although not with consciousness.

"[H]alf-wild, half-civilized" Lyra has been brought up by the Scholars at Oxford, "left among them by chance" (*Golden Compass*, 17). "[C]onfounded by her sly indifference and insincere repentances," the Intercessor of the Church had decided that Lyra was not "spiritually promising" (*Golden Compass*, 45), and lost interest in her welfare. In fact, a kitchen servant had watched over her as a baby, raised her insofar as any adult "raised" her; essentially, Lyra was free to roam

over the College roofs with Roger, the kitchen boy who was her particular friend, to spit plum stones on the heads of passing Scholars or to hoot like owls outside a window where a tutorial was going on, or racing through the narrow streets, or stealing apples from the market, or waging war. Just as she was unaware of the hidden currents of politics running below the surface of College affairs, so the Scholars, for their part, would have been unable to see the rich seething stew of alliances and enmities and feuds and treaties which was a child's life in Oxford. (*Golden Compass*, 31–2)

Following the pattern Otto Rank identified in his essay, *The Myth of the Birth of the Hero*,[20] Lyra is ignorant of the class into which she was born. Cast out at birth and raised by a lower set of parents, she moves comfortably among various social classes. Unbeknown to her, she is destined to liberate her fallen world. Of course, the classical hero is recast here in light of Pullman's antichurch, antisexist, and anticlassist values. Pullman shows the children of the poor to be most vulnerable, most unprotected from the lure of the rich and privileged. At its most powerful, Pullman's writing propels us into the immediacy of the seduction—its terrifying and realistic movement. He says, "It would happen like this."

This is the Limehouse, and here is the child who is going to disappear. He is called Tony Makarios. His mother thinks he's nine years old, but she has a poor memory that the drink has rotted; he might be eight, or ten. . . . Tony's not very bright, but he has a sort of clumsy tenderness that sometimes prompts him to give his mother a rough hug and plant a sticky kiss on her cheeks. The poor woman is usually too fuddled to start such a procedure herself; but she responds warmly enough, once she realizes what's happening. (*Golden Compass*, 36)

This, in contrast to Mrs. Coulter, "the lady in a long yellow-red fox-fur coat, whose dark hair falls, shining delicately, under the shadow of her fur-lined hood . . . standing in the doorway of the oratory, half a dozen steps above him. It might be that a service is finishing, for light comes from the doorway behind her, an organ is playing inside, and the lady is holding a jeweled breviary" (*Golden Compass*, 37). Pullman continues, "Tony knows nothing of this" (*Golden Compass*, 37). But his daemon, now in the form of a mouse, now a sparrow, succumbs to her daemon, the golden monkey, who "reaches out slowly . . . his movements gentle and inviting. The sparrow can't resist" (*Golden Compass*, 37).

It is from the working poor, the marginalized gyptians, boat people who "got little stand in the law" (*Golden Compass*, 109), that Lyra learns about her origins. And here she gets her first sense of a moral and committed adult community. John Faa, drawn in opposition to Lyra's cold, unremittingly selfish father, is the gyptian leader who undertakes the task of rescuing the kidnapped children. When asked by a member of his constituency if they should have to risk saving " 'landloper kids as well as gyptians [who have] been taken captive,' " he says, " 'are you saying we should fight our way through every kind of danger to a little group of frightened children, and then say to some of them that they can come home, and to the rest that they have to stay? No, you're a better man than that' " (*Golden Compass*, 103). So the privileged, for the most part, are the perpetrators, and the oppressed, for the most part, the rescuers. Lyra aligns herself, to the extent that she is able to distinguish between the two, with the forces of liberation.

In many ways, Lyra follows the archetypal hero cycle Joseph Campbell set forth in *The Hero With A Thousand Faces*,[21] in which the quest is envisioned as circular, inclusive, and promising the restoration of order to the community. Lyra's quest takes her through darkness to the Northern Lights, the bear kingdom, so that she spans both human and animal realms. The bears represent the hero's connection with an untamed, primal world; and although they are the familiar fairy tale talking beasts, Pullman gives them an original animal vitality. Iorek Byrnison is the deposed bear ruler whose throne has been usurped by another warrior bear, who lusts after what is distinctly human—a daemon, and what is falsely human—gold and power. In Iorek's presence, Lyra feels "close to coldness, danger, brutal power, but a power controlled by intelligence. . . . This strange hulking presence gnawing its meat was like nothing she had ever imagined, and she felt a profound admiration and pity for the lonely creature" (*Golden Compass*, 157).

It is precisely Lyra's child-state of innocence, the intuition she has not lost altogether, that provides this insight. However, there are times when she forgets to trust her natural impulses, and then her daemon, Panthalaimon, affectionately called "Pan," offers a reminder. Before Lyra knows anything about Mrs. Coulter, she is easily seduced by her as was Tony, the child of the destitute mother. Mrs. Coulter's charm and vitality appeal to Lyra, who has been raised by the dull and matronly women at Oxford. Initially, we are told, Lyra "could hardly take her eyes off her" (*Golden Compass*, 59). When Lyra goes to live with her, not only is everything in Mrs. Coulter's flat aesthetically pleasing—the pictures, mirrors, antique furniture, rooms "full of light," porcelain shepherdesses and harlequins— but in the "rose light" of the bathroom mirror, Lyra sees herself transformed into "a softly illuminate figure." However, Pan in his ermine shape, sits in Lyra's lap, "trembling violently." Ironically, her very wish, that Mrs. Coulter and Lord Asriel will meet, fall in love, get married, and adopt her—some of which, the meeting and falling in love, unbeknown to Lyra, has already occurred. The rest, the marriage and the adoption, never happen. And this last omission, their refusal to recognize and accept Lyra as their daughter, their utter unconcern for her welfare, marks their deadly narcissism. They, each in a distinct way, exploit her for their own purposes. For a short time, Lyra becomes Mrs. Coulter's mascot, "almost as if she were a daemon herself" (*Golden Compass*, 72), but Pan makes her aware of the danger of being socialized away from her own sense of knowing. A brilliant scene in which Mrs. Coulter gently washes Lyra's hair in her bath reveals the beginnings of the separation of child from her intuitive self, as Pan turns his eyes away from her for the first time in her nakedness. Here, shame is connected with the socialization of a false and duplicitous mother. And, conversely, Pullman implies that the natural sensuality and beginnings of sexuality, if accompanied by love, a natural support, and a healthy environment, might not invoke shame, that the origins of sin lie elsewhere. How we are civilized away from our animal/instinctual selves is dramatized in Mrs. Coulter's treacherous monologue to Lyra:

> "Darling, no one would ever dream of performing an operation on a child without testing it first. And no one in a thousand years would take a child's daemon away altogether! All that happens is a little cut, and then everything's peaceful. Forever! You see, your daemon's a wonderful friend and companion when you're young, but at the age we call puberty, the age you're coming to very soon, darling, daemons bring all sort of troublesome thoughts and feelings, and that's what lets Dust in. A quick little operation before that, and you're never troubled again. And your daemon stays with you, only . . . just not connected. Like a . . . like a wonderful pet, if you like. The best pet in the world! Wouldn't you like that?" (*Golden Compass*, 248)

In this world, children are always accompanied by their own soul-spirit-animal, who knows to take the appropriate shape, in fact, knows before the conscious child does whom to trust and whom to distrust. Highly intuitive, the daemon protects, teaches, inspires, illuminates—Pullman shows that the unconscious forces are what we need to rely on. As Lyra learns to distrust and dissemble, Pan takes "his most inexpressive shape, a moth, [so as not to] betray her feeling" (*Golden Compass*, 84). Caught by the powerful adults who deceive and manipulate, Pullman tells us, "[s]he had to be careful not to say anything obviously impossible; she had to be vague in some places and invent plausible details in others; she had to be an artist, in short" (*Golden Compass*, 246).

As hero Lyra must go beyond, must essentially *be* beyond those who surround her, the one among many. No matter how many helpers she has, she is the single force who can revitalize her community. Lyra, alone, learns to read the alethiometer, the golden compass. It is a solitary gift, a task that involves a poetic grasp, a deep and "wise passivity." Its name, which contains the word "lethe," suggests a movement against forgetfulness and points to its truth-telling function. " 'As for how to read it,' " she is told, " 'you'll have to learn by yourself' " (*Golden Compass*, 65). Lyra uses her intuition and her intellect to decode the meanings the machine offers, in layers: there are meanings below the surface meanings. For example, in answer to a question, the aletheiometer, much like a ouija board, points to an anchor, which first means " 'hope,' " she explains, " 'because hope holds you fast like an anchor so you don't give way. The second meaning is steadfastness. The third meaning is snag, or prevention. The fourth meaning is the sea. And so on, down to ten, twelve, maybe a never-ending series of meanings.' " John Faa, the gyptian leader, asks her, " 'But how does it know what level you're a thinking of when you set the question?' " And she replies, suggesting a deep, meditative state: " 'It only works if the questioner holds the levels in their mind. You got to know all the meanings, first, and there must be a thousand or more. Then you got to be able to hold 'em in your mind without fretting at it or pushing for an answer . . . ' " (*Golden Compass*, 112). The heroic tests and ultimately the survival of the children and of the world will involve a fine honing of intuitive skills. Pullman shows Lyra deeply engaged with reading the alethiometer as her eyes move like those of a chess player, who seems "to see lines of force and influence on the board . . . [noticing] the important lines, ignor[ing] the weak ones" (*Golden Compass*, 134). "Then she sat still," he tells us, "letting her mind hold the three levels of meaning together in focus, and relaxed for the answer, which came at once" (*Golden Compass*, 153).

The American title focuses on the alethiometer, the golden compass, and the original British title, *Northern Lights*, focuses on the final destination of the quest in this book. But the daemon, as an expression of the various levels of consciousness and of the development of consciousness, is the overarching metaphor of the book. Pullman shows Lyra's senses "magnified and mingled with Pantalaimon's" (*Golden Compass*, 87); when Pan is hurt she feels the pain "in her own flesh." When growing up, Pullman tells us, it was natural for children to pull away from their daemons, "seeing how far they could pull apart, [but always] coming back with intense relief" (*Golden Compass*, 171). After Lyra is recaptured by Mrs. Coulter, while she lies moaning and trembling, we are told, "Pantalaimon simply lay against her bare skin, inside her clothes, loving her back to herself" (*Golden Compass*, 245). A devastating moment is when Lyra comes upon a little boy, "huddled . . . clutching a piece of fish to him as Lyra was clutching Pantalaimon . . . against her heart; but that was all he had, a piece of dried fish; because he had no daemon at all. The Gobblers had cut it away. That was *intercision*, and this was a severed child" (*Golden Compass*, 187). Pullman goes on to establish the most unimaginable horror—"[a] human being with no daemon [which] was like someone without a face, or with their ribs laid open and their heart torn out: something unnatural and uncanny that belonged to the world of night-ghasts, not the waking world of sense" (*Golden Compass*, 188). It is taboo to touch someone's daemon. So sacred is this representation, that when Lyra is discovered hiding and is grabbed by two men, the description sounds as defiling and forbidden as rape. Pullman writes, "The men were gasping and grunting with pain or exertion. . . . And suddenly all the strength went out of her. It was as if an alien hand had reached right inside where no hand had a right to be, and wrenched at something deep and precious. She felt faint, dizzy, sick, disgusted, limp with shock. One of the men was *holding* Pantalaimon" (*Golden Compass*, 241). Lyra does escape, time and again, from the deadly clutches of various cruel adults. But she is still a child, and needs the help of the more powerful forces of good in the world.

Like the archetypal classical hero, Lyra receives the aid and wisdom of the supernatural world, the witches who in their reversal of female dependency on men, represent a liberation ideology. They are "ragged figures of such elegance," loved by mortals but immortal themselves, so that they enjoy their male partners but these relationships carry no expectations of permanence. As they say, " '[T]here are men we take for lovers or husbands . . . men [who] pass in front of our eyes like butterflies, creatures of a brief season. We love them; they are brave, proud, beautiful, clever; and they die almost at once' " (*Golden Compass*, 275). One special helper, Serafina Pekkala, tells Lyra how she once loved a mortal: " 'I would have changed my nature,' " she says, to marry him, but then, " 'I would never have flown again. . . . [Y]ou cannot change what you are, only what you do' " (*Golden Compass*, 276). Witches are creatures of freedom, they can live separately from their daemons, can send them far away to do their bidding. They own nothing, and are " 'not interested in preserving value or making profits' " (*Golden Compass*, 270). They have no "notion of honor," no concept of insult. As Serafina tells Lyra, " 'How could you insult a witch? What would it matter if you did?' " (*Golden Compass*, 270–1). " 'To fly is to be perfectly ourselves' " (*Golden Compass*, 271). As they live for hundreds of years, beyond location in the "real" world, they can embody what I suspect is Pullman's visionary agenda. At times this feels schematic, although there is a playfulness in Serafina's story that rescues the tone from didacticism.

In the human realm, the daemon functions as an echo of an inner self—the Butler's daemon "trotting submissively at his heels" (*Golden Compass*, 10), the Scholars with "their daemons strutting or fluttering alongside or perching calmly on their shoulders" (*Golden Compass*, 55). And for the adventurous spirit, for the child, Lyra, the daemon leads her into unchartered or forgotten territory. Pullman writes, "Lyra found her heart moving out toward the deep dark of the arctic night and the clean coldness, leaping forward to love it as Pan was doing, a hare now delighting in his own propulsion" (*Golden Compass*, 255). In its stable state, Pullman's daemon represents a prevailing quality of its owner, and he has been accused by some critics of a kind of fatalistic sense of character. In an interview he claimed that,

The concept doesn't determine outcomes, it suggests a nature . . . a picture of what we're all like. We're not all gifted in the same way. Some of us have great courage, but others don't. Some of us have physical skills, and others don't. Some of us are predisposed towards melancholy . . . and there's nothing we can do about those characteristics. But the things we *can* do something about still remain within our path. (Parsons, 129)

When asked what if you don't wish to have the nature you have, Pullman said, " 'Tough . . . we human beings have to find out what we are . . . because we're stuck with it, and we can't change it. . . . That doesn't say anything about . . . the morality or giftedness or attractiveness of anything. It's a basic sort of attitude to the world" (Parsons, 128–9). Lyra resists this solidity. She asks, " 'Why do daemons have to settle? . . . I want Panthalaimon to be able to change forever. So

does he' " (*Golden Compass*, 146). She's told, " 'That's part of growing up.' "
And when she asks about what "compensations" there are in adulthood, she is
told, " 'Knowing what kind of person you are' " (*Golden Compass*, 147).

When Pullman was asked during another interview where he got the idea of
the daemon from, he replied, "Daemons came into my head suddenly and unexpectedly, but they do have a sort of provenance. One clear origin is Socrates' daimon. Another is the old idea of the guardian angel."[22] James Hillman, in *The
Soul's Code*: *In Search of Character and Calling*, claims,

> The soul of each of us is given a unique daimon before we are born, and it has
> selected an image or pattern that we live on earth. This soul-companion, the daimon,
> guides us here; in the process of arrival, however, we forget all that took place and
> believe we come empty into this world. The daimon remembers what is in your
> image and belongs to your pattern, and therefore your daimon is the carrier of your
> destiny.[23]

He sees it as an ancient "figure from somewhere else, neither human nor divine,
something in between the two belonging to a 'middle region' (metaxu) to which
the soul also belonged. The daimon was more an intimate psychic reality than a
god; it was a figure who might visit in a dream or send signals as an omen, a
hunch, or an erotic urge" (Hillman, 258). Essentially, Pullman's daemon seems in
concert with Hillman's.

At the end, the majestic Lord Asriel pleads with the passionate Mrs. Coulter
to accompany him on his quest to find the Dust. "[T]heir mouths were fastened
together with a powerful greed," their daemons acting out the underside of their
struggle. "[T]he snow leopard rolled over on her back, and the monkey raked his
claws in the soft fur of her neck, and she growled a deep rumble of pleasure"
(*Golden Compass*, 348). Lyra, their child, watches this intensity, "wrenched apart
with unhappiness. And with anger, too; she could have killed her father; if she
could have torn out his heart, she would have done so there and then" (*Golden
Compass*, 349).

Finally, Lyra is left alone, with Pan, reimagining the quest, which she will
undertake in the sequel, *The Subtle Knife*.[24] Pan, the most imaginative part of her,
says: " 'We've heard them all talk about Dust, and they're so afraid of it, and you
know what? We *believed* them, even though we could see that what they were
doing was wicked and evil and wrong. . . . We thought Dust must be bad too
because they were grown up and they said so. But what if it isn't?' " (*Golden
Compass*, 350). Then, like Milton's Adam and Eve at the end of *Paradise Lost*,
who "hand in hand with wand'ring steps and slow,/ Through Eden took their solitary way," Lyra and Pan "turn away from the world they were born in, and looked
toward the sun, and walked into the sky" (*Golden Compass*, 351)—solitary also
because they alone know the pain and death and fear that lay behind them. And

alone they will enter the "doubt, and danger, and fathomless mysteries" that lie ahead of them. But Pullman reassures his readers that they weren't alone. They always had each other. And there is hopefulness in this vision. Children may not be born to the parents they need, Pullman suggests. Whether parents are cruel and calculating, like Lyra's, or weak and destitute like Tony's mother, Pullman here gives children a poetics of the self in the daemon figure, a source of hope that restores them to an early harmony with the world, while at the same time distinguishing them, releasing them from it.

## 6. *Harry Potter* and the Extraordinariness of the Ordinary

I don't think the world has ever seen a meteoric rise in a book's popularity quite like that of J. K. Rowling's *Harry Potter* books. Readers of all ages and "levels" have plowed through all four books and still, even after the very mediocre movie version, they anxiously await the fifth. Walking through the airport in Portland, Oregon, last year, I saw children of varied ages carrying that fat hardback edition of *Harry Potter and the Goblet of Fire*.[25] One eight-year-old told me, proudly, "I read all 732 pages." There are many children who have entered the reading world through Rowling's series, and you'd think adults would look kindly, gratefully on such initiation. And many do and have. But others seem angry at such success. Whatever the concerns of adults, clearly children love these books. As my goddaughter Melissa said when she was fourteen, "I like the Harry Potter books because they are like real life but more interesting."

Harry begins his journey at eleven years old, an age associated with coming into consciousness, particularly for boys, and particularly in England, when children begin their "serious" study to prepare them for adult life. What Harry discovers on his eleventh birthday is that he is a wizard, that he has powers he intuits but, as is true of most childhood knowledge, does not consciously recognize. He had noticed that strange things happened to him: his hair grew back overnight after his aunt sheared it off; the sweater she tried to force him to wear kept getting smaller when she tried to pull it over his head. A most hilarious scene occurs at the zoo, where the caged boa winked at him, after sleeping through his cousin Dudley's command to " 'Make it move,' " and, as it made its escape amidst "howls of horror," Harry "could have sworn a low hissing voice said, 'Brazil, here I come. . . . Thanksss, amigo.' "[26] He does not connect these events with his own power. Like most orphans, Harry has little sense of having any power at all.

And also like most orphan heroes, he will need to be unusually sensitive, almost vigilant, particularly because he has been raised by hostile relatives against whom his sensibility absolutely grates. He has to make his own choices, as Rowling points out, without the benefit of "access to adults," the "safety net of many children who have loving parents or guardians."[27]

However extreme this situation, it only epitomizes what at one time every child feels—that she is on her own, unacknowledged, unappreciated, unseen, and unheard, up against an unfair parent, and by extension, an unfair world. Justice and the lack of it, as we have seen, reign supreme in the literature of childhood, where our first sense of the world is often so astutely recorded. "But it's not fair" is a phrase that stands out from my childhood and continues to resonate for me even now. I am reminded of E. B. White's opening to the beloved classic, *Charlotte's Web*: " 'Where's Poppa going with that axe?' " White's hero, Fern, protests against the adults' Darwinian treatment of animals, those creatures closest to her child-sensibility: " 'But it's unfair! . . . The pig couldn't help being born small. . . . If *I* had been very small at birth,' " she accuses, " 'would you have killed *me*?' "[28]

And what could be more unfair than losing your parents as a baby? The orphan archetype embodies the childhood task of learning to deal with an unfair world. I also am reminded of Jane Eyre at ten years old, thrashing around in her awareness of her unjust treatment at the hands of her aunt and cousins. Harry, like his great Victorian predecessors, is a kind of Everychild, vulnerable in his power-lessness, but, as he discovers his strengths, he releases a new source of vitality into the world. He becomes the child-hero of his own story, like Dickens's "favorite child," the orphan hero of *David Copperfield*, whose story begins, "Whether I shall turn out to be the hero of my own life, or whether that station will be held by anybody else, these pages must show."[29] One of the most intriguing things about the *Harry Potter* stories is how they chronicle the process of the child's movement from the initial consciousness of himself as the central character in his story, a singular preoccupation with self, to a sense of his own power and responsibility to a larger community.

Harry Potter has been raised by the Dursleys who pride themselves on being "perfectly normal" (*Sorcerer's Stone*, 1)—a sign that this story will assert the unconventional, even the eccentric. Harry will provide a resistance to normality which, Rowling suggests, is necessary for inclusiveness, for the individual and the community to prosper. Mr. Dursley, director of Grunnings, which makes drills, is a brutal, "beefy man with hardly any neck" (*Sorcerer's Stone*, 1). His equally nasty opposite, Mrs. Dursley, is "thin . . . [with] nearly twice the usual amount of neck . . . [good for] spying on the neighbors" (*Sorcerer's Stone*, 1). These are the caretakers of "the boy who lived" through the murder of both his parents and the attempt on his own life. Many are the injustices heaped upon him: he is kept under the stairs, half-starved and half-clothed, is "small and skinny for his age . . . [his] glasses held together with a lot of Scotch tape because of all the times Dudley had punched him on the nose" (*Sorcerer's Stone*, 20). The Dursleys are also psychologically abusive and provide, conversely, a model of how not to treat children. They treat Harry "as though he wasn't there . . . as though he was something very nasty that couldn't understand them, like a slug" (*Sorcerer's Stone*, 22). They withhold the truth of Harry's birth, in violation of a basic tenet of children's rights—one of the many indications that Rowling sees children as people with rights. What they hate in Harry's behavior, "even more than his asking questions [is] his talking about anything acting in a way it shouldn't, no matter if it was in a dream or even a cartoon" (*Sorcerer's Stone*, 26). Here Rowling emphasizes the preeminence of the imagination of childhood and the need for children to question and dream. So when Harry dreams of a flying motorcycle, it foreshadows his success at Quidditch, a kind of soccer in the sky, and his imminent rise above the chains of conventionality. Normal, Muggle (nonmagical) school is a system that teaches children to use "knobbly sticks for hitting each other . . . [as if it were] good training for later life" (*Sorcerer's Stone*, 32). There Harry is persecuted by Dudley's "normal" friends, like Piers, "a scrawny boy with a face like a rat . . . who held people's arms behind their backs while Dudley hit them" (*Sorcerer's Stone*, 23)—because he is different, because he is an orphan, because he is dressed in Dudley's old, shrunken uniforms, looking "like he was wearing bits of old elephant skin" (*Sorcerer's Stone*, 33). Aside from his dark cupboard under the stairs, nowhere is Harry safe. And nowhere is he loved, which only provides the urgency for a compensatory endowment of magical powers.

Belying Harry's puny appearance and weak position in the Muggle world is his bolt of lightning scar, which marks him, like Cain, for difference and protection against antagonism to that uniqueness. When Harry is most vulnerable, his scar burns painfully, which serves to warn him against proximity of danger. A particularly touching image of Harry's vulnerability occurs at the end of the first chapter, where he is curled fetuslike in sleep, "not knowing he was special, not knowing he was famous . . . that at this very moment, people meeting in secret all over the country were holding up their glasses and saying in hushed voices: 'To Harry Potter—the boy who lived!' " (*Sorcerer's Stone*, 17).

Harry embodies this state of injustice frequently experienced by children, often as inchoate fear and anger—and its other side, desire to possess extraordinary powers that will overcome such early and deep exile from the child's birthright of love and protection. That every child experiences himself as special is obvious, if for no other reason than that everything that happens to him is inherently significant. The world revolves around him; each moment resonates with the potential vitality of the first time, of unexplored territory. As the child grows into consciousness, an inner world serves to witness the extraordinary quality of experience recorded, sorted through, and reflected on. Along with this consciousness comes the recognition that others may share that experience, in part at least, and that ultimately each child is just another human being on this large, multitudinous planet. I remember looking up at the stars one night in the country and coming to a sudden understanding that contained both terror and relief. My epiphany turned on how small and insignificant I was, coupled with the insight that I was not responsible for the world. I had only a small part to play; the world was long in the making before I entered it and would go on long after I was gone. I remember that my ordinariness, then, offered a perspective and put into sharp relief my need to be special.

The *Harry Potter* series opens with the infiltration of the ordinary world by the luminous and magical as "a large, tawny owl flutters past the window" unobserved by the blunted Dursleys. Mr. Dursley "noticed the first sign of something peculiar—a cat reading a map," but assumed that "[i]t must have been a trick of the light . . . and put the cat out of his mind" (*Sorcerer's Stone*, 2–3). He was aware of "a lot of strangely dressed people . . . in cloaks. Mr. Dursley couldn't bear people who dressed in funny clothes . . . [and] was enraged to see that a couple of them weren't young at all," dismissed them as "people [who] were obviously collecting for something [and put] his mind back on drills" (*Sorcerer's Stone*, 3). He was oblivious to "the owls swooping past in broad daylight, though people down in the street . . . pointed and gazed open-mouthed as owl after owl sped overhead" (*Sorcerer's Stone*, 4). With this startling image of the nocturnal in bright light, Rowling establishes three groups defined by their response to the magic of the world. The Dursleys represent those who are hostile to anything imaginative, new, unpredictable. The Muggles, who notice the owls but are remote from their magical aura, represent a kind of conventional center. Professor Dumbledore, Head of Hogwarts School of Witchcraft and Wizardry, an old man, whose silver hair and beard "were both long enough to tuck into his belt . . . [who wore] long robes, a purple cloak that swept the ground, and high-heeled, buckled boots" (*Sorcerer's Stone*, 8), and Professor McGonagall, who has shape-shifted from cat to woman, indicated by her glasses with "exactly the shape of the markings the cat had had around its eyes" (*Sorcerer's Stone*, 9), embody the childhood world of magic and awe.

In most earlier children's fantasies, the magical world is entirely separate from the daily life. In C. S. Lewis's *Narnia Chronicles*,[30] for example, entry into the supernatural takes place through a wardrobe at the back of a strange house during the bombings of World War II, and represents the child-heroes' escape into a reimagined and revitalized Christian realm. In Madeline L'Engle's *A Wrinkle in Time*[31] and its successors, *A Wind in the Door*[32] and *A Swiftly Tilting Planet*,[33] the magical world is celestial, in keeping with science fiction and L'Engle's strong religious allegorical allusions. Tolkien's *The Hobbit*[34] and *Lord of the Rings* trilogy[35] take place entirely in a magical world and represent a refuge, an alternative to the real world.

Rowling noted the genius of Lewis and Tolkien, those predecessors with whom she has been frequently compared, but claimed she was "doing something slightly different."[36] Although her stories contain the usual global battle between the forces of good and evil, Rowling, I believe, is essentially a novelist, strongest when writing about the real world. Harry has a psychology; his problems need resolution in the real world. Insofar as he is a real child, with little relief at home, at Hogwarts School of Witchcraft and Wizardry, where the supernatural reigns, he is freer to discover his own powers. In Rowling's stories, the interpenetration of the two worlds suggests the way in which we live, not only in childhood though especially so—on more than one plane, with the life of the imagination and daily life moving in and out of our consciousness. The two realms, romance and realism, located in the imagination, are always created by and rooted in the details of everyday life. In fantasy, always we are grounded; the unconscious invents nothing, or, as Freud put it, "In the psychic life, there is nothing arbitrary, nothing undetermined."[37]

The need for both realms and their interdependence was recognized by Wordsworth and Coleridge in their plan for the *Lyrical Ballads*. Coleridge wrote:

> my endeavors should be directed to persons and characters supernatural, or at least romantic—yet so as to transfer, from our inward nature, a human interest and a semblance of truth sufficient to procure for these shadows of imagination that willing suspension of disbelief for the moment, which constitutes poetic faith. . . . [Wordsworth was] to give the charm of novelty to things of every day, and to excite a feeling analogous to the supernatural, by awakening the mind's attention to the lethargy of custom, and directing it to the loveliness and wonders of the world before us—an inexhaustible treasure but for which . . . we have eyes yet see not, ears that hear not, and hearts that neither feel nor understand.[38]

In the *Harry Potter* books, magic calls attention to the awe and wonder of ordinary life. Rowling ingeniously enhances and amplifies the vitality of ordinary objects. For example, at Hogwarts, the walls are "covered with portraits of old headmasters and headmistresses, all of whom were snoozing gently in their frames."[39] Books bite and argue; "locked together in furious wrestling matches and snapping aggressively"[40]—a literary joke about the Battle of the Books or other debate literature, reminiscent of the *Wonderland* and *Looking Glass* landscapes. Along with magical wands, cloaks of invisibility, maps that reproduce and mirror actual journeys as they are taking place (like the virtual reality of technology), the things of children's culture—treats like candy, and kids' own particular kind of humor, like jokes about bodily fluids—are featured. Some of children readers' favorite aspects of life at Hogwarts include Bertie Bott's Every Flavor Beans, consisting of such flavors as spinach, liver, tripe, grass, sardine, vomit, ear wax, and "even a booger-flavored one" (*Sorcerer's Stone*, 104). Words themselves suggest the magical power of language to mean, as well as to evoke and connote. Such passwords as "pig snout," "scurvy cur," "oddsbodkin," suggest treasure and mystery. The characters' names are appropriately allusive and inviting. As Sharon Moore points out:

> There are sneaky-sounding s's: Slytherins, Snape, Severus, Sirius and Scabbers. The h's are kind of heroic: Hogwarts, Hedwig, Hermione and Hagrid. The f's are often unpleasant types: Filch and Fllitwick. . . . The names that sound French are usually difficult people: Madam Pince, Madam Pomfrey, and Malfoy.[41]

Alison Lurie notes,

> As in many folk tales, you can often tell a character's character from his or her
> name, and "Voldemort" neatly combines the ideas of theft, mold, and death. Harry
> Potter, on the other hand, has a name that suggests not only craftsmanship but both
> English literature and English history: Shakespeare's Prince Hal and Harry Hotspur,
> the brave, charming, impulsive heroes of *Henry IV*, and Beatrix Potter, who created
> that other charming and impulsive classic hero, Peter Rabbit.[42]

As Harry embodies both the ordinary and the extraordinary, his narratives
contain realistic and romantic elements. Like other questing heroes, Harry must
prove himself through a series of tests, each increasingly more difficult, a pattern
Joseph Campbell saw as corresponding to the dynamic movement through life
stages, particularly the development of consciousness and the discovery of identity. Like the simpler fairy tale heroes, Harry must break some taboo to create
change and, like other child heroes such as Lyra of *The Golden Compass*, he is
unaware of his destiny. For example, Cinderella, Perrault's and the Grimms's
most virtuous Christianized and domesticated girl-hero, must revolt against the
wishes of the good fairy godmother. She must forget to leave the ball by midnight, in order that the prince find her and that her rightful place be restored. This
tale acknowledges the hero's paradoxical struggle to maintain tradition and to
subvert it for evolution to occur. Some taboo must be broken, some boundary
crossed—this is at the heart of the hero's quest. Harry, who is, as Lurie points out,
a kind of Cinderlad himself, must break the very rules at Hogwarts needed to
maintain order and its basic values.

The fairy tales of childhood illustrate a most significant aspect of that earliest stage, the centrality of play and the imagination, which, though it receives
prominence in childhood, often gets lost along the way to adulthood. Consider
"Jack and the Beanstalk," in which Jack, a lazy child, refuses to do his mother's
bidding and "forgets" to sell the cow for money, but instead is enchanted by the
magic beans. The tale asserts his right to journey into the sky (the world above the
world), and solve the earthbound adult problem of money by stealing the golden
harp, hen, eggs—the means to achieving ever-regenerating money and power.
This is precisely what he never could have gotten by selling the cow. Once having
used up the modest sum he would have gotten from the cow, he would have had,
inevitably, to go out again to market with whatever was left to sell, only to return
home with fewer resources, thus moving into the cycle of poverty—from which
the poor rarely have the power to emerge, any more than children have the power
to overcome the authority of adults. The magic beans in this story represent relief
from the real problems that are quite beyond the child to solve, but can be, as the
story suggests, imagined. And the magic here embodies the imagination and
stands in for what is beyond the power of children, perhaps anyone, to actualize.

Just as we often can envision long before we can create the means to flee or resolve what feels overwhelming, it is even more so for children.

Harry's supernatural powers invite children to imagine beyond the boundaries of their limitations: what if I could see and hear without being seen or heard; what if I could fly; what if I could read another's mind. With his magic cloak, Harry is invisible; with his Nimbus 2000 racing broomstick, he can fly; he can even, in the fourth book, project himself into Dumbledore's siphoned-off thoughts. Also, like every child, Harry is one among many, represented here by the fact that his classmates are also wizards. While he is good at playing Quidditch, he is just an ordinary player at his school work; nor is he particularly insightful in the way he relates to or understands others. His classmate Hermione Granger, the girl Rowling most closely identifies with,[43] is smarter and more sensitive. Hermione has the most highly developed sense of justice; even though Harry has freed Dobby, the house-elf, Hermione alone understands the oppression of the house-elves, as they serve their masters without pay, "beaming, bowing, and curtsying" (*Goblet*, 379). Part of Rowling's genius is the creation of stories about the development of the ordinary boy, as he grows from the start of the series at ten years old to the age of seventeen. There will be one book for each year, Rowling has announced, with the "hormones kicking in."[44] Gender informs Rowling's vision in that she blends the male questor with the feminized hero of tales of school and home; these stories are relational, psychologically nuanced, and in that sense realistic.

During a recent radio interview, a child called in to ask if Rowling could please bring back Harry's parents. Respectfully and sorrowfully, she said she regretted that she couldn't do that. "You can't bring dead people back," she said.[45] She had to set limits on what magic could and couldn't do, since it was important to her to keep these characters real. Even the magical ones are defined by their human as well as magical traits. The real world, then, becomes somewhat illuminated by these characters who can span both worlds. For example, teachers at Hogwarts can be imaginative and compassionate; they are also flighty, vindictive, dim-witted, indulgent, lazy, frightened, and frightening. Students are clever, kind, weak, cruel, snobbish. Lessons are inspiring and tedious—as in the best and worst of real schools.

Harry's guide into the magic school at Hogwarts, Hagrid, is a larger than life figure, the giant from the fairy tales of childhood, deliverer of the annunciation: " 'Yeh don' know what yeh *are* . . . Harry—yer a wizard' " (*Sorcerer's Stone*, 50). He is "almost twice as tall as a normal man and at least five times as wide . . . simply too big to be allowed, and so *wild*—long tangles of bushy, black hair and beard hid most of his face . . . [with] hands the size of trash can lids, and . . . feet . . . like baby dolphins" (*Sorcerer's Stone*, 14). He is also careless, drinks too much, humanized by his sentimental and indulgent love for bizarre and grotesque creatures, such as the dragons and Blast-Ended Skrewts, who threaten the safety of Hogwarts. Even these creatures suggest the two sides of imaginative writing: dragons are recognizable as mythical fire-breathing creatures, although here Rowling makes them distinct, almost realistic:

> The baby dragon flopped onto the table. It wasn't exactly pretty; Harry thought it looked like a crumpled, black umbrella. Its spiny wings were huge compared to its skinny jet body, it had a long snout with wide nostrils, the stubs of horns and bulging, orange eyes. (*Sorcerer's Stone*, 235)

The Skrewts, sluglike and slimy, are also described in vivid detail, while their size mythicizes them. The movement here between these two poles suggests the force of the imagination of childhood to illuminate reality.

Most of the adventures take place at school, seen here as the transitional world situated between childhood and adulthood. It is a liminal space that tests the mettle of the child hero and, like all liminal landscapes, it represents the not-as-yet-conscious,[46] what is yet-to-be, possibility itself, and chance. A burning question for Harry, who has never fit in, not at home, not at "Muggle" school, who has never had the chance to experience friendship and all that it entails—loyalty, competition, finding a place among peers—is how will he succeed in this home away from home? Particularly when he has never been at home at home?

Situating the train that takes people to Hogwarts at $9\frac{3}{4}$, between tracks 9 and 10, reinforces the central location of these stories between the earth-bound and magical worlds. As Harry transports himself beyond the boundaries of the real world, between tracks 9 and 10, one can viscerally feel his body brace against the shock, his mind unbelieving, as he breaks through what appears to be a solid barrier, as the imaginary may seem in real life. The school and its various accoutrements epitomize, at the same time, the imagination of childhood and the real concerns of children. At Hogwarts, everything is adorned with the magic so that, for example, the point of entry into the bank, a warning against greed and snobbishness—a worldly concern—is heightened by the poetic language on the sign: *Enter, stranger, but take heed/ Of what awaits the sin of greed* (*Sorcerer's Stone*, 72). There are many such indications of Rowling's abhorrence of the class system, its divisiveness and the negative potential of specialness. Malfoy, the pale boy with the pointed face, whose sense of self is based on embracing his father's money and social position, is early established as Harry's enemy, just as Ron Weasley, who has to share the little his family has with his six siblings, and Hermione, the racially mixed daughter of a Muggle and a wizard, are his best friends.

While Hogwarts contains all the offensive and irritating aspects of real life—it in fact mirrors its elitism and petty power struggles—it is also a wondrous and humorous world. Required reading, for example, abounds with hilarious matches, such as *One Thousand Magical Herbs and Fungi* by Phyllida Spore and *Fantastic Beasts and Where to Find Them* by Newt Scamader. The magical Sorting Hat

matches each child with her proper house (Harry and his friends are assigned to
Gryffindor for their courage), and wands intricately fit their owners. The phoenix
that provided the feathers for Harry's wand did the same for Voldemort, the
"brother [who] gave you that scar" (*Sorcerer's Stone*, 85), Harry is told, linking
him, as Lucifer was God's fallen angel, to his dark enemy. And there is much
darkness in these books. However, it is always rooted in the psychological darkness associated with childhood and with human development: with anger, loss,
death, grief, fear, and with desire. Although initially Harry is elated when he hears
the news of his powers, he is also alarmed and bewildered. Hagrid notes that it's
hard to be singled out and Harry protests, " 'Everyone thinks I'm special . . . but I
don't know anything about magic at all. . . . I can't even remember what I'm
famous for' " (*Sorcerer's Stone*, 86). Fear of his power, unsure of how to control
desire, or how to recognize and use his gifts wisely—Harry, as Everychild, needs
guidance.

Rowling is adept at providing paradigms for thoughtful, courageous, and
moral behavior for children, with clear explanations of the states of feeling that
accompany the process. These deeper moments of reflection serve as pauses in
the rapid pace of these page-turners. It seems to me that the best mysteries, adventure stories, and romances represent a negotiation between the reckless pace of
the narrative moving forward and the meditative pockets that provide the space
and time to turn inward—to affirm our sense that something memorable is happening to us, something we can retrieve for later, after the book is ended. As is
true of our best writers, Rowling draws these opposing realms so seamlessly that
they appear to have always been there, side by side, the event and its meaning
exquisitely illuminated.

In *Harry Potter and the Sorcerer's Stone*, the scene in which Harry comes
upon the Mirror of Erised (thinly disguised so children will discover that it represents desire) and sees, for the first time in his life, his family, "he had a powerful
kind of ache inside him, half joy, half terrible sadness" (*Sorcerer's Stone*, 209).
How fascinating that his friend Ron sees only himself decked out as Head Boy,
his own "deepest, most desperate desire" (*Sorcerer's Stone*, 213). Ron, whose
strongest wish is to stand out from his five brothers and from Harry as well,
assumes he is seeing the future, just as Harry believed he was looking into his
past. However, this mirror, says Dumbledore, "will give us neither knowledge or
truth" (*Sorcerer's Stone*, 213). It can drive us mad, "not knowing if what it shows
is real or even possible." He warns against "dwell[ing] in dreams" as one could
"forget to live." However, he offers, "If you ever *do* run across it, you will now be
prepared" (*Sorcerer's Stone*, 214). Rowling has, essentially, taken the great test of
Odysseus, who must hear the song of the sirens, but not act on that calling, and
reimagined it for children. At its core, Rowling suggests, desire can be both allur-
ing and dangerous. Children need to understand, on whatever level, its complexity. Rowling does not minimize childhood longing. She offers this small allegory

with the understanding that the search for identity is reflected in that mirror—as Harry sees his family behind him, and desires only to return again and again to that vision of himself, supported by those who resemble him, smiling at and waving to him. This scene prepares for the ones that follow, in which Harry comes into deeper and darker knowledge, though always returning to this central issue of identity and the protection it promises.

If the Mirror reflects what we most long for, it also evokes the fear that accompanies such desire and the loss that engendered it. In *Harry Potter and the Prisoner of Azkaban*, Rowling focuses on this fear, beginning with the boggarts who take the shape of "whatever each of us most fears" (*Prisoner*, 133). For Harry, as his Dark Arts teacher tells him, it is fear itself, embodied in the dementors, the prison guards of Azkaban. What tortures Harry is his overwhelming guilt and sorrow at his mother's death. At the sight of these grey hooded figures, Harry hears his mother's desperate cries: " 'No, take me, kill me instead.' " Haunted by her pain and guilty that she died to save him, Harry is drawn into intense ambivalence, which Rowling explains:

> Terrible though it was to hear his parents' last moments replayed inside his head, these were the only times Harry had heard their voices since he was a very small child. . . . "They're dead," he told himself sternly . . . "and listening to echoes of them won't bring them back. You'd better get a grip on yourself if you want that Quidditch Cup." (*Prisoner*, 243)

The desire to be reunited with his parents, though natural and inevitable, serves as a warning, as with the Mirror, against remaining in the past, lost in memory or desire. Of course, in addition to exploring Harry's inner demons, here Rowling connects despair with madness and suggests that it is the loss of hope that makes us demented, that promotes criminality and destroys the heart. The dementors, those who are supposed to guard prisoners,

> drain peace, hope, and happiness out of the air around them. Get too near a dementor and every good feeling, every happy memory will be sucked out of you. . . . [S]oul-less and evil . . . you'll be left with nothing but the worst experiences of your life. . . . [S]et on a tiny island, way out to sea . . . they don't need walls and water to keep the prisoners in, not when they're all trapped inside their heads, incapable of a single cheerful thought. Most of them go mad within weeks. (*Prisoner*, 188)

The antidote for such haunting is happy memories, that which makes children feel safe, loved, confident, good about themselves. More than anything, a sense of self is exactly what Hagrid was denied in prison, as he tells Harry: " 'Yeh can' really remember who yeh are after a while' " (*Prisoner*, 221). Knowing who you are is at the heart here, the development of the child's consciousness, the narrative of

Everychild—the right to knowledge and expression of self. Rowling has spoken about depression as the loss of hope, how it has been her enemy, and how it has informed her depiction of the dementors here.[47] I remember fits of depression as a child, although without any name for that state of mind, it went unrecognized and was buried, along with the shame that accompanied all my unacknowledged feelings. As Sendak claimed, when he was called upon to defend his depictions of frightening monsterlike figures in *Where the Wild Things Are*, most frightening to children is to dream their own figures of fear and find no analogue in anything they hear about or read. Children need to see their feelings, particularly the darkest ones, reflected in their stories. Mitigating the darkness of the fairy tales takes away their power to reassure children that they are not alone in their fearful imaginings, that they are shared and can be addressed.[48]

As Harry gets older in the books, the emotional challenges become more complex, which Rowling attempts to help children understand. She has captured the familiar sense of childhood shame with the Howlers—loud, public scoldings sent by parents to humiliate and ultimately to control children. For example, Neville receives a letter in the audible form of his "grandmother's voice, magically magnified to a hundred times its usual volume, shrieking about how he had brought shame on the whole family" (*Prisoner*, 272). Such exposure is handled with a kind of empathic humor, reminiscent of Woody Allen's adult projection in "Oedipus Wrecks," one of the short films in *New York Stories*, of his mother's face in the sky, publicly denouncing him, a metaphor of adult shame and its roots in childhood. This externalized projection mirrors Harry's private, internal moments following his collapse at the sight of the dementors, when he "felt the beginnings of shame. Why had he gone to pieces like that, when no one else had?" (*Prisoner*, 36). Shame separates us, makes us feel less than, different from others. This aspect of difference, Rowling demonstrates, is deadly. At times she handles it with the acceptance that comes from humor; at times, with a kind of respect that accompanies our most difficult emotional trials.

Children also are led beyond the simple concept of evil as purely bad guys whose struggles abound in the earlier books. With *Harry Potter and the Prisoner of Azkaban*, what appears evil turns out to be a paradoxical figure, Lupin, who is a werewolf, a force of good that can be dangerous as well. Rowling's use of the werewolf as metaphor for the split self here is astute and in keeping with the earliest known Red Riding Hood variant in which the werewolf—a fusion of animal and human—rather than the wolf, tries to seduce the young girl.[49] What is most interesting here is that the potentially destructive part of the werewolf is humanized and offered with understanding. Rowling establishes his innocence and evokes compassion for him, as he tells his story. Lupin says, " 'I was a very small boy when I received the bite. My parents tried everything, but in those days there was no cure. . . . My transformations . . . were terrible. It is very painful to turn into a werewolf. I was separated from humans to bite, so I bit and scratched myself instead' " (*Prisoner*, 352–3). As Lupin becomes a werewolf when he doesn't take his potion, madness and self-destructive impulses are depicted with a kind of psychological truth. Rowling attempts to humanize the demonic, rather than demonize the human.

The servants of evil are recognizable as frail humans who have grown large because they are adults who are out of control—what is often most terrifying to children. Peter Pettigrew, in *Harry Potter and the Prisoner of Azkaban*, is "horrible to watch, like an oversized, balding baby, cowering on the floor" (*Prisoner*, 374), and Voldemort, who represents the generating power of evil, the force of discord and enmity, bears "the shape of a crouched human child, except Harry had never seen anything less like a child. It was hairless and scaly-looking. . . . Its arms and legs were thin and feeble, and its face—no child alive ever had a face like that. . . . The thing seemed almost helpless; it raised its thin arms, put them around Wormtail's neck, and Wormtail lifted it" (*Goblet*, 640–1). The infantile adult, a kind of perverted innocence, childish without anything childlike, is most horrifying when, as a child, it is the controlling force of your life.

How children take control of their lives—most crucial and central here—is metaphorically represented in several ways. Harry and Hermione watch themselves in "a Time-Turner," able to redo an event, to be in more than one place at a time, to go back in time while remaining in the present, to redo their mistakes and save the lovely hippogriff, Buckbeak. Harry tells Hermione, " 'I knew I could do it this time . . . because I'd already done it. . . . Does that make sense?' " (*Prisoner*, 412)—expressing the paradoxical sense of knowing what we didn't know we knew. Even more psychologically profound is the way in which Rowling demonstrates what can be retrieved, even in the final loss, the death of a parent. To protect himself from fear, Harry conjures up a "Patronus," an image of his father. As an orphan, Harry will have to provide for himself the father he has never known. Here is a kind of child vision of father atonement. Dumbledore, in such a vision as a father figure, tells Harry: " 'You think the dead we loved ever truly leave us? You think that we don't recall them more clearly than ever in times of great trouble? Your father is alive in you, Harry . . . you did see [him] last night. . . . You found him inside yourself' " (*Prisoner*, 427–8).

This scene represents the only real consolation as well as a possible direction for healing such an early fracture. There are many father/son atonement scenes. Most awful is Mr. Crouch's son, rejected by his father, even as he stands before him, pleading in his innocence, " 'Father! Father, I wasn't involved! . . . I'm your son! . . . I'm your son!' " (*Goblet*, 596). We are not surprised that, in his confusion and despair, he becomes a servant of evil. Rowling also helps children to understand how Neville's parents, "tortured for information about Voldemort's whereabouts" (*Goblet*, 602), go insane, and so, although they are alive, when Neville visits them with his grandmother, they do not recognize him. Harry is more fortunate than the others in that he has been able to retrieve something, a touchstone for protection he can carry with him, although he has never had access to his parents. But it is not enough in his relative state of privilege to be isolated from the misfortune of others. Harry feels for Crouch's son, as images of the pale-faced boy swim up to him from his imagination. His compassion extends to Neville too, as he imagines how it must feel "to have parents still living but unable to recognize you" (*Goblet*, 607).

The *Harry Potter* stories center on what children need to find internally—the strength to do the right thing, to establish a moral code. As hero, Harry must go beyond the apparent truth of things and, ultimately, learn to trust what he sees and to act on what is right. The tournament of the fourth book, *Harry Potter and the Goblet of Fire*, departs from the rather simple victory of Quidditch tournaments, in which one house at Hogwarts beats the others, Harry serving as Seeker, the primary position, for Gryffindor. In this book, as Hermione points out, " 'This whole tournament's supposed to be about getting to know foreign wizards and making friends with them.' " Although Ron with partial truth responds, " 'No it isn't. It's about winning' " (*Goblet*, 423), more is at stake here. The community is larger, more global. What it means to "win" is interrogated. In an expansive leap of feeling, Harry saves his rivals, along with his friends. Voices tell him: " 'Your task is to retrieve your own friend . . . leave the others' " (*Goblet*, 499). He wonders, "Why hadn't he just grabbed Ron and gone? He would have been first back. . . . Cedric and Krum hadn't wasted time worrying about anyone else" (*Goblet*, 505). In response, he resists such individualism with " 'an equally strong bond of friendship and trust. Differences of habit and language are nothing at all,' " Dumbledore tells him, " 'if our aims are identical and our hearts are open' " (*Goblet*, 723). Harry and his closest rival, Cedric (who took Cho Chang, the object of Harry's desire, to the ball), help and support each other, and finally decide to reach the Cup at the same time, thus producing two winners. While Cedric dies, and thus Harry alone bears the reward, the boys' rejection of the school's either/or policy establishes a new paradigm of sharing, building community, and inclusiveness.

Sharing thoughts and passing on experience is brilliantly depicted in the Pensieve, a basin which holds thoughts. " 'I sometimes find,' " Dumbledore tells Harry, " 'that I simply have too many thoughts and memories crammed into my mind. . . . At these times, I use the Pensieve. One simply siphons the excess thoughts from one's mind, pours them into the basin, and examines them at one's leisure. It becomes easier to spot patterns and links . . . when they are in this form' " (*Goblet*, 597). Harry is literally drawn through a substance that was either "liquid or gas . . . a bright, whitish silver . . . moving ceaselessly; the surface of it became ruffled like water beneath wind, and then, like clouds, separated and swirled smoothly. It looked like light made liquid—or like wind made solid" (*Goblet*, 583). To understand another's history one must enter into a liminal state;

one must move beyond the established boundaries of self and other, represented by the indistinguishable states of matter. In *Harry Potter and the Chamber of Secrets*, Harry had fallen "through a page in an enchanted diary, right into some-one else's memory" (*Chamber*, 586). But here the idea is more developed. Thought is depicted as tangible, progressive, dynamic—a series of landscapes to be visited, returned to, and discovered as patterns of meaning. Harry falls through Dumbledore's thoughts about his past, the subjectivity of memory extended to history. When he lands in the courtroom of Dumbledore's memory, "not one of [the adults] noticed that a fourteen-year-old boy had just dropped from the ceil-ing . . ." (*Goblet*, 585), reminiscent of Auden's Icarus, who falls unnoticed out of the sky. But unlike Icarus, who, in his youthful optimism, flew too high so that his wings melted from the heat of the sun, Harry's fall is a descent into conscious-ness, and, rather than cautionary, it is visionary. It suggests connection, that we can participate in another's experience, explore another's past, albeit only through the subjectivity of our own vision.

Even the child, without the experience of the adult, without perspective afforded by hindsight, can glean something valuable from the lessons of the past—not those set in stone to be received unquestioningly, but to make meaning of, the way Harry must make sense of the events he witnesses. In this scene of Dumbledore's younger days, Harry first notices how Dumbledore has aged, a per-spective that reveals Harry's developing consciousness of time. Each person car-ries a unique history, some of which can be shared, as when Dumbledore joins Harry in reviewing his thoughts.

Even the idea of reviewing thoughts supports the value of interrogation and reflection. Surely this runs counter to what we are currently being told by televi-sion, video games, fast-paced cutting images of MTV, and the superficial content of pulp fiction. The *Harry Potter* books satirize for children the superficiality of this world, its pretenses and human failures, the narcissism of popular culture, the stupidity and cruelty of the press, the rigidity and fraudulence embedded in our institutions, particularly the schools, framed by the unrelenting snobbery and elit-ism of our social world. The unprecedented popularity of the *Harry Potter* sto-ries—not only with sophisticated readers of a wide range of ages but also with new readers, those who previously resisted reading—suggests that rather than flat, knee-jerk responses, children are capable of and drawn to complexity and reflection, accompanied by the spectacular and integrated, always, in the real and recognizable world it is the child's mission to negotiate and struggle through.

# Afterword

I began this book with the Romantics' conception of childhood—with their configurations of innocence and wisdom, which they conflated into a higher innocence. I end with a contemporary vision of the child, who serves not as a spirit-guide for adults, but may need to be guided by them. When children's needs conflict with the needs of adults, or when adults cannot meet their needs, the literature of childhood can serve as a refuge from disappointment with the world. Stories, with their way of making sense of the world, can be powerful healers. To engage in moving a plot through time and space, to feel a sense of context and character, is in itself a healthy and generative experience. Stories of childhood create the space for an intimate and imaginative reciprocity between child and adult.

In her article, "The Narration of Metaphor in Children's Lives," therapist Kate Fincke discusses the mutually healing quality of the shared creation of story between child and adult. She writes,

> I have sought to describe the ingenious variety of ways in which a child's imaginative life can grapple with the tasks of living, from ordinary tasks like falling asleep to horrible ones like grieving. I have striven as well to point out that the child's imaginative life exerts a power over adult states of being. . . . I have made a stab at exploring the murky realm of human receptivity where narrative's strange ability to loosen the constraints of an individual's personality by transporting him or her across time and space and into other personas creates greater personal reflexivity.[1]

For adults, the poetics of childhood recalls the deep and early sources of feelings, not just as nostalgia but also with their original intensity. It provides a safe place to reclaim those feelings. It suggests, in fact compels a further look at the many aspects of childhood injustice that generated those feelings and continue to inform the recurring themes of this literature. Perhaps we are calling on the child in yet another way to guide us forward out of the "archetypal space of human injury,"[2] to restore us to our capacity for empathy not only for others, but for ourselves—an inevitable movement, I believe, toward wholeness. Perhaps the child guide, whether a real child or what psychologists have called the "inner child," also requires of us a new consideration of the world into which we were brought and the world into which we bring children.

In its broadest sense, then, the literature of childhood represents a challenge to the world. In the voices of children, in their questions about things that seem unfair, this literature demands that we look again at the crippling and divisive forces of racism and sexism. In its depiction of children suffering and struggling against the bleakest and most unstable conditions, it is an indictment of the barbaric effects of poverty on their lives. In response to our current world that criminalizes them, in response to our polluted, wartorn, power-hungry world, the literature of childhood, in its varied imagined landscapes, suggests an inclusive society in which children can find a safe and creative way to live.

# Endnotes

## Introduction

1. Gaston Bachelard, "Reveries Toward Childhood," in *Reclaiming the Inner Child*, ed. Jeremiah Abrams (New York: G.P. Putnam's Sons, 1990), 48; hereafter cited in text.
2. Alice Miller, *The Drama of the Gifted Child: How Narcissistic Parents Form and Deform the Emotional Lives of Their Talented Children*, trans. Ruth Ward (New York: Basic Books, 1981).
3. Alice Miller, *Pictures of a Childhood: Sixty-six Watercolours and an Essay*, trans. Hildegarde Hannum (New York: Meridian, 1995).
4. Carolyn Steedman, *Strange Dislocations: Childhood and the Idea of Human Interiority 1780–1930* (Cambridge, Mass.: Harvard University Press, 1995), 14; hereafter cited in text.
5. Peter Abbs, *A is for Aesthetic: Essays on Creative and Aesthetic Education* (London: Falmer Press, 1989), 4.
6. Johann Wolfgang von Goethe, *Wilhelm Meister's Apprenticeship*, ed. and trans. Eric A. Blackall (1839; rpt., Princeton, N.J.: Princeton University Press, 1989).
7. Mary Shelley, *Frankenstein, or the Modern Prometheus*, ed. Marilyn Butler (1818; rpt., New York: Oxford University Press, 1994).
8. James R. Kincaid, *Child-Loving: The Erotic Child and Victorian Culture* (New York: Routledge, 1992), 79.
9. Charles Dickens, *The Old Curiosity Shop* (1841; rpt., New York: Penguin Books, 1972), 56; hereafter cited in text as *Curiosity Shop*.
10. Lewis Carroll, *Alice's Adventures in Wonderland* and *Through the Looking Glass*, ed. Donald J. Gray (1865, 1871; rpt., New York: W.W. Norton, 1971).
11. Juliet Dusinberre, *Alice to the Lighthouse: Children's Books and Radical Experiments in Art* (1987; rpt., New York: St. Martin's Press, 1999), xxi; hereafter cited in text.

12.   Gertude Stein, *The World Is Round*, illus. Clement Hurd (1939; rpt., San Francisco: North Point Press, 1988).

13.   Christopher Bollas, quoted in *Transitional Objects and Potential Spaces: Literary Uses of D. W. Winnicott*, ed. Peter L. Rudnytsky (New York: Columbia University Press, 1993), xxi; hereafter cited in text.

14.   Gaston Bachelard, *The Poetics of Space* (1958; rpt., Boston: Beacon Press, 1969), xxiii.

15.   Northrop Frye, "Blake's Treatment of the Archetype," in *Blake's Poetry and Designs*, eds. Mary Lynn Johnson and John E. Grant (New York: W.W. Norton, 1979), 513; hereafter cited in text.

16.   See Philippe Ariès, *Centuries of Childhood: A Social History of Family Life*, trans. Robert Baldick (New York: Vintage Books, 1962), for a full discussion of the history of childhood. Jackie Wullschlager, *Inventing Wonderland: Victorian Childhood as Seen Through the Lives and Fantasies of Lewis Carroll, Edward Lear, J. M. Barrie, Kenneth Grahame, and A. A. Milne* (New York: The Free Press, 1995), 12, writes about the connection between childhood as a special state and children's literature in the nineteenth century. See Allison James, Chris Jenks, and Alan Prout, *Theorizing Childhood* (Cambridge, U.K.: Polity Press, 1998), for a recent study of the construction of childhood.

## Chapter 1

1.   Peter Ackroyd, *Blake* (London: Vintage, 1995), 3; hereafter cited in text.

2.   Harold Pagliaro, *Selfhood and Redemption in Blake's* Songs (University Park: Pennsylvania State University Press, 1987), 9; hereafter cited in text.

3.   Jean Hagstrum, "On Innocence and Experience," in *Blake's Poetry and Designs*, eds. Mary Lynn Johnson and John E. Grant (New York: W.W. Norton, 1979), 526.

4.   Thomas R. Frosch, "The Borderline of Innocence and Experience," in *Approaches to Teaching Blake's* Songs of Innocence and Experience, eds. Robert F. Gleckner and Mark L. Greenberg (New York: Modern Language Association of America, 1989), 75; hereafter cited in text.

5.   David Wagenknecht, *Blake's Night: William Blake and the Idea of Pastoral* (Cambridge, Mass.: Harvard University Press, 1973), 6.

6.   See the collection of essays edited by Steve Clark and David Worrall, *Blake in the Nineties* (New York: St. Martin's Press, 1999), for a full discussion of current perspectives.

7.   See Jean Hagstrum, *William Blake: Poet and Painter* (Chicago: University of Chicago Press, 1964), 78–87, for a full discussion of this process and of the distinction between illustration and illumination.

8.   According to Ackroyd, Blake's engraving technique was revealed to him by his brother Robert in a vision, 111.

9.   William Wordsworth, *Selected Poems and Prefaces*, ed. Jack Stillinger (Boston: Houghton Mifflin, 1965), 505; hereafter cited in text as *Selected Poems*.

10.   See discussion in Notes, *Selected Poems and Prefaces*, 505.

11.   See discussion in Notes, *Selected Poems and Prefaces,* 508. In contrast to this reading as sentimental, Ross Woodman "The Idiot Boy as Healer" in *Romanti-*

*cism and Children's Literature in Nineteenth-Century Enlgand,* ed. James Holt McGavran, Jr. (Athens, Ga.: University of Georgia Press, 1991), 72–95, sees the poem as mock heroic, although for him the boy is clearly a romantic hero.

12. John Turner, "Wordsworth and Winnicott in the Area of Play," *Transitional Objects and Potential Spaces: Literary Uses of D. W. Winnicott,* ed. Peter L. Rudnytsky (New York: Columbia University Press, 1993), 163; hereafter cited in text.

13. Steven Marcus, "Some Representations of Childhood in Wordsworth's Poetry," *Opening Texts: Psychoanalysis and the Culture of the Child,* eds. Joseph H. Smith and William Kerrigan (Baltimore, Md.: Johns Hopkins University Press, 1985), 11; hereafter cited in text.

14. Marcel Proust, *Swann's Way,* trans. C. K. Scott Moncrieff (1922; rpt., New York: Penguin Books, 1957), is the first volume of *Remembrance of Things Past.*

15. Charlotte Brönte, *Villette* (1853; rpt., New York: Penguin Books, 1979), 486.

16. George Eliot, *The Mill on the Floss* (1860; rpt., New York: Penguin Books, 1979), 94.

17. Herbert Lindenberger, "The Structural Unit: 'Spots of Time,' *William Wordsworth's* The Prelude," ed. Harold Bloom (New York: Chelsea House Publishers, 1986), 77; hereafter cited in text.

18. This refers to M. H. Abrams, *The Mirror and the Lamp: Romantic Theory and the Critical Tradition* (New York: Oxford University Press, 1953).

19. Opal Whiteley, *The Diary of Opal Whiteley* (1920; rpt., Brentwood, Tenn.: September Productions, 1995), xx; hereafter cited in text as *Diary.*

20. See Juliet McMaster, "Opal's Legacy," *Peter Paul Rubens and Other Friendly Folk* by Opal Whiteley, eds. Laura Cappello, Juliet McMaster, Lesley Peterson, and Chris Wangler (Edmonton: Juvenilia Press, 2001), n.5, where she mentions the Opal Whiteley Memorial (*http://www.efn.org*~opal) and the Opal Whiteley Diary Project (*http://intersect.uoregon.edu/opal/*).

21. See Introduction to *Peter Paul Rubens and Other Friendly Folk,* ix.

22. Laura Cappello, "Opal as Literary Artist," *Peter Paul Rubens and Other Friendly Folk,* xix; hereafter cited in text.

## Chapter 2

1. Morton N. Cohen, *Lewis Carroll: A Biography* (New York: Vintage Books, 1996), 108; hereafter cited in text.

2. Lewis Carroll, *Alice's Adventures in Wonderland* and *Through the Looking Glass,* ed. Donald J. Gray (New York: W.W. Norton, 1971), 120; hereafter cited in text as *Looking Glass.*

3. Lewis Carroll, *Alice's Adventures in Wonderland* and *Through the Looking Glass,* 3, hereafter cited in text as *Wonderland.*

4. William Empson, "The Child as Swain," excerpted from *Some Versions of Pastoral,* in *Alice's Adventures in Wonderland* and *Through the Looking Glass,* 344.

5. Martin Gardner, ed., *The Annotated Alice* (New York: Clarkson N. Potter, 1960), 38n3.

6.  From *Divine and Moral Songs for Children*, quoted in Gardner, 38n4, which was well known to Victorian children.

7.  See Phyllis Greenacre's *Swift and Carroll: A Psychoanalytic Study of Two Lives* (New York: International Universities Press, 1955); Peter Coveney's *The Image of Childhood: The Individual and Society, a Study of the Theme in English Literature* (Baltimore, Md.: Penguin Books, 1967); and, more recently, James R. Kincaid's *Child-Loving: The Erotic Child and Victorian Culture* (New York: Routledge, 1992), and Morton N. Cohen, *Lewis Carroll: A Biography.*

8.  A few years ago, I was giving a talk on Carroll to the Children's Writers section of the PEN Congress. Those who attended—children's book authors and illustrators—insisted that the mood of the *Alice* stories was triumphant, particularly for children, as Alice persists in her own sense of things and dismisses the adult world at the end. This seems to be the dominant view among critics such as Donald Rackin, "Alice's Journey to the End of Night," and Judith Bloomingdale, "Alice as *Anima*: The Image of Woman in Carroll's Classic," both in *Aspects of Alice: Lewis Carroll's Dreamchild as Seen Through the Critics' Looking Glasses,* ed. Robert Phillips (New York: Vintage Books, 1971). Bloomingdale says, "The heroic task that Alice as child-heroine must perform in *Wonderland* is to assert in the face of a primitive threatening universe the reasonableness of her own . . . right to exist" (386). She further claims that it is "her capacity for compassion" that "distinguishes" Alice the Queen (390).

9.  Alwin L. Baum, "Carroll's *Alices*: The Semiotics of Paradox," *Lewis Carroll*, ed. Harold Bloom (New York: Chelsea House Publishers, 1987), 67.

10. Lois R. Kuznets, *Kenneth Grahame* (New York: Twayne Publishers, 1987), 1; hereafter cited in text.

11. Kenneth Grahame, *The Wind in the Willows* (New York: Charles Scribner's Sons, 1908; rpt., 1960), 41; hereafter cited in text as *Wind.*

12. In Kuznets, 27, both Peter Hunt and Kuznets point out that Grahame chooses to ignore the "brutal sexuality" associated with Pan, which was "emphasized by many of Grahame's contemporaries."

13. Geraldine Poss, "An Epic in Arcadia: The Pastoral World of *The Wind in the Willows*," *Children's Literature,* 4 (1975): 80–90.

## Chapter 3

1.  Julia Kristeva, "*Stabat Mater*," *The Kristeva Reader*, ed. Toril Moi (New York: Columbia University Press, 1986), 180; hereafter cited in text as "*Stabat Mater*."

2.  For further information, see Mary D. Ainsworth, *Patterns of Attachment: A Psychological Study of the Strange Situation* (Hillsdale, N.J.: Lawrence Erlbaum, 1978); also John Bowlby, *Attachment and Loss* (London: Hogarth Press, 1977).

3.  Winifred Gallagher, *The Power of Place: How Our Surroundings Shape Our Thoughts, Emotions, and Actions* (New York: HarperCollins, 1993); hereafter cited in text.

4.  Mark Johnson, *The Body in the Mind: The Bodily Basis of Meaning, Imagination, and Reason* (Chicago: University of Chicago Press, 1987), xiv.

5. Christopher Bollas, "The Aesthetic Moment and the Search for Transformation," *Transitional Objects and Potential Spaces: Literary Uses of D. W. Winnicott*, ed. Peter L. Rudnytsky (New York: Columbia University Press, 1993), 40–1; hereafter cited in text.

6. Clare Kahane, "Gender and Voice in Transitional Phenomena," *Transitional Objects and Potential Spaces: Literary Uses of D. W. Winnicott*, ed. Peter L. Rudnytsky (New York: Columbia University Press, 1993), 280; hereafter cited in text.

7. Margaret Wise Brown, *The Runaway Bunny*, illus. Clement Hurd (New York: Harper & Row, 1972).

8. D. W. Winnicott, *Playing and Reality* (New York: Basic Books, 1971), 134.

9. Patricia Seator Skorman, *Nature as Holding Environment and Other Themes: A Heuristic Investigation into the Experience of Nature Using Sensory Awareness and Creative Process* (Ph.D. diss., The Union Institute, 2000), 167.

10. Else Minarek, *Little Bear*, illus. Maurice Sendak (New York: Harper & Row, 1957); hereafter cited in text as *Little Bear*.

11. Faith Ringgold, *Tar Beach* (New York: Crown Publishers, 1991).

12. From the last page of text, unpaginated.

13. Maurice Sendak, *In the Night Kitchen* (New York: Harper & Row, 1970).

14. Randall Jarrell, *The Bat-Poet*, illus. Maurice Sendak (New York: Macmillan, 1963); hereafter cited in text as *Bat-Poet*.

15. Jerome Griswold, *The Children's Books of Randall Jarrell* (Athens, Ga.: University of Georgia Press, 1988), 52.

16. Leo Zanderer, "Randall Jarrell: About and For Children," *The Lion and the Unicorn*, 2,1 (Spring 1978): 73; hereafter cited in text.

17. Randall Jarrell, *Fly By Night*, illus. Maurice Sendak (New York: Farrar, Straus, & Giroux, 1976).

18. From an unpublished interview with Maurice Sendak conducted by Geraldine DeLuca and me in 1977.

19. Susan Griffin, *What Her Body Thought* (San Francisco: HarperCollins, 2000), 308–9.

20. Nancy Chodorow, *The Reproduction of Mothering: Psychoanalysis and the Sociology of Gender* (Berkeley: University of California Press, 1978).

21. Luce Irigaray, *This Sex Which Is Not One*, trans. Catherine Porter (Ithaca, N.Y.: Cornell University Press, 1985), 215.

22. Julia Kristeva, "Revolution in Poetic Language," in *The Kristeva Reader* ed. Toril Moi (New York: Columbia University Press, 1986), 96.

23. Shirley Nelson Garner, Claire Kahane, and Madelon Sprengnether, eds., *The (M)other Tongue: Essays in Feminist Psychoanalytic Interpretation* (Ithaca, N.Y.: Cornell University Press, 1985), 10.

24. Jamaica Kincaid, *Annie John* (New York: Farrar, Straus, & Giroux, 1983), 4; hereafter cited in text as *Annie John*.

25. Erik H. Erikson, *Childhood and Society* (New York: W.W. Norton, 1950), 79, connects the belief that "once upon a time one destroyed one's unity with a maternal matrix" to the "biblical saga of paradise" and the Fall.

26. Julia Kristeva, "About Chinese Women," in *The Kristeva Reader*, 157.

27. Lyda Clifton, from an unpublished interview with Jamaica Kincaid (Summer 1986); hereafter cited in text.

28. Jamaica Kincaid, *At the Bottom of the River* (New York: Farrar, Straus, & Giroux, 1978), 60.

29. Susan Willis, "Black Women Writers: Taking a Critical Perspective," in *Making a Difference: Feminist Literary Criticism*, eds. Gayle Greene and Coppelia Kahn (London: Methuen, 1985), 211–37, associates the theme of community with mothers in black women's work. Alice Walker, *In Search of Our Mothers' Gardens* (San Diego: Harcourt Brace Jovanovich, 1983), 240, says, "Yet so many of the stories that I write, that we all write, are my mother's stories." Paule Marshall, "From the Poets in the Kitchen," in *Reena and Other Stories* (Old Westbury, N.Y.: Feminist Press, 1983), 11–2, claims that her mother and her mother's friends were the major influences on her as a writer: "They taught me my first lessons in the narrative art. They trained my ear. They set a standard of excellence . . . the best of my work must be attributed to them; it stands as a testimony to the rich legacy of language and culture they so freely passed on to me in the wordshop of the kitchen."

30. Jamaica Kincaid, in an interview insert by Patricia T. O'Connor in the Book Review section of the *New York Times*, April 7, 1985, 6, emphasizes the significance of her mother in her conception of herself as an artist.

31. Jamaica Kincaid, *The Autobiography of My Mother* (New York: Farrar, Straus, & Giroux, 1996), 227–8.

## Chapter 4

1. In *The Enlightened Heart: An Anthology of Sacred Poetry*, ed. Stephen Mitchell (New York: Harper & Row, 1989).

2. Terry Gifford, *Pastoral* (New York: Routledge, 1999), 11; hereafter cited in text.

3. Frances Hodgson Burnett, *The Secret Garden* (New York: Dell, 1962; rpt., 1911); hereafter cited in text as *Secret Garden*.

4. Quoted in Maria Nikolajeva, *From Mythic to Linear: Time in Children's Literature* (Lanham, Md.: Scarecrow Press, 2000), 30.

5. Philippa Pearce, *Tom's Midnight Garden* (New York: HarperCollins Publishers, 1992, rpt., 1958); hereafter cited in text as *Midnight Garden*.

6. See Maria Nikolajeva's study of time in children's literature, *From Mythic to Linear*.

7. William Steig, *The Amazing Bone* (New York: Farrar, Straus, & Giroux, 1976).

8. Jonathan Cott, *Pipers at the Gates of Dawn: The Wisdom of Children's Literature* (New York: Random House, 1981), 106.

9. Roni Natov, "Internal and External Journeys: The Child Hero in *The Zabajaba Jungle* and *Linnea in Monet's Garden*," *Children's Literature in Education*, 20, 2 (June 1989): 92.

10. William H. Gass, "Stein: Portraits and Repetition," *Modern Critical Views: Gertrude Stein*, ed. Harold Bloom (New York: Chelsea House, 1986), 147; hereafter cited in text.

11. Marianne DeKoven, "Melody," *Modern Critical Views*, 174; hereafter cited in text.

12. Edith Thacher Hurd, "The World Is Not Flat," Afterword, *The World Is Round*, illus. Clement Hurd (1939; rpt., San Francisco: North Point Press, 1988), wrote that, "Gertrude Stein had very definite ideas about the design and printing of the book," 131, including colors for pages and illustrations. She oversaw all the illustrations, Clement Hurd added, " 'making very specific criticisms of my pictures,' " 133. All further references will be to this edition; hereafter cited in text as *World*.

13. Christina Björk, *Linnea in Monet's Garden*, illus. Lena Anderson (Stockholm: R&S Books, 1985); hereafter cited in text as *Linnea*.

14. Quoted from the back flap of the above edition, which speaks of both author and illustrators as, "Like Linnea, they were nature-loving city girls, born and raised in Stockholm, Sweden."

15. Linnaeus, an eighteenth-century botanist, often called "the Father of Taxonomy," had a deep love of plants and a fascination with their names from an early age. His ideas on classification have influenced generations of biologists.

16. Jean Craighead George, *Julie of the Wolves* (New York: HarperCollins, 1972); hereafter cited in text as *Julie*.

17. From Alfred Lord Tennyson, "In Memoriam," 56, l. 15.

18. Jean Craighead George, *Julie* (New York: HarperCollins, 1994).

19. Jean Craighead George, *Julie's Wolf Pack* (New York: HarperCollins, 1997).

# Chapter 5

1. E. T. A. Hoffmann, *The Golden Pot*, in *The Golden Pot and Other Tales*, trans. Ritchie Robertson (New York: Oxford University Press, 1992), 20; hereafter cited in text as *Golden Pot*.

2. Maria Tatar, ed., *The Classic Fairy Tales* (New York: W.W. Norton, 1999), 25; hereafter cited in text.

3. Maurice Sendak, *Where the Wild Things Are* (New York: Harper & Row, 1963).

4. Kenneth Negus, *E. T. A. Hoffmann's Other World: The Romantic Author and His "New Mythology"* (Philadelphia: University of Pennsylvania Press, 1965), 120; hereafter cited in text.

5. Ritchie Robertson, "Introduction," *The Golden Pot and Other Tales*, xii.

6. This term "orientalism" was used in this defining way by Edward Said, *Orientalism* (New York: Vintage Books, 1979).

7. Sigmund Freud, "The Uncanny (1919)," *The Complete Works of Sigmund Freud, XVII (1917–1919)*, trans. James Strachey (London: Hogarth Press, 1955).

8. Maria Tatar, *Spellbound: Studies on Mesmerism and Literature* (Princeton, N.J.: Princeton University Press, 1978), 146.

9. E. T. A. Hoffmann, *Nutcracker and the King of Mice*, in *The Best Tales of Hoffmann*, ed. E. F. Bleiler (New York: Dover Publications, 1967); hereafter cited in text as *Nutcracker*.

10. E. T. A. Hoffmann, *The Sandman*, in *The Golden Pot and Other Tales*; hereafter cited in text as *Sandman*.

11. See E. F. Bleiler's Introduction in *The Best Tales of Hoffmann*, xxiv–xxv.

12. See Iona Opie and Peter Opie, eds., *The Oxford Dictionary of Nursery Rhymes* (London: Oxford University Press, 1951), for various interpretations and scholarship on the nursery rhymes.

13. See *The Collins Large German Dictionary* (New York, HarperCollins, 1999).

14. See Walter Benjamin's discussion of the storyteller in *Illuminations*, ed. Hannah Arendt, trans. Harry Zohn (New York: Schocken Books, 1968), 84–5.

15. Lois R. Kuznets, in her excellent study, *When Toys Come Alive: Narratives of Animation, Metamorphosis, and Development* (New Haven, Conn.: Yale University Press, 1994), sees the story of Marie's development into a sexual creature as a male construction of female sexuality. Her biographical note grounds this assertion, 214, n. 14.

16. The nurse's version of the sandman is earlier than the mother's. A painting dated 1554/5 by Bosch, Rotterdam Museum, of the sandman shows him with a huge bag of eyeballs falling out of the bag.

17. Quoted from Jackie Wullschlager's translation of this biblical passage in *Hans Christian Andersen: The Life of a Storyteller* (New York: Alfred A. Knopf, 2000), 256; hereafter cited in text.

18. Jack Zipes, *Fairy Tales and the Art of Subversion: The Classical Genre for Children and the Process of Civilization* (New York: Methuen, 1983), 85.

19. See Jackie Wullschlager, his most recent biographer, *Hans Christian Andersen*, 249, who calls his behavior toward royalty "obsequious," noting his "unquestioning reverence for kings and princes." She says, "While fame and fortune consoled him, they also threatened to isolate him further, as he climbed the social ladder and left behind the world which had created him," 258.

20. See Wullschlager on his relationship with Dickens, for example, in *Hans Christian Andersen*, 357–60.

21. See Wullschlager, in *Hans Christian Andersen*, on Andersen's well-known relationship with Jenny Lind, the Swedish singer, in "Jenny," 218–41 and 269–70.

22. Wolfgang Lederer, *The Kiss of the Snow Queen: Hans Christian Andersen and Man's Redemption By Women* (Berkeley: University of California Press, 1986), 6; hereafter cited in text.

23. Hans Christian Andersen, "The Snow Queen," in *The Complete Fairy Tales and Stories*, trans. Erik Christian Haugaard (New York: Anchor Doubleday, 1983); hereafter cited in text as *Snow Queen*.

24. Hans Christian Andersen, "The Ice Maiden," in *The Complete Fairy Tales and Stories*, 739; hereafter cited in text as *Ice Maiden*.

25. Hans Christian Andersen, "The Red Shoes," in *The Complete Fairy Tales and Stories*.

26. Nesca A. Robb, *Four In Exile* (Port Washington, N.Y.: Kennikat Press, 1948), 123–4; hereafter cited in text.

27. Hans Christian Andersen, "The Little Mermaid," in *The Compete Fairy Tales and Stories*; hereafter cited in text as *Mermaid*.

28. Charles Dickens, *The Old Curiosity Shop* (1841; rpt., New York: Penguin Books, 1972), 45; hereafter cited in text as *Curiosity Shop*.

29. Charles Dickens, *Bleak House* (1853; rpt., New York: Penguin Books, 1971).

30. Charles Dickens, *Little Dorrit* (1857; rpt., New York: Penguin Books, 1967).

31. See Baruch Hochman and Ilia Wachs, *Dickens: The Orphan Condition* (Madison, N.J.: Fairleigh Dickinson University Press, 1999), 12–3; hereafter cited in text as Hochman, on the popularity of the nineteenth-century orphan in fiction and on Dickens's own use of this central motif in *Oliver Twist, David Copperfield, Bleak House, Little Dorrit*, and *Great Expectations*.

32. See Alice Miller's landmark study, *Prisoners of Childhood or The Drama of the Gifted Child*. See also Joyce Zoriana, "Nell and I," *The Hudson Review*, 50 (Winter 1998): 573–90.

33. See Malcolm Andrews's discussion of the origins of *The Old Curiosity Shop*, in the Introduction, *The Old Curiosity Shop*, 11–9.

34. See Andrews's discussion throughout the Introduction, 11–31.

35. See Hochman and Wachs on the "paranoid plot" of the orphan novel.

## Chapter 6

1. Elizabeth Sewell, *The Field of Nonsense* (London: Chatto & Windus, 1952).

2. Edward Lear, *The Nonsense Books of Edward Lear* (New York: New American Library, 1964).

3. Florence Parry Heide, *The Shrinking of Treehorn*, illus. Edward Gorey (New York: Holiday House, 1971).

4. Florence Parry Heide, *Treehorn's Treasure*, illus. Edward Gorey (New York: Holiday House, 1981).

5. Florence Parry Heide, *Treehorn's Wish*, illus. Edward Gorey (New York: Holiday House, 1984).

6. Joseph Zornado, *Inventing the Child: Culture, Ideology, and the Story of Childhood* (New York: Garland Publishing, 2001), 186; hereafter cited in text.

7. William Steig, *The Zabajaba Jungle* (New York: Farrar, Straus, & Giroux, 1987).

8. Maurice Sendak, *Higglety Pigglety Pop! or There Must Be More To Life* (New York: Harper & Row, 1967); hereafter cited in text as *Higglety*.

9. Quoted in Ellen Pifer, *Demon or Doll: Images of the Child in Contemporary Writing and Culture* (Charlottesville, Va.: University Press of Virginia, 2000), 73; hereafter cited in text.

10. Vladimir Nabokov, *The Annotated Lolita*, ed. Alfred Appel (New York: Vintage Books, 1991, rpt. 1955); hereafter cited in text as *Lolita*.

11. Appel claims that "parody provides the main basis for Nabokov's involution. . . . In a novel such as *Lolita* . . . the involution is sustained by the parody and the verbal patterning" (quoted in *Lolita*, xxvii); for a full discussion of Nabokov's use of parody, see xlix–lv.

12. See M. M. Bakhtin, "Discourse in the Novel," in *The Dialogic Imagination: Four Essays*, trans. Caryl Emerson and Michael Holquist (Austin: University of Texas Press, 1981), 259–422.

13. See Pifer on comparisons between Humbert and Frankenstein, 81–6.

14. Julia Bader, "*Lolita*: The Quest for Ecstasy," in *Vladimir Nabokov's* Lolita, ed. Harold Bloom (New York: Chelsea House, 1987), 59; hereafter cited in text.

15. Doris Lessing, *The Fifth Child* (New York: Vintage Books, 1989); hereafter cited in text as *Fifth Child*.

16. Doris Lessing, *The Golden Notebook* (New York: Simon & Schuster, 1962).
17. Doris Lessing, *The Four-Gated City* (New York: Alfred A. Knopf, 1969).
18. Doris Lessing, *The Summer Before the Dark* (New York: Alfred A. Knopf, 1973).
19. Doris Lessing, *The Memoirs of A Survivor* (New York: Alfred A. Knopf, 1975).
20. Doris Lessing, *Love, Again* (New York: HarperCollins, 1996).
21. Pifer gives a detailed reading of the Frankenstein myth in "New Versions of the Idyll: Lessing's *The Fifth Child* and Kundera's Infantocracy," 129–46.
22. Doris Lessing, *Ben, in the World* (New York: HarperCollins, 2000).

## Chapter 7

1. Arundhati Roy, *The God of Small Things* (New York: Random House, 1997), 219; hereafter cited in text as *God of Small Things*.
2. From an interview, http://website.lineone.net/~jon.simmons/roy/tgost4.htm.
3. Barbara Kingsolver, *The Poisonwood Bible* (New York: HarperCollins, 1998); hereafter cited in text as *Poisonwood*.
4. Joseph Conrad, *The Heart of Darkness* (1902; rpt., New York: Signet, 1950).
5. Mary Galbraith, "Hear My Cry: A Manifesto for an Emacipatory Childhood Studies Approach to Children's Literature," *The Lion and the Unicorn*, 25, 2 (April, 2001): 187–205, urges an investigation of "childhood in an adult dominated world."

## Chapter 8

1. Kimberly Reynolds, Introduction, *Frightening Fiction*, eds. Kimberley Reynolds, Geraldine Brennan, and Kevin McCarron (London: Continuum, 2001); hereafter cited in text.
2. Geraldine Brennan, "The Game Called Death: Frightening Fictions by David Almond, Philip Gross and Lesley Howarth," in *Frightening Fictions*, 97.
3. Annie Ernaux, *Shame*, trans. Tanya Leslie (New York: Seven Stories Press, 1998), 92.
4. Vera B. Williams, *Amber Was Brave, Essie Was Smart* (New York: Greenwillow Books, 2001); hereafter cited in text as *Amber*.
5. In a recent telephone interview, Vera B. Williams told me that this is her most autobiographical work.
6. Vera B. Williams, *Cherries and Cherry Pits* (New York: Greenwillow Books, 1986).
7. An Na, *A Step From Heaven* (Asheville, N.C.: Front Street, 2001); hereafter cited in text as *Step From Heaven*.
8. Sapphire, *Push* (New York: Random House, 1997); hereafter cited in text as *Push*.
9. See, for example, Anson M. Green, "Risky Materials in the Classroom: Using Sapphire's Novel *Push*," http://www.2.wgbh.org/MCBWEIS/LTC/ALRI/using-push.html.
10. See Scott Carlon's "Preciouswords—Sapphire speaks about *Push*," interview by Darius Casey, http://www.daily.umn.edu/ae/Print/ISSUE38/special23.html.

11.   This book had a profound effect on my students when I taught it in two different seminars, "The Imagination of Childhood" and "Living Women Visionary Writers." Most moving to me was a poem written by one of my students, a young poet/teacher, who said that *Push* changed the way she sees the world. She writes:

"I'm alive inside. A bird is my heart."
 (from *Push*)
That which doesn't kill us makes us fly.
I wonder you. Still you have wings,
And courage and strength.
The truth is, I know you are alive—
Not just a fictional character, but real silent.
Survivor.
I see you everywhere—on the streets,
At three when the schools let out.
The girls that got big mouths, and then look down
With solemn knowledge.
They don't wanna lash out.
But when your building is burning
You wanna be heard screamin "Help!"
Naaaa . . . it's even deeper than that.
God they pile in the bus.
One girl pushing another:
"Get out of my way!!"
"Hold your horses motherfucker."
The back of the bus laughs.
Is that you Precious?
Or are you the girl sitting in the front
Who is charmingly quiet?
Escape. Try to fly to a higher branch.
I have cried for you . . .
                         Nicole Vislocky

12.   David Almond, *Heaven Eyes* (New York: Delacorte Press, 2000).
13.   Laurie Halse Anderson, *Speak* (New York: Farrar, Straus, & Giroux, 1999).
14.   David Almond, *Skellig* (New York: Delacorte Press, 1998); hereafter cited in text as *Skellig*.
15.   Gabriel Garcia Marquez, "The Very Old Man With Enormous Wings," *Leaf Storm and Other Stories*, trans. Gregory Rabassa (New York: Harper & Row, 1972).
16.   Bram Stoker, *The Essential Dracula*, ed. Leonard Wolf (New York: Plume, 1993, rpt. 1897), 298.
17.   Philip Pullman, *The Golden Compass* (New York: Ballantine Books, 1995); hereafter cited in text as *Golden Compass*.
18.   From "The Marriage of Heaven and Hell," in *The Portable Blake* (New York: Viking, 1946), 251.

19.  From Wendy Parsons and Catriona Nicholson, "Talking to Philip Pullman: An Interview," *The Lion and the Unicorn*, 23, 1 (January, 1999): 119; hereafter cited in text.
20.  Otto Rank, *The Myth of the Birth of the Hero and Other Writings* (New York: Vintage Books, 1959).
21.  Joseph Campbell, *The Hero with a Thousand Faces* (1949, rpt., Princeton, N.J.: Princeton University Press, 1972).
22.  From the website ACHUKA, http://www.achuka.co.uk/ppint.htm.
23.  James Hillman, *The Soul's Code: In Search of Character and Calling* (New York: Random House, 1996), 8; hereafter cited in text.
24.  Philip Pullman, *The Subtle Knife* (New York: Ballantine Books, 1999).
25.  J. K. Rowling, *Harry Potter and the Goblet of Fire* (New York: Scholastic, 2000); hereafter cited in text as *Goblet*.
26.  J. K. Rowling, *Harry Potter and the Sorcerer's Stone* (New York: Scholastic, 1997), 28; hereafter cited in text as *Sorcerer's Stone*.
27.  From a radio interview with J. K. Rowling, WNPR, 820 AM, December 28, 1999.
28.  E. B. White, *Charlotte's Web* (New York: Harper & Row, 1952), 3.
29.  Charles Dickens, *David Copperfield* (1850; rpt., Oxford: Oxford University Press, 1994), 1.
30.  C. S. Lewis, *The Lion, the Witch, and the Wardrobe* (New York: Macmillan, 1950).
31.  Madeline L'Engle, *A Wrinkle in Time* (New York: Farrar, Straus, & Giroux, 1962).
32.  Madeline L'Engle, *A Wind in the Door* (New York: Farrar, Straus, & Giroux, 1973).
33.  Madeline L'Engle, *A Swiftly Tilting Planet* (New York: Farrar, Straus, & Giroux, 1978).
34.  J. R. R. Tolkien, *The Hobbit; or There and Back Again* (Boston: Houghton Mifflin, 1966).
35.  J. R. R. Tolkien, *The Lord of the Rings* (Boston: Houghton Mifflin, 1954–1956).
36.  From the radio interview with J. K. Rowling noted above.
37.  Quoted in Tzvetan Todorov, *The Fantastic: A Structural Approach to a Literary Genre*, trans. Richard Howard (Cleveland, Oh.: Case Western Reserve University Press, 1973), 161.
38.  Samuel Coleridge, *Biographia Literaria*, in *The Longman Anthology of British Literature* 2 (New York: Addison-Wesley, 1999), 531.
39.  J. K. Rowling, *Harry Potter and the Chamber of Secrets* (New York: Scholastic, 1999), 203; hereafter cited in text as *Chamber*.
40.  J. K. Rowling, *Harry Potter and the Prisoner of Azkaban* (New York: Scholastic, 1999), 52; hereafter cited in text as *Prisoner*.
41.  Sharon Moore, ed., *We Love Harry Potter!* (New York: St. Martin's Press, 1999), 2.
42.  Alison Lurie, "Not for Muggles," Archives, December 16, 1999, available from: http://www.nybooks.com/nyrev/WWWarchdisplay.cgi?19991216006R@p4; hereafter cited in text.
43.  The debate over Rowling's choice and use of a boy hero has been extensive. Christine Schoefer, for example, writes about "Harry Potter's girl trouble," where

she claims that "[n]o girl is brilliantly heroic the way Harry is, no woman is experienced and wise like Professor Dumbledore . . . [that] the range of female personalities is so limited that neither women nor girls play on the side of evil," [and that Rowling] depicts Hermione as working "hard to be accepted by Harry and his sidekick Ron, who treat her like a tag-along until Volume 3" (http://www.salon.com/books/feature/2000/01/13/potter/print.html). Along with her many supporters, Rowling complains, "What irritates me is that I am constantly, increasingly, being asked 'Can we have a strong female character, please?' Like they are ordering a side order of chips. I am thinking 'Isn't Hermione strong enough for you?' She is the most brilliant of the three and they need her. . . . But my hero is a boy and at the age he has been girls simply do not figure that much . . . I think that it would be extremely contrived to throw in a couple of feisty, gorgeous, brilliant-at-math and great-at-fixing-cars girls." From an interview from *The Times*, June 30, 2000, entitled "Harry and me," available from: http://www.the-times.co.uk/onlinespecials/features/harrypotter/story18.html.

44. From the radio interview with J. K. Rowling of December 28, mentioned above.
45. Ibid.
46. This phrase was used by Ernst Bloch, *The Utopian Function of Art and Literature*, trans. Jack Zipes and Frank Mecklenburg (Cambridge, Mass.: MIT Press, 1988).
47. In an interview on June 30, 2000, in the London *Times*, Rowling was quoted as describing the dementors as "a description of depression . . . entirely from my own experience. Depression is the most unpleasant thing I have ever experienced. . . . It is that absence of being able to envisage that you will ever be cheerful again. The absence of hope. That very deadened feeling, which is so very different from feeling sad. Sad hurts but it's a healthy feeling. It is a necessary thing to feel. Depression is very different," available from http://www.the-times.co.uk/onlinespecials/features/harrypotter/story18.html.
48. From an unpublished interview with Maurice Sendak conducted by Geraldine DeLuca and me in 1977.
49. See Jack Zipes, *The Trials and Tribulations of Little Red Riding Hood: Versions of the Tale in Sociocultural Perspective* (South Hadley, Mass.: J. F. Bergin, 1983).

## Afterword

1. Kate Fincke, "The Narration of Metaphor in Children's Lives," *The Lion and the Unicorn*, 25, 2 (April, 2001):275–6.
2. I quote Ellen Tremper, my friend and colleague, here from a recent conversation we had.

# Bibliography

## PRIMARY WORKS

Almond, David. *Heaven Eyes*. New York: Delacorte Press, 2000.

———. *Skellig*. New York: Delacorte Press, 1998.

Andersen, Hans Christian. *The Complete Fairy Tales and Stories*. Trans. Erik Christian Haugaard. New York: Anchor Doubleday, 1983.

Anderson, Laurie Halse. *Speak*. New York: Farrar, Straus, & Giroux, 1999.

Björk, Christina. *Linnea in Monet's Garden*. Illus. Lena Anderson. Stockholm: R&S Books, 1985.

Blake, William. *Blake's Poetry and Designs*. Eds. Johnson, Mary Lynn and John E. Grant. New York: W.W. Norton, 1979.

———. *The Portable Blake*. New York: Viking, 1946.

Brönte, Charlotte. *Villette*. 1853. New York: Penguin Books, 1979.

Brown, Margaret Wise. *The Runaway Bunny*. Illus. Clement Hurd. New York: Harper & Row, 1972.

Burnett, Frances Hodgson. *The Secret Garden*. 1911. New York: Dell Co., 1962.

Carroll, Lewis. *Alice's Adventures in Wonderland* and *Through the Looking Glass*. 1865. 1871. Ed. Donald J. Gray. New York: W.W. Norton, 1971.

Conrad, Joseph. *Heart of Darkness*. 1902. New York: Signet, 1950.

Dickens, Charles. *Bleak House*. 1853. New York: Penguin Books, 1971.

———. *David Copperfield*. 1850. Oxford: Oxford University Press, 1994.

———. *Little Dorrit*. 1857. New York: Penguin Books, 1967.

———. *The Old Curiosity Shop*. 1841. New York: Penguin Books, 1972.

Eliot, George. *The Mill on the Floss*. 1860. New York: Penguin Books, 1979.

George, Jean Craighead. *Julie*. New York: HarperCollins Publishers, 1994.

———. *Julie of the Wolves*. New York: HarperCollins Publishers, 1972.

———. *Julie's Wolf Pack*. New York: HarperCollins Publishers, 1997.

Goethe, Johann Wolfgang von. *Wilhelm Meister's Apprenticeship.* 1839. Ed. and Trans. Eric A. Blackall. Princeton, N.J.: Princeton University Press, 1989.

Grahame, Kenneth. *The Wind in the Willows.* 1908. New York: Charles Scribner's Sons, 1960.

Heide, Florence Parry. *The Shrinking of Treehorn.* Illus. Edward Gorey. New York: Holiday House, 1971.

———. *Treehorn's Treasure.* Illus. Edward Gorey. New York: Holiday House, 1981.

———. *Treehorn's Wish.* Illus. Edward Gorey. New York: Holiday House, 1984.

Hoffmann, E.T.A. *The Golden Pot and Other Tales.* Trans. Ritchie Robertson. New York: Oxford University Press, 1992.

———. *The Best Tales of Hoffmann.* Ed. E. F. Bleiler. New York: Dover Publications Inc., 1967.

Jarrell, Randall. *The Bat-Poet.* Illus. Maurice Sendak. New York: Macmillan, 1963.

———. *Fly By Night.* Illus. Maurice Sendak. New York: Farrar, Straus, & Giroux, 1976.

Kincaid, Jamaica. *Annie John.* New York: Farrar, Straus, & Giroux, 1983.

———. *At the Bottom of the River.* New York: Farrar, Straus, & Giroux, 1978.

———. *Autobiography of My Mother.* New York: Farrar, Straus, & Giroux, 1996.

Kingsolver, Barbara. *The Poisonwood Bible.* New York: HarperCollins, 1998.

Lear, Edward. *The Nonsense Books of Edward Lear.* New York: New American Library, 1964.

L'Engle, Madeleine. *A Swiftly Tilting Planet.* New York: Farrar, Straus, & Giroux, 1978.

———. *A Wind in the Door.* New York: Farrar, Straus, & Giroux, 1973.

———. *A Wrinkle in Time.* New York: Farrar, Straus, & Giroux, 1962.

Lessing, Doris. *Ben, in the World.* New York: HarperCollins, 2000.

———. *The Fifth Child.* New York: Vintage Books, 1989.

———. *The Four-Gated City.* New York: Alfred A. Knopf, 1969.

———. *The Golden Notebook.* New York: Simon & Schuster, 1962.

———. *Love, Again.* New York: HarperCollins, 1996.

———. *The Memoirs of A Survivor.* New York: Alfred A. Knopf, 1975.

———. *The Summer Before the Dark.* New York: Alfred A. Knopf, 1973.

Lewis, C. S. *The Lion, the Witch, and the Wardrobe.* New York: Macmillan, 1950.

Marquez, Gabriel Garcia. "The Very Old Man With Enormous Wings," *Leaf Storm and Other Stories.* Trans. Gregory Rabassa. New York: Harper & Row, 1972.

Minarek, Else. *Little Bear.* Illus. Maurice Sendak. New York: Harper & Row, 1957.

Na, An. *A Step From Heaven.* Asheville, N.C.: Front Street, 2001.

Nabokov, Vladimir. *The Annotated Lolita.* 1955. Ed. Alfred Appel. New York: Vintage Books, 1991.

Pearce, Philippa. *Tom's Midnight Garden.* 1958. New York: HarperCollins, 1992.

Proust, Marcel. *Swann's Way.* Trans. C. K. Scott Moncrieff. 1922. New York: Penguin Books, 1957.

Pullman, Philip. *The Golden Compass.* New York: Ballantine Books, 1995.

———. *The Subtle Knife.* New York Ballantine Books, 1999.

Ringgold, Faith. *Tar Beach.* New York: Crown Publishers, 1991.

Rowling, J. K. *Harry Potter and the Chamber of Secrets.* New York: Scholastic, 1999.

———. *Harry Potter and the Goblet of Fire.* New York: Scholastic, 2000.

————. *Harry Potter and the Prisoner of Azkaban.* New York: Scholastic, 1999.

————. *Harry Potter and the Sorcerer's Stone.* New York: Scholastic, 1997.

Roy, Arundhati. *The God of Small Things.* New York: Random House, 1997.

Sapphire. *Push.* New York: Random House, 1997.

Sendak, Maurice. *Higglety Pigglety Pop! or There Must Be More To Life.* New York: Harper & Row, 1967.

————. *In the Night Kitchen.* New York: Harper & Row, 1970.

————. *Where the Wild Things Are.* New York: Harper & Row, 1963.

Shelley, Mary. *Frankenstein, or the Modern Prometheus.* 1818. Ed. Marilyn Butler. New York: Oxford University Press, 1994.

Steig, William. *The Amazing Bone.* New York: Farrar, Straus, & Giroux, 1976.

————. *The Zabajaba Jungle.* New York: Farrar, Straus, & Giroux, 1987.

Stein, Gertrude. *The World Is Round.* Illus. Clement Hurd. 1939. San Francisco: North Point Press, 1988.

Stoker, Bram. *The Essential Dracula.* 1897. Ed. Leonard Wolf. New York: Plume, 1993.

White, E. B. *Charlotte's Web.* New York: Harper & Row, 1952.

Whiteley, Opal. *The Diary of Opal Whiteley.* 1920. Brentwood, Tenn.: September Productions, 1995.

Williams, Vera B. *Amber Was Brave, Essie Was Smart.* New York: Greenwillow Books, 2001.

————. *Cherries and Cherry Pits.* New York: Greenwillow Books, 1986.

Wordsworth, William. *Selected Poems and Prefaces.* Ed. Jack Stillinger. Boston: Houghton Mifflin, 1965.

## SECONDARY WORKS

Abbs, Peter. *A is for Aesthetic: Essays on Creative and Aesthetic Education.* London: Falmer Press, 1989.

Abrams, M. H. *The Mirror and the Lamp: Romantic Theory and the Critical Tradition.* New York: Oxford University Press, 1953.

ACHUKA. Http://www.achuka.co.uk/ppint.htm.

Ackroyd, Peter. *Blake.* London: Vintage, 1995.

Ainsworth, Mary D. *Patterns of Attachment: A Psychological Study of the Strange Situation.* Hillsdale, N.J.: Lawrence Erlbaum, 1978.

Andrews, Malcolm. Introduction, *The Old Curiosity Shop.* New York: Penguin Books, 1972.

Ariès, Philippe. *Centuries of Childhood: A Social History of Family Life.* Trans. Robert Baldick. New York: Vintage Books, 1962.

Bachelard, Gaston. *The Poetics of Space.* 1958. Boston: Beacon Press, 1969.

————. "Reveries Toward Childhood," *Reclaiming the Inner Child.* Ed. Jeremiah Abrams. New York: G.P. Putnam's Sons, 1990.

Bader, Julia. "*Lolita*: The Quest for Ecstasy," *Vladimir Nabokov's* Lolita. Ed. Harold Bloom. New York: Chelsea House, 1987.

Bakhtin, M. M. "Discourse in the Novel," *The Dialogic Imagination: Four Essays.* Trans. Caryl Emerson and Michael Holquist. Austin: University of Texas Press, 1981.

Baum, Alwin L. "Carroll's *Alices*: The Semiotics of Paradox," *Lewis Carroll.* Ed. Harold Bloom. New York: Chelsea House Publishers, 1987.

Benjamin, Walter. *Illuminations*. Ed. Hannah Arendt. Trans. Harry Zohn. New York: Schocken Books: 1968.

Bleiler, E. F. Introduction, *The Best Tales of Hoffmann*. New York: Dover Publications, 1967.

Bloch, Ernst. *The Utopian Function of Art and Literature*. Trans. Jack Zipes and Frank Mecklenburg. Cambridge, Mass.: MIT Press, 1988.

Bloomingdale, Judith. "Alice as *Anima*: The Image of Woman in Carroll's Classic," *Aspects of Alice: Lewis Carroll's Dreamchild as Seen Through the Critics' Looking Glasses*. Ed. Robert Phillips. New York: Vintage Books, 1971.

Bollas, Christopher. "The Aesthetic Moment and the Search for Transformation," *Transitional Objects and Potential Spaces: Literary Uses of D. W. Winnicott*. Ed. Peter L. Rudnytsky. New York: Columbia University Press, 1993: 40–9.

Bowlby, John. *Attachment and Loss*. London: Hogarth Press, 1977.

Brennan, Geraldine. "The Game Called Death: Frightening Fictions by David Almond, Philip Gross and Lesley Howarth," *Frightening Fictions*. Eds. Kimberley Reynolds, Geraldine Brennan, and Kevin McCarron. London: Continuum, 2001.

Campbell, Joseph. *The Hero with a Thousand Faces*. 1949. Princeton, N.J.: Princeton University Press, 1972.

Cappello, Laura. "Opal as Literary Artist," *Peter Paul Rubens and Other Friendly Folk* by Opal Whiteley. Eds. Laura Cappello, Juliet McMaster, Lesley Peterson, and Chris Wangler. Edmonton, Alb: Juvenilia Press, 2001.

Carlon, Scott. "Preciouswords—Sapphire speaks about *Push*," Interview by Darius Casey, http://www.daily.umn.edu/ae/Print/ISSUES38/special23.html.

Chodorow, Nancy. *The Reproduction of Mothering: Psychoanalysis and the Sociology of Gender*. Berkeley: University of California Press, 1978.

Clark, Steve and David Worrall, eds. *Blake in the Nineties*. New York: St. Martin's Press, 1999.

Clifton, Lyda. Interview (unpublished), 1986.

Cohen, Morton N. *Lewis Carroll: A Biography*. New York: Vintage Books, 1996.

Coleridge, Samuel. *Biographia Literaria. The Longman Anthology of British Literature* 2. New York: Addison-Wesley, 1999.

*The Collins Large German Dictionary*. New York: Harper Collins, 1999.

Cott, Jonathan. *Pipers at the Gates of Dawn: The Wisdom of Children's Literature*. New York: Random House, 1981.

Coveney, Peter. *The Image of Childhood: The Individual and Society, a Study of the Theme in English Literature*. Baltimore, Md.: Penguin Books, 1967.

DeKoven, Marianne. "Melody," *Modern Critical Views: Gertrude Stein*. Ed. Harold Bloom. New York: Chelsea House, 1986.

Dusinberre, Juliet. *Alice to the Lighthouse: Children's Books and Radical Experiments in Art*. 1987. New York: St. Martin's Press, 1999.

Empson, William. "The Child as Swain," excerpted from *Some Versions of Pastoral* in *Alice's Adventures in Wonderland and Through the Looking Glass*. Ed. Donald J. Gray. New York: W.W. Norton, 1971.

Erikson, Erik H. *Childhood and Society*. New York: W.W. Norton, 1950.

Ernaux, Annie. *Shame*. Trans. Tanya Leslie. New York: Seven Stories Press, 1998.

Freud, Sigmund. "The Uncanny (1919)," *The Complete Psychological Works of Sigmund Freud, XVII (1917-1919)*. Trans. James Strachey. London: Hogarth Press, 1955.

Frosch, Thomas R. "The Borderline of Innocence and Experience," *Approaches to Teaching Blake's* Songs of Innocence and Experience. Eds. Robert F. Gleckner and Mark L. Greenberg. New York: Modern Language Association of America, 1989.

Frye, Northrop. "Blake's Treatment of the Archetype," *Blake's Poetry and Designs.* Eds. Mary Lynn Johnson and John E. Grant. New York: W.W. Norton, 1979.

Galbraith, Mary. "Hear My Cry: A Manifesto for an Emancipatory Childhood Studies Approach to Children's Literature," *The Lion and the Unicorn* 25, 2 (April, 2001): 187–205.

Gallagher, Winifred. *The Power of Place: How Our Surroundings Shape Our Thoughts, Emotions, and Actions.* New York: HarperCollins, 1993.

Gardner, Martin, ed. *The Annotated Alice.* New York: Clarkson N. Potter, 1960.

Garner, Shirley Nelson, Claire Kahane, and Madelon Sprengnether, eds. *The (M)other Tongue: Essays in Feminist Psychoanalytic Interpretation.* Ithaca, N.Y.: Cornell University Press, 1985.

Gass, William H. "Stein: Portraits and Repetition," *Modern Critical Views: Gertrude Stein.* Ed. Harold Bloom. New York: Chelsea House, 1986.

Gifford, Terry. *Pastoral.* New York: Routledge, 1999.

Green, Anson M. "Risky Materials in the Classroom: Using Sapphire's Novel *Push.*" Http://www.2.wbgh.org/MCWEIS/LTC/ALRI/usingpush.htm.

Greenacre, Phylllis. *Swift and Carroll: A Psychoanalytic Study of Two Lives.* New York: International Universities Press, 1955.

Griffin, Susan. *What Her Body Thought.* San Francisco: HarperCollins, 2000.

Griswold, Jerome. *The Children's Books of Randall Jarrell.* Athens, GA.: University of Georgia Press, 1988.

Hagstrum, Jean. "On Innocence and Experience," *Blake's Poetry and Designs.* Eds. Mary Lynn Johnson and John E. Grant. New York: W.W. Norton, 1979.

———. *William Blake: Poet and Painter.* Chicago: University of Chicago Press, 1964.

Hillman, James. *The Soul's Code: In Search of Character and Calling.* New York: Random House, 1996.

Hochman, Baruch and Ilia Wachs. *Dickens: The Orphan Condition.* Madison, N.J.: Fairleigh Dickinson University Press, 1999.

Hurd, Edith Thacher. "The World Is Not Flat," Afterword, *The World Is Round* by Gertrude Stein. Illus. Clement Hurd. 1939. San Francisco: North Point Press, 1988.

Irigaray, Luce. *This Sex Which Is Not One.* Trans. Catherine Porter. Ithaca, N.Y.: Cornell University Press, 1985.

James, Allison, Chris Jenks, and Alan Prout. *Theorizing Childhood.* Cambridge, U.K.: Polity Press, 1998.

Johnson, Mark. *The Body in the Mind: The Bodily Basis of Meaning, Imagination, and Reason.* Chicago: University of Chicago Press, 1987.

Kahane, Clare. "Gender and Voice in Transitional Phenomena," *Transitional Objects and Potential Spaces: Literary Uses of D.W. Winnicott.* Ed. Peter L. Rudnytsky. New York: Columbia University Press, 1993: 278–91.

Kincaid, James R. *Child-Loving: The Erotic Child and Victorian Culture.* New York: Routledge, 1992.

Kristeva, Julia. "About Chinese Women," *The Kristeva Reader.* Ed. Toril Moi. New York: Columbia University Press, 1986.

————. "Revolution in Poetic Language," *The Kristeva Reader*. Ed. Toril Moi. New York: Columbia University Press, 1986.

————. *"Stabat Mater,"* *The Kristeva Reader*. Ed. Toril Moi. New York: Columbia University Press, 1986.

Kuznets, Lois R. *Kenneth Grahame*. New York: Twayne Publishers, 1987.

————. *When Toys Come Alive: Narratives of Animation, Metamorphosis, and Development*. New Haven, Conn.: Yale University Press, 1994.

Lederer, Wolfgang. *The Kiss of the Snow Queen: Hans Christian Andersen and Man's Redemption By Women*. Berkeley: University of California Press, 1986.

Lindenberger, Herbert. "The Structural Unit: 'Spots of Time,' " *William Wordsworth's* The Prelude. Ed. Harold Bloom. New York: Chelsea House Publishers, 1986.

Lurie, Alison. "Not for Muggles," Archives, December 16, 1999: http://www.nybooks. com/nyrev/WWWaarchdisplay.cgi?1999121600R@p4.

Marcus, Steven. "Some Representations of Childhood in Wordsworth's Poetry," *Opening Texts: Psychoanalysis and the Culture of the Child*. Eds. Joseph H. Smith and William Kerrigan. Baltimore, Md.: Johns Hopkins University Press, 1985.

Marshall, Paule. "From the Poets in the Kitchen," *Reena and Other Stories*. Old Westbury, N.Y.: Feminist Press, 1983.

McMaster, Juliet. "Opal's Legacy," *Peter Paul Rubens and Other Friendly Folk* by Opal Whiteley. Eds. Laura Cappello, Juliet McMaster, Lesley Peterson, and Chris Wangler. Edmonton: Juvenilia Press, 2001.

Miller, Alice. *Prisoners of Childhood, or The Drama of the Gifted Child: How Narcissistic Parents Form and Deform the Emotional Lives of Their Talented Children*. Trans. Ruth Ward. New York: Basic Books, 1981.

————. *Pictures of a Childhood: Sixty-six Watercolours and an Essay*. Trans. Hildegarde Hannum. New York: Meridian, 1995.

Mitchell, Stephen, ed. *The Enlightened Heart: An Anthology of Sacred Poetry*. New York: Harper & Row, 1989.

Moore, Sharon, ed. *We Love Harry Potter!* New York: St. Martin's Press, 1999.

Natov, Roni. "Internal and External Journeys: The Child Hero in *The Zabajaba Jungle* and *Linnea in Monet's Garden*," *Children's Literature in Education*, 20, 2. (1989): 91–101.

Negus, Kenneth. *E. T. A. Hoffmann's Other World: The Romantic Author and His "New Mythology."* Philadelphia: University of Pennsylvania Press, 1965.

Nikolajeva, Maria. *From Mythic to Linear: Time in Children's Literature*. Lanham, Md.: The Scarecrow Press, 2000.

O'Connor, Patricia T. Book Review section of the *New York Times*, 7, April 1985.

Opie, Iona and Peter Opie, eds. *The Oxford Dictionary of Nursery Rhymes*. London: Oxford University Press, 1951.

Pagliaro, Harold. *Selfhood and Redemption in Blake's* Songs. University Park, Pa.: Pennsylvania State University Press, 1987.

Parsons, Wendy, and Catriona Nicholson. "Talking to Philip Pullman: An Interview," *The Lion and the Unicorn*, 23, 1 (January, 1999): 116–34.

Peterson, Lesley. *Peter Paul Rubens and Other Friendly Folk* by Opal Whiteley. Eds. Laura Cappello, Juliet McMaster, Lesley Peterson and Chris Wangler. Edmonton, Alb: Juvenilia Press, 2001.

Pifer, Ellen. *Demon or Doll: Images of the Child in Contemporary Writing and Culture.* Charlottesville, Va.: University Press of Virginia, 2000.

Poss, Geraldine. "An Epic in Arcadia: The Pastoral World of *The Wind in the Willows.*" *Children's Literature,* 4 (1975): 80–90.

Rackin, Donald. "Alice's Journey to the End of Night," *Aspects of Alice: Lewis Carroll's Dreamchild as Seen Through the Critics' Looking Glasses.* Ed. Robert Phillips. New York: Vintage Books, 1971.

Rank, Otto. *The Myth of the Birth of the Hero and Other Writings.* New York: Vintage Books. 1959.

Reynolds, Kimberly. Introduction, *Frightening Fiction: Contemporary Classics of Children's Literature.* Eds. Kimberley Reynolds, Geraldine Brennan, and Kevin McCarron. London: Continuum, 2001.

Robb, Nesca A. *Four In Exile.* Port Washington, N.Y.: Kennikat Press, 1948.

Robertson, Ritchie. Introduction, *The Golden Pot and Other Tales.* Trans. Ritchie Robertson. New York: Oxford University Press, 1992.

Said, Edward. *Orientalism.* New York: Vintage Books, 1979.

Sewell, Elizabeth. *The Field of Nonsense.* London: Chatto & Windus, 1952.

Simmons, Jon. Interview with Arundhati Roy. http://www.lineone.net/~jon.simmons/roy/tgost4.htm.

Skorman, Patricia Seator. *Nature as Holding Environment and Other Themes: A Heuristic Investigation into the Experience of Nature Using Sensory Awareness and Creative Process.* Ph.D. Diss. The Union Institute, 2000.

Steedman, Carolyn. *Strange Dislocations: Childhood and the Idea of Human Interiority 1780–1930.* Cambridge, Mass.: Harvard University Press, 1995.

Tatar, Maria, ed. *The Classic Fairy Tales.* New York: W.W. Norton, 1999.

———. *Spellbound: Studies on Mesmerism and Literature.* Princeton N.J.: Princeton University Press, 1978.

Todorov, Tzvetan. *The Fantastic: A Structural Approach to a Literary Genre.* Trans. Richard Howard. Cleveland, Oh.: Case Western Reserve University Press, 1973.

Turner, John. "Wordsworth and Winnicott in the Area of Play," *Transitional Objects and Potential Spaces: Literary Uses of D. W. Winnicott.* Ed. Peter L. Rudnytsky. New York: Columbia University Press, 1993: 161–88.

Wagenkneckt, David. *Blake's Night: William Blake and the Idea of Pastoral.* Cambridge, Mass.: Harvard University Press, 1973.

Walker, Alice. *In Search of Our Mothers' Gardens.* San Diego: Harcourt Brace Jovanovich, 1983.

Willis, Susan. "Black women Writers: Taking a Critical Perspective," *Making a Difference: Feminist Literary Criticism.* Eds. Gayle Greene and Coppelia Kahn. London: Methuen, 1985.

Winnicott, D. W. *Playing and Reality.* New York: Basic Books, 1971.

Woodman, Ross. "The Idiot Boy as Healer," *Romanticism and Children's Literature in Nineteenth-Century England.* Ed. James Holt McGavran, Jr. Athens, Ga.: University of Georgia Press, 1991: 72–95.

Wullschlager, Jackie. *Hans Christian Andersen: The Life of a Storyteller.* New York: Alfred A. Knopf, 2000.

————. *Inventing Wonderland*: *Victorian Childhood as Seen Through the Lives and Fantasies of Lewis Carroll, Edward Lear, J. M. Barrie, Kenneth Grahame, and A. A. Milne*. New York: Free Press, 1995.

Zanderer, Leo. "Randall Jarrell: About and for Children," *The Lion and the Unicorn*, 2, 1 (Spring 1978): 73–93.

Zipes, Jack. *Fairy Tales and the Art of Subversion*: *The Classical Genre for Children and the Process of Civilization*. New York: Methuen, 1983.

————. *The Trials and Tribulations of Little Red Riding Hood*: *Versions of the Tale in Sociocultural Perspective*. South Hadley, Mass.: J.F. Bergin, 1983.

Zoriana, Joyce. "Nell and I," *The Hudson Review*, 50 (Winter 1998): 573–90.

Zornado, Joseph. *Inventing the Child*: *Culture, Ideology, and the Story of Childhood*. New York: Garland Publishing, 2001.

# Index